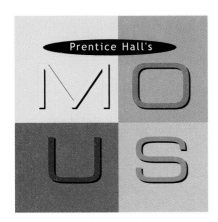

Prentice Hall's

MO
US

TEST PREPARATION GUIDE FOR

⤑ Excel 2000

TEST
PREPARATION
GUIDES
SERIES

**Emily Ketcham,
Series Editor**

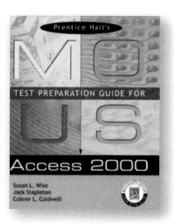

Prentice Hall's

M O U S

TEST PREPARATION GUIDE FOR

Excel 2000

Emily Ketcham
Carolyn Monroe

Prentice Hall

Upper Saddle River, New Jersey

Editor-in-Chief: Mickey Cox
Acquisitions Editor: Lucinda Gatch
Assistant Editor: Jennifer Cappello
Development Editor: Cecil Yarbrough
Managing Editor: Monica Stipanov
Editorial Assistant: Mary Toepfer
Director of Strategic Marketing: Nancy Evans
Marketing Manager: Kris King
AVP/Director of Production & Manufacturing: Michael Weinstein
Manager, Production: Gail Steier de Acevedo
Project Manager: Tim Tate
Manufacturing Buyer: Natacha St. Hill Moore
Associate Director, Manufacturing: Vincent Scelta
Book Design: David Levy
Cover Design: Pisaza Design Studio, Ltd.
Full Service Composition: Impressions Book and Journal Services, Inc.

© 2001 by Prentice Hall

Printed in the United States of America

ISBN: 0-13-027744-4

Library of Congress Cataloging-in Publication Data

Ketcham, Emily.
  Prentice Hall's MOUS test preparation guide for Excel 2000 / Emily Ketcham,
    Carolyn Monroe.
    p. cm. – (Prentice Hall's MOUS test preparation guides series)
  Includes index.
  ISBN 0-13-027744-4
  1. Microsoft Excel for Windows—Examinations—Study guides. 2. Microsoft
software—Examinations—Study guides. 3. Business—Computer programs—Study and
teaching. 4. Electronic data processing personnel—Certification. I. Title: MOUS test
preparation guide for Excel 2000. II. Title: Excel 2000. III. Monroe, Carolyn.
IV. Title. V. Series.

HF5548.4.M523 K485 2000
005.369—dc21   00-056679

Contents

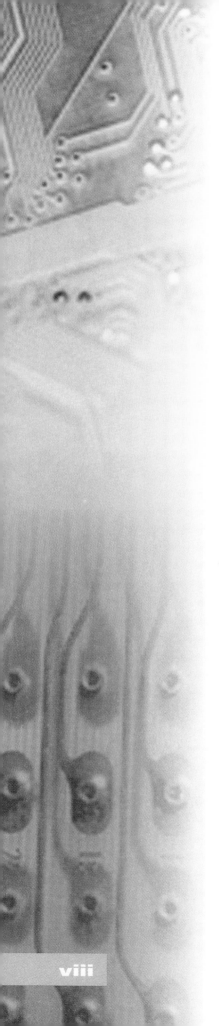

■ 15 *Use Excel with the Web*   329

■ 16 *Work with Templates and Macros*   348

■ 17 *Collaborate with Workgroups*   367

Appendix

Preface

A flash of insight—

...and I saw the kind of book that people would really use—even enjoy using—and that would help them learn. That insight led to the creation of this new series, Prentice Hall's MOUS Test Preparation Guides for Office 2000.

This series has two main objectives: to provide students with a clear, direct and comprehensive source for gaining computer expertise, and to support instructors with superior resources to enhance their teaching.

This book is designed for people like these:

- Busy adults who want to get right to the point.
- Beginners who don't want to be overwhelmed with jargon and unnecessary details.
- Experienced users whose goal is to pass the MOUS certification exam.

Five elements combine to make this series so effective:

Condensed steps cover each skill precisely, without burying you in unnecessary examples and too many words.

Thought Questions challenge students to apply what they've learned.

Tips from a Pro give inside information about the application. More than just a way to cram for the exam, this book provides expert guidance so you can use Microsoft Office like a professional.

MOUS objectives are specifically addressed and clearly labeled in each chapter so you will be ready for certification.

MOUS PinPoint software supplies interactive tutorials and timed tests so you gain hands-on experience using the software and taking the MOUS exams.

IMPORTANT: The CD-ROM accompanying this book contains the PinPoint software as well as all the data files for you to use as you work through the chapters. It contains separate folders for each chapter. Please refer to the Readme file on the CD to review how to use the student data files.

○ **Feature: You cover the subject without getting covered up.**

Straightforward guide to learning—Short, pithy explanations for each skill take a What-Why-How-Results approach. You'll find it easy to learn these key aspects:

- The core concepts for each skill
- Why it's important, or why you'll use it
- How to do it, step-by-step
- What to expect as a result

This means you can quickly find answers, see how to do a skill, and gain expertise. The tasks are covered, but not covered up. Just the facts, ma'am.

○ **Feature: You gain insight into how professionals use the skills.**

Use your skills like a master—The **Tips from a Pro** feature adds to your knowledge so you can handle tasks like a professional. You not only learn how to perform each skill, but also how to select and use the features appropriately, along with some alternatives and shortcuts to the traditional method. For example, **Tips from a Pro** cover these topics:

- How to format a document so people will want to read it.
- What to include when adding a chart to a document.
- Ways to set up a form so people will fill it out correctly and completely every time.
- The best way to use lines and borders in a table.
- Pitfalls to avoid in proofing spelling.
- And many more.

○ **Feature: You zero in on MOUS objectives for success.**

A MOUS bible—For each application, we cover every MOUS objective—at both Core and Expert levels—in one slim book. This means the answer you need for every MOUS skill is close at hand. You can use this book to teach yourself or to help you review your skills.

○ **Feature: You learn hands-on with PinPoint.**

MOUS PinPoint Software—This series is designed to work hand in hand with the engaging PinPoint Software, created by Kelly Temporary Services for training professionals. It matches the book with its short, to-the-point approach, and strongly reinforces the skills you need to prepare for the certification exam.

MOUS PinPoint software contains these elements:

- *Trainers:* Over a hundred interactive computer-based skill drills for each application, with demonstrations and immediate feedback
- *Evaluations:* Sample MOUS certification exams with real-life testing conditions.

I'm hooked on MOUS PinPoint, and here's why:

- It zeroes in on a single skill. When you can successfully complete each task, you can utilize these skills in your real life to help get your work done.
- Instant feedback lets you know whether you've performed the task correctly.
- Not sure how to do it? Click Show Me, and a short explanation and demonstration models the skill, then lets you try it yourself.
- It times how long it takes you to complete a single skill. Like Beat The Clock, this brings out a spirit of competition, and makes you want to try harder and work faster than the timer!

Result: accomplishment and expertise

Learners who use this MOUS Test Prep Guide and its accompanying MOUS PinPoint software are well prepared to pass the MOUS certification exam. Not merely a way to cram for the test, this series expertly guides you to competent use of Microsoft Office to accomplish your day-to-day tasks.

Supplements Package

Student Supplements

Companion Web site (www.prenhall.com/phmoustest) Includes student data files as well as test questions that allow students to test their knowledge of the material and get instant assessment.

Instructor Supplements

Instructor's Resource CD-ROM Includes Instructor's Manuals, Test Manager, PowerPoint slides, and data and solutions files for all four Office applications.

Companion Web site (www.prenhall.com/phmoustest) Includes the Instructor's Manuals, PowerPoint slides, and data and solutions files for all four Office applications, all available for download.

Acknowledgments

I am blessed to be surrounded by so many smart and capable professionals who took a part in producing this book. Dean Terry Maness and department chair G.W. Willis at Baylor's Hankamer School of Business supported this project with a good schedule and computer resources. Several other colleagues at Baylor University provided components of the book: Carolyn Monroe wrote a number of the end-of-chapter exercises and projects, Pati Milligan produced the instructions for the final chapter, and Colene Coldwell served as able cohort in composing and creating this new series. Three friends permitted me to use their enjoyable writings as samples in the exercises and projects: Elizabeth Vardaman, Christy Garner, and Laurel Naversen.

A true partner, Cecil Yarbrough worked carefully through every chapter, providing direction and correction and helping to shape the series. Lucinda Gatch deserves the credit for championing these new books and, with her gentle humor, encouraging superhuman efforts from all who had a hand in its production: Kris King, Monica Stipanov, Tim Tate, and Jennifer Cappello.

My husband Don supports both body and soul with every comfort. How grateful I am for having all of them in my life.

Emily Ketcham
Baylor University

Features and Benefits

Why the books in this series are the ultimate interactive MOUS test preparation guides:

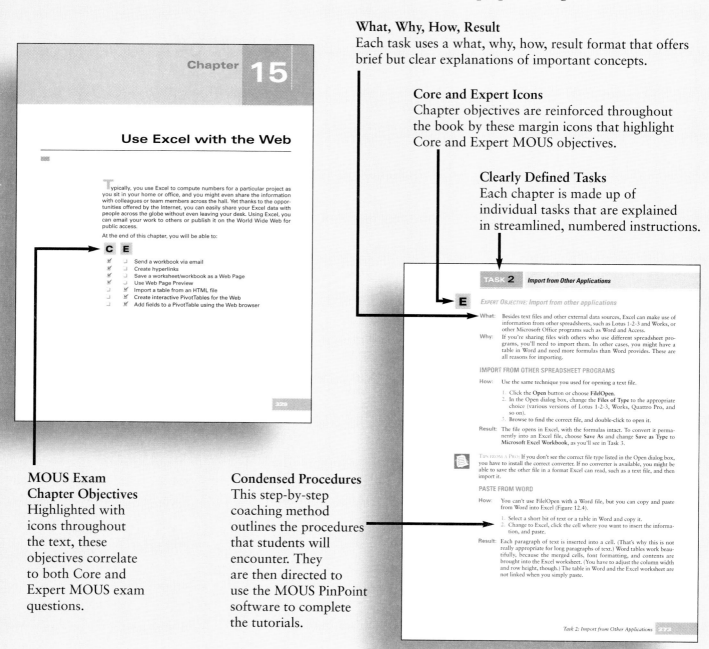

What, Why, How, Result
Each task uses a what, why, how, result format that offers brief but clear explanations of important concepts.

Core and Expert Icons
Chapter objectives are reinforced throughout the book by these margin icons that highlight Core and Expert MOUS objectives.

Clearly Defined Tasks
Each chapter is made up of individual tasks that are explained in streamlined, numbered instructions.

MOUS Exam Chapter Objectives
Highlighted with icons throughout the text, these objectives correlate to both Core and Expert MOUS exam questions.

Condensed Procedures
This step-by-step coaching method outlines the procedures that students will encounter. They are then directed to use the MOUS PinPoint software to complete the tutorials.

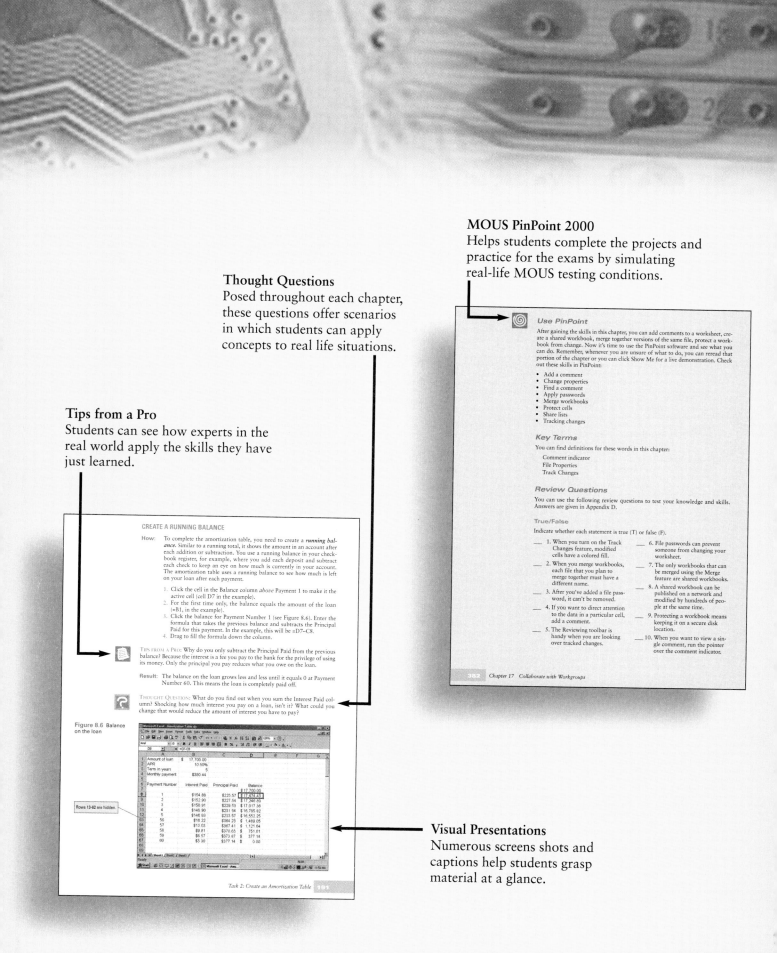

MOUS PinPoint 2000
Helps students complete the projects and practice for the exams by simulating real-life MOUS testing conditions.

Thought Questions
Posed throughout each chapter, these questions offer scenarios in which students can apply concepts to real life situations.

Tips from a Pro
Students can see how experts in the real world apply the skills they have just learned.

Visual Presentations
Numerous screens shots and captions help students grasp material at a glance.

Figure 8.6 Balance on the loan

Rows 13-62 are hidden.

Start with Windows

Before you begin using the Microsoft Office 2000 programs, you need to know a little bit about Windows. What you see when your computer is first turned on and ready to use is Windows. It is a type of software known as the operating system, and it is what the computer uses to direct its computing processes.

We humans use the operating system for starting programs we want to use for work or pleasure (such as Word, Excel, PowerPoint, Access, or Solitaire) and for managing the contents of our computers.

This chapter will cover the basic skills for all of these versions of Windows:

- ○ Windows 2000
- ○ Windows Millennium Edition (ME)
- ○ Windows 98

At the end of this chapter you will be able to:

- ❑ Explain what an operating system does
- ❑ Name items on the Windows desktop
- ❑ Start programs
- ❑ Handle windows
- ❑ Use menus and dialog boxes
- ❑ Manage the contents of your computer
- ❑ Customize the desktop

TASK 1 — Turn on the Computer

What: The first step in learning to use the computer is to turn it on.

Why: Well, I guess you know why.

How: Follow these steps to turn on the computer and start Windows.

1. Look on the front of the computer for a button to push. Often the button is marked with a circle with a vertical line, like this: ⏻ Alternatively, you may have a switch labeled with a line and circle. The line means On, and the circle means Off. If you've found the correct button, you'll hear the computer begin to hum and perhaps see some lights flash.

2. You may have to turn on the monitor as well. Often the switch is under its "chin." When you're successful, you'll see a green light, and after a little warm-up time, you'll see something appear on the monitor.

3. Watch as some numbers and words go by, and then a colorful screen appears while Windows is loading.

4. Depending on how Windows is set up on your computer, you may have to *log on*, that is, type in your user name and password. Check with your instructor to find out what you should type. Here's how to log on:

   1. Type your name in the first box.
   2. Press the Tab key on the keyboard.
   3. Type your password in the second box.
   4. Press **Enter**.

⧖ 5. Do you see the small hourglass on your screen? That means that Windows is busy.

Result: When the computer has finished *booting up*, or starting, you will see the Windows screen shown in Figure 1. The hourglass image you may have noticed earlier has changed into a small arrowhead.

TASK 2 — Explore the Windows Desktop

What: Examine Figure 1 to see the names of each of the items on the screen.

Why: You will need to learn the names of the elements shown on the screen so you can refer to them quickly when they are mentioned in this book or on the MOUS exam. The Windows desktop shown in Figure 1 contains the following elements:

Desktop is the term for the entire Windows screen, including the background. Like your physical desk, it contains the documents you're working on, as well as handy tools to help you get your work done.

Icons are small pictures that represent tools, programs, or documents you can use. This desktop has the following icons:

○ *My Documents* is a handy folder where you can store documents that you work on.

○ *My Computer* is a way to view and manage the contents of your computer.

○ *My Network Places* is a way to view and manage your computer's connections to a network or the Internet. (In Windows 98, you'll see **Network Neighborhood** instead. It's used to manage all the resources connected by a network to your computer.)

○ *Recycle Bin* is a temporary storage place for items you discard or delete from your computer.

○ *Internet Explorer* is a computer program known as a *browser*, which is used to see information found on the World Wide Web.

○ *Microsoft Outlook* is Office 2000's program for sending e-mail and managing personal information such as schedules, contacts, and tasks.

Mouse pointer is controlled by your mouse, touchstick, touchpad, or other pointing device.

Start button, when you click it, reveals a menu or list of choices of things to do.

Quick Launch toolbar contains buttons that, when you click them, start programs.

Taskbar contains a button for each task your computer is currently processing. (There are none shown here.)

The *clock* helps you keep track of how long till lunchtime or your next appointment.

 TIPS FROM A PRO: What you see on your computer may look a little different from what you see here. You may have different icons, different pictures, or different colors. You may see underlined words and additional images.

Figure 1 The Windows screen

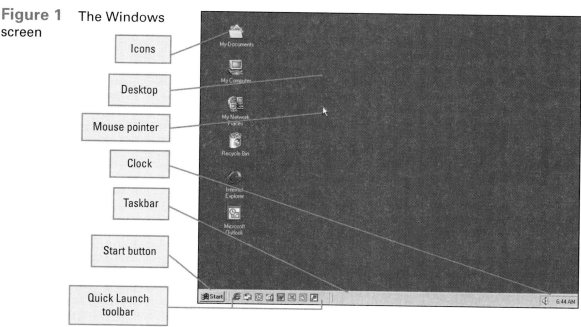

Icons

Desktop

Mouse pointer

Clock

Taskbar

Start button

Quick Launch toolbar

What: A major strength of using Windows is being able to use a pointing device. All pointing devices use similar techniques: point, click, double-click, right-click, and drag. Common pointing devices include these:

1. A mouse, a rolling device you use with your entire hand, consisting of buttons and possibly a wheel;
2. A touchstick, a small, rubbery knob in the middle of a laptop computer's keyboard you wiggle with your fingertip, combined with one or two buttons you click with your thumb;
3. A touchpad, a rectangular area often found below the keyboard of a laptop computer that you use by touching or tapping with your finger.

You use the pointing device to control the ***mouse pointer*** on screen, that little picture that often resembles an arrow or an hourglass.

Why: When you use the mouse (or other pointing device) to give directions to the computer, you don't have to type a million commands. Instead, use the mouse to indicate things on screen that you want to use or actions you want to do.

How: Every pointing device has five major techniques. Read about these techniques for the pointing device that you have (Tables 1 through 3).

Table 1   Mouse Techniques

Technique	*How to do it*	*Effect on screen*
Point	Roll the mouse on the surface in a certain direction.	The mouse pointer (often an arrow) moves in the same direction. Try pointing to the clock. You will see today's date appear.
Click	Tap the left mouse button with your index finger (assuming you're right-handed).	Selects (or sometimes opens) whatever the mouse pointer is pointing to on screen. Click the Start button to see the menu appear. Click again to make it disappear.
Double-click	Same as above, only do it two times quickly. If it doesn't work, try holding the mouse very still and clicking twice in a row even more quickly.	Opens whatever the mouse pointer is pointing to on the screen. You'll use this later.
Right-click	Click the right mouse button with your middle finger (assuming you're right-handed).	Shows a ***shortcut menu***, a short menu with a variety of commands. Try this out: Point to the middle of the desktop and right-click. Click a blank area to get rid of the shortcut menu.

Technique	How to do it	Effect on screen
Drag	Point to something on screen, and then click and hold down the left button while you move the mouse.	Moves the item you pointed to from one place to another. Also used to select more than one item. You'll use this later.
Scroll	Rotate the wheel toward or away, or click the wheel button and move the mouse. (Available only on a mouse that has a wheel button between the left and right buttons)	Moves the contents of a list or window up or down. You'll use this later.

Table 2 Touchstick Techniques

Technique	How to do it	Effect on screen
Point	Push the touchstick in a certain direction.	The mouse pointer (often an arrow) moves in the same direction. Try pointing to the clock. You will see today's date appear.
Click	Tap once quickly on a button below the keyboard.	Selects (or sometimes opens) whatever the mouse pointer is pointing to on screen. Click the Start button to see the menu appear. Click again to make it disappear.
Double-click	Same as above, only do it two times quickly. If it doesn't work, try tapping twice in a row even more quickly.	Opens whatever the mouse pointer is pointing to on the screen. You'll use this later.
Right-click	Tap once on the right button.	Shows a shortcut menu, a *short menu* with commands you can choose from. Try this out: Point to the middle of the desktop and right-click. Click a blank area to get rid of the shortcut menu.
Drag	Point to something on the screen, and then hold down the left button while you push the touchstick in a certain direction.	Moves the item you pointed to from one place to another. Also used to select more than one item. You'll use this later.

Table 3 Touchpad Techniques

Technique	How to do it	Effect on screen
Point	"Draw" with your finger on the touchpad in a certain direction.	The mouse pointer (often an arrow) moves in the same direction. Try pointing to the clock. You will see today's date appear.
Click	Tap once lightly on the touchpad, or tap the button.	Selects (or sometimes opens) whatever the mouse pointer is pointing to on screen. Click the Start button to see the menu appear. Click again to make it disappear.
Double-click	Tap two times quickly. If it doesn't work, try tapping twice in a row even more quickly.	Opens whatever the mouse pointer is pointing to on the screen. You'll use this later.
Right-click	Tap once quickly on the right button.	Shows a shortcut menu, a **short menu** with commands you can choose from. Try this out: Point to the middle of the desktop and right-click. Click a blank area to get rid of the shortcut menu.
Drag	Place the mouse pointer on something, and then hold down the left button while you "draw" on the touchpad with your finger in a certain direction.	Moves the item you pointed to from one place to another. Also used to select more than one item. You'll use this later.

 TIPS FROM A PRO: Do you see underlined words beneath each icon when you point to it? If so, you're using Web-style Windows, rather than classic Windows. With Web-style Windows, you use slightly different techniques with your pointing device. Table 4 shows the main differences. You'll learn how to change from one style to the other in Task 9.

Table 4 Pointing and Clicking in Classic and Web-style Windows

When you do this . . .	What happens in classic Windows	What happens in Web-style Windows
Point	No effect	Selects an item
Click	Selects an item	Opens an item
Double-click	Opens an item	Unnecessary—just click once

Result: As you become proficient in using your pointing device, you will be able to tell the computer what you want to do with little effort. You'll learn when to use each of these techniques for using Windows and Office 2000.

Note: From this point on, this book will use the term "mouse" for all pointing devices.

What: An obvious place to start using Windows is the Start button. (A *button* is a rectangular area you can click to access a command or action.) When you move the mouse pointer to the Start button and click, the *Start menu* appears, as you see in Figure 2. It contains a list of choices or commands. Some of the choices are followed by a right-pointing triangle. That means when you choose them, another menu will appear.

Figure 2   Start menu

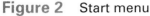

Programs menu

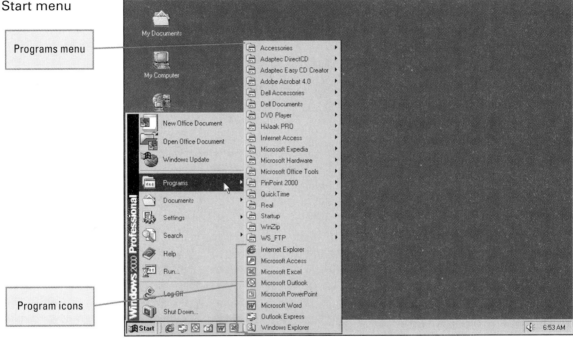

Program icons

Why: A menu provides a set of choices for you. You don't have to remember what command to type to tell the computer what to do.

How: Use a menu this way.

1. Click the **Start** button, and the Start menu appears.
2. Move the mouse up or down to highlight or select different items on the menu.
3. Point to **Programs**, and the Programs menu appears. Point to **Accessories**, and the Accessories menu appears. You can click a program icon (something without a right-pointing triangle) to start a program. For example, you could click **Calculator** on the Accessories menu.
4. Or click away from the menu to make it go away without starting anything.

Result: When you choose something from the menu, the menu disappears, and the computer gets busy doing what you told it to do. You can choose from items listed on the Start menu to begin working on your computer. These are the ones you'll use often:

- ○ **Programs** gives a list of programs you can access and use.
- ○ **Help** offers information and assistance for any technique or feature of Windows.
- ○ **Log Off** enables someone else to use the same computer. If you're working in a computer lab, you'll probably use this command instead of Shut Down.
- ○ **Shut Down** is what you choose when you're ready to turn off your computer.

TIPS FROM A PRO: Always choose **Shut Down** before turning off the power to your computer. See Task 10 to learn how to do this.

TASK **5**	*Handle Windows*

What: When you start a program or open a folder, it opens in a rectangular area called a *window*, shown in Figure 3. On the taskbar, you will also see a button associated with the window. You can open several different items, each in its own window. For every open window, a button appears on the taskbar.

All windows have the same elements, some more and some less, that you can use to change the window's size, move it around on the screen, see what's in it, and close it.

Figure 3   Two windows

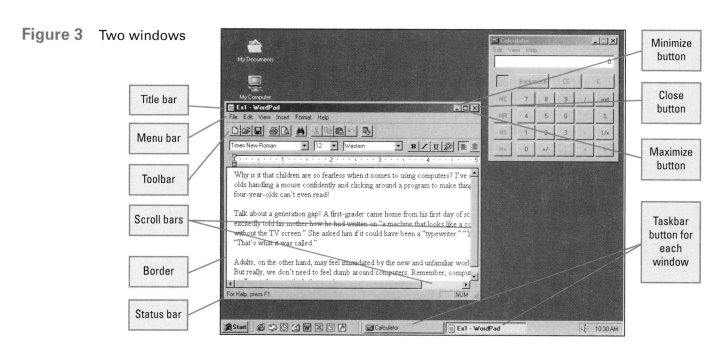

Start with Windows

Why: All windows have certain elements in common, and once you learn to use them, you will feel comfortable in any program.

MAXIMIZE A WINDOW

How: A window can be *maximized* or enlarged so that it fills the entire screen (Figure 4). You can do this two ways:

- ❍ Click the **Maximize** button.
- ❍ Double-click the **title bar**.

Figure 4 Two windows, one maximized

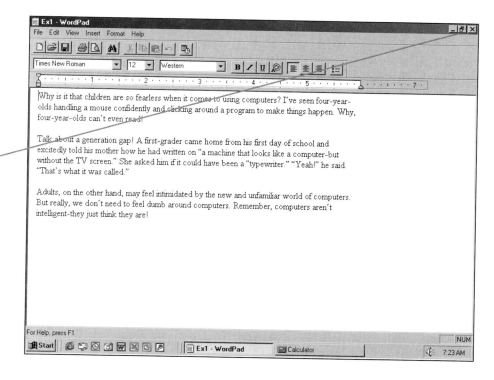

Restore button replaces Maximize button.

Result: The window fills the screen, and the Maximize button disappears, as it no longer applies. In its place is the Restore button that you can click to restore the window to its intermediate size. The maximized window covers the other windows, but you can tell what's open by the buttons on the taskbar.

TIPS FROM A PRO: When you maximize a window, can you still see the taskbar? If not, you can still access it. Try moving the mouse pointer to the bottom edge of the screen. Sometimes the taskbar will pop into view. If not, you can see it again when you minimize the window, as you'll learn shortly. You'll learn how to customize the taskbar in Task 9 to make it appear or always remain on screen.

RESTORE A WINDOW

How: You may want to *restore* a maximized window to its intermediate size. You can do this in two ways:

○ Click the **Restore** button (the one that replaced the Maximize button).
○ Double-click the **title bar**.

Result: The window shrinks back to its original size, an intermediate size that does not fill the entire desktop. The Restore button is replaced with the Maximize button.

 THOUGHT QUESTION: Look back at Figure 3. Why do you suppose the Calculator does not have a Maximize or Restore button?

MINIMIZE A WINDOW

How: Whether a window is maximized or middle-sized, you may find that it is in the way when you want to look at something else on the screen. To *minimize* a window so that it appears only as a button on the taskbar, click the **Minimize** button, near the top-right corner of the window.

Figure 5 Two windows, one minimized.

This window is minimized.

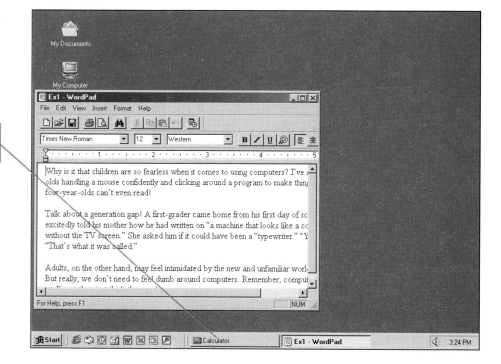

Result: The window seems to disappear, but it is still available. It's just put aside temporarily while you do other things on your Windows desktop.

SWITCH AMONG SEVERAL WINDOWS

How: With two or more windows open at a time, you can work on more than one thing at a time. This is called **multitasking**. The windows may overlap each other or one may be maximized or minimized, but no matter what, a button for each appears on the taskbar. To tell the computer which window you want to use, do one of these:

❍ Click the window's button on the taskbar.
❍ Click somewhere within the window you want, if you can see it.

Result: The window you choose immediately comes to the front of all the other windows. Its title bar has a brighter color, and its button on the taskbar appears pushed in. This window is called the **active window**.

MOVE A WINDOW

How: When one window overlaps another, or perhaps covers an icon on the desktop that you want to use, you can move the window on the desktop. To do this, place the mouse pointer on the title bar and drag.

Result: The window moves in the direction you drag it. (Of course, this doesn't work on a window that has been maximized or minimized.)

SIZE A WINDOW

How: Besides maximizing or minimizing a window, you can change its height and width to suit your needs.

1. Place the mouse pointer over the border until it turns into a two-headed arrow, as you see in Figure 6.
2. Drag the border inward or outward to change the dimensions of the window.

TASK 5: Handle Windows   **11**

Figure 6 Change the size of a window

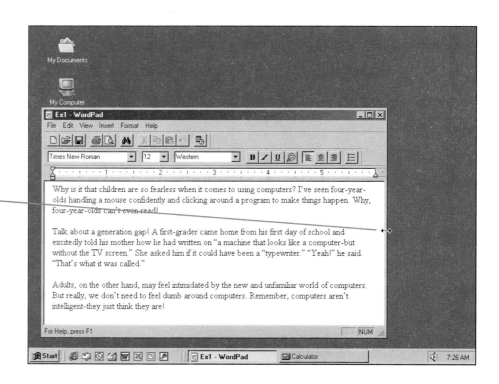

Mouse pointer becomes a two-headed arrow.

Result: The height or width of the window changes, so you can see more or less of the window's contents.

TIPS FROM A PRO: If you place the mouse pointer on the corner, it turns into a diagonal two-headed arrow. Now when you drag, you can change both the height and width at the same time.

SCROLL IN A WINDOW

How: When the contents of a window do not entirely fit within a window, *scrollbars* appear along the right or bottom edge, as in Figure 7. Use your mouse along with the scrollbars to bring the other contents of the window into view:

○ Click an arrow at either end of the scrollbar to move a little bit at a time. Click and hold the arrow to scroll slowly.
○ Drag the box from one end to the other or anywhere in between to see a different part of the contents.
○ Click above or below the box to scroll up or down one screen.
○ Rotate the mouse wheel, if you have one, to look at the contents above or below at the current screen.

Figure 7 Window with scrollbars

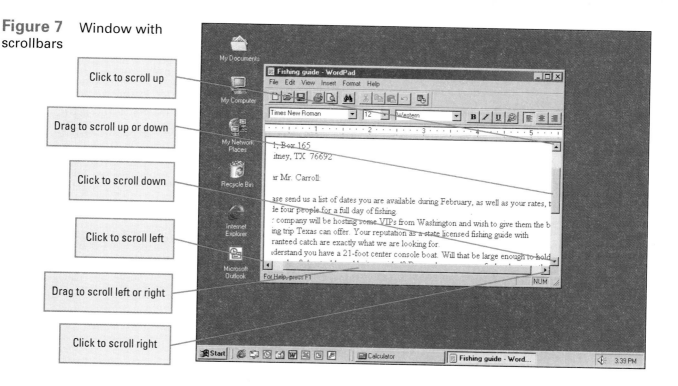

Click to scroll up

Drag to scroll up or down

Click to scroll down

Click to scroll left

Drag to scroll left or right

Click to scroll right

Result: You can view all the contents of a window, even the material that is currently out of view.

CLOSE A WINDOW

How: When you are completely through using a window, click the **Close** button on the top-right corner.

Result: This removes the window from the screen and removes its button from the taskbar. It is no longer using the computer's processing resources.

TASK 6   *Interact with Programs*

What: When you've got a program open in a window, no matter what program it is, you interact with it the same general way. Just below the title bar is the *menu bar*, containing a series of words that drop down a menu of commands when you click them.

Some commands require you to make more specific choices. For example, the Print command enables you to specify answers to these questions: What pages do you want to print? What printer do you want use? What order do you want the pages printed? To make your choices, the program presents you with a *dialog box*, a rectangular message box that you can click or type in.

Why: Using menus and dialog boxes is how we humans tell the computer what we want it to do. When you can quickly find the commands you need and make choices easily in the dialog box, you'll be showing your expertise.

USE MENUS

How: Here's how to use a menu on the menu bar.

1. Click a word on the menu bar to drop down the menu.
2. Click a command to choose it, or click away from the menu to make it go away without choosing anything.

Look at Figure 8 to see how to read a menu.

Figure 8   Menu commands

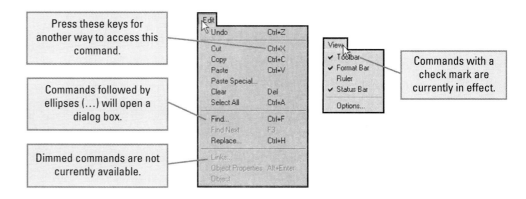

Press these keys for another way to access this command.

Commands followed by ellipses (...) will open a dialog box.

Dimmed commands are not currently available.

Commands with a check mark are currently in effect.

Result: When you choose a command, the program obeys or, if the command is followed by ellipses (...), opens a dialog box for you to make more choices.

   TIPS FROM A PRO: Typical commands that appear in many programs are always found on the same menu. For example, you can count on finding the Print command on the File menu, and the Copy command on the Edit menu.

USE DIALOG BOXES

How: Although the choices that appear in various dialog boxes are specific to the command, the way you interact with any dialog box is the same. Each element shown in Figure 9 works a different way to make it easy for you to specify what you want.

❍ Type in a ***text box*** to give the computer your information.
❍ Click a ***check box*** to insert or remove a check next to a choice.
❍ Click the down arrow on a ***drop-down list*** to see more choices to click.
❍ Click a choice in a ***list box***, or scroll to see more choices.
❍ Click one ***option button*** among the choices given.
❍ Click the up or down arrows on a ***spin box*** to increase or decrease a number.
❍ Use a ***command button*** just as you use the Start button. Click OK to accept the choices and put them into effect, or click Cancel to make the dialog box go away without making any change.
❍ Click a ***tab*** to see another screen of choices on a related topic.

○ Click the *Help* button (the question mark in the title bar) and then click any element in the dialog-box for pop-up help on what it does.

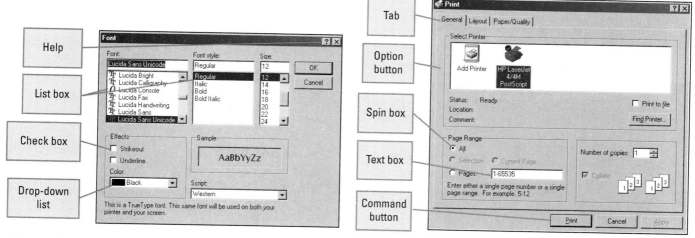

Figure 9 Typical dialog box elements

Result: When you make your choices in the dialog box and click **OK**, the command takes effect. If instead you want the dialog box to go away and not make changes, click **Cancel** or press the **Esc** key.

 TIPS FROM A PRO: To advance from one text box to another, press the **Tab** key. This is faster than clicking with the mouse because you leave your hands on the keyboard and continue typing your information.

TASK 7 | *View the Contents of Your Computer*

What: Computers store information such as documents, pictures, spread-sheets, databases, and programs in *files*. Files are organized into *folders*, and folders can be placed inside other folders, just as pieces of paper are placed into manila folders and then in hanging folders and organized in the various drawers of a filing cabinet. A folder that contains another folder is called a *parent folder*, and a folder that is inside another folder is often called a *subfolder*.

Like the separate drawers of a filing cabinet, the computer has several *disk drives* that read the information stored there. The drives available on your computer are named with letters of the alphabet:

1. A 3 1/2-inch floppy disk drive is named drive A.
2. An internal hard disk drive is named drive C (a second hard disk, if you have one, would be named drive D).
3. A CD-ROM or DVD-ROM drive is usually named drive D (or E, if you have two hard disks).

4. Other drives, such as a Zip drive and ones available over a network, will be named with subsequent letters.

Windows offers two resources that let you see the contents of the computer: My Computer and Windows Explorer. In both of these, when you look at what's stored in your computer, you can view it several different ways.

Why: You need to see the contents of your computer to know what's stored on it and where everything is, just as you know what's found in the various drawers and closets of your home. When you see a file or folder listed, you can open it, copy it, rename it, or delete it, or you can make a shortcut to it. You'll learn all these skills in the next tasks.

 TIPS FROM A PRO: As you view the file contents of your computer, you'll notice a variety of icons. The icon is a way to see what kind of file it is. Some common icons are shown in Table 5.

Table 5   Common Windows Icons

Icon	File type
	Folder
	Word document
	Excel worksheet
	PowerPoint presentation
	Access database
	Web page
	Text file

USE MY COMPUTER

How: Follow these steps to open My Computer and view its contents various ways.

1. Move the mouse pointer to the **My Computer** icon on the desktop. (If you are using Web-style Windows, the mouse pointer will turn into a pointing hand.)
2. Double-click (or if you are using Web-style Windows, click once) on the icon. My Computer opens in a window on the screen, similar to Figure 10.

Figure 10 My Computer

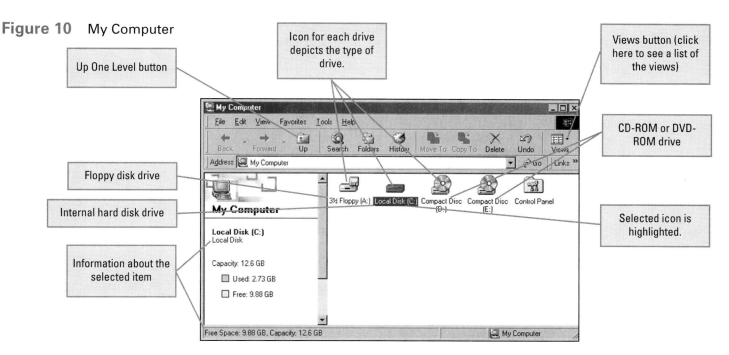

Up One Level button

Icon for each drive depicts the type of drive.

Views button (click here to see a list of the views)

CD-ROM or DVD-ROM drive

Floppy disk drive

Internal hard disk drive

Information about the selected item

Selected icon is highlighted.

3. Click to *select* an icon for a drive (for Web-style Windows, just point to it with the mouse pointer and pause). The icon appears darker, and information appears on the left and on the status bar.

4. Double-click an icon (or click once in Web-style Windows) to open it and see its contents. *Note*: You have to insert a disk into the floppy, CD, or DVD drive before you try to open it.

5. Click the **Views** button several times in succession to get the views shown in Figure 11. You can also click the arrow next to the button and choose a view from the list that appears.

   ○ **Large Icons view** shows all the folders and files in alphabetical order across the rows.

   ○ **Small Icons view** lists across the rows all the folders and then the files in alphabetical order.

   ○ **List view** lists all the folders and then the files in alphabetical order vertically, down the column.

   ○ **Details view** shows not only the file name and type, but also the size and date it was created or last modified. You can click the column headings to sort the files in order by name, by type, by size, and by date.

   ○ **Thumbnails view** displays a small version of the file. This is particularly useful for pictures and other graphics.

Figure 11 Five views

Back

Address bar

Forward

Up One Level

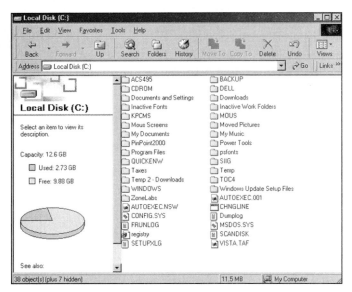

(a) Large icons view

(b) Small icons view

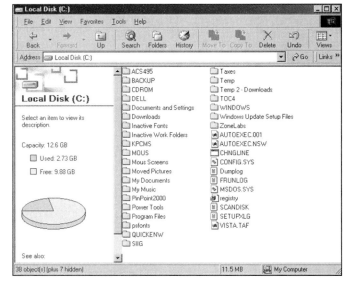

(c) List view

Click a column heading to sort the files on that column; click it again to reverse the sort order.

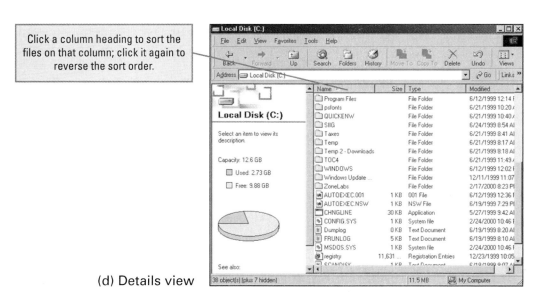

(d) Details view

Start with Windows

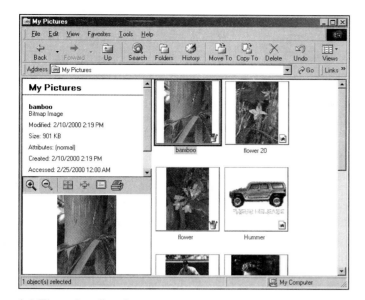

(e) Thumbnails view

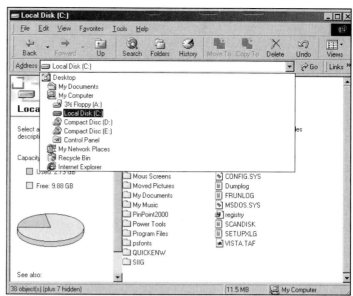

Figure 12 Address bar shows a list of drives

6. Double-click a folder to see its contents (click once in Web-style Windows).
7. Click the **Up One Level** button on the toolbar to see the parent folder or drive that contains the items you are currently viewing.
8. Click the **Back** button to retrace your steps in viewing various drives and folders in reverse order. Click the **Forward** button to step through them again.
9. Click the **Address** bar's down arrow to choose a different drive, as you see in Figure 12.

Result: You can click buttons to change views, and you can control which folder or drive's contents are on display. Viewing the contents is the first step to managing the contents of your computer, which you'll learn in Task 8.

TIPS FROM A PRO: You can also use the Address bar to access the Web. Just type the address for a Web page and press **Enter**, and My Computer will transform into the Web browser, Internet Explorer.

ACCESS WINDOWS EXPLORER

How: To access Windows Explorer do one of these:

○ Click the **Start** button, choose **Programs**, and then click **Windows Explorer**. (You may have to click the downward-pointing triangle on the bottom of the Programs menu to see more choices.) In Windows ME, click the Start button, choose Programs, select Accessories, and then click Windows Explorer.

TASK 7: View the Contents of Your Computer   **19**

○ Open **My Computer** and transform it into Windows Explorer. To do this, click the **Folders** button. (In Windows 98, click the **View** menu, choose **Explorer Bar**, and click **Folders**.)

Windows Explorer adds one feature to My Computer: the *Folders pane*. As you see in Figure 13, the Folders pane shows a list of drives and folders, with the folders indented beneath the drive, and subfolders indented even more, something like an outline.

To use Windows Explorer, use these techniques:

○ Scroll up and down to see more drives and folders.
○ Click a **+** next to a drive or folder to expand it to show the folders contained inside.
○ Click a **–** next to a drive or folder to collapse the subfolders and take up less space in the Folders pane.
○ Click a drive or folder to see its contents on the right side of the window.

Result: Using the Folders pane makes it easy to navigate around the various drives and folders to view their contents. When you click a drive or folder, it appears dark, or selected. This is the *current drive* or *current folder*, the one whose contents are listed in the right side of the window. Click a different drive or folder in the Folders pane to change which one is current.

 TIPS FROM A PRO: The name of the current drive or folder also appears on the title bar of the window, on the address bar, and on its taskbar button as well.

 THOUGHT QUESTION: Can you have both a current drive *and* a current folder? Can you change the current folder without changing the current drive?

Figure 13 Windows Explorer

Folders pane

Click + to expand.

Click – to collapse.

This has been expanded to show subfolders.

This is collapsed to hide subfolders.

Folders pane has its own scrollbar.

What: Besides just looking around, you can use My Computer and Windows Explorer to manage the contents of your computer. Here are some of the tasks you can easily do:

- ❍ Create a folder to organize your stuff.
- ❍ Rename a file or folder.
- ❍ Copy a file or folder to another location.
- ❍ Move a file or folder to a different drive or folder.
- ❍ Use Send To as a quick way to make a copy.
- ❍ Delete a file or folder.

Why: You can use these skills to get organized. For example, you might take all the files, including pictures, charts, and documents, that pertain to a certain project and place them in a new folder you've created to specifically hold them. Or you can look on the CD that accompanies this book and copy the files needed for the exercises and projects to your hard disk or floppy disk so you can work on them. You can delete unwanted files, and when you have an important item you've been working on, you can use these skills to create a *backup* copy to store it in a separate location, just in case something happens to the original.

CREATE A FOLDER

How: Follow these steps to create a folder.

1. Open My Computer or Windows Explorer.
2. Choose where you want the folder to be.

   - ❍ In My Computer, view the drive or folder that you want to contain the new folder.
   - ❍ In Windows Explorer, use the Folders pane to select the drive or folder that you want to contain the new folder.

3. Click **File** and choose **New** and then click **Folder**. A new folder named *New Folder* appears, with its name surrounded by a rectangle, as you see in Figure 14.
4. Type the name of the folder and press **Enter**.

Type the folder's name.

Figure 14 Creating a folder in Windows Explorer

Result: The new folder appears both in the window and in the Folders pane.

TIPS FROM A PRO: If you happen to click away before you type the name for the new folder, you can still rename it later.

RENAME A FILE OR FOLDER

How: Follow these instructions to rename a file or folder.

1. Select the item you want to rename.
2. Right-click to see the shortcut menu shown in Figure 15.
3. Click (with either button) the **Rename** command. The menu goes away, and a rectangle appears around the name, indicating that you can type.
4. Type the new name and press **Enter**.

Result: The rectangle disappears from around the name, and the file or folder is renamed.

 TIPS FROM A PRO: The shortcut menu is *context-sensitive*, meaning that the choices shown on it depend on what you were pointing to when you right-clicked. This type of menu is sometimes called a context menu. The commands in Figure 15 are the ones you can use for managing files and folders. You'll see other commands on the shortcut menu when you right-click other items on screen.

Figure 15 Shortcut menu

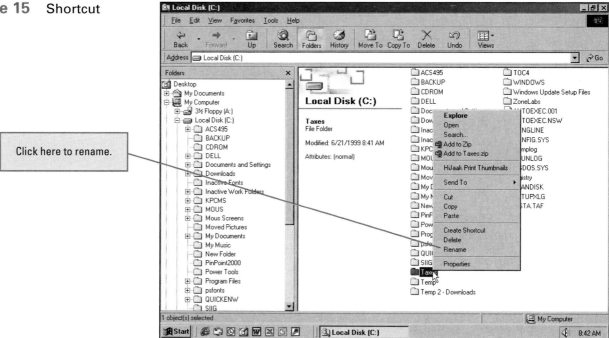

Click here to rename.

COPY OR MOVE A FILE OR FOLDER USING THE FOLDERS PANE

How: The Folders pane makes it easy to copy or move items. You can simply drag the items from the right side to the left.

 TIPS FROM A PRO: You can copy and move several items at the same time, if you want. To do this, you first have to select several items. Here are some techniques for selecting several items at once:

○ Drag a rectangular area surrounding the items you want to select.
○ Press and hold the **Shift** key and click the first and last items; the items you clicked and all the items in between will be selected.
○ Press and hold the **Ctrl** key and click each item you want, without selecting items between.

These techniques are for selecting items in classic Windows; if you're using Web-style Windows, hold down **Shift** or **Ctrl** while you point rather than clicking to select.

1. Scroll up or down the Folders pane, and expand as necessary until you see the destination for the file or folder.
2. Select on the right side of the window the file or folder you want to copy or move.
3. Right-drag (that is, drag while holding down the right mouse button) the selected item to the Folders pane until the destination is highlighted or selected. You can see this operation in Figure 16.

Figure 16 Dragging to the Folders pane

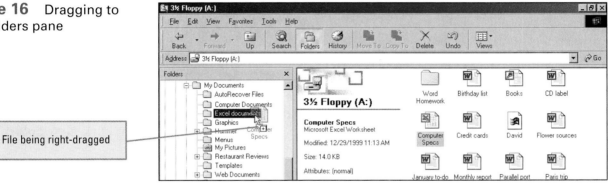

File being right-dragged

4. Release the mouse button, and a shortcut menu appears with several choices, as you see in Figure 17:

○ **Move here.** This is a good choice for organizing your files and folders.
○ **Copy here.** This is the choice when you want a second copy as a backup.
○ **Create shortcut(s) here.** You'll learn about shortcuts in Task 9.
○ **Cancel.** Choose this if you don't want to do any of the above.

Figure 17 Choose whether to move or copy

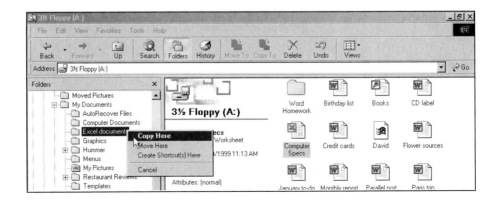

5. Click to choose **Move** or **Copy**, or click **Cancel** to change your mind.

Result: If you chose Move, the file or folder is removed from one location and placed in the new location. This is a good choice for when you are rearranging and organizing your files and folders on your hard disk. If you chose Copy, the file or folder is duplicated and appears in both locations. This is good for making backups on another disk.

  TIPS FROM A PRO: If you make a mistake in the copy or move process, click the **Undo** button and then try again.

COPY OR MOVE A FILE OR FOLDER IN MY COMPUTER

How: Windows provides several methods for copying. The instructions below use the buttons on the toolbar, but the Copy to Folder and Move to Folder commands are also available on the Edit menu. Select the item(s) you want to copy.

1. Click either the **Copy To** or **Move To** button. This opens the dialog box shown in Figure 18.
2. Expand the drives and folders as necessary, and scroll until you see the destination.
3. Click the destination and click **OK,** or click **New Folder** to create a new folder to contain the items.

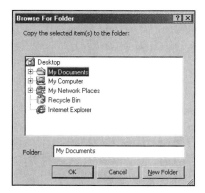

Figure 18 Browse for Folder dialog box

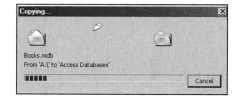

Figure 19 Copying in progress

Result: You may see an animation of the move or copy process, as shown in Figure 19. This is called a progress bar.

 TIPS FROM A PRO: Here's another way to create a folder. Click the **New Folder** button, as you see in Figure 18, if you want to create a new folder to contain the items you are moving or copying.

How: Working in Windows 98 is just a little different from working in newer versions of Windows. Instead of the Copy To button, you use the Copy and Paste buttons, and in place of the Move To button, you use the Cut and Paste buttons, shown in Figure 20. The Cut, Copy, and Paste commands are also available on the Edit menu.

Figure 20 Windows 98 toolbar has Cut, Copy, and Paste buttons

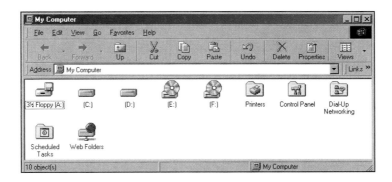

1. Select the item you want to copy.
2. To make a duplicate of an item, click **Copy**; to move an item, click **Cut**.
3. Navigate to and select the destination where you want the item to be placed. (In classic Windows, each folder may open in its own My Computer window, and therefore the Back and Forward buttons may be disabled.)
4. Click **Paste**.

Result: When you paste, you see an animation of the process.

TIPS FROM A PRO: You can use these same Cut, Copy, and Paste commands to move and duplicate lots of things besides just files and folders. For example, you can copy or cut a picture or a bit of text from inside one document and paste it into another. The copied or cut item is placed on the *clipboard*, a temporary storage place provided by Windows. Then you can paste it wherever you want.

USE SEND TO

How: An easy way to make a backup copy of the file is to use the Send To command.

1. Select the file or folder you want to back up.
2. Right-click the file, and then choose **Send To** on the shortcut menu, as shown in Figure 21.
3. Click the destination from the submenu. *Note:* you must first insert a floppy disk into the drive before you choose 3 1/2 Floppy A:.

Figure 21 Send To command

Choose **3 1/2 Floppy (A)** to make a backup onto a floppy disk.

Choose **My Briefcase** to coordinate files between two computers.

Result: The Copying dialog box appears, showing the process, just as you saw when you used the Copy To button.

DELETE A FILE OR FOLDER

How: When you've got unwanted files or folders on your disk, it's easy to remove them in My Computer or Windows Explorer.

1. Select the file or folder you want to delete.
2. Click the **Delete** button, or press the **Delete** key on the keyboard, or choose **Delete** from the **Edit** menu.
3. Click **OK** to confirm the delete, or **Cancel.**

Result: A dialog box appears, as in Figure 22, confirming whether you want to delete the selected item. When you click OK, the item will be deleted.

If you're deleting an item from your hard disk, Windows will move it to the Recycle Bin instead of permanently deleting it. This Windows feature temporarily stores deleted items, giving you a chance to change your mind and retrieve them, just as you can paw through the wastepaper basket looking for a bill or letter you've tossed by mistake.

Figure 22 Confirming
the delete

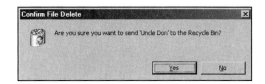

THOUGHT QUESTION: Why is the Recycle Bin only available on your hard disk, and not for files deleted from a floppy disk?

USE THE RECYCLE BIN TO RESTORE A DELETED FILE

How: To recover a file you've deleted from your hard disk, open the Recycle Bin.

1. Double-click the **Recycle Bin** on the Windows desktop, in My Computer, or in Windows Explorer's Folders pane. (Click once to open, if you are using Web-style Windows.)
2. Select the item you want to retrieve.
3. Right-click and choose **Restore**, as you see in Figure 23.

Figure 23 Restoring a deleted file from the Recycle Bin

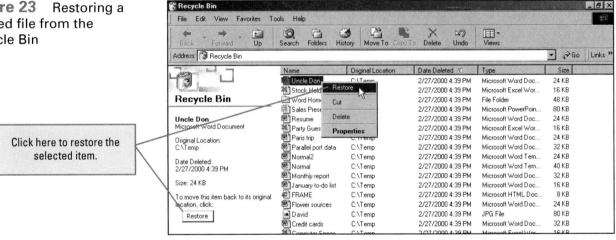

Click here to restore the selected item.

Result: The file is restored to the folder from which it was originally deleted.

TIPS FROM A PRO: If you delete a folder, you delete all the files contained in it. Only the folder is shown in the Recycle Bin, but the files are there also, even though their names aren't listed. Restoring the folder restores the files as well.

EMPTY THE RECYCLE BIN

How: Deleted items sent to the Recycle Bin are still taking up space on your hard disk. You must empty the Recycle Bin to permanently delete the files and thus make room on your hard disk.

1. Right-click the **Recycle Bin.**
2. Choose **Empty Recycle Bin** from the shortcut menu, shown in Figure 24a.
3. Click **Yes** to confirm that you want to permanently delete the files, or click **No** if you're not sure (Figure 24b).

Figure 24 Emptying the Recycle Bin

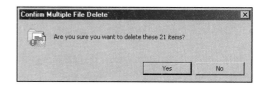

(a) Using the shortcut menu   (b) Confirming the delete

Result: The files are now permanently deleted, making more space available on your hard disk. If you wanted to restore them now, you have to go to the trouble and expense of getting and using special recovery software.

TASK 9   *Customize Windows*

What: One of the nice features of using Windows is the capability to customize it. This task covers just a few of the items you can customize.

Why: You can show your personality or just get things arranged the way you like so you can work efficiently.

CHANGE THE MOUSE

How: If you're left-handed, you'll especially like the capability to customize the way the mouse works.

1. Click the **Start** button, choose **Settings,** and click **Control Panel.** This opens the window shown in Figure 25.

Figure 25 Control Panel is used to customize the features of your computer

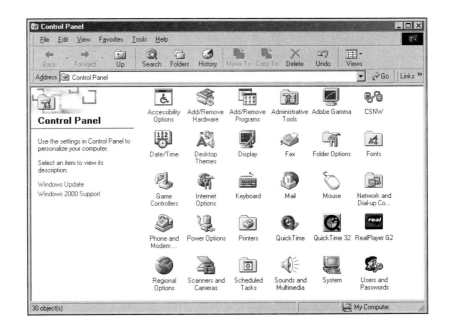

2. Double-click the icon for **Mouse** (or click once if you are using Web-style Windows). This opens the Mouse Properties dialog box.

3. Click the **Buttons** tab, if necessary, to see the dialog box shown in Figure 26. *Note:* Your dialog box may have different options.

4. Specify whether you prefer to use the mouse right-handed or left-handed, that is, which button you want to use regularly to choose things and which button you want to use to get the shortcut menu. Look through the various tabs in the dialog box, and make other adjustments you need, such as changes to the double-click speed or the motion of the mouse, or even the appearance of the mouse pointer.

5. When you're finished making choices, click one of the following buttons:

   ○ **Apply** to make the change and see its effect immediately, leaving the dialog box open for more changes.
   ○ **OK** to make changes and close the dialog box.
   ○ **Cancel** to close the dialog box without making any changes.

Figure 26 Customize the mouse

Choose other tabs to see more options.

Result: If you clicked OK, the choices you made in the Mouse dialog box are put into effect. Enjoy the new settings for your mouse!

 TIPS FROM A PRO: The *Control Panel* contains a number of other icons for you to customize to best fit your computer's hardware and your own preference. Open them up, explore a little, and click **Cancel** to leave without making any changes.

CHANGE THE DISPLAY

How: You can access the Display Properties dialog box to customize its appearance without even opening the Control Panel.

1. Right-click an empty area of the Windows desktop.
2. Choose **Properties** from the shortcut menu.
3. Look through the various tabs on the dialog box to see choices for customizing all sorts of features of the desktop. Here are some of the things you can do:

   ○ Change the design that appears on the desktop (Figure 27).
   ○ Set a screen saver to come on when your computer is idle.
   ○ Change the colors of the window elements, such as the title bar.
   ○ Change the resolution and number of colors that your monitor displays.

4. After you've made your choices, click one of the following buttons:

   ○ **Apply** to make the changes and see its effect immediately, leaving the dialog box open for more changes.
   ○ **OK** to make the changes and close the dialog box.
   ○ **Cancel** to close the dialog box without making any changes.

Figure 27 Customize the display

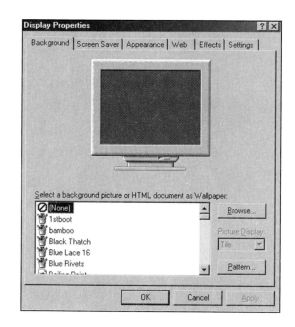

Result: You can show your individuality by your choices and make Windows a more pleasant environment to work in.

TIPS FROM A PRO: Here's how you change to (or from) Web-style Windows:

For Windows 2000

1. In My Computer or Windows Explorer, choose the **Tools** menu and click **Folder Options**.
2. Click the **General** tab, if necessary, to see the dialog box in Figure 28a.
3. Click to choose the top choice of each pair for Web-style windows, or the bottom choice of each pair for classic Windows, or any combination of Web-style and classic style that you prefer.

For Windows 98

1. In My Computer or Windows Explorer, choose the **View** menu, and click **Folder Options**.
2. Click the **General** tab if necessary, to see the dialog box in Figure 28b.
3. Choose **Web-style** (or **Classic style**, if you want to use that instead); or choose **Custom** and click **Settings** to open the Custom Settings dialog box, where you can choose any combination of Web-style and Classic style.
4. Click **OK**.

Figure 28 Folder Options dialog box

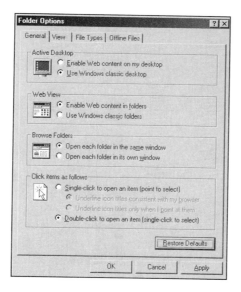

(a) In Windows 2000

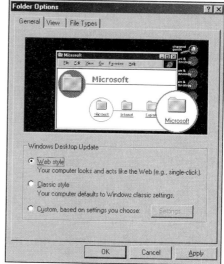

(b) In Windows 98

How: You have to change the settings for the taskbar before you can use the PinPoint tutorials and tests. Here's how to do that:

1. Place the mouse pointer on a blank area of the taskbar and right-click to see the shortcut menu in Figure 29.

Figure 29   Taskbar shortcut menu

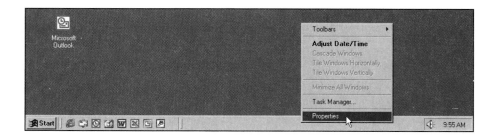

2. Click Properties to see the dialog box shown in Figure 30.

Figure 30   Taskbar properties

To use PinPoint, click to remove checks from these two boxes.

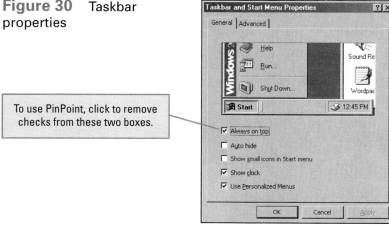

3. Choose one or more of these choices, and click **OK**:

   ○ **Always on Top** keeps the taskbar on screen even when a window is maximized.
   ○ **Auto Hide** minimizes the taskbar so that it appears as a line on the bottom of the screen. When you move the mouse pointer to it, the taskbar reappears.
   ○ **Show Small Icons in Start Menu** makes the Start menu shorter in height. (Not too useful.)
   ○ **Show Clock** displays the digital clock in the tray on the right side of the taskbar. (Very handy.)
   ○ **Show Personalized Menus** (not available in Windows 98) enables you to see only the menu selections on the Programs menu that you use most often, hiding the rest until you click the down arrow at the bottom of the Programs menu.

Result: The taskbar and Start menu behave the way you prefer.

TIPS FROM A PRO: Before you use the PinPoint software, you must remove checks from the Always on Top and Auto Hide choices in the Taskbar Properties dialog box.

ADD SHORTCUT ICONS TO THE DESKTOP

How: The Windows desktop, like your physical tabletop, should keep all the things you use often close at hand. You can create a *shortcut icon* right on the desktop as a way to quickly access your favorite file, folder, program, or Web page.

1. Use My Computer or Explorer and look around the various drives and folders to find the item you want to access quickly.
2. Right-click and from the shortcut menu choose **Send To** and then click **Desktop (Create Shortcut)**.

Figure 31
Shortcut icon

Result: A shortcut icon appears on the desktop. You can tell that it's a shortcut not only by its name, but by the small crooked arrow that appears on the corner, as in Figure 31.

You can rename a shortcut by right-clicking and choosing **Rename**, as you did before. You can delete shortcuts from the desktop by selecting it and pressing the **Delete** key. *Warning:* Do NOT delete icons from the desktop if they are not shortcut icons. This might delete a program. A better way to remove unwanted programs is through the Control Panel.

 THOUGHT QUESTION: Examine your Windows desktop. Which icons are shortcuts, and which are the actual programs?

ADD BUTTONS TO THE QUICK LAUNCH TOOLBAR

How: Rather than cluttering up your desktop with shortcut icons, you can put buttons on the Quick Launch portion of the taskbar (Figure 32). They'll be handy all the time, even when a window is maximized.

Figure 32
Quick Launch toolbar

1. Use My Computer or Windows Explorer and look around the various drives and folders to find the item you want to access quickly.
2. Select the item and right-drag (that is, drag with the right mouse button) to the Quick Launch toolbar.
3. To rearrange the icons, drag left or right. To delete an icon, drag it to the Recycle Bin.

Result: Your favorite programs, files, or folders are always handy.

 TIPS FROM A PRO: Do you want to add the icons for Word, Excel, PowerPoint or Access to the Quick Launch toolbar? Find them quickly with the Windows Search feature.

IN WINDOWS 2000

1. Click **Start**, choose **Search**, and click **For Files or Folders** (or in My Computer, click the **Search** button). This opens the Search Assistant, shown in Figure 33.
2. In the **Search for Files or Folders Named** box, type one of the following names:

   ○ **Winword.exe** for Word
   ○ **Powerpnt.exe** for PowerPoint
   ○ **Excel.exe** for Excel
   ○ **Msaccess.exe** for Access

3. Right-drag the program icon down to the Quick Launch toolbar, as you see in Figure 33.
4. On the menu that appears, choose **Create Shortcut Here**.

Figure 33 Find the Word program

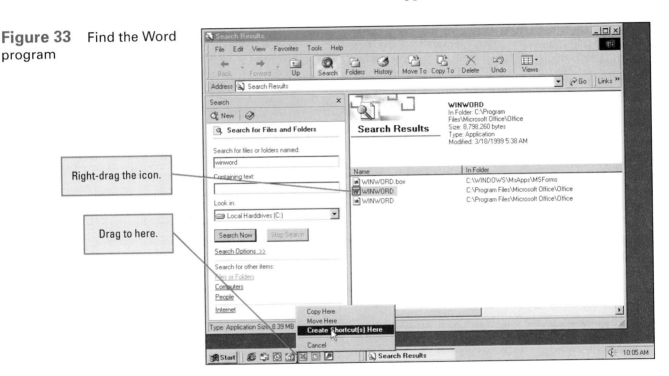

FOR WINDOWS 98

1. Click **Start**, choose **Find**, and click **Files or Folders**.
2. In the Find window, type the name of the program you want (same as above) and press **Enter**. In the bottom of the dialog box, you'll see the results.
3. Right-drag the program icon down to the Quick Launch toolbar, as you see in Figure 33.
4. On the menu that appears, choose **Create Shortcut Here**.

Start with Windows

TASK 10 *Exit Windows*

What: At the end of the workday, before you turn off your computer, you must exit Windows properly.

Why: If you don't exit before turning off the computer, Windows doesn't have a chance to store everything in its proper place. Sometimes files or programs are still in *RAM*, (Random Access Memory, the temporary storage place a computer uses for processing), and when you turn the power off, RAM evaporates. The next time you turn on your computer, Windows will have to do lots of checking and cleaning up to get everything put into place—or worse, some files may be damaged.

How: Follow these steps to shut down your computer safely.

1. Close all open windows by clicking their **Close** buttons.
2. Click the **Start** button and choose **Shut Down**.
3. A dialog box similar to that of Figure 34 asks what you want to do. Choose **Shut Down** and click **OK**.

Figure 34 Shut Down Windows dialog box for Windows 2000

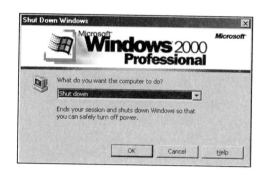

Result: Windows takes a few moments to put everything away and then either turns off your computer for you or gives you permission to turn it off yourself.

TIPS FROM A PRO: Does your computer seem to keep locking up or having trouble? Sometimes you can fix it by restarting it. Choose **Shut Down** from the Start menu, but this time, choose **Restart**. This will force Windows to clear everything up and start over, so you can continue to work.

Key Terms

Note: you can find definitions for these words in this chapter:

Active window	Menu bar
Backup	Minimize
Boot up	Mouse pointer
Buttons	Multitasking
Check box	My Briefcase
Clipboard	My Computer
Clock	My Documents
Collapse	My Network Places
Command button	Operating system
Control panel	Option button
Context-sensitive	Parent folder
Current drive	Quick Launch toolbar
Current folder	RAM
Desktop	Recycle Bin
Details view	Restore
Dialog box	Scroll bars
Disk drives	Select
Drop-down list	Shortcut icon
Expand	Shortcut menu
File	Small Icons view
Folder	Spin box
Folders pane	Start button
Icons	Start menu
Large Icons view	Subfolder
List box	Tab
List view	Taskbar
Log in	Text box
Maximize	Window

Review Questions

You can use the following review questions and exercises to test your knowledge and skills. Answers are given in Appendix D.

True/False

Indicate whether each statement is true (T) or false (F).

___ 1. An operating system is a special type of software you use to type a document.

___ 2. When the computer is busy, such as when it's booting up, the mouse pointer resembles an hourglass.

___ 3. The rectangular strip containing the Start button is called the taskbar.

___ 4. When you want to access a context-sensitive shortcut menu, double-click something.

___ 5. When you click the **Start** menu, you can see the files and folders contained in your computer.

___ 6. When one window is maximized and another is minimized, you can access the minimized one by choosing from the Start menu.

___ 7. To make a dialog box go away without making any changes, click **Cancel**.

___ 8. The main difference between My Computer and Windows Explorer is the Folders pane.

___ 9. To create a folder, click the **File** menu and choose **New** and then **Folder**.

___ 10. When you select a file on the hard disk of your computer and press the **Delete** key or **Delete** button, it is permanently deleted.

Multiple Choice

Select the letter that best completes the statement.

___ 1. A word for the entire windows screen that contains the taskbar and icons is:
  a. Background.
  b. Desktop.
  c. Explorer.
  d. My Computer.
  e. Operating system.

___ 2. When you choose a command on a menu that is followed by ellipses (...):
  a. A dialog box appears.
  b. A window appears.
  c. The menu disappears and the command is immediately put into effect.
  d. The window is minimized.
  e. Nothing happens, because the command is not currently available.

___ 3. Several documents or programs may be organized and stored together in a:
  a. Button.
  b. Desktop.
  c. File.
  d. Folder.
  e. Shortcut.

___ 4. The main hard disk on your computer is usually named:
  a. Drive A.
  b. Drive C.
  c. Drive 0.
  d. Drive 1.
  e. the Parent drive.

___ 5. The view to use when you want to sort the files in order by the date they were created is:
  a. Details view.
  b. Large icons view.
  c. List view.
  d. Small icons view.
  e. Sort view.

___ 6. A copy of an important file or folder stored on a separate disk in case something happens to the original is called a:

    a. Backup.
    b. Bootup.
    c. Keeper.
    d. Safety.
    e. Subfile or Subfolder.

___ 7. To copy a file or folder, first select it and then:

    a. Right-drag it to the destination in the Folders pane.
    b. Click the **Copy To** button and choose the destination.
    c. Right-click and choose **Send To**.
    d. All of the above.
    e. Either a or b.

___ 8. The temporary storage place for items deleted from the hard disk is called the:

    a. Desktop.
    b. Keeper.
    c. Trashcan.
    d. Wastepaper Basket.
    e. None of the above.

___ 9. To change the color or design of the desktop:

    a. Right-click the desktop and choose **Properties**.
    b. Double-click **My Computer**.
    c. Scroll up or down in the window.
    d. Click the **OK** button on the Quick Launch portion of the taskbar.
    e. Click the **Maximize** button on the window.

___ 10. To use PinPoint software, you must make sure these settings for your taskbar *do not* have a check mark:

    a. Always on Top and Auto Hide.
    b. Auto Hide and Show Clock.
    c. Always on Top and Minimize.
    d. Auto Clock and Quick Launch.
    e. Minimize and Start.

Screen Review

Match the letters in Figure 35 with the correct items in the list.

Figure 35

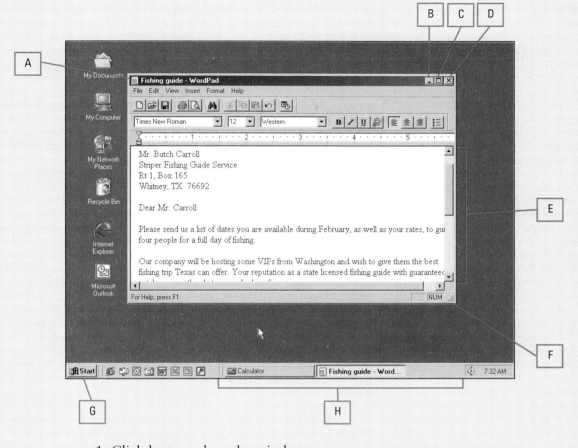

___ 1. Click here to close the window.

___ 2. Click here to access a minimized window.

___ 3. Click here to make the open window fill the screen.

___ 4. Drag here to move the window to the right.

___ 5. Click here to see a menu of the available programs.

___ 6. Drag here to make the window slightly smaller or larger.

___ 7. Click or drag here to see the contents of the window that are not currently in view.

___ 8. Click here so the open window will disappear and show only as a button on the toolbar.

Exercise and Project

Follow these step-by-step instructions to practice using your Windows skills. If you are working in a computer lab, ask your instructor how to log in and exit Windows.

Exercise

1. With your computer on, make a quick sketch of your desktop. Label several icons.
2. Open **My Computer**. On your paper, write down whether or not the window is maximized.
3. Make a list of the drives available on your computer. Write down both the drive name and the type of drive.
4. Insert the PinPoint CD from the back of your book into the CD drive. View the contents of the CD. Write down the names of the first four folders you see.
5. Change the view to see all of the views. Use Details view to find the date that one of the files or folders was last modified. Write the date on your paper.
6. Turn on the Folders pane (Windows 98 users: choose **View**, then **Explorer Bar** and click **Folders**). View the contents of the PinPoint CD. In the Folders pane, expand all the folders and subfolders. Make a sketch of their organization on your paper.
7. View the contents of the Chapter 2 folder. Write down the name of a file contained in it.
8. Insert a floppy disk into Drive A. Use the **Copy** or **Send To** command to place a copy of the file you viewed in Step 7 onto the floppy disk.
9. Make drive A the current drive. Write on your paper how much free space the disk has available.
10. Delete the file you copied to the floppy disk. On your paper, write down whether it is sent to the Recycle Bin or permanently deleted.

Project

Try out the features of both Web-style Windows and classic Windows. Compare the way you interact with Windows in the two styles. Use the Help feature to find out more about these two options; learn about the Active Desktop as well. Explain the benefits of these features, which style you prefer, and why.

Get Started with Excel

Create a budget and financial statements, calculate loan payments, chart sales, or handle lists of data—imagine facing any of these chores without using a calculator or a computer! Yet these tasks are easy to perform when you use Excel 2000. With Excel, you can quickly enter the information and do simple or sophisticated calculations with all the speed and accuracy that make computers so powerful. The skills you learn in this chapter are the starting point.

At the end of this chapter, you will be able to:

*

C **E**

C	E	
☐	☐	Start Excel
☐	☐	Explain what's on the screen
☐	☐	Customize the Excel screen
☐	☐	Move around in a workbook
☑	☐	Go to a specific cell
☑	☐	Move to other worksheets
☑	☐	Enter text, dates, and numbers into a worksheet
☑	☐	Use AutoSum
☑	☐	Save a workbook the first time
☑	☐	Save another version of the file
☑	☐	Create a folder from Excel
☐	☐	Print using the Print button
☑	☐	Use the Office Assistant
☐	☐	Start a new workbook
☐	☐	Close worksheets and exit Excel

*Whenever you see one of these icons, you know that's a skill you have to perform specifically on the certification exam to become a Microsoft Office User Specialist. Core objectives are marked with the C icon, and the Expert objectives are labeled with the E.

What: Start the Excel 2000 program.

Why: You can use Excel to make calculations, chart information, and manage data.

How: Several methods can be used to start Excel:

- ❍ Click the **Start** button, point to **Programs**, and click **Excel** (Figure 1.1).
- ❍ If the Excel icon is on the Quick Launch area of the Windows taskbar, click it, or if a shortcut to Excel is on the Windows desktop, double-click it.
- ❍ Double-click the name of an Excel file, and Excel automatically opens along with the file. (You can use My Computer or Windows Explorer to see the contents of your computer.*)

Figure 1.1 Two ways to start Excel

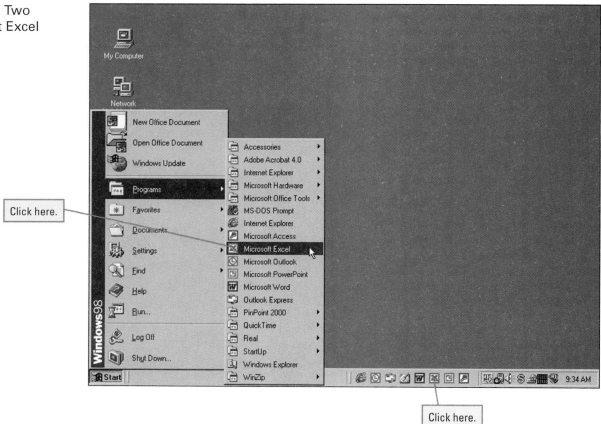

Result: When you start Excel, the screen shown in Figure 1.2 on pages 44 and 45 appears.

*You should have some general knowledge about Windows before you start this chapter. See the chapter titled "Start with Windows."

TASK 2 — Explore the Excel Screen

What: When Excel opens, you immediately see an empty grid of rows and columns. At the intersection of a row and column is a rectangular unit called a *cell*. The overall grid is called a *worksheet*. Several worksheets may be contained in a single Excel file, which is called a *workbook*. Examine Figure 1.2 to see the names of each of the screen elements. Some items are familiar to you from your experience in Windows.

- ○ Title bar
- ○ Menu bar
- ○ Toolbar
- ○ Minimize button
- ○ Maximize button
- ○ Close button
- ○ Scroll bars
- ○ Status bar
- ○ Taskbar button for each open window

Some items are characteristic of all Microsoft Office programs, and some are unique to Excel.

- ○ The particular tools on the toolbars
- ○ The particular information shown on the status bar
- ○ The work area where you will type your data

Because many elements are located in the same place and work the same way in Word, Excel, PowerPoint, and Access, we say they have a *common user interface*. This means that when you learn one of these programs, you have a head start in learning others because many elements are familiar to you.

THOUGHT QUESTION: As you look at the menu, what items seem familiar to you? From your experience with other Windows programs, what commands can you predict will appear on the menus?

Why: You need to learn the names of the elements shown on the screen so you can refer to them quickly when they are mentioned in this book or on the exam.

Title bar contains the name of the current file. Excel names files Book1, Book2, and so on, until you give them a name.

Menu bar shows lists of commands when you click the menu names.

Standard and Formatting toolbars share a row. Standard toolbar (at left) contains buttons that perform common commands with the click of a mouse. Formatting toolbar (at right) contains buttons to change the appearance of the text. More buttons appear when you click the More Buttons button at the toolbar's right side. Double-click the vertical bar at the left edge of either toolbar to expand it and see more buttons.

Active cell is where your typing is placed. It has a bold border.

This mouse pointer is used to select items in Excel. Click to select a single cell. Drag to select several cells.

Office Assistant gives quick access to Excel's built-in Help.

A cell is referred to by its column letter and row number. The cell at the intersection of column A and row 5 is cell A5.

Rows are numbered from 1 to 65,536.

Status bar gives information about a command or process.

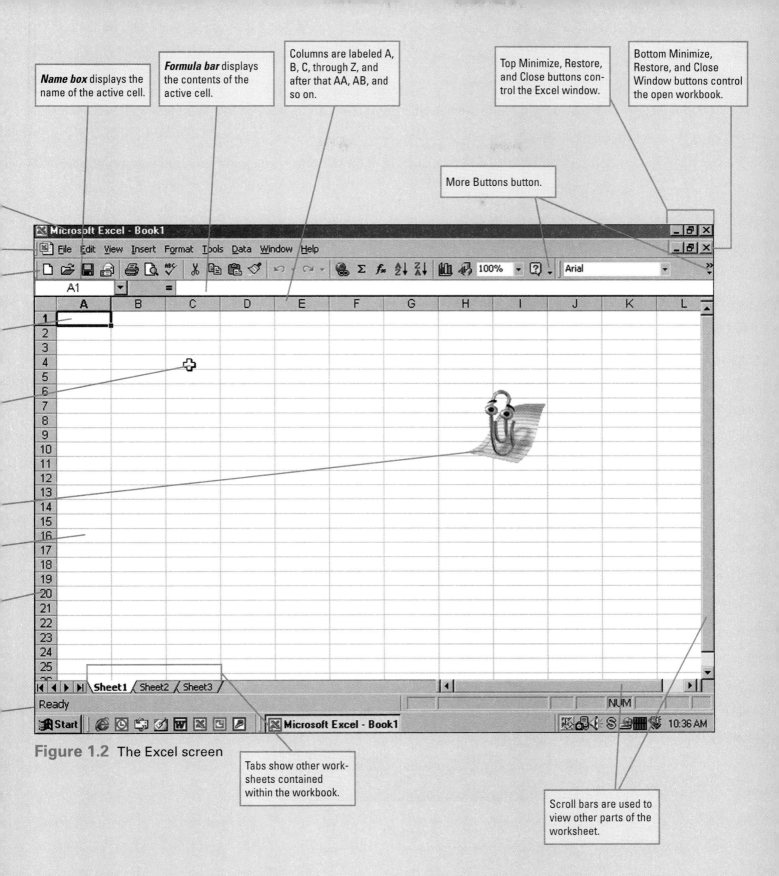

Name box displays the name of the active cell.

Formula bar displays the contents of the active cell.

Columns are labeled A, B, C, through Z, and after that AA, AB, and so on.

Top Minimize, Restore, and Close buttons control the Excel window.

Bottom Minimize, Restore, and Close Window buttons control the open workbook.

More Buttons button.

Tabs show other worksheets contained within the workbook.

Scroll bars are used to view other parts of the worksheet.

Figure 1.2 The Excel screen

Task 2: Explore the Excel Screen **45**

How: You can find out about each element of the Excel screen by using the mouse.

1. Click the **Help** menu name and choose **What's This?** (From now on when this book refers to menus and commands, you'll see them tied together, like this: Help|What's This?) The mouse pointer changes to a big question mark.
2. Click anywhere on the screen you want more information about.
3. Repeat steps 1 and 2 to find out about something else.

Result: The information appears in a yellow box on screen. When you're done reading it, click anywhere to make it go away.

TASK 3   *Show Full Menus and Toolbars*

What: As you saw in Figure 1.2, the *default* Excel screen (that is, the one you see before you make changes) contains a single row of buttons to help you quickly accomplish common tasks. As you work, Excel automatically customizes the toolbar to display the buttons that you use most.

In addition, when you begin to use Excel, you see only commonly used commands on the menus. Other commands appear after a short pause, or when you click the double down arrows at the bottom of the menus.

You can customize many areas of the program to suit your unique work habits by using the Customize dialog box shown in Figure 1.3. When you modify the settings in this dialog box, the changes take effect immediately and remain in effect until you change them again.

Figure 1.3 The Customize dialog box

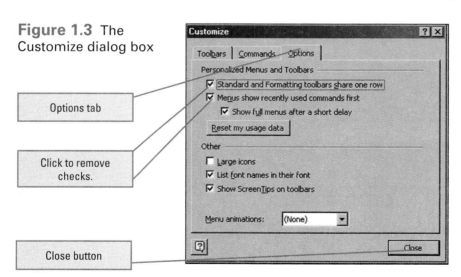

You can customize these items:

○ Display the toolbars on two rows
○ Show all the menu selections immediately without having to pause

Why: Some people like the way Excel personalizes the screen. Others want to have handy access to all the buttons and the full menus. While putting your toolbars on two rows does cut down on the space available for viewing your work, you'll learn to use all the buttons on the toolbars and will want to keep them all in view.

How: Use the following steps:

1. Choose **Tools|Customize**.
2. Click the **Options** tab (refer to Figure 1.3).
3. Clear the top two check boxes.
4. Click **Close**.

Result: Excel now displays two rows of buttons, with the Standard toolbar on top and the Formatting toolbar on bottom (Figure 1.4). In addition, when you display the menus, all the commands appear immediately.

Figure 1.4 Standard and Formatting toolbars on separate rows

Note: For consistency, the figures in the remainder of the book show Excel with both toolbars and full menus displayed. If you work on different computers in a laboratory, you may have to do this procedure each time you use Excel to display the toolbars on two rows and have the full menus appear when you click a menu name.

TIPS FROM A PRO: When you're working with the toolbars on a single row, you can quickly expand to see more of the buttons. To do this, double-click the vertical bar on the left side of either toolbar. This Tip will be especially handy when you are working in the PinPoint software, because in PinPoint you can't customize the toolbars so that they appear on separate rows.

TASK **4**   *Move Around in a Workbook*

What: When you begin a new workbook, the *active cell* (the one surrounded by the bold border, where any typing will appear) is in the top-left corner of the worksheet, in cell A1. To create your worksheet or make changes to it, you must move around in it.

Why: Getting around in a worksheet quickly is the mark of a confident, experienced Excel user. Learn the fastest way to get from place to place so you can use your time efficiently.

USE THE KEYBOARD TO MOVE THE ACTIVE CELL

How: Move around in the worksheet by pressing the arrow keys and other direction keys on the keyboard.

Table 2.1 shows some handy keyboard shortcuts for moving around in a worksheet; you will use several of these often.

Table 2.1 Keyboard Shortcuts for Moving Around in a Worksheet

Press this key...	To move here
Left arrow	One cell to the left
Right arrow	One cell to the right
Up arrow	Up one row
Down arrow	Down one row
Home	The cell in column A of the current row
Page Up	Up one screen
Page Down	Down one screen
Ctrl+Home	Cell A1
Ctrl+End	The cell at the intersection of the right-most used column and the bottom-most used row (the lower-right corner of your work area)
Ctrl+arrow key	Jump to end of a series of blank or nonblank cells in a given direction

Result: When you use the keyboard to move around in the worksheet, you move the location of the active cell. You then begin adding or editing the contents of the active cell.

USE THE SCROLL BAR

How: You can also use the mouse to click or drag the scroll bars to view different parts of a worksheet. The movements are shown in Figure 1.5. If your mouse has a wheel button, you can also use it to scroll through the document. Rotate away from you to scroll up; rotate toward you to scroll down.

Result: The difference between using the keyboard and the scroll bars is that when you use the keyboard, you are moving the active cell. On the other hand, using the mouse to scroll up or down in the worksheet merely changes the view. You must click the mouse in the worksheet to move the active cell.

GO TO A SPECIFIC CELL

CORE OBJECTIVE: Go to a specific cell

How: To jump directly to a specific cell, click the **Name box** on the left side of the formula bar, and type the *cell address* (that is, its column letter and row number, such as A1 or B5) and press **Enter**.

Result: As soon as you press Enter, the Excel screen displays that cell (and the ones near it) and makes it the active cell.

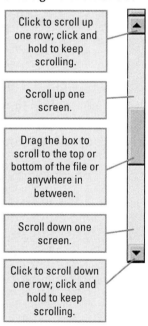

Figure 1.5 Scrolling through a worksheet

Click to scroll up one row; click and hold to keep scrolling.

Scroll up one screen.

Drag the box to scroll to the top or bottom of the file or anywhere in between.

Scroll down one screen.

Click to scroll down one row; click and hold to keep scrolling.

MOVE TO OTHER WORKSHEETS

CORE OBJECTIVE: *Move between worksheets in a workbook*

How: Workbooks typically contain three worksheets (although you can easily add or delete sheets, as you'll learn in Chapter 12, "Handle Multiple Worksheets"). To use or view a different worksheet, click the tab on the bottom of the worksheet. The tabs are labeled Sheet1, Sheet2, and Sheet3 until you rename them.

Result: When you click a worksheet's tab, the sheet is displayed so you can work on it.

> **TASK 5**   *Enter Text, Numbers, and Dates*

CORE OBJECTIVE: *Enter text, dates, and numbers*

What: Cells in a worksheet can contain five kinds of entries. You can see examples of these in Figure 1.6. Each one is handled a little differently.

- ○ *Text* is any word or combination of letters and numbers. Text is automatically left-aligned in the cell. The text too long for the cell overlaps any blank cells to the right.
- ○ *Numbers*, such as 5,280 or 97%, form the basis for all your calculations. They're automatically right-aligned in the cell to keep the columns of numbers lined up, just as your fourth-grade teacher insisted.
- ○ *Dates and times* are curious types of number. Although they may contain words, such as *January* and *PM*, Excel knows what you mean and changes them into values you can use in calculations.
- ○ *Formulas*, for example the **x + y** that you used in algebra, specify the calculations you want Excel to make based on numbers in the worksheet. They always begin with an equal sign (=).
- ○ *Comments* are a way to communicate directions or information without typing directly in a cell. You can tell a comment is in a cell by a small red triangle in the upper-right corner. Read comments by placing the mouse pointer over the cell and pausing.

TIPS FROM A PRO: You'll learn all about handling comments in Chapter 17, "Collaborate with Workgroups," but they're easy to create. Simply click the cell where you want the comment to be and choose **Insert|Comment**. In the comment box that appears, type the comment. When you are finished, click elsewhere. The red triangle appears in the corner of the cell.

Why: To build a worksheet, you must first enter numbers and the text that describes them. Later you'll use formulas to perform calculations.

Figure 1.6 A sample Excel worksheet

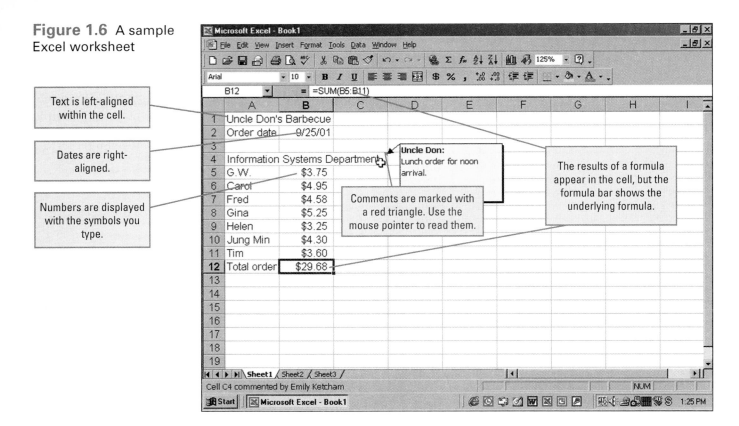

Text is left-aligned within the cell.

Dates are right-aligned.

Numbers are displayed with the symbols you type.

Uncle Don:
Lunch order for noon arrival.

Comments are marked with a red triangle. Use the mouse pointer to read them.

The results of a formula appear in the cell, but the formula bar shows the underlying formula.

ENTER TEXT

How: Text you type always appears in the active cell.

1. Click the cell where you want the text to appear. The bold border moves to this cell, showing that it is the active cell.
2. Type the text. What you type appears in the active cell and in the formula bar. If you make a mistake while typing, press **Backspace** and correct it.
3. When you have completed the contents for one cell, press **Enter**.

Result: The text you typed is deposited into the cell. The bold border moves down to the next row. (If it remains in the same cell, use the down arrow key to move it down to the next row.)

If the text is longer than the width of the cell, it flows to the right and overlaps any blank cells. However, if something is in the cell to the right, the text appears to be cut off (Figure 1.7). Don't worry—the text is intact and will appear when you widen the column. You'll learn how to do this in Chapter 2, "Edit Worksheet Contents."

 TIPS FROM A PRO: After you are done typing, you can complete the cell entry any of these ways:

- Press Enter to move down one cell.
- Press Tab to move to the right one cell.
- Press an arrow key to move one cell any direction.
- Click any other cell to move directly there.
- Click the check mark on the formula bar.

Figure 1.7 Entering long text in a cell

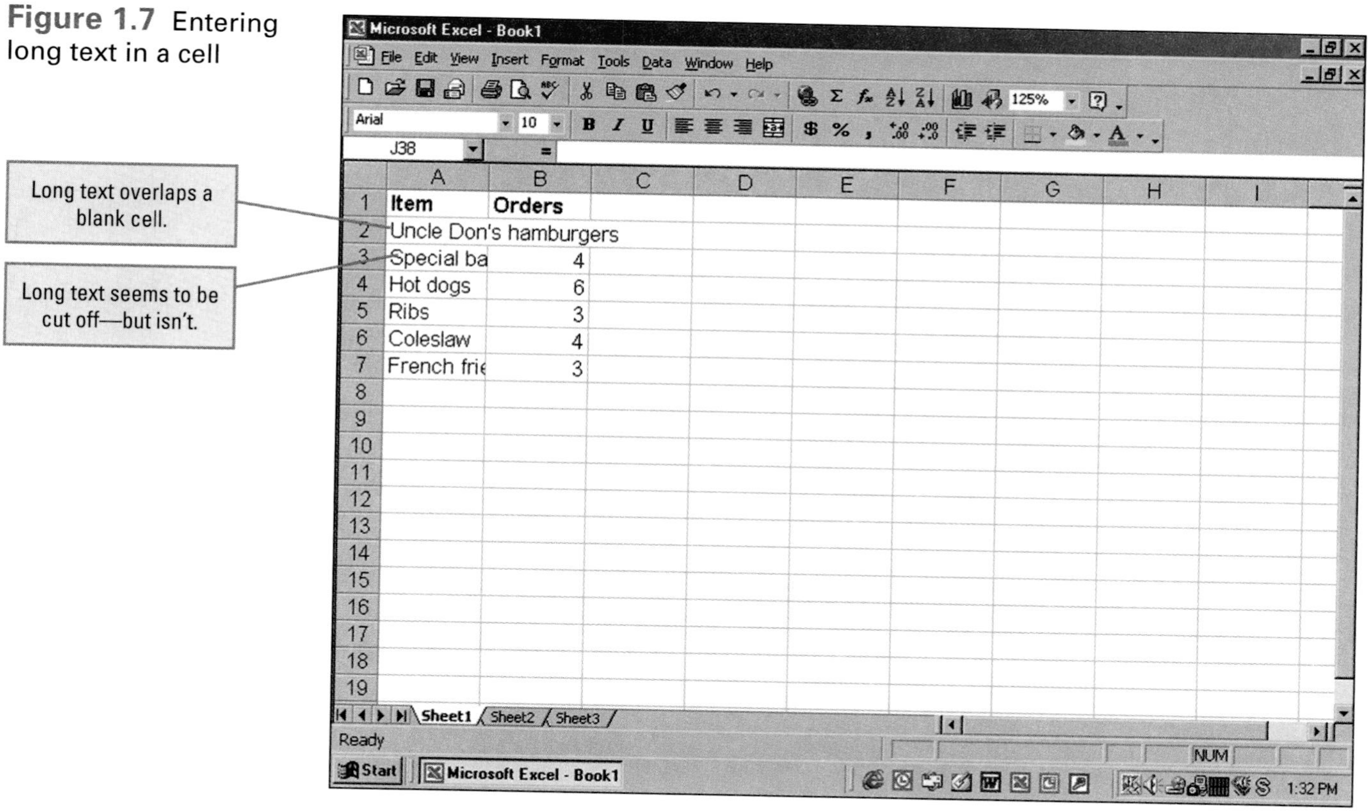

Long text overlaps a blank cell.

Long text seems to be cut off—but isn't.

	A	B	C	D	E	F	G	H	I
1	**Item**	**Orders**							
2	Uncle Don's hamburgers								
3	Special ba	4							
4	Hot dogs	6							
5	Ribs	3							
6	Coleslaw	4							
7	French frie	3							

ENTER NUMBERS

How: Type numbers into a cell by using the keys on the top row of the keyboard or, if Num Lock is turned on, by using the keypad on the right side of the keyboard.

- ○ Type the numbers in the cell and press **Enter**.
- ○ If you type decimals, such as 1.5000, Excel often eliminates the trailing zeros and displays 1.5. (You'll learn how to control this in Chapter 3, "Modify Worksheet Structure.")
- ○ You can also type dollar signs, commas, or percent signs, and Excel displays them with the numbers. Even when you type these symbols, Excel interprets your entry as numbers. (You'll learn how to add these symbols to plain numbers in Chapter 3.)
- ○ Type a negative number by typing a minus sign or by surrounding the number with parentheses.

Result: The numbers appear right-aligned within the cell.

ENTER DATES AND TIMES

How: You type dates and times just as you do text. How you type them determines how they will appear. You can type them several different ways:

- ○ Type **9/25** or **9/25/01** or **9/25/2001** and press **Enter**, and Excel displays 9/25/01. (If you don't include the year, Excel assumes the current year.)
- ○ Type **Sep 25**, **Sept 25**, **September 25**, or **September 25, 2001** and press **Enter**, and Excel displays 25-Sep.

Task 5: Enter Text, Numbers, and Dates **51**

- Type **8:00** and press **Enter**, and Excel displays 8:00 (and assumes AM).
- Type **8:00 a** and press **Enter**, and Excel displays 8:00 AM.
- Type **8:00 p** and press **Enter**, and Excel displays 8:00 PM.

 TIPS FROM A PRO: Excel provides a number of *shortcut keys* you can press to do something quickly. Often they involve holding down the Ctrl key while pressing another key. Those of you who are fast typists will especially like to use shortcut keys because they save time by allowing you to keep your hands on the keyboard. Here are two handy shortcut keys for entering dates and times:

- To enter today's date, hold down the **Ctrl** key and press ; (semicolon). (This shortcut key is written **Ctrl+;**.)
- To enter the current time, hold down the **Ctrl** and **Shift** keys and press ; (semicolon). (This shortcut key is written **Ctrl+Shift+;**.)

Result: Like numbers, dates are right-aligned within the cell, and you can use dates in calculations.

TASK **6**   *Use AutoSum*

 C CORE OBJECTIVE: *Use basic functions (Sum)*

What: Suppose your worksheet has a long list of numbers to add up. You can sum them instantly by clicking using Excel's AutoSum feature.

Why: Don't count on your fingers or pull out a calculator; Excel can calculate it more quickly and more accurately. Even more importantly, whenever a number changes, Excel instantly recalculates and displays the corrected sum.

How: You can use either of these two methods to total the numbers:

1. Click the cell below the list to make it the active cell.
    2. Click the **AutoSum** button. Excel surrounds the cells it thinks you want to total with a moving border, as you see in Figure 1.8.
3. Press **Enter** or click the check mark on the formula bar to accept the suggestion.

Here's another, even faster method.

1. Click and drag to select all the cells you want to total. *Selected* cells are shown with shading and a bold border, as you see in Figure 1.9.
2. Click the **AutoSum** button or press the shortcut key **Alt+=**.

 TIPS FROM A PRO: The status bar displays the sum of cells you select, but only while they are selected.

Result: The numbers are automatically totaled, and the total is placed either in the active cell (if you used the first method), or in the cell just below the list. Like the numbers it adds, the result is right-aligned within the cell.

Riding behind the sum is a formula. You can always see the formula for the active cell in the formula bar. You'll learn more about formulas in Chapter 2.

Figure 1.8 Using AutoSum

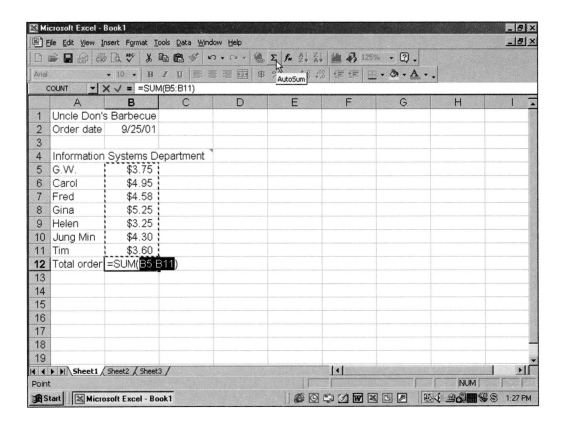

Figure 1.9 Selecting cells before using AutoSum

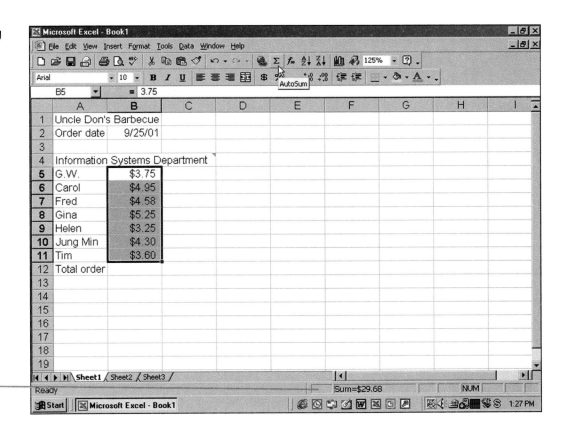

Sum is displayed here temporarily.

TIPS FROM A PRO: You can also total up a horizontal row of numbers using the AutoSum button.

TASK **7**	*Save a Workbook*

 C CORE OBJECTIVE: *Use Save*

What: When you have completed a worksheet, you must save it on a disk.

Why: While you are building a worksheet, it is held in a temporary storage place within the computer called RAM, or random access memory. Unlike human memory, the computer won't "remember" unless you save your work. If you turn off the computer or if the power goes out, all your work disappears. To store your work permanently, you must save it on a disk.

THE FIRST TIME YOU SAVE

How: You can save by any of these methods:

- ○ Choose **File|Save**.
- ○ Click the **Save** button on the toolbar.
- ○ Use the shortcut key **Ctrl+S**.

 THOUGHT QUESTION: Why do you suppose Excel offers three ways to do the same thing, such as saving a file?

The first time you save, the Save As dialog box appears (Figure 1.10), prompting you for a file name and destination. Follow the steps shown in the figure.

Figure 1.10 Save As dialog box

2. Click here to change the destination disk or folder.

1. Type the file name here.

3. Press **Enter** or click **Save** to finish.

Figure 1.11 File name of a saved workbook

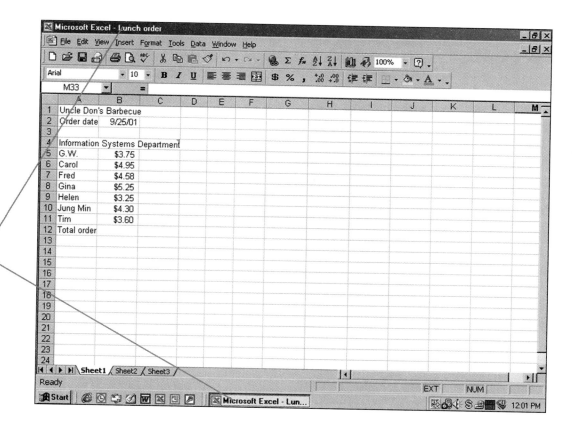

File name appears here.

Result: The workbook's name appears on the title bar and on the taskbar button (Figure 1.11).

TIPS FROM A PRO: Shortcut keys, such as Ctrl+S, are often easy to remember—in this case, S is for Save.

SUBSEQUENT SAVES

How: Click the **Save** button or press **Ctrl+S**.

Result: After you save the workbook the first time, saving it again bypasses the Save As dialog box. Excel simply saves the latest version with the same name in the same location. You might see an animation of the saving process on the status bar.

TIPS FROM A PRO: Because you never know when the power will suddenly go out, it's a good idea to save your workbook every ten minutes or so. Luckily, Excel has a feature called AutoSave that prompts you to save your workbook every so often. You can turn on this feature and customize how often Excel prompts you to save by choosing **Tools|AutoSave**. This opens the dialog box shown in Figure 1.12, where you can specify the interval.

If AutoSave does not appear on the Tools menu, follow these steps:

1. Choose **Tools|Add-Ins**. This opens the dialog box shown in Figure 1.13.
2. Click to check the box next to **AutoSave Add-in**, and click **OK**.
3. If a prompt asks if you want to install the add-in now, insert the Microsoft Office CD and click Yes.

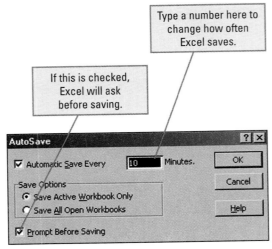
Type a number here to
change how often
Excel saves.

If this is checked,
Excel will ask
before saving.

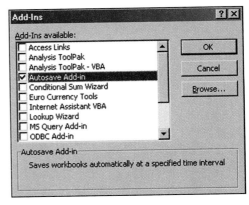

Figure 1.12 AutoSave

Figure 1.13 Installing Add-Ins

TASK **8**	*Save Another Version of the File*

C

CORE OBJECTIVE: *Use Save As (different name, location)*

What: You use the Save As command to save the file under a new name or in a new location.

Why: After a file has been saved the first time, using the Save command or clicking the Save button saves it to the same location under the same name. What do you do if you need to make a copy of the file on another disk as a backup or to use on a different computer? What do you do if you want to make some changes to the worksheet for a different purpose but keep both versions? For example, after you create a budget for one department, you might adapt it for another department. To keep both versions of the budget, you can't simply save; the new version replaces the old one on the disk. Instead, you have to store it with a different name.

How: Choose **File|Save As** to show the dialog box you used the first time you saved it.

1. To give the new version a different name, type the new name in the **File Name** box.
2. To save the file in a new location, click the **Save In** drop-down list to see the disks and folders available on your computer (Figure 1.14). For example, to save the file on a floppy disk, you would look through the list and choose drive A: 3 ½ Floppy.

Figure 1.14 Saving to a new drive or folder

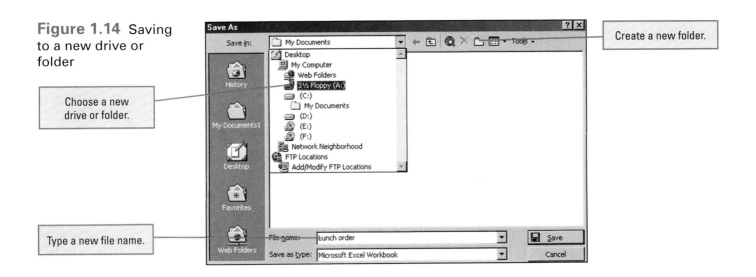

Create a new folder.

Choose a new drive or folder.

Type a new file name.

Note: Your computer may show different drives or folders than those shown here.

Result: You now have another version of your workbook saved in a different place or with a different name. You can use My Computer or Windows Explorer to see both files.

TASK 9   *Create a New Folder*

C   *CORE OBJECTIVE: Create a folder*

What: You can create a new folder in which to save your files.

Why: As you begin to create more and more workbooks, you need a way to keep them organized. One way to do this is to make a system of folders. You don't have to leave Excel when you realize you need a new folder. You can create a folder right in the Save As dialog box.

How: To create a folder to organize your files, follow these steps:

1. Choose **File|Save As**.
2. Inside the dialog box, click the **Create New Folder** button.
3. In the New Folder dialog box that appears (Figure 1.15), type the name for the folder. Press **Enter** or click **OK**.

Result: Excel automatically creates the folder and opens it so you can save your workbook, as you see in Figure 1.16. Type a file name and then press **Enter** or click **Save** to finish saving the workbook in the new folder.

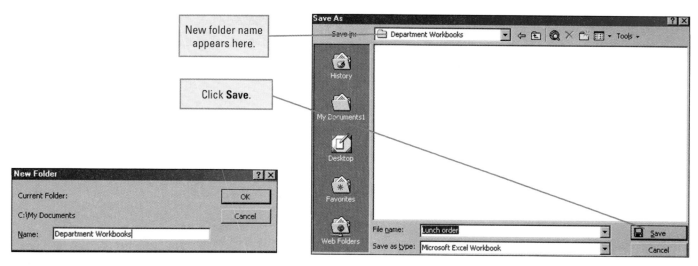

New folder name
appears here.

Click **Save**.

Figure 1.15 New Folder dialog box

Figure 1.16 Workbook ready to save in a new folder

What: After you've spent time creating a workbook, you'll want to print a copy on paper.

Why: Although many files are only viewed electronically, paper copies are still used for several reasons:

- ❍ To be able to examine the file away from the computer
- ❍ To keep a copy as a permanent record
- ❍ To send it in the mail or by fax

 How: Click the **Print** button.

Result: As soon as you click the Print button, you might see these items on your screen:

- ❍ A dialog box opens explaining what is being printed. To stop the printing process, click Cancel.
- ❍ A printer icon appears on the right side of the taskbar, near the clock

A single copy of the worksheet you see on the screen will come rolling out of the printer—assuming, of course, that your computer is attached to a printer, the printer is on, and the printer has paper in it.

TASK **11** *Use the Office Assistant*

C

CORE OBJECTIVE: *Use the Office Assistant*

What: The Office Assistant provides help when you need to know how to do something in Excel. This help is available at the click of a button and in every dialog box. You can ask a question, or you can look through the table of contents or index for relevant topics. Sometimes the Office Assistant suggests ways to help before you even ask for it.

You can get help four ways:

❍ Click the Office Assistant, if it's available.
❍ Click the **Help** button on the toolbar or in the dialog box.
❍ Choose an item from the Help menu.
❍ Press the **F1** key.

Why: When you're looking for an answer, you don't have to ask someone else or read through a book. Even experienced users use Help to learn more about a certain technique or feature of Excel.

How: The Office Assistant is easy to use. If you don't see it on your screen, you must turn it on.

1. To turn on the Office Assistant, choose **Help|Show the Office Assistant**.
2. To get help, click the Office Assistant. As you see in Figure 1.17, a yellow speech balloon suggests topics that might be relevant to what you're doing. Click one of these to get more information.
3. You can also type a topic or a question in the box. A few words are all that is needed. In the example, we're looking for help on how to save. Press **Enter** or click **Search**.

Result: After you choose a topic or type a question, Help opens in a window next to your worksheet, as you see in Figure 1.18. Here you can browse through the topics and, as on the Web, click topics (in blue or purple) to display the information. If you want to print the topic, you can click the Print button. When you are finished reading the information, click the Close button to close Help and return to your worksheet.

Figure 1.17 Office Assistant ready to help

Figure 1.18 Help topics

Click here to print the topic.

Click a topic (in blue or purple) to see relevant information.

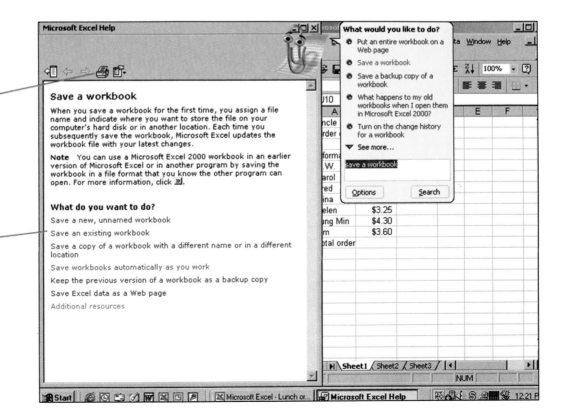

Tips from a Pro: You can turn off the Office Assistant if you find it gets in the way or asks too many annoying questions. To do so, choose **Help|Hide the Office Assistant**. In addition, you can customize the way the Office Assistant works and even choose a different assistant by clicking the Options button in the Office Assistant's yellow speech balloon.

TASK 12 *Start a New Workbook*

What: Excel doesn't limit you to having just one workbook open at a time. If you want to, you can start fresh with a new workbook containing three blank worksheets.

Why: You wouldn't want to start Excel over again just to get a new file.

How: Click the **New** button on the toolbar.

Result: Three things happen:

- ❍ A new workbook appears, ready for you to type.
- ❍ The title bar shows the name of the workbook as Book2 (or Book3, and so on).
- ❍ The taskbar may show an *additional* button with an Excel icon, along with the workbook name, as you see in Figure 1.19.

Figure 1.19 New workbook covers the previous one

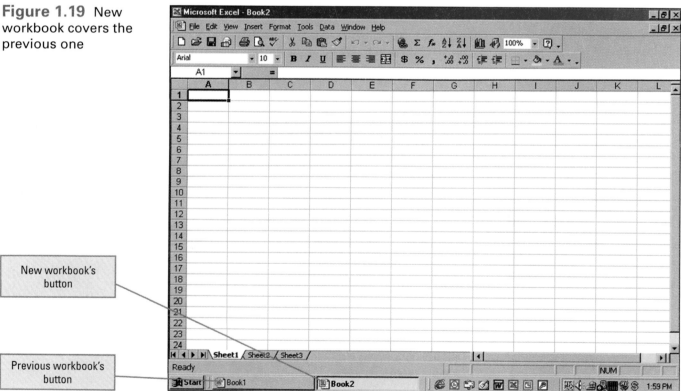

New workbook's button

Previous workbook's button

When you create a new workbook, it hides the previous workbook, just as you can cover one piece of paper by putting another sheet on top of it. You can still access the previous workbook, though. When you click its button on the taskbar, it appears on screen and hides the new, blank workbook, just like pulling a piece of paper from the bottom of a stack of papers and placing it on top.

 TIPS FROM A PRO: If an additional Excel button doesn't appear on the taskbar for each Excel file, you can still switch among them easily. Click the Window command to see a list of open files. Choose the file you want to work on.

 TIPS FROM A PRO: If you don't see an additional Excel button on the taskbar for each new file you create, change this option. Choose **Tools|Options** and click the **View** tab. In the Show section, select the check box next to **Windows in Taskbar** and click **OK**.

TASK **13** *Close Files and Exit Excel*

What: When you are done with a workbook and ready to turn to a new task, you need to save and close it. When you're finished for the day you need to exit Excel.

The Excel window has two sets of sizing buttons (Figure 1.20). The top set controls the Excel program; the bottom set controls the open workbook. When you have several workbooks open, you can close the active one by clicking its Close Window button. The next open workbook appears in the window. Clicking the Close Window button for the last open workbook closes it but leaves Excel open.

Clicking the upper Close button closes all open files and exits Excel at the same time.

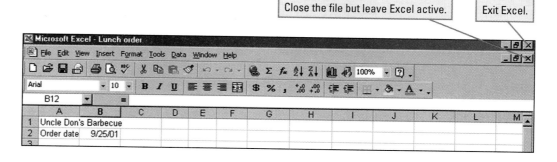

Figure 1.20 Closing files and exiting Excel

Why: Because each file and the Excel program use some of your computer's processing power, it's a good idea to close them when you're finished. When you close and exit, you'll be sure all your workbooks are safely stored on a disk so you can work on them again in the future.

CLOSE FILES WITHOUT EXITING EXCEL

How: You can close files in two ways:

○ Click the **Close Window** button at the right end of the menu bar.
○ Choose File|Close.

Result: If you have not saved your workbook, Excel prompts you to do so. Then the window closes, removing the button from the taskbar. This lets you know the file is no longer in the computer's RAM.

When you close the last open workbook, the Excel window remains open, but the worksheet area is gray.

EXIT EXCEL

How: You can exit Excel in two ways:

○ Click the **Close** button at the right end of the title bar.
○ Choose **File|Exit**.

Result: Again, if you have not saved all open workbooks, Excel prompts you to do so. Then all open files close and the Excel window closes. The application is removed from the computer's RAM.

Use PinPoint

After gaining the skills in this chapter, you can start Excel, enter text, dates, and numbers, add them up, print and save a worksheet, start a new file, and exit Excel. Now it's time to use the PinPoint software and see what you can do. Remember: Whenever you are unsure of what to do, you can reread that portion of the chapter or you can click Show Me for a live demonstration. Check out these skills in PinPoint:

- Close workbook
- Create a folder
- Enter text and numbers
- Save a workbook
- Save As
- Use AutoSum

Key Terms

You can find definitions for these words in this chapter:

Active cell	Cell
Comment	Common user interface
Default	Formula
Formula bar	Name box
Number	Selection
Shortcut keys	Text
Workbook	Worksheet

Review Questions

You can use the following review questions to test your knowledge and skills. Answers are given in Appendix D, "Answers to Review Questions."

True/False

Indicate whether each statement is true (T) or false (F).

___ 1. To start Excel, double-click the Start button.

___ 2. The intersection of a row and column is called a cell.

___ 3. To make the toolbars appear on two separate rows, choose Tools|Customize.

___ 4. If you see only a short list of choices on a menu, the rest of the choices will appear after a short pause.

___ 5. The bold rectangle that shows where your typing will appear is called the mouse pointer.

___ 6. When you type text, it appears left aligned within the cell.

___ 7. You should finish creating a worksheet completely before you save it.

___ 8. If you want to create a new folder and save your workbook to it, you must first minimize Excel and use My Computer to create the new folder.

___ 9. If you want to save a file with a new name or location, choose File|Save As.

___ 10. You can tell the Office Assistant is working if you see its button on the taskbar.

Multiple Choice

Select the letter that best completes the statement.

___ 1. If text is too long to fit within the cell:
   a. It overlaps any blank cells to the right.
   b. The extra letters get chopped off.
   c. The words will wrap to a second line within the cell.
   d. The computer will beep.
   e. It doesn't work, because you can only put one word into each cell.

___ 2. Which of the following will Excel consider to be a number:
   a. 255b Baker St.
   b. $5.25.
   c. 98.6.
   d. All of the above.
   e. Both b and c.

___ 3. You can tell a comment is within a cell because:
   a. The cell is highlighted in yellow.
   b. The cell is highlighted in red.
   c. A red triangle appears in the corner.
   d. A yellow triangle appears in the corner.
   e. The mouse pointer gets a red triangle on it.

___ 4. When you save a workbook the first time, you must:
   a. Name it.
   b. Print it.
   c. Use AutoSave.
   d. Make a new folder for it.
   e. All of the above.

___ 5. The Save As dialog box allows you to:
   a. Specify a new name for a workbook.
   b. Specify the drive or folder where you want to save a workbook.
   c. Create a new folder.
   d. All of the above.
   e. Both a and b.

___ 6. To get a single copy of the worksheet on paper:
   a. Click the Office Assistant.
   b. Double-click the Office Assistant.
   c. Click the Print button.
   d. Save it, and a copy is automatically printed.
   e. Use AutoSum, and a copy is automatically printed.

___ 7. If you want to change the worksheet and save the new version with a different name:
   a. Click the Save button.
   b. Use the shortcut key Ctrl+S.
   c. Choose File|Save As.
   d. Turn on AutoSave.
   e. Any of the above.

___ 8. When you click the Office Assistant, type a question, and click Search:
   a. The Office Assistant lists relevant topics.
   b. A demonstration occurs on screen.
   c. You will hear a spoken answer to your question.
   d. Your worksheet is covered up by a new Help window.
   e. The Office Assistant blinks at you or dances around.

___ 9. If you have saved a file, the name of the file appears:
   a. In the title bar.
   b. On the taskbar button.
   c. In the Save As dialog box.
   d. All of the above.
   e. Only a and c.

___ 10. When you exit Excel:
   a. The workbook is automatically saved.
   b. The workbook is automatically printed.
   c. The numbers are automatically summed.
   d. The button is removed from the taskbar.
   e. All of the above.

Match the letters in Figure 1.21 with the correct items in the list.

Figure 1.21

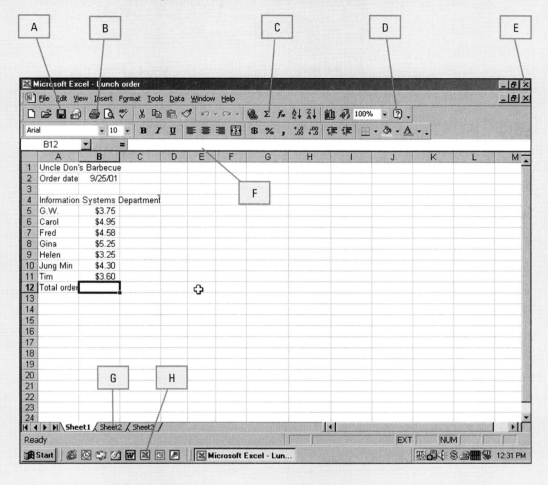

___ 1. Click here to exit Excel.

___ 2. Click here to print the workbook.

___ 3. Click here to save the workbook.

___ 4. Click here to total the numbers in the list.

___ 5. Look here to see a formula after you total the numbers.

___ 6. Click here to get help.

___ 7. The fastest way to start Excel is to click here.

___ 8. Click here to view another worksheet in the workbook.

Exercise and Project

Follow these step-by-step instructions to create a worksheet. If you are working in a computer lab, ask your instructor where you should save and print your file.

Exercise

1. Start Excel.

2. Customize the screen so that the Standard and Formatting toolbars appear on separate rows and so that full menus appear.

Figure 1.22
Results of exercise

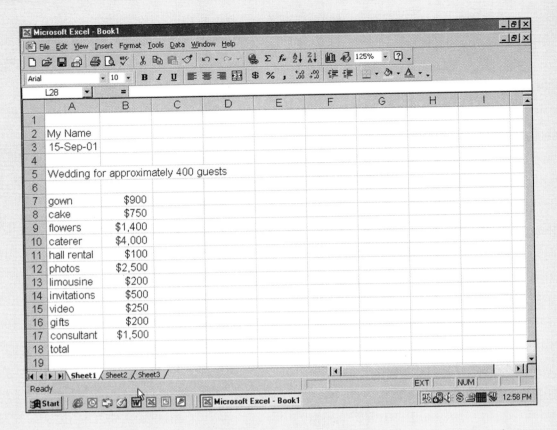

3. Match the screen shown in Figure 1.22. To begin, go to cell A2 and type your name. In cell A3, insert today's date. Leave row 4 blank. In cell A5 type the heading shown. Leave row 6 blank, and then follow the figure to type the text and numbers in rows 7 through 18.

4. In cell B18, use the AutoSum button to total up the cost of the wedding.

5. Save the workbook with the name **Wedding**, and leave it open on the screen.

6. Create a new workbook and type your name at the top. Make a list of expenses for the groom. Include such things as tux, clergy, rings, gifts, and trip. Sum up these expenses.

7. Save the workbook as **Groom** and print.

8. Return to the *Wedding* workbook. Change the cost of the gown to **$1,100**.

9. To the right of the current list, add a new list titled **Elope**. Include costs such as suitcase and ladder. Sum these up.

10. Insert a comment telling which option you prefer.

11. Save the new version of the *Wedding* workbook in a new location and with a new name. Create a folder called **Excel 2000** on your disk, and save the workbook as **Marry**.

12. Print. Close all the files and exit Excel.

Project

Use your new Excel skills to create a worksheet. Put your name and date on the top rows, and then type a list of items and sum them up. Use the Office Assistant to find out several ways to get assistance while you work in Excel. (*Hint:* Search for **Help**.) Below your list, type a line explaining one way to get help.

Chapter 2

Edit Worksheet Contents

Now that you've used Excel to create a simple worksheet, you can use the same skills for many tasks. Sometimes you can open a worksheet you've already created and adapt it for a new use. This chapter shows you how to open and locate files, add and revise formulas, and duplicate the cell contents for several time periods.

At the end of this chapter, you will be able to:

C E

☑	❑	Locate and open an existing workbook
☑	❑	Enter formulas in a cell
❑	❑	Create a budget
☑	❑	Apply currency and comma formats
☑	❑	Adjust the decimal place
☑	❑	Edit cell content
☑	❑	Work with series (use AutoFill)
☑	❑	Clear cell content
☑	❑	Use the Undo and Redo features
☑	❑	Use Find and Replace
☑	❑	Check spelling

C   CORE OBJECTIVE: *Locate and open an existing workbook*

What: To edit or use a workbook you have previously created and saved, you will have to locate and open it.

Why: As you learned in the chapter "Start with Windows," a computer uses disks to store files, such as Excel workbooks. Your computer's hard disk may contain thousands of files. You need to know the best methods for finding a file you created previously so you can get to work on it.

How: You can open files several ways.

IN WINDOWS

❍ Find the file listed in My Computer or Windows Explorer and double-click it.
❍ Click the Start menu and click Open Office Document.
❍ Click the Start menu, point to Documents, and click the name of the file (if you used the file recently). See the first screen in Figure 2.1.

IN EXCEL

❍ Choose **File|Open**.
❍ Click the **Open** button on the toolbar.
❍ Press **Ctrl+O**.
❍ Click the workbook's name in the list of recently used files at the bottom of the File menu (see the second screen in Figure 2.1).

Figure 2.1
Recently used files

On the Documents
menu in Windows

On the File
menu in Excel

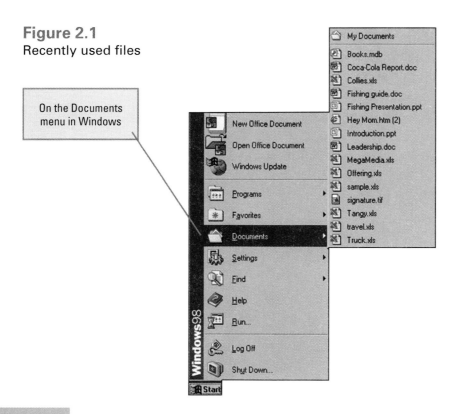

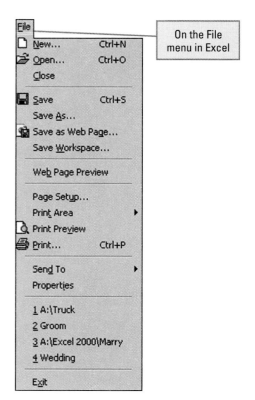

Figure 2.2 Open dialog box

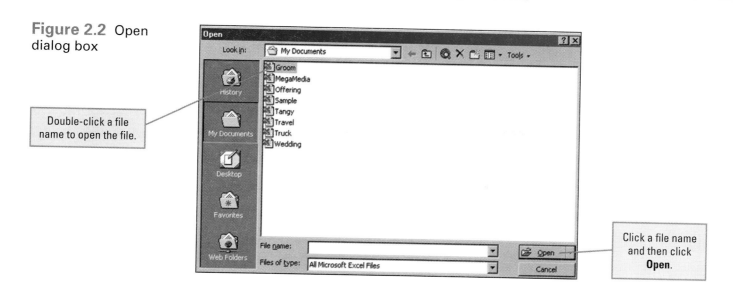

Double-click a file name to open the file.

Click a file name and then click **Open**.

Result: When you use the Open command or Open button, the Open dialog box appears, as you see in Figure 2.2. It looks familiar to you because it resembles the Save As dialog box you used in Chapter 1.

The major difference in the way you use the Open dialog box compared to Save As is that instead of typing the name of the file to save it, you must find the name of the file listed and double-click it to open it. If you see the file listed, that is easy to do.

TIPS FROM A PRO: By default, the first time you use the Open dialog box each day, Excel displays the contents of the My Documents folder. After you change to another drive or folder, Excel displays the contents of that folder the next time you use the dialog box.

TASK 2 — Locate a Workbook

C

CORE OBJECTIVE: *Locate and open an existing workbook*

What: Sometimes a file is not located in the current drive or folder (that is, the one whose contents you are currently viewing). The file may be located on another drive, such as the floppy disk (drive A) or a networked drive. It might also be located on the current drive but in a different folder.

Why: Like finding a piece of paper on your desk or your favorite shoes, locating a file on your computer may be easy or difficult, depending on how neat and organized you are. If you set up a system of folders for each type of file and carefully put each one where it belongs when you save it, finding the file is simply a matter of navigating through the various drives and folders until you locate it.

How: The Open dialog box (Figure 2.3) contains tools to make it easy for you to look in other places to find your document.

○ Use the **Look In** drop-down list to change to a different drive.
○ Use the **Up One Level** button to see the contents of the folder that contains the current folder.

Figure 2.3 Open
dialog box in Details
view

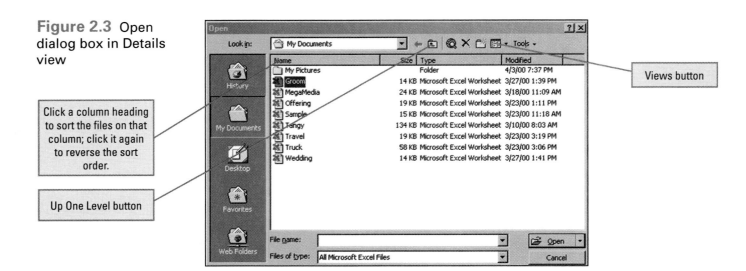

Click a column heading
to sort the files on that
column; click it again
to reverse the sort
order.

Up One Level button

Views button

○ Use the icons in the Places bar along the left side to jump quickly to
the **My Documents** folder or a place listed in **Favorites**, or to access
recently used files under **History**.

○ Change views with the **Views** button.

The Views button offers four views for the Open dialog box. You can
click the button to cycle through the four views, or you can click the
drop-down arrow to see the choices.

○ **List** shows a compact listing of all the files in the current folder.

○ **Preview** sometimes shows the contents of the selected file.

○ **Details** shows the size and date created or last modified for all the
files in the current folder.

○ **Properties** shows a few statistics about the selected file.

Result: When you see the name of the workbook, double-click it and it opens in
Excel, with the file name displayed in the title bar.

TIPS FROM A PRO: If you still can't find your file after looking around the various
folders, you can use the Search feature in Windows 2000 or the Find feature in
Windows 98. Excel also has a Find feature, but it is not as easy to use as the one
in Windows. To access it, open the Open dialog box, click Tools to open a menu,
and then click Find.

TASK **3**   *Enter Formulas in a Cell*

C CORE OBJECTIVE: *Enter formulas in a cell*

What: In Chapter 1, "Get Started with Excel," you learned how to insert text,
dates, and numbers into a cell. You also learned how to sum up the
numbers using the AutoSum button. You can also type formulas in a cell
to do all sorts of calculations.

Formulas always begin with an equal sign (=). Then, to calculate the result,
they combine numbers, cell references, and these arithmetic operators:

```
+ to add                    / to divide
– to subtract               % to take a percent
* to multiply               ^ to raise to a power (or exponent)
( ) to change the order of calculation
```

Excel calculates formulas from left to right, following a set order of operations. Enclosing part of a formula in parentheses changes the order in which the items are calculated. Look at this example:

= (48 – 12)*2/9 + 1

This formula equals 9 because the calculations inside the parentheses happen first, multiplication and division next, and then addition and subtraction. Table 2.1 shows the order in which Excel performs operations in formulas.

Table 2.1 Order of Operations, from First to Last

Operator	Effect
–	Negation (as in –1)
( )	Parentheses
%	Percent
^	Exponentiation
* and /	Multiplication and division
+ and –	Addition and subtraction

Why: Creating formulas is the most common skill used in building worksheets. Suppose you have a simple budget for the coming year, such as the one in Figure 2.4, for a lemonade stand. Every budget lists income on the top and expenses on the bottom. Below that comes the "bottom line," the difference between the two. You use a formula to calculate the income minus the expenses. AutoSum won't work for subtraction.

Figure 2.4 Sample budget

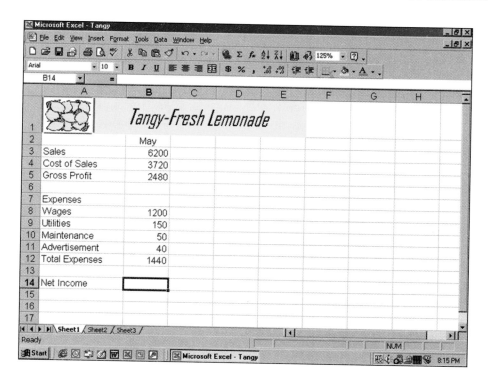

THOUGHT QUESTION: Why can't you use AutoSum to subtract one number from another?

How: In the example in Figure 2.4, to calculate the Net Income you must subtract Total Expenses from Gross Profit. Let's use two methods to create the formula for cell B14.

To type the formula, follow these steps:

1. Click **cell B14** to make it the active cell.
2. Type **=B5-B12** and press **Enter**.

To use the *pointing method*, you type the arithmetic symbols but click each cell instead of typing its cell address.

1. Click **cell B14** to make it the active cell, where you want the formula placed.
2. Press **=**. This begins the formula in the active cell.
3. Click **cell B5**. This surrounds the cell with a moving border. At the same time, the cell address is added to the formula. You can see the formula in the cell as well as on the formula bar at this point.
4. Press **–**, either on the keyboard or the keypad.
5. Click **cell B12**. Now the moving border appears around this cell, and its address is added to the formula. You can see an example of this in Figure 2.5.
6. Press **Enter**. This deposits the formula into the cell, and Excel calculates the result.

Figure 2.5 Building a formula by pointing

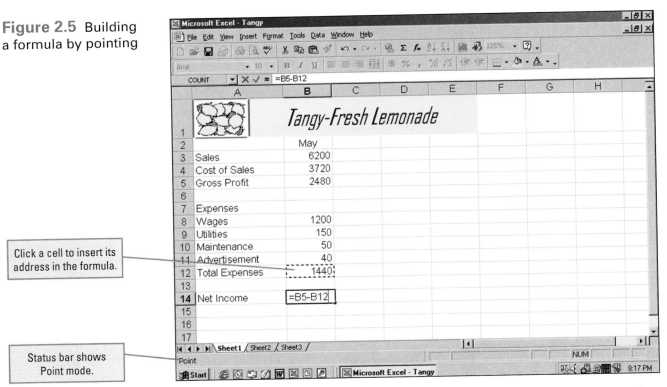

Click a cell to insert its address in the formula.

Status bar shows Point mode.

Result: After you press **Enter**, the results appear in the cell, but the formula appears in the formula bar, as you see in Figure 2.6. The best thing about using formulas is that when the numbers change, Excel calculates the results for you—automatically, instantly, and accurately.

Figure 2.6 Formula and results

The formula appears in the formula bar.

Results appear in the cell.

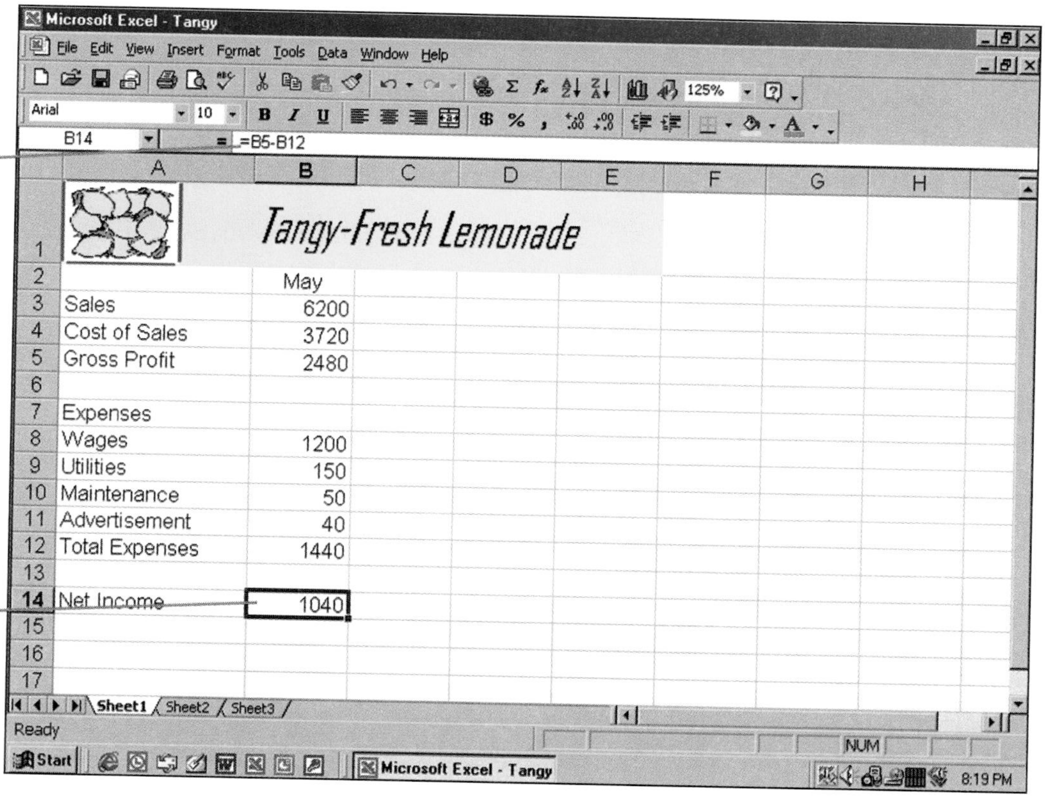

TASK 4   *Create a Budget*

What: You use formulas to create all sorts of worksheets, but knowing what formula to create is the hard part. Budgets have certain calculations you make repeatedly after you know each part's definition.

Why: Budgets help an individual or organization plan its finances. As you learned previously, you must examine income and expenses and the difference between them. If you have more income than expenses, good—you're expecting a profit. If your income is less than expenses—well, sometimes that happens, but a budget helps you plan for the future.

How: Let's define a few more budget items for the lemonade stand example.

- **Sales** is the amount in the cash register. You'll just estimate what you think the sales will be and type the number.
- **Cost of Sales** is the amount it costs you to create the product or service you are selling. For the lemonade stand example, you must purchase lemons, sugar, paper cups, ice, and water. Cost of Sales is usually calculated as a percent of the sales. If we assume the cost is 60 percent of sales, the formula will be =B3*60%. (Another way to calculate the same thing is =B3*.60. You must use either the decimal or the percent sign.)
- **Gross Profit** is the amount of profit after paying for the raw materials. The formula to calculate this will be =B3-B4.
- **Expenses** are usually estimates, simply typed numbers, although they also can be calculated as a percent of sales, if they vary.

- ○ **Total Expenses** is calculated by using the AutoSum button.
- ○ **Net Income,** as you just learned, is **Gross Profit** minus **Total Expenses,** or =B5–B12

Now suppose we project that sales will increase by 10% each month during the summer. What will the formula for June sales be?

=B3*10%? No! That only gives us 10 percent, and we want to *increase* by 10%. You must add the 10 percent to the original sales figure.

=B3 + B3*10% is the correct formula. Here are other ways to calculate the same thing:

=B3*1.1

=B3*110%

Use whichever form makes mathematical sense to you, as they are all the same.

Result: The formulas for the finished budget worksheet are shown in Figure 2.7

Figure 2.7 Sample budget

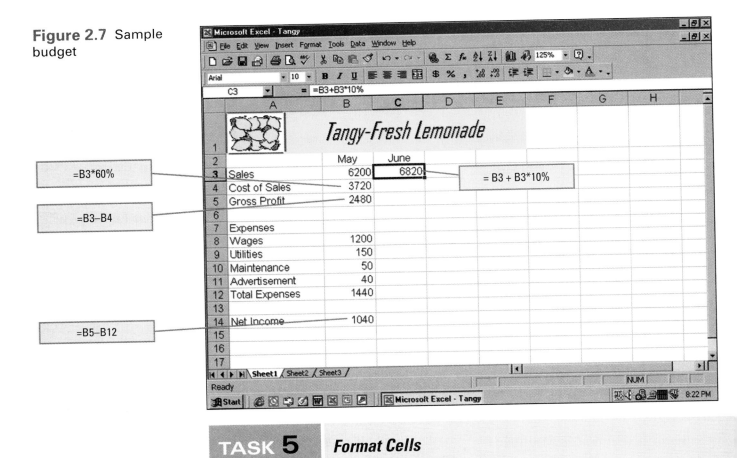

=B3*60%

=B3–B4

=B5–B12

TASK 5 **Format Cells**

C CORE OBJECTIVE: *Apply currency and comma formats*

C CORE OBJECTIVE: *Adjust the decimal place*

What: To make your budget more readable, you must *format* it, or change its appearance. To do this, you can click buttons on the Formatting toolbar. If you've used Word or PowerPoint, several of these buttons are already familiar to you.

Why: Widen columns so that all the text appears. Add dollar signs to help the reader know you are talking about money, and add commas to make it easy to read numbers over 1,000. Make some headings stand out by making them bold or italic, and separate numbers from the total by underlining.

How: The Formatting toolbar has lots of buttons you can use to change the appearance of your worksheet. Here are some you can easily use on a budget.

$ ○ **Add dollar signs.** Click the **Currency Style** button to add dollar signs to the numbers on the top and bottom rows.

, ○ **Add commas.** Click the **Comma Style** button to add commas to numbers where dollar signs aren't needed.

TIPS FROM A PRO: When you format the top row of numbers with dollar signs, the numbers no longer line up correctly with the other numbers in the column. To correct this, use Comma formatting on the other numbers, even if they are less than 1,000.

.00 ○ **Decrease decimals.** Click the **Decrease Decimal** button two times to eliminate the decimal places. In a budget, you are just estimating dollars, so cents aren't needed.

U ○ **Add underlines.** Click the **Underline** button to add an underline on the cell above the total.

B **I** ○ **Add bold or italic.** Click the **Bold** or **Italic** button to emphasize headings.

○ **Indent text.** Click the **Increase Indent** button to indent subordinate items from the left edge of the cell. (Click the Decrease Indent button to reduce the amount of indent.)

○ **Widen columns.** When your text is too long to fit within a cell, it extends into a blank column to the right or appears cut off. To widen the column, place the mouse pointer over the right border of the column heading until it turns to a two-headed arrow, as you see in Figure 2.8. Then you can drag right or left to change the column width, or double-click to make it fit the widest item in the column.

Figure 2.8 Changing column width

Two-headed pointer

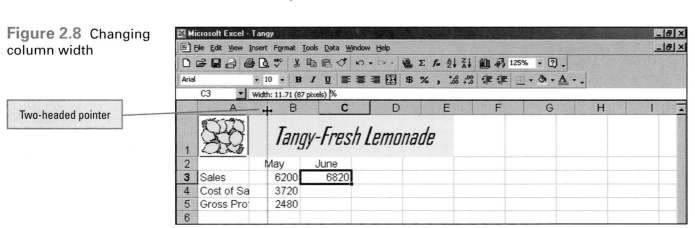

Figure 2.9
Formatted cells

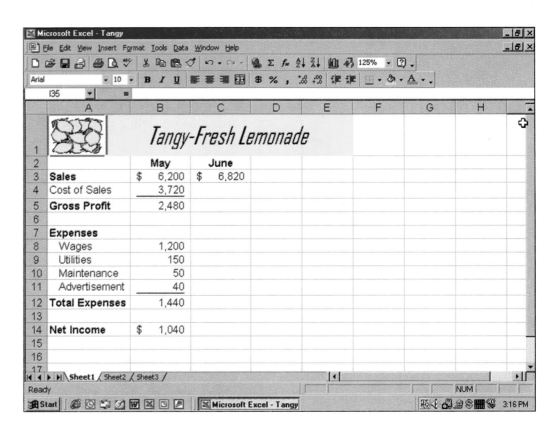

Result: Although the numbers have a different appearance, the contents of the cells have not changed. The formatting of a cell is separate from its contents. Figure 2.9 shows a sample budget with formatting.

Go ahead and experiment with the effects of using the buttons on the Formatting toolbar. You'll learn about how and when to use all of them and many other formatting techniques in Chapter 6, "Format Worksheets."

TIPS FROM A PRO: When you type a number with dollar signs and commas, Excel automatically formats the cells for you. You don't have to click the buttons.

TASK 6   *Edit Cell Content*

CORE OBJECTIVE: *Edit cell content*

What: After you enter text, numbers, or a formula into a cell, you may need to change it. You can always retype the entry, if it's short. If it's long, you can easily edit it instead.

One way to do this is to click in the formula bar and make changes. When the mouse pointer is over the formula bar, it appears as an I-beam. This makes it easy for you to click between letters to place the insertion point where you want to begin making corrections.

Why: Sometimes it's easier to make a minor change to the contents of a cell rather than start over from scratch.

How: You can edit the contents of a cell three ways.

○ Move the mouse pointer to the formula bar and click to place the insertion point. Make changes by pressing **Backspace** or **Delete** and retyping.

○ Double-click the cell, and the mouse pointer turns into an I-beam. Click to place the insertion point within the cell, and make changes.

○ Press the **F2** key and make the changes.

When you edit the contents of the cell, two new buttons appear on the formula bar, as you see in Table 2.2 and Figure 2.10. You can use these buttons to finish editing. The status bar shows Edit status until you click one of these, when it changes back to Ready, meaning you can work on any cell in the worksheet.

Table 2.2 Completing an Edit

Result desired	Keyboard	Mouse
Make the change permanent	Press **Enter**	Click ✔
Stop editing and make no change	Press **Esc**	Click ✘

Figure 2.10 Edit cell contents

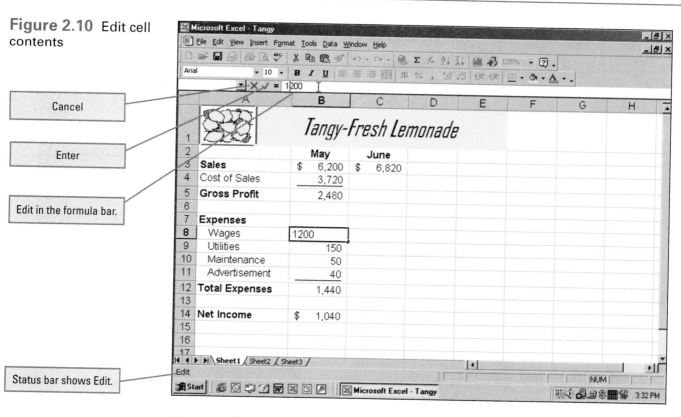

Cancel

Enter

Edit in the formula bar.

Status bar shows Edit.

Result: If you press Enter or click the Enter button on the formula bar, the changes are made permanent. If you press Esc or click the Cancel button on the formula bar, the contents of the cell are left unchanged. In either case, the status bar shows Ready, and you can then work on other cells in the worksheet.

TIPS FROM A PRO: When you format a number with dollar signs, you can't remove the dollar signs by editing the cell contents because the formatting is stored separately from the contents of the cell. One way to remove dollar signs where they are not needed is to click the Comma Style button.

TASK 7 Use AutoFill

 C CORE OBJECTIVE: *Work with series (AutoFill)*

What: After you've built a budget for a single period of time, you often have to repeat the process for several other time periods, say the next month, quarter, or year. Excel provides the *AutoFill* feature to copy text, numbers, and formulas to adjacent cells. You can also use the feature to create a sequence.

Why: AutoFill saves you the trouble of typing the same text, numbers, and formulas repeatedly.

COPY DATA

How: The active cell is surrounded by a bold rectangle, and on the lower-right corner is a small black square called the *fill handle*.

1. Select the cell you want to copy.
2. Place the mouse pointer over the fill handle. It turns into a black cross (rather than the normal fat plus), as you see in Figure 2.11.
3. Drag across or down adjacent cells.

Figure 2.11 Using AutoFill to copy data

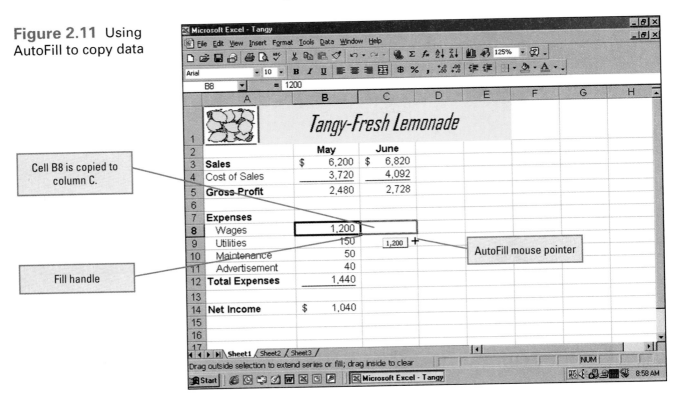

Cell B8 is copied to column C.

Fill handle

AutoFill mouse pointer

Result: Using AutoFill you can quickly and easily build a large worksheet by copying text and numbers to adjacent cells. Excel is so smart: When you copy formulas using AutoFill, they automatically adjust to refer to the correct items. As you see in Figure 2.12, the formula to calculate Net Income for June has changed to refer to the cells in column C.

Figure 2.12
Formulas
automatically adjust

Formula for June

Formula for May is
=B5–B12.

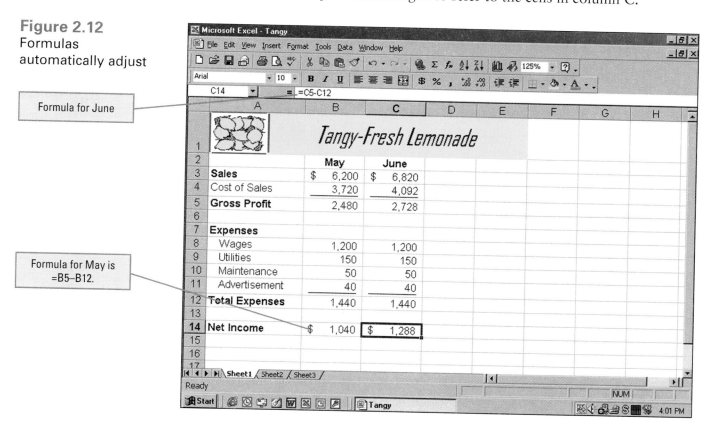

FILL A SERIES

How: The AutoFill feature is amazing; it correctly figures out what you want to put in adjacent cells. How it works depends on what you select.

To continue a sequence of dates, times, or certain time periods from a single cell:

1. Select the cell containing the beginning value.
2. Place the mouse pointer over the fill handle.
3. Drag across or down adjacent cells.

As you see in Figure 2.13, numbers are copied, but dates and times change to the next value.

Figure 2.13
AutoFilling a series
down from a single
cell

Select row 1.

Drag down to get
these preset results.

	A	B	C	D	E	F	G	H	I
1	1	Jan	January	Mon	Monday	Q1	Quarter 1	8:00	
2	1	Feb	February	Tue	Tuesday	Q2	Quarter 2	9:00	
3	1	Mar	March	Wed	Wednesday	Q3	Quarter 3	10:00	
4	1	Apr	April	Thu	Thursday	Q4	Quarter 4	11:00	
5									

TIPS FROM A PRO: If you hold down the Ctrl key as you drag the fill handle, numbers increase by 1 and dates and times are copied as is, instead of changed to the next value.

To continue a sequence of numbers, dates, or time periods based on data in two or more adjacent cells:

1. Type the first few items of the sequence in adjacent cells.
2. Select the cells.
3. Drag the fill handle to adjacent cells.

As you see in Figure 2.14, the series extends based on the cells you have selected.

Select rows 1 and 2.

Drag down with the fill handle to continue the sequence.

	A	B	C	D	E	F	G	H	I
1	1	1	2	5	Monday	Jan-00	Jan	8:00	
2	1	2	4	10	Wednesday	Jul-00	Apr	8:15	
3	1	3	6	15	Friday	Jan-01	Jul	8:30	
4	1	4	8	20	Sunday	Jul-01	Oct	8:45	
5	1	5	10	25	Tuesday	Jan-02	Jan	9:00	
6									

Figure 2.14
AutoFilling a series down from two or more cells

Result: As you drag, the yellow ScreenTip shows the contents of the cells. When you select more than one cell, the sequence continues according to the first few items.

 TIPS FROM A PRO: You can also create a custom fill series, such as "high, medium, low," or "strongly agree, agree, neutral, disagree, and strongly disagree." You'll learn how to do this in Chapter 13, "Manage Data and Lists."

 TIPS FROM A PRO: You can also use the AutoFill feature to project the future based on past numbers. In the budget, for example, you can select all the Net Income amounts and then fill them to the right to make a projection about future earnings. (Excel does this on the fly through a complex mathematical computation called regression analysis.)

TASK 8 | Clear Cell Content

 CORE OBJECTIVE: Clear cell content

What: You can remove a cell entry, and leave the cell or cells empty. You might be tempted to press the Spacebar to make a cell look blank, but the cell wouldn't be empty in that case. To empty a cell completely, you *clear* it.

Why: You may put something into a cell by mistake and want to have it empty.

How: You can clear selected cells using any of these methods:

○ Press **Delete**.
○ Choose **Edit|Clear|Contents**.

- ○ Right-click the cells and choose **Clear Contents** from the shortcut menu.
- ○ Drag the fill handle up and in, so that the cell is shaded, as you see in Figure 2.15.

Figure 2.15 Using the fill handle to clear

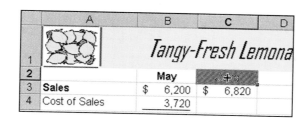

Result: As you drag the fill handle inward and upward, the selected cell or cells become shaded. When you release the mouse button, the cells are emptied.

TIPS FROM A PRO: The Edit|Clear command has other options. You can also use it to remove the formatting or any comments from the selected cells. Choose **All** to remove the contents, the formatting, and the comments.

| TASK **9** | *Use the Undo and Redo Features* |

C CORE OBJECTIVE: *Use Undo and Redo*

What: When you make a small mistake in entering data in a cell, you can easily retype, but if you make a larger error, such as clearing cells by mistake, you need to use the Undo feature. Undo brings back the information that you thought was gone.

Excel keeps a record of changes you make to your worksheet, and you can choose to undo the last one—or as many as you want—in reverse order. Then if you change your mind and want to do the changes again, you can simply use Redo.

Undo only works on changes that you've made during this session, so you can't undo procedures if you closed the worksheet and opened it again. It also doesn't work on operations that do not result in changes, such as printing or saving.

Why: It's common enough to make a mistake and immediately regret it. Excel enables you to backtrack.

How: The Undo and Redo buttons work for a single operation or for multiple actions.

- ○ To reverse the last action, click the **Undo** button.
- ○ To undo several actions, click the down arrow next to the Undo button and drag to select as many actions as you want to reverse (Figure 2.16).
- ○ To redo the last item you used Undo on, click the **Redo** button.
- ○ To redo several actions you used Undo on, click the down arrow next to Redo and drag to select as many actions as you want to restore.

Figure 2.16
Undoing several
actions at once

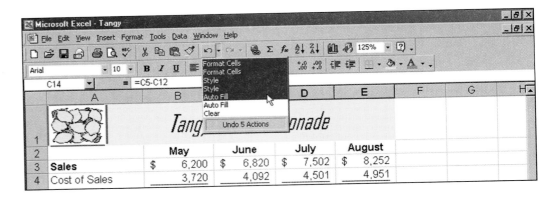

The methods for using the Undo and Redo commands are summarized in Table 2.3.

Table 2.3 Undo and Redo Commands

Command	Button	Shortcut key
Edit|Undo		Ctrl+Z
Edit|Redo		Ctrl+Y

Result: The change you made by mistake is reversed. You'll find the Undo and Redo features quite handy as you continue to modify and format worksheets.

TASK **10** *Use Find and Replace*

CORE OBJECTIVE: *Use Find and Replace*

What: When you are building worksheets, you will sometimes find that a repeated item needs to be changed every time it's mentioned. For example, if you need to prepare a budget similar to another department's budget, you open the original file and wherever the previous department is mentioned, you must replace it with the current one. The Find and Replace feature helps you quickly find every occurrence of the department and replace it with the correct one.

Why: Making these sorts of changes one by one might lead to errors. For example, it would be easy to miss one mention of the department, or you might transpose some letters when typing the same text repeatedly. That's why automating the process is a good idea—not only to keep you from tiresome, repetitive tasks, but also to ensure that the task is done without error.

FIND TEXT

How: Use the Find command to locate certain text or numbers, or the Replace command to find it and replace it with an alternative.

1. Choose **Edit|Find** or press **Ctrl+F.** This opens the dialog box shown in Figure 2.17.
2. Type the text or data you are searching for.
3. Specify the direction of the search—down the columns or across the rows (searching columns is usually faster).
4. Click **Match Case** to find and replace items with the exact same capitalization.
5. Click **Find Entire Cells** so Excel will only find cells that contain an exact match of what you typed in the **Find What** box.
6. Click **Find Next.**

Result: When you use the Find command, Excel jumps the active cell to the next instance of the item you are seeking.

REPLACE TEXT

How: You can combine the find action with the process of replacing.

1. Choose **Edit|Replace** or click the Replace button on the Find dialog box to see the dialog box shown in Figure 2.18.
2. Type the text or data you wish to find in the **Find What** box.
3. Type the replacement in the **Replace With** box.
4. Click **Find Next** and then **Replace** to review each selection one at a time, or click **Replace All** to do every instance all at one time.

Figure 2.17 Find dialog box

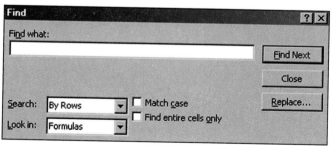

Figure 2.18 Replace dialog box

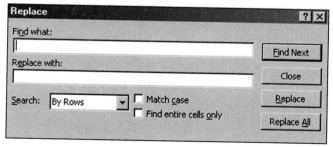

Result: What happens depends on which button you click:

○ To step through the entire document, deciding each time whether to make the replacement, use **Find Next** and **Replace.**

○ Alternatively, you can save time and click **Replace All** to do the job without having to confirm each one. However if you use this, be sure to check that you didn't replace something that shouldn't have been changed.

When you've seen all the instances, Excel loops back to the beginning and starts over (or if there's only one instance, just stays in one place). Close the Find box when you're finished.

TASK 11 *Check Spelling*

 C CORE OBJECTIVE: *Check spelling*

What: Whether you don't know the proper spelling of a word or simply stumble in your typing, the spelling checker helps correct errors.

Why: Anyone can inadvertently misspell a word. Isn't it annoying to find an error after you work so hard on a project?

How: Follow these steps to check the spelling in your worksheet:

1. Press **Ctrl+Home** to move the insertion point to cell A1, or drag specific cells to specify which ones to check.
2. Click the **Spelling** button, press the **F7** shortcut key, or choose **Tools|Spelling**. This opens the dialog box shown in Figure 2.19. Excel checks the Office dictionary, finds the first possible error, and shows one or more suggestions for correcting it.
3. Respond to the Spelling dialog box in one of these ways:
   - Click **Ignore** if you want to leave the item as it is.
   - Click **Ignore All** to avoid having to click Ignore repeatedly for the same item. Ignore All affects only this file.
   - Select the correction you want and click **Change**.
   - Use **Change All** if you want to make the same correction repeatedly throughout.
   - Click **Add** if you want this item included in a custom dictionary. This way the spelling checker bypasses it from now on.
   - **AutoCorrect** adds this mistake and its correction to the list of items that Excel automatically corrects as you type.

Figure 2.19 Spelling dialog box

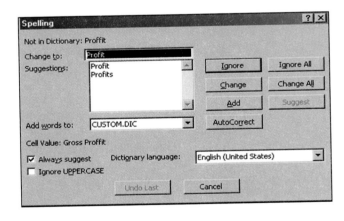

TIPS FROM A PRO: Does your name or your organization's name constantly come up in the spelling checker? Click **Add** to add it to the dictionary.

Result: When all the cells have been checked and you've responded with Change or Ignore, Excel notifies you that the spelling check is complete. Click **OK** to continue working. Be sure to proofread, though. You may have words incorrectly spelled that the spelling checker doesn't see as an error, such as *form* instead of *from*.

Use PinPoint

After gaining the skills in this chapter, you can find an existing workbook and open it and modify the cell contents. You can create a budget, build its formulas, and use the fill handle to fill and clear cells. Now it's time to use the PinPoint software and see what you can do. Remember, whenever you are unsure of what to do, you can reread that portion of the chapter or you can click Show Me for a live demonstration. Check out these skills in PinPoint:

- Check spelling
- Clear cell contents
- Decimal places
- Edit cell contents
- Enter a formula
- Fill a range
- Find and replace
- Indent cell text
- Numeric format
- Open a workbook
- Undo

Key Terms

You can find definitions for these words in this chapter:

AutoFill
Clear
Fill handle
Pointing method

Review Questions

You can use the following review questions to test your knowledge and skills. Answers are given in Appendix D, "Answers to Review Questions."

True/False

Indicate whether each statement is true (T) or false (F).

___ 1. In My Computer, if you double-click the name of an Excel file, it opens in Excel.

___ 2. When you type a cell entry and press Enter, the active cell jumps to the cell below.

___ 3. You can see the formula for the active cell in the formula bar, but the cell shows the result.

___ 4. You can edit a formula either in the formula bar or in the cell itself.

___ 5. Click the Cancel button on the formula bar to complete editing and return the status to Ready.

___ 6. Gross Profit is calculated by taking Total Income minus Total Expenses.

___ 7. Net Income is calculated by taking Gross Profit minus Total Expenses.

___ 8. To have cell B2 grow by 20%, use the formula =B2*20%.

___ 9. To copy the contents of a cell to adjacent cells, drag the fill handle.

___ 10. To reverse the last changes you've made, click the Reverse button.

Multiple Choice

Select the letter that best completes the statement.

___ 1. To open an Excel file you've used recently:
a. Click the file name on the bottom of the File menu.
b. Click the file name on the bottom of the Edit menu.
c. Choose Start|Documents and click the file name.
d. Click the Start button and choose Recent.
e. Either a or c.

___ 2. If you click Open and can't see the file you want listed in the dialog box:
a. Click the Views button to see all the files on the computer.
b. Click the Up One Level button to see the contents of the parent folder.
c. Click the Look In drop down list to change the file type.
d. Click the My Computer button on the left side of the dialog box to see all the files on your computer.
e. All of the above.

___ 3. To begin a formula, type:
   a. +.
   b. -.
   c. =.
   d. /.
   e. F.

___ 4. The formula to calculate Cost of Sales so that it equals 60% of the Sales in cell B2 is:
   a. = B2+60%.
   b. = B2*60%.
   c. = B2/60%.
   d. = B2^60%.
   e. = B2%60.

___ 5. If the Sales number in cell B2 changes, the formula for Cost of Sales:
   a. Immediately recalculates the results.
   b. Flashes on and off, reminding you to recalculate.
   c. Must be updated.
   d. Should be retyped.
   e. Changes to refer to column C.

___ 6. If you type Jan into a cell and then drag the fill handle to adjacent cells, what you see is:
   a. Jan, Jan, Jan.
   b. Jan, Feb, Mar.
   c. January, January, January.
   d. January, February, March.
   e. Jan 1, Jan 2, Jan 3.

___ 7. To remove the contents of a cell and empty it completely:
   a. Press Delete.
   b. Drag in and up with the fill handle.
   c. Press Spacebar.
   d. All of the above.
   e. Either a or b.

___ 8. You can use the Undo button:
   a. To undo actions one at a time.
   b. To reverse several changes at once.
   c. To correct spelling mistakes.
   d. To stop printing a worksheet by mistake.
   e. Both a and b.

___ 9. When you want to change October to November throughout a monthly report wherever it appears, click the Edit menu and choose:
   a. Change.
   b. Find.
   c. Replace.
   d. Undo.
   e. Redo.

___ 10. When checking a worksheet for spelling errors, choose:
   a. Ignore if the word is just fine as it is.
   b. Change after you click the correct spelling.
   c. Add if you don't want the spelling checker to see this as an error.
   d. AutoCorrect to have Excel change this error automatically next time.
   e. All of the above.

Screen Review 1

Match the letters in Figure 2.20 with the correct items in the list.

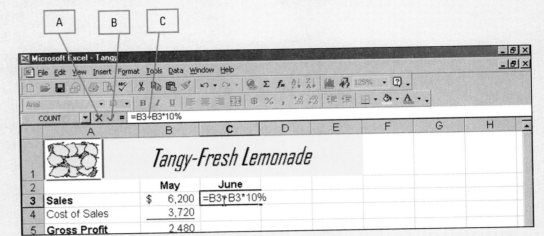

Figure 2.20

_____ 1. Click here to finish the formula.

_____ 2. Click here to stop editing the cell without making any changes.

_____ 3. Click here to edit the contents of the current cell.

Screen Review 2

Match the letters in Figure 2.21 with the correct items in the list.

Figure 2.21

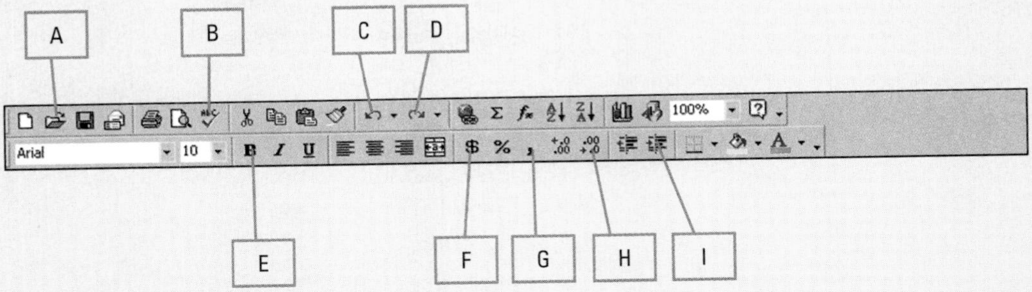

_____ 1. Click here to check the spelling.

_____ 2. Click here to open a different file.

_____ 3. Click here to reverse changes you've made.

_____ 4. Click here to redo the change you just reversed.

_____ 5. Click here to emphasize headings.

_____ 6. Click here to add dollar signs to numbers.

_____ 7. Click here to indent subheadings.

_____ 8. Click here to align plain numbers with those formatted with $.

_____ 9. Click here to reduce the number of decimal places.

Exercise and Project

Follow these step-by-step instructions to create a worksheet. If you are working in a computer lab, ask your instructor where you should save and print your file.

Exercise

1. Open **Collies.xls** from the *Student\Chapter 2* folder on your PinPoint CD-ROM.
2. Type **Q1** in cell B3 and use AutoFill to complete the four Quarter headings. Type **Total** in cell F3.
3. Enter a formula in cell C4 to make the Sales grow by 2% each quarter.
4. Fill the formula across for Quarters 3 and 4.
5. Enter a formula into cell B5 to calculate Cost of Sales by taking 20% of Sales.
6. Enter a formula into cell B7 to calculate Gross Profit.
7. Change the Pedigrees expense in cell B12 to **400**.
8. In cell B18, enter a formula to total the expenses.
9. Enter a formula in B20 to calculate Net Profit.
10. Format the Sales row and Net Profit row with **dollar signs** and **no decimal places**.
11. Format all the other rows with **Comma** format and **no decimal places**.
12. **Indent** the names of the expenses in cells A10 through A16.
13. **Underline** the numbers for Cost of Sales and Shows.
14. Select B5 through B20 and use AutoFill to copy the values and formulas through Quarter 4.
15. In cell F4, enter a formula to calculate the total sales for the four quarters.
16. Fill the formula in F4 down through F20.
17. Remove the contents of the blank rows. Remove the dollar signs from all the cells except the top and bottom ones, and add underlines where appropriate.
18. Use Edit Replace to change **Housing** to **Kennels**.
19. Check the spelling in the worksheet.
20. Save the file as **Kennel Budget.xls**. Print.

Project

Suppose you have started a small business where you create Web pages for friends and businesses. Create a budget for the business, including expenses such as Software (Front Page), Hardware (digital camera, CD-R drive, MP3 player . . .), Internet Service Provider, Graphics, and any other items you may need. Show the budget on a quarterly basis, and be sure you show a profit by the end of the year. Save and print the worksheet.

Modify Worksheet Structure

E xcel's power comes from its flexibility. You've seen how Excel understands what you mean to do when you fill a formula to adjacent cells. In the same way, you can add new columns, rows, or individual cells and delete unwanted ones. You can rearrange or duplicate the cells in other parts of the worksheet. If you're working on a very long or very wide worksheet, you can freeze one part of the sheet and move around in another part to view two separate parts of the sheet at one time.

At the end of this chapter, you will be able to:

C   E

☐	☐	Select ranges, rows, or columns
☑	☐	Duplicate cells (copy and paste)
☑	☐	Move cells (cut)
☑	☐	Use drag-and-drop to move cells
☑	☐	Use Paste Special
☑	☐	Use the Office Clipboard to collect and paste
☑	☐	Insert and delete rows and columns
☑	☐	Insert and delete selected cells
☐	☐	Insert and paste
☑	☐	Modify the size of rows and columns
☑	☐	Hide and unhide rows and columns
☑	☐	Freeze and unfreeze rows and columns
☑	☐	Change the zoom setting
☑	☐	Calculate an average

What: When you want to restructure your worksheet or rearrange it, you must first specify what parts you want to work with, just as you click cells to specify which ones to include in a formula. You do this by *selecting* with either the mouse or the keyboard. When an item is selected, Excel surrounds it with a dark border and makes it appear shaded.

When you are working on a worksheet, the active cell, surrounded by the dark border, is automatically selected. You can also select a *range* (a group of several cells). A range of adjacent cells is named according to the cells in the top-left corner and the bottom-right corner, with a colon between, for example A1:B4.

To select rows, columns, or the entire worksheet, you use the row and column headings.

Why: You must select something before you can rearrange or copy. Selecting also speeds the process of inserting and deleting rows and columns. You'll also need to select items when building certain formulas or charts.

Figure 3.1 Selecting

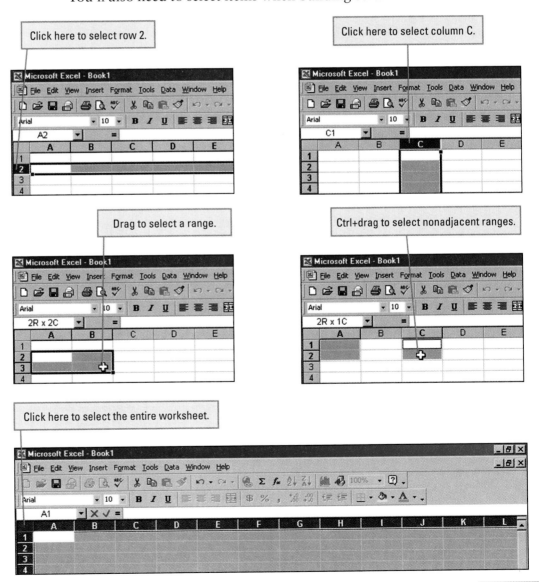

How: Here's how to select larger portions of a worksheet.

- ○ To select a range, click and drag with the mouse, or hold down the **Shift** key and press the **arrow keys.**
- ○ To select a row, click the row heading number.
- ○ To select a column, click the column heading letter.
- ○ To select the entire worksheet, click the **Select All** button at the intersection of the row numbers and column headings, as in Figure 3.1.
- ○ To extend a selection, click the first item, hold down the **Shift** key, and click the last item. Everything in between is also selected.
- ○ To select nonadjacent items, click the first, hold down the **Ctrl** key, and click the next item. Nothing between is selected.

 THOUGHT QUESTION: When would it be handy to select several nonadjacent cells or ranges?

Result: The first item in the selection is the active cell, so it does not appear shaded, although it is surrounded by the dark border, as seen in Figure 3.1.

 TIPS FROM A PRO: When you have a range selected and begin to type cell entries, the active cell moves only within the selection. To make a cell entry in another cell, click or use the arrow keys to move the cell.

TASK **2** *Rearrange Text*

 CORE OBJECTIVE: *Cut, copy, paste, paste special, and move selected cells*

What: You can rearrange a cell, range, or an entire row or column. To do this, you must first select what you want to rearrange.

You use the copy-and-paste process to duplicate cells and put the copy in another location. If instead you want to remove the cell from its place and put it elsewhere, you use the cut-and-paste technique. The commands for doing each are summarized in Table 3.1.

A feature new to Office 2000 is the collect-and-paste process, where you can cut or copy multiple items to the Office Clipboard. You'll learn about that in Task 3.

Table 3.1 Cut, Copy, and Paste Commands

Command *	Button	Shortcut key	Effect
Edit|Cut	✂	Ctrl+X	Removes selected material, puts it on the Clipboard
Edit|Copy	📋	Ctrl+C	Puts duplicate of selected material on the Clipboard
Edit|Paste	📋	Ctrl+V	Inserts contents of Clipboard beginning with the active cell

*You can also right-click and choose the Cut, Copy, or Paste command from the shortcut menu.

TIPS FROM A PRO: It makes sense that Ctrl+C is for Copy, but why the X and V for Cut and Paste? Well, the X may call to mind the shape of the scissors on the Cut button. But the real reason is that these three keys are located next to each other along the bottom row of the keyboard. This way you can perform the cut-and-paste or copy-and-paste process with just one hand.

Why: In the process of creating or refining a worksheet, you often want to move a block of cells to another location or to duplicate them and then make a few changes. It would be time-consuming to retype it all from scratch, particularly if the selection is a large one. Besides, when you recreate the text, numbers, and formulas, you might make an error.

The procedures for duplicating and moving cells are similar. They both begin with selecting.

DUPLICATE CELLS (COPY AND PASTE)

How: Follow these steps:

1. Select the cell, range, row, or column (using techniques you learned in Task 1) that you want to copy.
2. Click the **Copy** button, choose **Edit|Copy**, press **Ctrl+C**, or right-click and choose **Copy**. The copied cells are surrounded by a moving border, as you see in Figure 3.2.
3. Move the active cell to the top-left corner of area where you want the item located.
4. To insert a single copy of the selection, press **Enter**. If you want to copy it several places, don't press Enter; instead, click the **Paste** button, choose **Edit|Paste**, press **Ctrl+V**, or right-click and choose **Paste**.
5. Repeat steps 3 and 4 to copy it multiple times.
6. When you're done, press **Esc**, if necessary, to get rid of the moving borders around the selection.

Figure 3.2 Copying cells

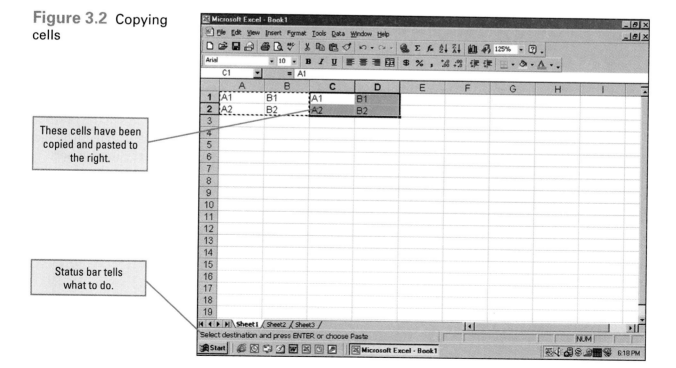

These cells have been copied and pasted to the right.

Status bar tells what to do.

Result: The contents appear in two or more locations. Using the Copy command makes a duplicate of the cells without removing them from the original location. Whenever you paste, the new information replaces any existing contents in the destination cells.

MOVE CELLS (CUT AND PASTE)

How: As with the copy-and-paste process, follow these steps:

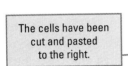

1. Select the cells you want to move.
2. Click the **Cut** button, choose **Edit|Cut**, press **Ctrl+X**, or right-click and choose **Cut**. The selected cells are surrounded by a moving border.
3. Move the active cell to the top-left corner of area where you want the item located.
4. Press **Enter**, click the **Paste** button, choose **Edit|Paste**, press **Ctrl+V**, or right-click and choose **Paste**. (When you cut, you can only paste once, not multiple times.)

Result: The text has been removed from the first location and inserted at the destination, as you see in Figure 3.3.

Figure 3.3 Moving cells

The cells have been cut and pasted to the right.

MOVE CELLS (DRAG AND DROP)

Another way to move cells—perhaps even easier to use than the cut-and-paste method—is the *drag-and-drop* method. All you have to do is drag with the mouse.

How: Pay attention to the shape of the mouse pointer when you use this techique.

1. Select the cells you want to move.
2. Move the mouse pointer over the dark selection border until it turns into a left-pointing arrow (not the fat plus or the black cross)
3. Hold down the left mouse button, and drag until you see the destination surrounded by the gray border. A yellow box also tells the exact address of the destination (see Figure 3.4). Release the mouse button.

Figure 3.4 Drag and drop

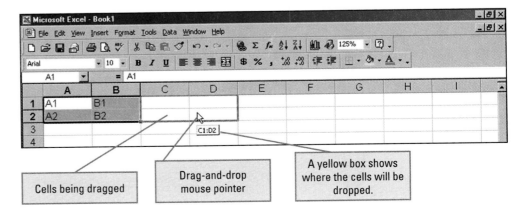

Cells being dragged

Drag-and-drop mouse pointer

A yellow box shows where the cells will be dropped.

Result: As soon as you release the mouse, the cells are dropped into the new location. If the destination cells are not empty, Excel prompts you to be sure you want to replace their contents with the new information.

 TIPS FROM A PRO: Did you notice the status bar as you used drag-and-drop to rearrange cells? It says "Use Alt key to switch sheets." You can use drag-and-drop to move cells to another worksheet in the workbook. To do this, hold down the **Alt** key, drag down to the tab of the destination worksheet, and when the new worksheet appears, move to the cell at the top-left corner of the destination on that new worksheet.

PASTE SPECIAL

How: On certain occasions, you'll use the **Edit|Paste Special** command, rather than pressing Enter or choosing Paste to paste material you've copied or cut. As you see in Figure 3.5, the Paste Special dialog box offers several options for pasting. Here are the main ones you'll use:

❍ **All** pastes both the formulas and formatting.
❍ **Formulas** pastes only the contents of the cells, with no formatting.
❍ **Values** pastes only text and numbers. Where you have formulas, the answers are pasted as numbers instead.
❍ **Formats** makes a copy of the formatting without the cell contents.
❍ **Operation** allows you to add the pasted items to the current cell contents (or subtract, multiply, or divide).
❍ **Transpose** is used to change a list of items down a column to a list across a row.
❍ **Paste Link** sets up a link between two worksheets or files, so that when you change the original, the copy changes too.

Result: Using the Paste Special dialog box, you can control exactly what is deposited in the destination while copying or moving material.

Figure 3.5 Paste Special dialog box

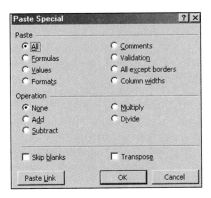

 TASK 3 **Collect and Paste**

C **CORE OBJECTIVE: Use the Office Clipboard**

What: As you know from the "Start with Windows" chapter, Windows provides a temporary storage place called the *Clipboard* to store a file—or, in this case, copied or cut cells—while you are rearranging things. The

Figure 3.6
Clipboard toolbar with
two items collected

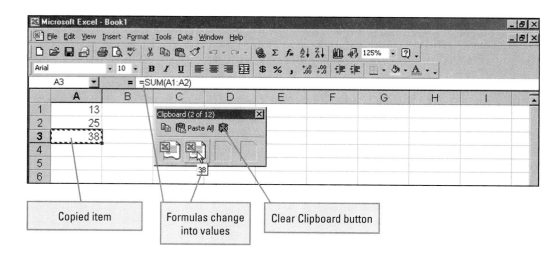

Copied item | Formulas change into values | Clear Clipboard button

Office Clipboard, however, improves on this by allowing storage of up to 12 items.

The Clipboard toolbar appears whenever you choose Copy or Cut two or more times without choosing Paste in between. You can also access the Clipboard toolbar, shown in Figure 3.6, by choosing View|Toolbars| Clipboard.

Why: Each time you copy or cut two or more items, you see an icon added to the Office Clipboard. This way you can collect several items and paste them all at once or one at a time.

Warning: When you copy a formula using the Office Clipboard, formulas are not retained. Instead, they turn into values—mere numbers.

How: The process of using the Office Clipboard to collect and paste multiple items at once is similar to the copy-and-cut processes.

TO COLLECT

1. Select the first cell or range you want to collect.
2. Choose **Copy** or **Cut**.
3. Select the second cell or range.
4. Choose **Copy** or **Cut**. At this point, the Clipboard toolbar should appear.
5. If the Clipboard toolbar doesn't appear, you must activate the feature. To do this, choose **View|Toolbars|Clipboard**, and then repeat steps 1 and 2.
6. To see the contents of each item, place the mouse pointer over its icon on the Clipboard toolbar and pause (don't click).

TO USE THE ITEMS YOU'VE COLLECTED

1. Move the insertion point to the destination where you want to paste.
2. To insert one item, click its icon.
3. To insert all the items at once into a single column, click **Paste All**.
4. When you finish with a series of edits, empty the Clipboard so that you can start fresh with a new operation. To do this, click the **Clear Clipboard** button.
5. To remove the Clipboard toolbar from the screen, click its **Close** button.

Result: The Paste All procedure inserts all the items you collected into a column of your worksheet. They are inserted in the same order in which you collected them. If any of the cells you collected contained formulas, they are converted into plain old numbers.

TASK 4 — Insert and Delete

C *CORE OBJECTIVE: Insert and delete rows and columns*

C *CORE OBJECTIVE: Insert and delete selected cells*

What: When you've forgotten something, you can easily make room for new items in your worksheet. You can either move the existing items using the skills you learned in Task 3, or you can insert new cells, rows, or columns. Alternatively, when you have extra cells, rows, or columns you want to get rid of, you can delete them. Using the Cut command or pressing the Delete key empties them; in contrast, deleting cells, rows, or columns removes them completely from the worksheet structure.

Why: You wouldn't want to erase the worksheet and start all over again just because you needed to rearrange or add new material.

INSERT ROWS AND COLUMNS

How: Use any of these techniques to insert rows and columns.

○ To insert a row:

  1. First select the row or rows that will move down to make room for the new row. (To do this, click the row number on the left side of the screen.)

  2. Choose **Insert|Rows** or right-click and choose **Insert**.

○ To insert a column:

  1. First select the column or columns that will move to the right to make room for the new column. (To do this, click the column heading on the top of the screen.)

  2. Choose **Insert|Columns** or right-click and choose **Insert**.

Result: A new row appears above the selected row, and a new column appears to the left of a selected column, as you see in Figure 3.7.

Figure 3.7 New column inserted

![Screenshot of Microsoft Excel - Book1 window showing a worksheet with A1, A2 in column A, an empty selected column B, and B1, B2 in column C]

TIPS FROM A PRO: What happens to the formulas in your worksheet when you insert rows or columns? Well, that depends.

If the formulas refer to specific cells, the formulas automatically reflect the new location of the cells, so you don't have to worry about those.

If the formulas refer to a range, such as when you use AutoSum, the formula might still be correct—but only if you inserted rows and columns into the middle. If you inserted them at one of the ends, the sum might not reflect the new cells. That's why it's important to go back and check each formula after adding new rows, columns, or cells.

DELETE ROWS AND COLUMNS

How: You may think you can delete a row or column by selecting it and pressing **Delete**. However, what that does is remove the contents of the cells, leaving empty cells behind. To remove a row or column completely, follow these steps:

1. First select the row or column you want to remove.
2. Choose Edit|Delete or right-click and choose Delete.

Result: The remaining columns and rows scoot together. Any formula that referred to a cell in the deleted row or column now shows #REF, meaning Excel can't find the cell reference anymore (Figure 3.8). You have to correct those by hand.

Figure 3.8 Formulas referring to deleted cells

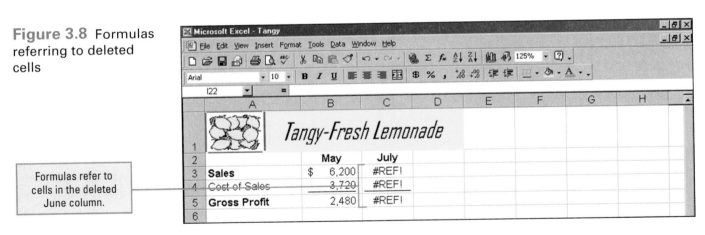

Formulas refer to cells in the deleted June column.

INSERT AND DELETE CELLS

How: You use a slightly different procedure when you want to insert or delete a few cells rather than an entire column or row.

1. Select the cells.
2. Choose **Insert|Cells** (to insert) or choose **Edit|Delete** (to delete). In the dialog boxes (Figure 3.9), specify how you want to shift the existing cells. As you see, you can also use this procedure to insert or delete entire rows or columns, even if you don't select them first.

Result: Inserting and deleting cells this way does not affect the entire worksheet, but affects only the cells in the highlighted columns or rows. When cells are added to or removed from the worksheet, the adjacent cells are

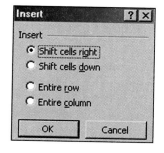

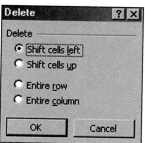

Figure 3.9 Insert and Delete dialog boxes

displaced horizontally or vertically, as you see in Figure 3.10, but the remaining cells are unaffected.

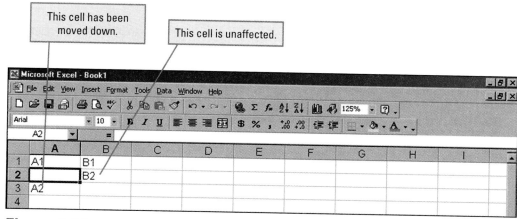

Figure 3.10 Inserting cells does not affect the entire row

 TIPS FROM A PRO: You can combine inserting cells with the copy-and-paste process. You can insert new cells and paste the contents in a single operation. To do this, after copying or cutting, move to the destination and choose **Insert|Copied Cells** or **Insert|Cut Cells**, a command that only appears after you copy or cut something. You may then have to specify whether to shift the cells down or to the right.

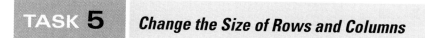

TASK **5**   *Change the Size of Rows and Columns*

 CORE OBJECTIVE: *Modify size of rows and columns*

What: After you've begun a worksheet, you will want to change the width of the columns and the height of the rows to fit the contents. You might want to hide them completely so they don't appear on screen or in the printed document.

Why: The columns and rows must be wide enough to show the contents of the cells. You hide rows or columns to keep them out of sight, but still use the data and formulas stored in them. When rows or columns are hidden, others are less likely to tamper with the contents.

CHANGE COLUMN WIDTH

How: Change the width of a column by using the mouse or the menus.

To use the mouse, place the mouse pointer on the boundary at the right side of the column heading until it turns into a two-headed arrow (Figure 3.11). Drag to adjust the width, or double-click to have Excel automatically make the column as wide as the widest item in that column.

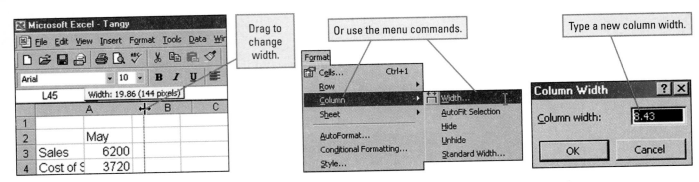

Figure 3.11 Changing column width

Alternatively, you can choose **Format|Column** and select one of the choices:

○ **Width** opens a dialog box where you can type the number of characters for the width of the column (assuming a standard character size).
○ **AutoFit Selection** is the same as double-clicking the line on the column heading. It makes the column just wide enough to contain the largest item in the column.
○ **Hide** sets the column width to 0. You learn about this in the next section.
○ **Unhide** restores a hidden column to its previous width.
○ **Standard width** enables you to type the number of characters of width for all the columns in the worksheet. (This does not affect columns where you have manually specified a width already.)

Result: The columns can have different widths, depending on their contents.

TIPS FROM A PRO: If you drag across column headings to select several columns, you can AutoFit all of them at once by double-clicking any column border.

CHANGE ROW HEIGHT

Figure 3.12 Drag row heading boundary to change height

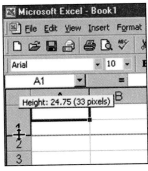

How: This is needed much less often than changes to the column width because you don't often insert tall items into a cell. You change the height of a row the same way you set the width of a column.

Place the mouse pointer on the boundary below the row heading until it turns into a two-headed arrow (Figure 3.12). Drag to adjust the height, or double-click to have Excel automatically size the row to contain the largest item in that row.

Alternatively, you can choose **Format|Row** and select one of the choices:

○ **Height** opens a dialog box where you can type the number of points for the height of the row. (The default is 12.75.)
○ **AutoFit Selection** is the same as double-clicking the boundary of the row heading. It makes the row just tall enough to contain the largest item in the row.
○ **Hide** sets the row height to 0. You learn about this in the next section.
○ **Unhide** restores a hidden row to its previous height.

Result: The rows can have different heights, depending on their contents.

HIDING AND UNHIDING

CORE OBJECTIVE: *Hide and unhide rows and columns*

How: When you want to remove a row or column from sight without permanently deleting it, you can hide it. To do this, select the rows or columns you want to hide, and then do one of these actions:

- ❍ Choose Format|Row|Hide, or press Ctrl+9.
- ❍ Choose Format|Column|Hide, or press Ctrl+0.

Result: What this does is set the column width to zero. You can tell by the column headings in Figure 3.13 that columns are missing.

Figure 3.13 Column C is hidden

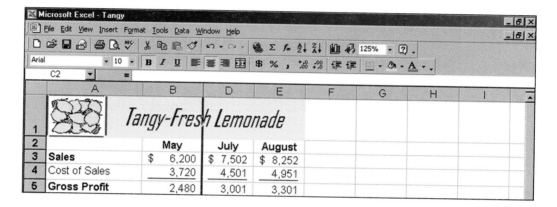

TIPS FROM A PRO. To restore the hidden columns or rows, how do you select them to change their size? Select several columns or rows, spanning the hidden one. If row 1 or column A is hidden, you can't use this method. Instead, jump to one of the hidden cells first. To do this, type the address of a hidden cell in the Name box at the left end of the formula bar and press **Enter**. The active cell is hidden, but the Unhide command now works on the hidden row or column.

TASK 6   *Freeze and Unfreeze*

CORE OBJECTIVE: *Freeze and unfreeze rows and columns*

What: When your worksheet has labels in the top row or left column to describe the data, you can *freeze* them so that they always appear on screen even when you scroll down or to the right.

When you use the Window|Freeze Panes command, everything above the current row or to the left of the current column is frozen in place. This way, it is always visible.

Why: When you have a large worksheet that contains more rows or columns than you can see on the screen at one time, you find yourself scrolling left and right or up and down to see the cells, which can become a hassle.

How: To freeze cells, follow these steps carefully:

1. Set up the screen the way you want it to appear when it is frozen. If necessary, scroll up or down, left or right, so that the correct rows and columns appear on the left and top of the screen.
2. Place the active cell in the specific location so that everything you want frozen is above it or to its left.
3. Choose **Window|Freeze Panes**.

Result: Excel places a thin, dark line above and to the left of the active cell. As you move around the worksheet, the columns and rows slide "behind" the frozen ones, so they always remain in place, as you see in Figure 3.14. To remove the effect, choose **Window|Unfreeze Panes**.

Figure 3.14 Frozen rows and columns

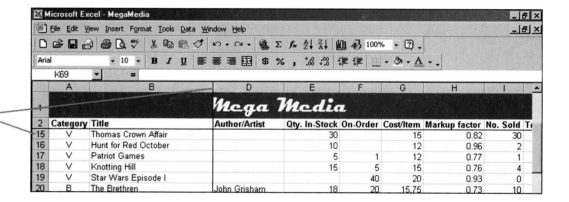

Column C and rows 3 through 14 are not shown.

TASK 7   *Use Zoom and Full Screen*

CORE OBJECTIVE: *Change the zoom setting*

What: Another way to view a large worksheet is to change the zoom setting or use Full Screen view. You can *zoom* in to magnify the sheet up to 400% (or four times the size), or zoom out to as small as 10% to see more cells in the window. Full Screen view requires no particular zoom setting, but instead removes the Excel title bar, toolbars, and even the taskbar from the screen, maximizing the amount of workspace you have available.

Why: You may want to be able to see more of the worksheet in the window, or perhaps you want a closer look at the cells.

USING ZOOM SETTINGS

How: To change the zoom settings, type a number in the Zoom box or click the arrow next to the box to see the choices (Figure 3.15).

- ❍ Choose 200 or type a number larger than 100 to magnify or zoom in on fewer cells.
- ❍ Choose 25, 50, or 75 or type a number less than 100 to zoom out to see the big picture of more cells. The cells will look smaller, though.
- ❍ Select a range of cells and then click the Zoom arrow and choose **Selection**. The magnification adjusts so that the selected cells fill the screen.

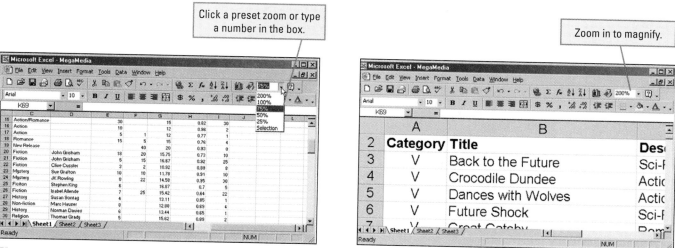

Figure 3.15 Changing the zoom

Result: When you zoom in, you see fewer cells, but they are larger. When you zoom out, you see more cells, but they are smaller.

USING FULL SCREEN VIEW

How: To maximize the work area, choose **View|Full Screen**.

Result: All that's left on the screen is the menu and the row and column headings, as you see in Figure 3.16. You get maximum space for building your worksheet. This is great when you're creating formulas, but not so handy for formatting the cells because the buttons aren't available. To return to another view, click the **Close Full Screen** button on the Full Screen toolbar.

Figure 3.16 Full Screen view

	A	B	C	D	E	F	G	H
1				*Mega Media*				
2	Category	Title	Description	Author/Artist	Qty. In-Stock	On-Order	Cost/Item	Markup fa
3	V	Back to the Future	Sci-Fi		1	2	12	
4	V	Crocodile Dundee	Action		4		12	
5	V	Dances with Wolves	Action		10		15	
6	V	Future Shock	Sci-Fi		3			
7	V	Great Gatsby	Romance		2			
8	V	Patch Adams	New Release		15			
9	V	Runaway Bride	New Release		20		15	
10	V	My Best Friend's Wedding	Comedy		15		12	
11	V	Goofy Movie	Children		25		15	
12	V	Tarzan	Children		25		15	
13	V	Zorro	Action/Romance		30		15	
14	V	Robin Hood	Action		10		11	
15	V	Thomas Crown Affair	Action/Romance		30		15	
16	V	Hunt for Red October	Action		10		12	
17	V	Patriot Games	Action		5	1	12	
18	V	Knotting Hill	Romance		15	5	15	
19	V	Star Wars Episode I	New Release			40	20	
20	B	The Brethren	Fiction	John Grisham	18	20	15.75	
21	B	Testament	Fiction	John Grisham	5	15	16.67	
22	B	Atlantis Found	Fiction	Clive Cussler	3	2	10.92	
23	B	O is for Outlaw	Mystery	Sue Grafton	10	10	11.78	
24	B	Harry Potter and the Doomspell	Mystery	JK Rowling	0	22	14.58	
25	B	Riding the Bullet	Ficiton	Stephen King	6		16.87	
26	B	Daughter of Fortune	Fiction	Isabel Allende	7	25	15.42	
27	B	In America	History	Susan Sontag	4		13.11	
28	B	Wild Minds	Non-fiction	Marc Hauser	8		12.88	
29	B	The Isles	History	Norman Davies	6		13.44	
30	B	Signatures of Grace	Religion	Thomas Grady	5		15.62	

C   CORE OBJECTIVE: *Use basic functions (Average)*

What: You know how to calculate a sum using the AutoSum button. Have you noticed the cell entry that Excel creates when you click the button? It is =SUM(A1:A4) or something like that, depending on which cells you are adding.

This is an example of a *function*, a predefined formula. All functions have these elements in common: equal sign, name, and parentheses. Most have something inside the parentheses.

Another function that's easy to use is the Average function.

Why: True, you can find an average by dividing the total by the number of items, but this is easier because it doesn't require you to count anything.

How: This formula is easy to type.

1. Make the active cell where you want the average to be.
2. Type the following entry (capitals don't matter): **=average(**
3. Click and drag to select the cells you want to average.
4. Press **Enter**.

Result: Excel puts on the final parenthesis, capitalizes AVERAGE, and places the result in the cell.

Use PinPoint

After gaining the skills in this chapter, you can restructure the worksheet by adding or deleting rows, columns, and cells, and change their size as well. You can also freeze panes and calculate an average. Now it's time to use the PinPoint software and see what you can do. Remember, if you are unsure of what to do, you can reread that portion of the chapter or you can click Show Me for a live demonstration. Check out these skills in PinPoint:

- Change zoom settings
- Column and row size
- Copy cells using the Clipboard
- Freeze panes
- Hide and display toolbars
- Hide rows and columns
- Insert and delete cells
- Insert rows and columns.
- Move cells

Key Terms

You can find definitions for these words in this chapter:

Clipboard   Drag-and-drop
Freeze   Function
Office Clipboard   Range
Selecting
Zoom

Review Questions

You can use the following review questions and exercises to test your knowledge and skills. Answers are given in Appendix D, "Answers to Review Questions."

True/False

Indicate whether each statement is true (T) or false (F).

___ 1. When a range is selected, it is surrounded by a dark border and appears shaded.

___ 2. To select cells with the keyboard, hold down the Shift key and press arrow keys.

___ 3. To select a row, click the letter A or B in the heading.

___ 4. After copying, use Paste instead of pressing Enter to duplicate the material multiple times.

___ 5. One reason to use the Paste Special command is to convert formulas into values.

___ 6. One drawback to using the Office Clipboard is that it converts formulas into values.

___ 7. You can insert new cells and deposit copied material into them in one operation.

___ 8. To change the standard width of the columns in a worksheet, you must highlight them first.

___ 9. Hiding a column is the same as setting its width to 0.

___ 10. You can hide columns but not rows.

Multiple Choice

Select the letter that best completes the statement.

___ 1. To select two nonadjacent ranges, hold down:
   a. Alt.
   b. Ctrl.
   c. Shift.
   d. F1.
   e. Spacebar.

___ 2. After you copy cells, to paste them in the destination:
   a. Choose Edit|Paste.
   b. Right-click and choose Paste.
   c. Press Enter.
   d. All of the above.
   e. Both a and b.

___ 3. Drag-and-drop is the same as:
   a. Copy.
   b. Cut.
   c. Paste.
   d. Copy and paste.
   e. Cut and paste.

___ 4. When you insert a row, the new row is placed:
   a. Above the current row.
   b. At the top of the worksheet.
   c. Below the current row.
   d. At the bottom of the current work area.
   e. Wherever you specify in the dialog box.

___ 5. When a cell containing a formula shows #REF, it means that the cells it referred to have been:
   a. Hidden.
   b. Emptied.
   c. Moved.
   d. Removed.
   e. All of the above.

___ 6. AutoFit means that the size of the column is:
   a. Wide enough to contain the largest entry.
   b. At least 2 inches wide.
   c. The widest column in the worksheet.
   d. Continually adjusted as you enter text in the cells.
   e. All of the above.

___ 7. When you want to keep some rows or columns from scrolling out of view:
   a. Press the Ctrl key to control where they stay.
   b. Freeze the panes.
   c. Immobilize the rows.
   d. Click the Stop Scroll button.
   e. Use AutoFit.

___ 8. When the active cell is cell B2 and you choose Window|Freeze Panes, what will be frozen is:
   a. Column A.
   b. Column A and row 1.
   c. Column B and row 2.
   d. Columns A and B and rows 1 and 2.
   e. Cells A1, A2, B1, and B2.

___ 9. You can tell that rows have been frozen because:
   a. An icicle icon appears in the top-left corner.
   b. The rows appear shaded.
   c. A dark line appears.
   d. You can't move the active cell into those rows.
   e. All of the above.

___ 10. To calculate an average of some numbers, use this function:
   a. Ave.
   b. Average.
   c. Avg.
   d. Mean.
   e. Median.

Match the letters in Figure 3.17 with the correct items in the list.

Figure 3.17

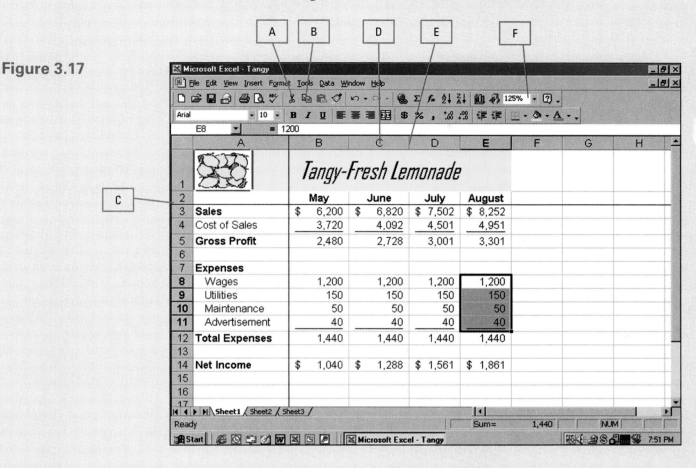

___ 1. Drag here to change the column width.

___ 2. Click here to cut the selected cells.

___ 3. Double-click here to use AutoFit.

___ 4. Look here to see that rows are frozen.

___ 5. Click here before inserting a new column.

___ 6. Click here to make a duplicate of the selected cells.

___ 7. Choose a different amount of magnification.

Exercise and Project

Follow these step-by-step instructions to create a worksheet. If you are working in a computer lab, ask your instructor where you should save and print your file.

Exercise

1. Open **Megamedia.xls** from the *Student\Chapter 3* folder on your PinPoint CD-ROM.

2. AutoFit the column widths.

3. AutoFit the height of row 1.

4. Insert a row between the title and the column labels.

5 Insert a column between Cost/Item and Markup Factor, and fill in a formula to calculate **Total Cost** (the sum of column E and F times the price in column G). Use AutoFill to fill this formula down the column.

6. Format both Cost columns using **Currency** style. Format the Markup Factor using **Percent** style.

7. Freeze the panes so that the title and the column labels are always visible on screen.

8. Insert a column between Markup Factor and No. Sold and fill in a formula to calculate **Selling Price** (the Cost/Item divided by the Markup Factor). Format this with **Currency** style and fill it down the column.

9. Calculate **Total Sales** (No. Sold times Selling Price) and fill down.

10. Hide **Markup** and all columns relating to **Cost** because you want to print a copy of the list for a customer. Print.

11. Turn on the Clipboard toolbar and collect (copy) the column labels (row 3) plus one item from each category (video, books, music).

12. Open a new workbook and Paste All. Check to see whether the contents of the hidden columns are included.

13. Return to the original worksheet. Turn off the Office Clipboard toolbar. Hold down the **Ctrl** key and click five titles you would like to order and their associated selling prices. Copy the 10 selected cells.

14. Go to the new worksheet and paste the cells into a blank area using the Paste Link option of the Paste Special command. You should have two columns, one with the titles, and the other with the prices.

15. Return to the original worksheet. Change the price of one of your choices.

16. Unhide all the columns. Save the workbook.

17. Return to the new worksheet containing your purchases. Find the total.

18. Below the total, calculate the amount of sales tax. Find the total amount of the sale (total of the prices plus tax). Format the cells appropriately. Save and print.

Project

Start a new worksheet with the following rows:

- Term
- Course
- Credit Hours
- Points
- Letter Grade

Enter the information for several classes you have taken (use pretend grades, if you'd rather). For **Points**, use whatever grading system your school uses, typically 4 for an A, 3 for a B, 2 for a C, and so on. Insert a new row labeled **Grade Points**. Calculate the grade points by multiplying Credit Hours times Points.

Copy the worksheet and use the Paste Special and Transpose option to change it from vertical to horizontal. Size the columns to fit exactly. Move the Points column so that it is after the Letter Grade column. Average the grade points to find your Grade Point Average (GPA). Insert a new row on the top of the worksheet and type your name and class information. Save and print the worksheet.

Chapter 4

Control Cell References

Excel can do more than simple sums or arithmetic. When you build a worksheet, you can use all sorts of complicated formulas that refer to other cells. When you do this, it's easy to get mixed up as to what cells you should refer to. Excel lets you name cells with regular words and refer to them by name, rather than by row and column. Alternatively, you can use Excel's auditing tools to help you figure out if an error has been made.

At the end of this chapter, you will be able to:

C **E**

☑	☐	Use absolute and relative cell references
☐	☐	Calculate percent of total
☐	☐	Calculate a running sum
☐	☑	Use a named range in a formula
☐	☑	Add and delete a named range
☐	☐	View all the formulas
☐	☑	Work with the Auditing toolbar
☐	☑	Trace precedents
☐	☑	Trace dependents
☐	☑	Trace errors

CORE OBJECTIVE: *Use references (absolute and relative)*

What: When you create a formula and fill it down a column or across a row, Excel automatically adjusts the formula to refer to the cells. For the example in Figure 4.1, when the total was filled across, the formula automatically changed from the sum of the items in column B to column C. And that's right!

Figure 4.1
Relative cell references change

	A	B	C
1	**Expenses**	**March**	**April**
2	Rent	185	185
3	Utilities	35	42
4	Groceries	62	56
5	Gas	40	58
6	Entertainment	84	143
7	**Total**	=SUM(B2:B6)	=SUM(C2:C6)
8			

> Formula filled across the row

> New column inserted

	A	B	C	D
1	**Expenses**	**March**		**April**
2	Rent	185		185
3	Utilities	35		42
4	Groceries	62		56
5	Gas	40		58
6	Entertainment	84		143
7	**Total**	=SUM(B2:B6)		=SUM(D2:D6)
8				

If you insert a column, the sum automatically changes to reflect the new column letter. Now it refers to column D. Excel is so smart! These are examples of what are known as *relative cell references*, and they are one reason why building formulas in Excel is so easy.

Now suppose you want to determine what percent each expense is of the total. To do that, you divide the expense by the total, as you see in cell C2 of Figure 4.2. What happens when you fill this down? Each row number changes, just as the column letter changes when you fill across.

But this is a disaster—the result of the formulas in the cells will show #DIV/0!, an error message meaning that you're trying to divide by zero. Although you want the B2 to change automatically to B3, B4, and on down the line, you want to divide each time by B7, not B8, B9, and so on. To keep Excel from changing the row number or column letter when you copy or fill, you must use *absolute cell references*. To do that, add $

Figure 4.2
Calculating percent of total

	A	B	C
1	**Expenses**	**March**	**Percent of Total**
2	Rent	185	=B2/B7
3	Utilities	35	=B3/B8
4	Groceries	62	=B4/B9
5	Gas	40	=B5/B10
6	Entertainment	84	=B6/B11
7	**Total**	=SUM(B2:B6)	
8			

Errors occur when relative cell references are filled down.

	A	B	C
1	**Expenses**	**March**	**Percent of Total**
2	Rent	185	=B2/$B$7
3	Utilities	35	=B3/$B$7
4	Groceries	62	=B4/$B$7
5	Gas	40	=B5/$B$7
6	Entertainment	84	=B6/$B$7
7	**Total**	=SUM(B2:B6)	
8			

Absolute cell reference is needed.

to the cell reference so that it becomes $B$7. This means absolutely Column B and absolutely Row 7, no matter what.

Why: You have to use absolute references to prevent the cell reference from changing from a specific location during the copy or fill process. (They aren't needed if you use the formula in only a single cell and won't copy or fill it).

How: You can create an absolute cell reference two ways:

○ Type the formula including dollar signs. For the example, in cell C2 type =B2/$B$7.

○ Enter the cell reference without dollar signs and immediately press the **F4** key. For the example, type =B2/B7 and press F4. B7 changes to $B$7.

% To complete the formula in cell C2 in the example, press **Enter**. Format it as a percent by clicking the **Percent Style button** on the toolbar (or press **Ctrl+Shift+%**). Then fill the formula down to the Total row.

Result: The reference to the total will not change when the formula is filled down. This means your answers will be correct, and you won't see the #DIV/0! error message. If you've done everything correctly, the percent next to Total will equal 100%.

TIPS FROM A PRO: You can also use what are called *mixed cell references*, when only the row or the column is absolute. To do this, apply a single dollar sign, either to the row (B$7) or to the column ($B7). The F4 key comes in handy here. It cycles through all the choices when you press it multiple times. Here's what it does each time you press it: $B$7, B$7, $B7, B7. Both, one, the other, none, and so on.

What: Another use for absolute cell references is to create the formula for a *running sum*. You use a running sum to see how much the total is each time you add a new item.

Why: For example, suppose you have the figures from a restaurant's cash register every hour, as in Figure 4.3. You could get a single total by clicking the AutoSum button, but suppose you want to keep track of the total so far, hour by hour.

One way to do this is to create a different sum for each row. But that's much too much trouble. Instead, you can use an absolute cell reference to fill a single formula down the column.

How: Set up the running total by typing the formula using an absolute cell reference.

1. Type the formula like this: **=sum($B$2:B2)**
2. Press **Enter**. This formula works by summing all the cells from the first reference to the last. B2 is both the first and last reference; therefore, the amount in B2 is the only number included.
3. Fill the formula down the column.

Result: The absolute reference remains on $B$2, but the relative reference changes as you fill it down to refer to the new row. This way the sum grows to include each new row. Figure 4.4 shows this, with the formulas in column C and the displayed results in column D.

Figure 4.3
Formula for a running sum

	A	B	C
1	Hour	Hourly total	Today's total
2	AM 6	69.58	=SUM($B$2:B2)
3	AM 7	173.25	
4	AM 8	202.15	
5	AM 9	195.56	
6	AM 10	211.77	
7	AM 11	250.01	
8	PM 12	431.95	

Figure 4.4 The running sum completed

	A	B	C	D
1	Hour	Hourly total	Today's total	Results of running sum
2	AM 6	69.58	=SUM($B$2:B2)	69.58
3	AM 7	173.25	=SUM($B$2:B3)	242.83
4	AM 8	202.15	=SUM($B$2:B4)	444.98
5	AM 9	195.56	=SUM($B$2:B5)	640.54
6	AM 10	211.77	=SUM($B$2:B6)	852.31
7	AM 11	250.01	=SUM($B$2:B7)	1102.32
8	PM 12	431.95	=SUM($B$2:B8)	1534.27

THOUGHT QUESTION: How is using a running sum different from using AutoSum?

| TASK 3 | **Use Named Ranges** |

EXPERT OBJECTIVE: *Use a named range in a formula*

What: Excel has the ability to use *named ranges*, real words to refer to a cell or cells, rather than the typical cell references. For example, instead of typing =Sum(B3:B48) or having to drag to define what you want to sum, you can type =Sum(Sales).

If your worksheet has labels across the top and down the left column, you can easily name the cells—in fact, you don't even have to name them yourself, as Excel can figure out what you mean. In addition, you can name cells yourself, or even give a name to a constant or formula you use often.

Why: Using named ranges rather than cell references in formulas offers two main advantages:

❍ The formulas are easier to read with regular words in place of cell references.
❍ The named ranges are absolute cell references, so you don't have to remember to press F4 or type $.

TURN ON AUTOMATIC NAMES

How: Excel lets you refer to cells using the names on the top row and left column, but you have to turn on this option.

❍ Choose **Tools|Options**, choose the **Calculation** tab, and select the check box to **Accept Labels in Formulas** (Figure 4.5).

Result: Well, nothing visible happens, but now you can try it out!

Figure 4.5 Turn on automatic named ranges

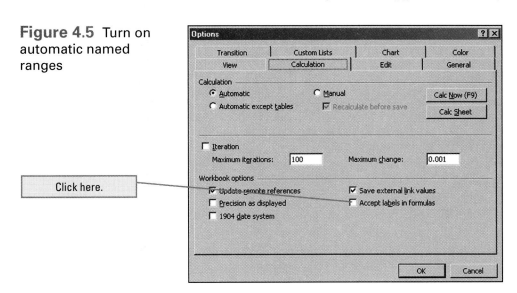

Click here.

Figure 4.6 Sample worksheet

	A	B	C	D
1		**Fri**	**Sat**	**Sun**
2	Cheesecake	104.25	109.45	116.85
3	Fudge brownie	43.86	28.44	46.15
4	Cherry pie	50.49	34.01	52.25
5	Apple turnover	65.34	41.32	63.33
6	Carrot cake	9.03	17.52	23.28
7	Oreo mint	80.30	53.40	76.85
8	Mocha slush	14.32	13.35	23.84
9	Shortcake	58.83	32.22	55.53
10	Lemtart	50.73	20.67	45.70
11				

USE NAMED RANGES

How: Now for the fun.

○ To refer to all the figures in a column or row, type the name.
○ To refer to a single cell, type the row name and the column name with a space between.

Using the example in Figure 4.6, let's build formulas using words instead of having to squint at the screen to figure out which cell to click.

Result: Compare the two approaches in Table 4.1. Which is easier to understand? Which is easier to check for errors?

Table 4.1 Using Range Names or Cell References

Sample formulas	Using names	Using cell references
To sum the sales for Friday	=sum(Fri)	=sum(B2:B10)
To sum the sales for Friday and Saturday	=sum(Fri:Sat)	=sum(B2:C10)
To sum the entire weekend sales	=sum(Fri:Sun)	=sum(B2:D10)
To add Friday's sales for cherry pie and cheesecake	=Fri cherry pie+ Fri cheesecake	=B4+B2
To find the total sales of cherry pie and cheesecake	=sum(cherry pie)+ sum(cheesecake)	=sum(B4:D4)+ sum(B2:D2)

ADD NAMES

EXPERT OBJECTIVE: Add and delete a named range

How: If you're not sure someone else who will be using this worksheet will have the Accept Labels in Formulas option turned on, you can specifically define the names yourself. Here are two ways:

○ Use the Name box:
1. Select the cell or cells you want to name.
2. Type a one-word name in the **Name box** on the left side of the formula bar, and press **Enter**.

○ Use the Create Name command:
1. Select the cell or cells you want to name as well as the corresponding labels in the top row and left column.
2. Choose **Insert|Name|Create**. This opens the dialog box shown in Figure 4.7.
3. Click to choose the top row or left column, or both, to name the cells.

Figure 4.7 Using the Create Names dialog box

	A	B	C	D	E	F	G	H	I
1		Fri	Sat	Sun					
2	Cheesecake	104.25	109.45	116.85					
3	Fudge brownie	43.86	28.44	46.15					
4	Cherry pie	50.49	34.01	52.25					
5	Apple turnover	65.34	41.32	63.33					
6	Carrot cake	9.03	17.52	23.28					
7	Oreo mint	80.3	53.4	76.85					
8	Mocha slush	14.32	13.35	23.84					
9	Shortcake	58.83	32.22	55.53					
10	Lemtart	50.73	20.67	45.7					
11									

Create Names

Create names in
☑ Top row
☑ Left column
☐ Bottom row
☐ Right column

OK   Cancel

Result: Excel adds the names to a list of named ranges for the worksheet. Any spaces in the names are changed to underlines to create a one-word name, such as Cherry_pie. You'll see how they are listed in the following few sections.

TIPS FROM A PRO: Named ranges are always absolute values. This can be a blessing for items you want to keep absolute, so you don't have to remember to press F4 or type dollar signs. However, if you use a name in the formula to sum a column, for instance, and then fill across, it will *not* change to refer to the neighboring column.

TIPS FROM A PRO: You can use the name to go to that location quickly. To do this, drop down the Name box at the left side of the Formula bar and choose the name. Another method is to choose Edit|Go To and select the name.

DEFINE A CONSTANT

How: When you want to define a specific numeric value instead of remembering it to type the number into a formula yourself, give it a name. For example, let's define a name for the sales tax multiplier.

1. Choose **Insert|Name|Define**. A list appears with the names you already defined .
2. Type the name you want, for example, **With_tax**, in the **Names in Workbook** box (Figure 4.8).
3. Type the number or formula you want the name to represent in the **Refers To** box. For our With_tax example, the number would be 1.0825 (or 100 percent plus whatever your sales tax rate is), as you see in Figure 4.8.
4. Click **Add**.

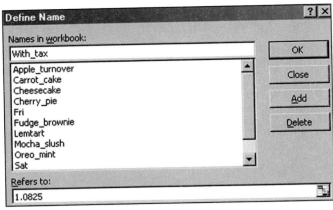

Figure 4.8 Define Name dialog box

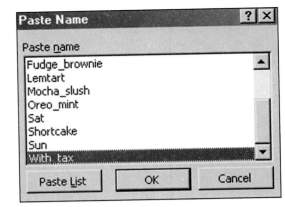

Figure 4.9 Paste Name dialog box

Result: The name is added to the list. Now you can see how much the price is with sales tax. Type =$48*With_tax and press Enter, and the calculation is done for you.

PASTE NAMES

How: When you want to use a name rather than a cell reference but can't remember the exact name or how to spell it, use the Paste Name command.

1. Begin to type the formula, for example, =sum(
2. Choose **Insert|Name|Paste** to see the list of all the range names you defined (Figure 4.9).
3. Click the name you want and then click **OK**. Continue the formula.

Result: You can build formulas without typing or even having to remember how to spell the name.

APPLY NAMES TO CONVERT EXISTING FORMULAS

How: If you really like using named ranges instead of cell references, you can convert existing formulas to refer to names.

1. Select the cell or cells containing formulas that are using cell references that now have names.
2. Choose **Insert|Name|Apply.** Select all the range names, if necessary, and click **OK**.

Result: Excel searches for cell references and replaces them with names, if the names exist.

DELETE NAMES

How: If you aren't using all the names and the list gets too long, you can delete some.

1. Choose **Insert|Name|Define**.
2. Click each name you want to get rid of and click **Delete**.
3. When you are finished, click **OK**.

Result: Extraneous names are removed from the list.

What: Although you can see one formula at a time in the formula bar, you might want to view all the formulas instead of the number results on screen.

Why: You'll use this feature when you need to check the formulas to make sure they're correct. When you have one or two simple sums, you can view one formula at a time, but for a complex worksheet this is easier.

How: Press **Ctrl+`** (the key to the left of the 1 on a standard keyboard). Alternatively you can choose **Tools|Options**, click the **View** tab, and select the check box for **Formulas**.

Result: As you see in Figure 4.10, Excel automatically doubles the column widths. If necessary, you can adjust them, but when you turn the formulas off by pressing Ctrl+` again, the column widths will be restored to the previous size.

Figure 4.10 Viewing formulas

	A	B	C	D	E
1		Fri	Sat	Sun	Total
2	Cheesecake	104.25	109.45	116.85	=SUM(Cheesecake)
3	Fudge brownie	43.86	28.44	46.15	=SUM(Fudge_brownie)
4	Cherry pie	50.49	34.01	52.25	=SUM(Cherry_pie)
5	Apple turnover	65.34	41.32	63.33	=SUM(Apple_turnover)
6	Carrot cake	9.03	17.52	23.275	=SUM(Carrot_cake)
7	Oreo mint	80.3	53.4	76.85	=SUM(Oreo_mint)
8	Mocha slush	14.32	13.35	23.835	=SUM(Mocha_slush)
9	Shortcake	58.83	32.22	55.525	=SUM(Shortcake)
10	Lemtart	50.73	20.67	45.7	=SUM(Lemtart)
11	Total	=SUM(Fri)	=SUM(Sat)	=SUM(Sun)	=SUM(Fri:Sun)
12					

TASK **5** **Use Auditing Tools**

E *EXPERT OBJECTIVE: Work with the Auditing toolbar*

What: Excel provides a number of tools to let you *audit* or examine the accuracy of your worksheet. You may have noticed when you click the formula bar to edit a formula, Excel color-codes the cells that are referred to in the formula (Figure 4.11).

Figure 4.11 Editing a formula

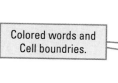

Colored words and Cell boundries.

This color coding may be too subtle. By using the Auditing feature, you can have Excel draw big bold tracer arrows to the cells the formula refers to, its *precedents* (pronounced *press*-edents). In addition, you can have Excel draw tracer arrows from a cell to show which formulas refer to *it* (its *dependents*).

Why: When you build a complex worksheet with lots of formulas, you might find it hard to read the formulas to determine whether you've made any errors. Or if you have error messages, it might be tricky to figure out what is causing the problem. The commands on the Auditing menu and the Auditing toolbar help you with this task.

VIEW THE AUDITING TOOLBAR

Figure 4.12
Auditing toolbar

How: Choose **Tools|Auditing** and click **Show Auditing Toolbar**.

Result: The toolbar (Figure 4.12) appears floating on screen. You can turn it off by clicking the Close button on its top-right corner. The toolbar provides buttons to use when auditing formulas in a worksheet.

TRACE PRECEDENTS

E

EXPERT OBJECTIVE: Trace precedents (find cells referred to in a formula)

How: Follow these steps to trace precedents:

1. Click the cell containing the formula you want to audit.
2. Choose **Tools|Auditing|Trace Precedents** or click the **Trace Precedents** button to trace the cells that directly provide the data for the formula you are auditing.
3. Choose the command or click the button again to go back one more level and see the precedents for *those* cells.

Result: Excel shows tracer arrows from the cells that are used in the formula (Figure 4.13). If the formula refers to a range, a single tracer arrow appears and the range is boxed.

If you find an error, edit the formula to refer to the correct cells. Remove the arrows by clicking the **Remove Precedent Arrows** button one or more times.

Figure 4.13 Tracing precedents

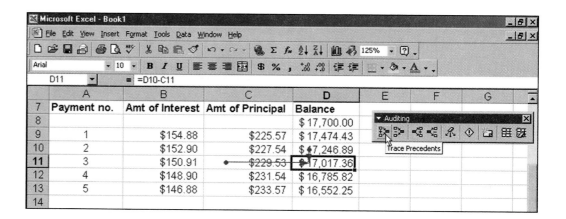

TRACE DEPENDENTS

EXPERT OBJECTIVE: Trace dependents (find formulas that refer to a cell)

How: Follow these steps to trace a cell's dependents:

1. Click the cell containing the formula you want to audit.
2. Choose **Tools|Auditing|Trace Dependents** or click the **Trace Dependents** button to trace the cells that refer to the formula you are auditing.
3. Choose the command or click the button again to go forward one more level and see the dependents for those cells as well.

Result: Excel shows tracer arrows to the cells that refer to the selected cell (Figure 4.14). If you find an error, edit the formula to refer to the correct cells. Remove the arrows by clicking the **Remove Dependent Arrows** button one or more times.

Figure 4.14 Tracing dependents

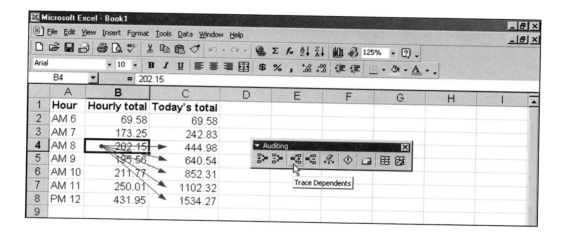

TIPS FROM A PRO: You can show tracer arrows for precedents and dependents for several cells and really clutter up the screen. To remove all the arrows at once, click the **Remove All Arrows** button.

CHECK FOR ERRORS

EXPERT OBJECTIVE: Trace errors (find and fix errors)

How: When the worksheet contains an error message such as #NA! or #DIV/0!, Excel helps you find the cause.

1. Click the cell containing the error.
2. Choose **Tools|Auditing|Trace Error** or click the **Trace Error** button.

Result: The arrows appear showing the cells that are referred to in the formula. When you edit the formula to fix it, the arrows automatically disappear.

Use PinPoint

After gaining the skills in this chapter, you can use relative and absolute cell references appropriately, use named ranges, and use the auditing tools. Now it's time to use the PinPoint software and see what you can do. Remember, whenever you are unsure of what to do, you can reread that portion of the chapter or you can click Show Me for a live demonstration. Check out these skills in PinPoint:

- Cell references
- Display formulas
- Go to a cell
- Labels in a formula
- Name a range
- Trace dependent
- Trace errors
- Trace precedent

Key Terms

You can find definitions for these words in this chapter:

Relative cell references
Absolute cell references
Mixed cell references
Running sum
Named ranges
Audit
Precedents
Dependents

Review Questions

You can use the following review questions to test your knowledge and skills. Answers are given in Appendix D, "Answers to Review Questions."

True/False

Indicate whether each statement is true (T) or false (F).

___ 1. It's important to use absolute cell references whenever you want to fill a formula down a column or across a row.

___ 2. To make a cell reference absolute, click the button with the $.

___ 3. If you will only use a formula in a single cell and will not copy or fill it, you never have to use absolute cell references.

___ 4. When you want to see a subtotal as you add each item, use a running sum.

___ 5. A named range is a group of cells you can refer to by a name, rather than by row and column.

___ 6. Named ranges are absolute.

___ 7. You can use labels to refer to cells without having to use the Insert|Name command.

___ 8. One way to name a cell is to type its name in the formula bar.

___ 9. When you name a range, it is surrounded by a bold blue border.

___ 10. The trouble with using named ranges is that you can't use them in a formula if you can't spell the names.

Multiple Choice

Select the letter that best completes the statement.

___ 1. The shortcut key to make a cell reference absolute is:
a. Ctrl+A.
b. Ctrl+R.
c. F2.
d. F4.
e. None of the above.

___ 2. When you type =$B$4 in a cell and fill it down, what will appear in the next cell below will be:
a. =B4.
b. =$B$4.
c. =B5.
d. =$B$5.
e. =$C$5.

___ 3. The formula to create a running sum to fill down a column beginning with cell B2 is:
a. =B2+$B$3.
b. =$B$2+B3.
c. =sum(Running).
d. =sum($B$2:B2).
e. Either b or d.

___ 4. One way to name ranges is to select the numbers and labels in a range and then choose:
a. Define|Name.
b. Insert|Name|Create.
c. Insert|Range.
d. Tools|Options.
e. View|Range Names.

___ 5. The Insert|Name|Apply command is used to:
a. Apply a range name to the selected cells.
b. Convert existing formulas to use range names.
c. Insert range names in a formula as you build it.
d. Delete range names that are no longer needed.
e. All of the above.

___ 6. When you want to be able to figure out what is wrong with your formulas, this feature will be a big help:
a. Named ranges.
b. View formulas.
c. View precedents.
d. Auditing tools.
e. All of the above.

___ 7. When you choose Tools| Auditing|View Precedents, what appears on screen is:
a. Red arrows pointing to error messages.
b. Blue arrows pointing to the current cell.
c. Arrows pointing to cells that refer to the current cell.
d. The formulas appear in all the cells.
e. Color-coded lines and boxes surrounding the cells that refer to the current cell.

___ 8. When a cell shows #DIV/0!, you can correct it by using this command:

    a. Trace Arrows.

    b. Trace Audit.

    c. Trace Dependents.

    d. Trace Error.

    e. Trace Zeros.

___ 9. If you click a second time on the Trace Dependent button (or choose the command a second time):

    a. The dependent arrows are applied on the next cell below the current one.

    b. The precedent arrows appear on the current cell.

    c. The dependent arrows appear for the cells depending on the current one.

    d. The existing arrows are removed from the screen.

    e. All of the above.

___ 10. If you've used a name in a formula:

    a. The auditing tools no longer work.

    b. The cell reference is absolute.

    c. The name is automatically capitalized.

    d. An error message will never occur.

    e. All of the above.

Screen Review

Match the letters in Figure 4.15 with the correct items in the list.

Figure 4.15

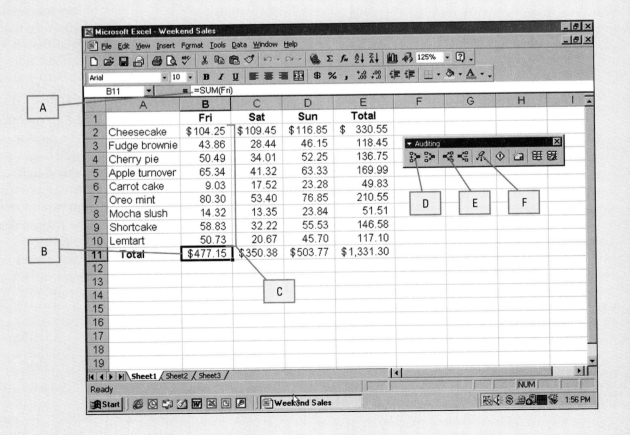

___ 1. Look here to see a formula using a named range.

___ 2. Look here to see what the name in the formula refers to.

___ 3. Click here to see what cells this formula refers to.

___ 4. Click here to see what other cells refer to the active cell.

___ 5. Click here to remove auditing arrows from the screen.

___ 6. Click here before using the auditing tools.

Exercise and Project

Follow these step-by-step instructions to create a worksheet. If you are working in a computer lab, ask your instructor where you should save and print your file.

Exercise

Note: You will need the file **Kennel Budget.xls,** which you created in the exercise for Chapter 2.

1. Go to row 21 and label it **Cumulative Net Profit**. Widen column A if needed.
2. Type a formula in B21 that can be copied across the row to calculate a running sum for **Net Profit**. Fill it across, but be careful not to copy it into the Total column. You'll know you entered it correctly if the Total Net Profit = Q4's Cumulative value.
3. Highlight A4:B21 and create range names using labels in the left column.
4. Go to cell B18 and replace the formula with this: **=Sum(Food:Shows)**.
5. Insert a new Expense called **Toys** between Grooming and Training. Give it a value of **$50** per quarter. What do you have to do in the Total column?
6. Convert the formula in B21 so that it uses the named ranges. (Use Insert| Names|Apply.)
7. Go back to B7 and deliberately make this mistake: **=B3-B5**. Leave cell B7 active. Now choose Tools|Auditing|Trace Error. Print the sheet.
8. Fix the error.
9. Now click cell E21 and trace the precedents. What cells are affected?
10. Remove the arrows.
11. Click Total Expenses for Q1. Choose Tools|Auditing|Trace Dependents. What cells are affected now?
12. View the formulas. Print the worksheet.
13. Toggle to show the calculated values again, and save the worksheet.

Project

As recording secretary for Peace Community Church, you have to create a report for the bimonthly meeting. Open **Offering.xls** from the *Student\Chapter 4* folder of the PinPoint CD. Either turn on the feature to allow you to use labels in formulas or use the Create command to name the ranges. Using the labels or range names, write formulas to sum each type of offering for the bimonthly meeting and also to total the offerings for each week. Write a running-sum formula to sum the year-to-date offerings. Format the worksheet using Currency and Comma styles and making the totals bold.

Show the formulas and print the worksheet. Turn off the formulas, save, and print.

Chapter 5

Manage Pages and Printing

So far, when you wanted a paper copy of the worksheet, you clicked the Print button and received a copy from the printer. Excel offers additional flexibility by enabling you to specify exactly what you want to print, the items that are included on the top or bottom of every page, and the way you want the pages to appear.

At the end of this chapter, you will be able to:

C　**E**

C	E	
✔	❑	Print a selection
✔	❑	Preview and print worksheets and workbooks
✔	❑	Set the print area and clear a print area
❑	❑	Print large worksheets
✔	❑	Change page orientation and scaling
✔	❑	Set page margins and centering
✔	❑	Set up headers and footers
✔	❑	Set print titles and sheet options
❑	❑	Collapse a dialog box
✔	❑	Insert and remove a page break

CORE OBJECTIVE: *Print a selection*

 CORE OBJECTIVE: *Preview and print worksheets and workbooks*

What: Sure, you've printed before by clicking the Print button, but that only gave you a single copy at a time. When you access the Print dialog box, however, additional options become available.

Why: You have more choices and more control over the printing process when you access the Print dialog box, shown in Figure 5.1.

Figure 5.1 Print dialog box

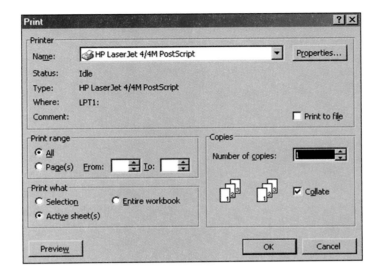

How: You can access the Print dialog box in two ways:

❍ Choose **File|Print**.
❍ Press **Ctrl+P**.

Result: When the Print dialog box appears, you have more control over printing choices. Here you can designate:

❍ Which printer to use (click to see a list of all the available printers)
❍ Which pages to print: all the pages, or just certain pages (just type in the first and last page number)
❍ Whether to print a selected range, the active worksheet, or all the non-empty sheets in the workbook
❍ How many copies to print
❍ Whether to collate the copies of multiple-page printouts

You can also click the Preview button to go to Print Preview. (You'll learn about that in Task 2.) When you finish making choices, press **Enter** or click **OK** to complete the process.

 TIPS FROM A PRO: To print a specific range rather than the entire worksheet, drag to select the range of cells before choosing File|Print. Then you can specify **Selection** under Print What.

TASK 2   *Use Print Preview*

CORE OBJECTIVE: *Preview and print worksheets and workbooks*

What: Before you print your worksheet, you can view its appearance on the page with the Print Preview feature.

Why: You can save time and the cost of printing if you quickly check the "big picture" to see the way the worksheet will appear on the page before you print.

How: To use Print Preview, click the **Print Preview** button or choose **File|Print Preview**.

TIPS FROM A PRO: If you hold down the Ctrl key and click the sheet tabs before you click the Print Preview button, you can use Print Preview to view all the worksheets in the workbook.

Result: The Print Preview screen, shown in Figure 5.2, shows you the overall look of the page. Notice that the mouse pointer has changed to a magnifier. This indicates that when you click anywhere on the page, you will zoom in or out again.

Along the top of the screen are a number of buttons.

- ❍ To view other pages, if any, press the **Next** button or **Previous** button.
- ❍ The **Zoom** button lets you get a closer look at the cells; it's the same as clicking with the mouse pointer.
- ❍ **Print** takes you to the Print dialog box, which you learned about in Task 1.
- ❍ **Setup** takes you to the Page Setup dialog box. You'll learn about its features in Tasks 4, 5, 6, and 7.

Figure 5.2 Print Preview

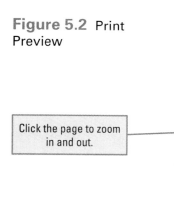

Click the page to zoom in and out.

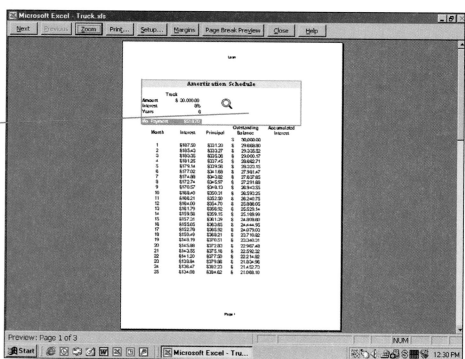

❍ **Margins** is great for setting the margins. You'll learn how to do this in Task 5.

❍ **Page Break Preview** let you set up where the pages divide. You'll learn about this in Task 8.

❍ Click **Close** to return to the normal Excel window, or **Help** to get help.

TASK **3**	*Set the Print Area*

CORE OBJECTIVE: *Set print area and clear print area*

What: When you want to print a range of cells rather than the entire work-sheet, you can always select the cells first and then choose File|Print and click Selection. But that's a lot of trouble if you have to do it every time. Instead, Excel lets you specify that only certain cells are the ones to print. To do this, you define the *print area*.

Why: When your worksheet has an input zone or a work area that is just for your calculations, you may not want that printed with the finished product. Setting the print area lets you specify exactly which cells to include in the printed copy.

How: Follow these simple steps to define the print area:

1. Select only the cells you want to include in the printed copy.
2. Choose **File|Print Area|Set Print Area**.

Result: The selected cells are surrounded by a thin dashed border, as you see in Figure 5.3, signifying that these cells are the ones that will be printed. If you use Print Preview, you will see that this is the only part of the work-sheet that appears on the printed page.

If you change your mind and want to print the entire sheet again, remove the print area by choosing **File|Print Area|Clear Print Area**.

Figure 5.3 Print area has been set

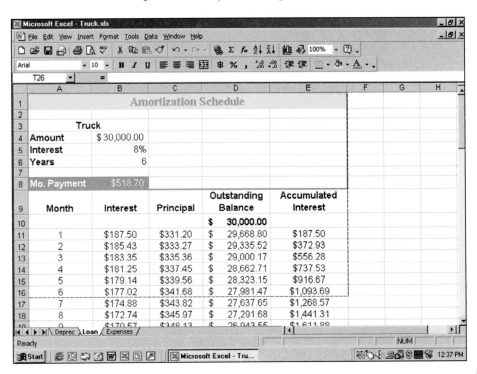

CORE OBJECTIVE: *Change page orientation and scaling*

What: When you are creating small worksheets, you don't think about changing the direction of the page, but some worksheets and charts require the page to be wider than it is tall. Like landscape paintings that typically are wider than they are tall, *landscape* orientation enables you to fit wider items on the page. A page that is taller than it is wide has what is called *portrait* orientation, like portraits of people.

Two other features are useful when you're trying to print a large worksheet.

○ *Scaling* lets you specify a certain percent to reduce or enlarge your worksheet.
○ The Fit To Page feature allows you to force the worksheet to print on a specific number of pages, without having to calculate the percent yourself.

Why: When you need to print a worksheet that is too large to fit on the page without making the font very small, you use the orientation and scaling features. For instance, you may have a worksheet with data for January through December, and so you need the extra width more than the height.

How: Use the Page Setup dialog box to adjust orientation and scaling.

1. Choose **File|Page Setup**.
2. Click the **Page** tab to access the dialog box shown in Figure 5.4.
3. Specify one of the following settings:
   • **Adjust to ___ % of normal size.** Click the arrows to change the percent or type a percent in the box to enlarge or reduce the size of the printout by a certain percent.

Figure 5.4 Page tab of the Page Setup dialog box

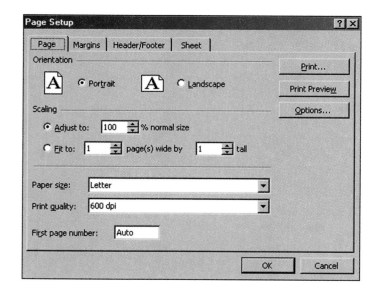

- **Fit to ___ page(s) wide by ___ tall.** Click the arrows or type the number of pages you want. For example, to squeeze the whole thing onto a single page, make it 1 page wide by 1 tall. To allow it to span two pages side by side, choose 2 pages wide by 1 tall. When you have a worksheet that is really long, but one little column runs over onto a second page wide, you can choose 1 page wide and leave blank the number of pages tall for it to flow as long as it wants.
- **Paper size.** If your printer can handle larger page sizes, such as legal size paper (8 1/2 × 14), you might be able to fit a large worksheet on one page.

Result: Using the options on the Page tab of the Page Setup dialog box, you can control how you fit a large worksheet on the printed page.

TIPS FROM A PRO: Here's a summary of ways to make a slightly-too-wide worksheet fit on a page.

- Change the orientation to landscape.
- Set the Fit to Page option to 1 page wide.
- Change the scaling to a smaller percent.
- Use legal-size paper (with landscape orientation).
- Make the margins narrower.
- Make the columns narrower.
- In Page Break Preview, drag the blue lines to the right to include more columns.

TASK 5	*Set Margins and Centering*

CORE OBJECTIVE: *Set page margins and centering*

What: In Print Preview, you might notice that a single column of your worksheet flows onto a second page. Although you can scrunch it in by reducing the scaling percent or by turning the orientation to landscape, sometimes all you have to do is adjust the *margins*, the distance between the edge of the paper and the printed information.

On the other hand, when you have a small worksheet, in Print Preview you might notice that it looks awkward in the top-left corner of the page, with the rest of the page empty. You can center the small worksheet on the page without having to adjust margins.

You can change margin settings two ways: by typing the exact measurements into a dialog box, or by dragging boundary lines in Print Preview by eye.

Why: For the most attractive page, you should strive to have the appropriate balance between the worksheet and the surrounding white space.

USE THE DIALOG BOX

How: In the dialog box, you can specify exact measurements for margins.

1. Choose **File|Page Setup.**
2. Click the **Margins** tab to access the dialog box shown in Figure 5.5.
3. Click the arrows to specify the margins (in inches) for the four sides of the page. (Header and footer measurements must be smaller than the margin settings. You'll learn about this in Task 6.) You can preview the settings in the dialog box.
4. Click the check boxes if you want horizontal or vertical centering. You can see a preview of this effect in the dialog box. Click **OK.**

Figure 5.5 Margins tab of the Page Setup dialog box

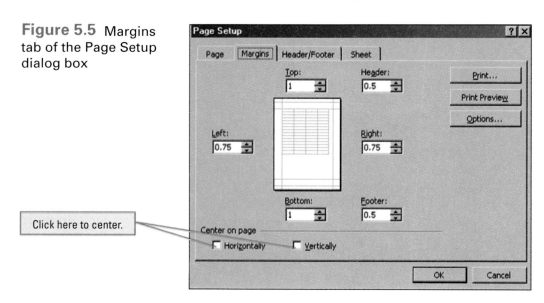

Click here to center.

Result: The distance between the printing and the edge of the page is increased or decreased, depending on the measurements you select.

SET MARGINS IN PRINT PREVIEW

How: In Print Preview, you can adjust the margins by eye.

1. Click the **Print Preview** button or choose **File|Print Preview.**
2. Click the **Margins** button.

As you see in Figure 5.6, boundary lines for the margins appear, as well as handles denoting each of the non-empty columns. Place the mouse pointer over the lines or handles until it turns into a two-headed arrow and drag to adjust the width of margins or columns.

Result: Unlike using the dialog box, when you drag to change the margins or column widths in Print Preview, the changes occur immediately so you can see them on screen. To undo changes in the margins or column widths, close Print Preview and click the Undo button one or more times.

Figure 5.6 Changing margins in Print Preview

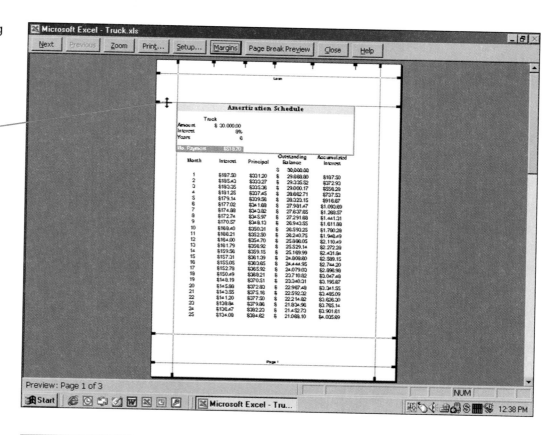

Drag two-headed pointer to change margins.

TASK 6   *Set Up Headers and Footers*

C   CORE OBJECTIVE: *Set up headers and footers*

What: When you want the same text, such as a title or a page number, to appear on the top of every page, you create a *header*. Text that appears on the bottom of every page is called a *footer*. Both headers and footers appear within the page margins. You set the measurement for headers and footers in the Margins tab of the Page Setup dialog box.

Why: For careful records, you might want to include the file name, author, or date on the page. For longer worksheets, you might want to include page numbers and the total number of pages. You wouldn't want to have to type the text at the top of every page. Instead, you can set up the information once and have Excel place the text on every page.

How: Excel has a number of standard headers and footers already set up for you. If none of these are what you want, you can create custom headers or footers.

1. Choose **File|Page Setup**, and click the **Header/Footer** tab.
2. Next to **Header** or **Footer**, click to open a drop-down list of standard choices, as shown in Figure 5.7. Scroll through to find one you like, or choose the one that comes closest.
3. To create a header or footer not on the list, click **Custom Header** or **Custom Footer** button to see the dialog box shown in Figure 5.8.

Figure 5.7 Setting up headers and footers

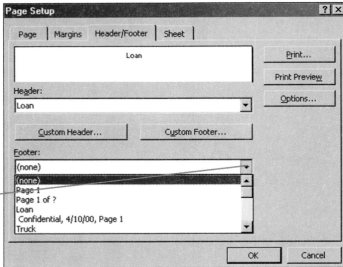

Click here to drop down a list of standard footers.

Figure 5.8 Creating a custom header

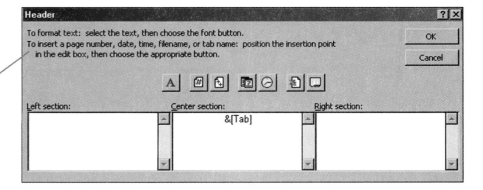

Text explains how to use the buttons.

Unlike a word processor, Excel doesn't have a way to set tabs. Instead, it provides three sections for you to use in setting up the information for the header. Click in each section to type text, or click the various buttons to insert the page number, total number of pages, date, time, file name, sheet tab, and so on.

Result: Whatever you choose for the header appears within the top margin of every page, and the footer appears within the bottom margin of every page. Use Print Preview to see how the header and footer will appear on the printed page.

To change their distance from the edge of the paper, use the Margins tab of the Page Setup dialog box or use Print Preview.

TASK 7 *Specify Sheet Options*

CORE OBJECTIVE: *Set print titles and options (gridlines, print quality, row and column headings)*

What: The Sheet tab of the Page Setup dialog box deals with elements you can add to the page to make it more useful. You might be used to seeing your worksheet with the gridlines delineating the rows and columns, yet when you print, the lines no longer appear. You might also want to see the ABCs for the columns and 123s for the rows. You can turn on the gridlines and the row and column headings from this dialog box.

Another feature you'll sometimes find useful is the ability to set *print titles*. Remember how you can freeze panes to keep some rows or columns on screen no matter where you scroll in the document? Print titles is the printed-page equivalent to freezing panes, where certain rows or columns appear at the top or left side of every piece of paper.

Why: You'll enjoy having a printout with the row and column headings and gridlines when you're trying to audit or debug your worksheet away from the computer.

Print titles, on the other hand, are handy because the headings repeat on the top or left side of every page of the printout without your having to copy and paste them each time.

How: Choose **File|Page Setup** and click the **Sheet** tab, as you see in Figure 5.9. This dialog box enables you to set the print area if you haven't already done so.

Figure 5.9 Sheet tab of the Page Setup dialog box

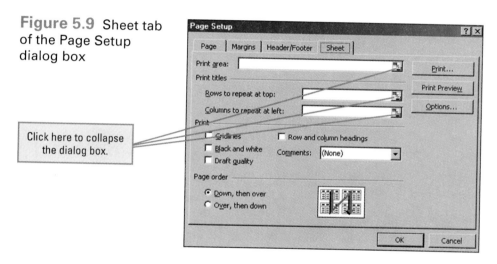

Do you see the red arrow on the button next to several of the choices in this dialog box? When you click the **Collapse Dialog** button, the dialog box shrinks to a single line, as you see in Figure 5.10. This lets you get the dialog box out of the way while you click or drag on the worksheet, for example, when you want to define the print area. Click the button again to restore the dialog box to its regular size.

- ❍ To specify a print area, click in the **Print Area** box, collapse the dialog box, and drag the print area.
- ❍ To designate a row to repeat at the top of every worksheet, collapse the dialog box and click the row heading number.
- ❍ To designate a column to repeat at the left of every worksheet, collapse the dialog box and click the column-heading letter.
- ❍ Click to select the other Print options.
- ❍ When you are finished, click **OK**, or click **Print Preview** to see the effect.

Result: Figure 5.11 shows the way the worksheet appears with row and column headings, gridlines, and print titles.

Figure 5.10
Collapsed dialog box

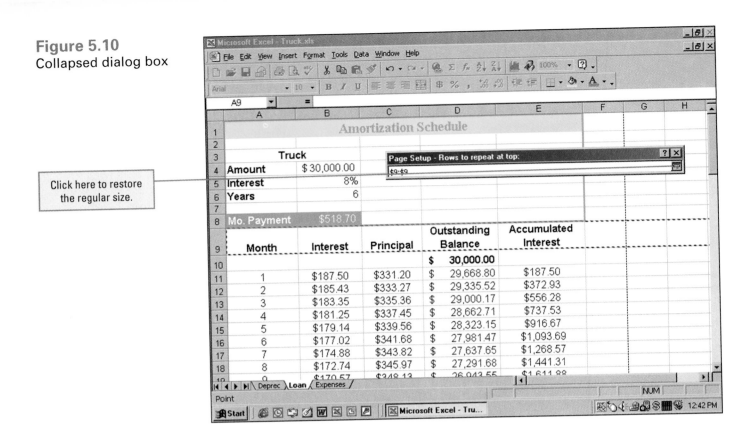

Click here to restore the regular size.

Figure 5.11 Row and column headings, gridlines, and print titles

Print Titles repeats row 9 on page 2.

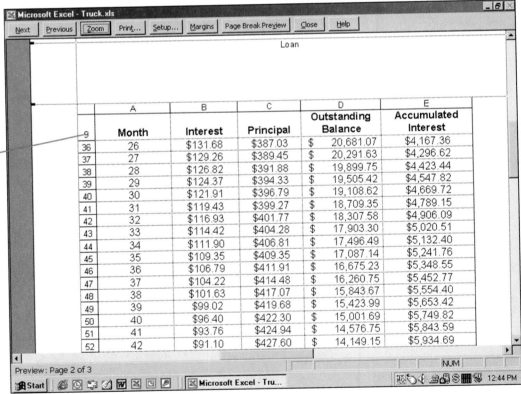

TIPS FROM A PRO: What could you do to get a printout of the formulas in a worksheet? (Hint: use Ctrl+`.)

Core Objective: Insert and remove a page break

What: When your worksheets are large, they might run to more than one page. You can control exactly which page contains the data by inserting *page breaks*. As worksheets grow longer and extend past one page, Excel automatically calculates how much room is available and starts a new page when needed. Automatic page breaks appear as dotted lines in the worksheet after you print or use Print Preview. Excel also enables you to specify where to begin a new page by inserting a manual page break where you want one. You can do this by using the Insert|Page Break command or by using Page Break Preview.

Why: Sometimes you want to place material on a separate page, even though it could fit on the same page. Other times you want to control exactly where the page break falls.

USE THE COMMAND

How: The trick to using the command is to specify its location first, by selecting a cell, row, or column.

- ❍ Select a row and choose **Insert|Page Break**, and the page break is inserted above the current row, so the selected row is now on the next page.
- ❍ Select a column and choose **Insert|Page Break**, and the page break is inserted to the left of the current column, so the selected column now appears on the next page.
- ❍ Click a cell and choose **Insert|Page Break**, and two page breaks are inserted above and to the left of the active cell.
- ❍ To remove a page break, select the item again and choose **Insert| Remove Page Break**.

Result: Manual page breaks, ones you insert, appear as dashed lines across or down the sheet, whereas automatic page breaks appear as dotted lines, as you see in Figure 5.12. When you use Print Preview, you can view the contents of each of the various pages.

USE PAGE BREAK PREVIEW

How: Another way to control where the page breaks fall is to use Page Break Preview. Access it one of these ways:

- ❍ Choose **View|Page Break Preview**.
- ❍ In Print Preview, click the **Page Break Preview** button.

Figure 5.12 Manual and automatic page breaks

Automatic page break

Manual page break

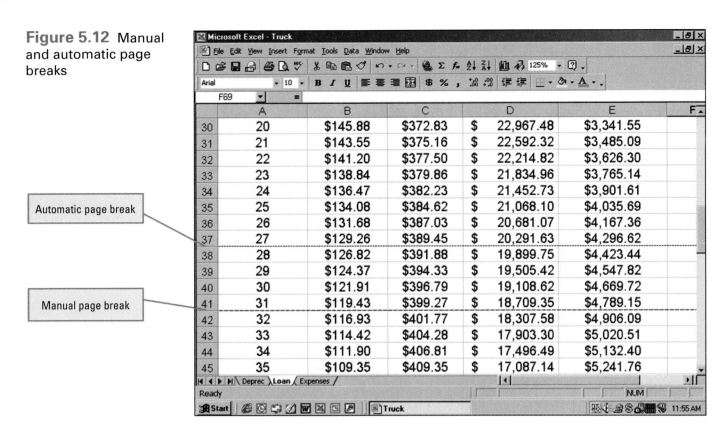

Figure 5.13 Page Break Preview

Automatic page break

Manual page break

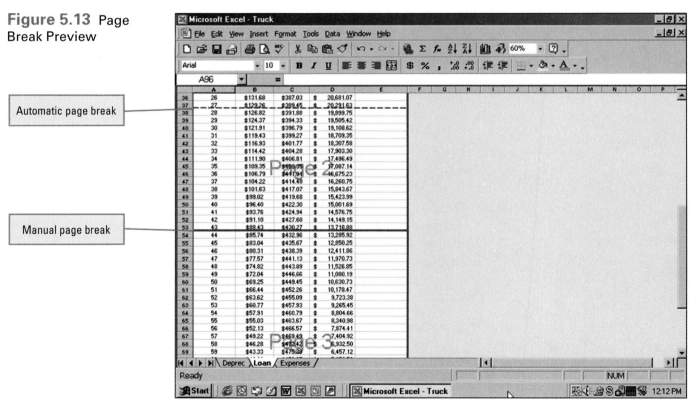

As soon as you do that, you see a new view of your worksheet, as shown in Figure 5.13. Here you can adjust both the print area and the page breaks. Use these techniques:

❍ To move page breaks, drag them. Automatic page breaks appears as dashed blue lines, and manual page break as solid blue lines.
❍ To reduce the print area, drag the blue boundary between the light and shaded areas inward or up.
❍ To enlarge the print area, select an area outside it, right-click, and choose **Add to Print Area**. This might not add more pages, however. It often squeezes the additional area onto the existing number of pages.
❍ To add a page break, select a location, right-click, and choose **Insert Page Break** from the shortcut menu.
❍ To reset page breaks or reset the print area, right-click and choose from the shortcut menu.

Result: Page Break Preview is a handy way to see exactly what parts of the worksheet will appear on the various pages when they are printed. To exit Page Break Preview, choose **View|Normal**.

 TIPS FROM A PRO: Another nice feature of Page Break Preview is that you can zoom out to see all the pages at one time. To do this, change the zoom percentage to a smaller number, such as 50%.

 ## Use PinPoint

After gaining the skills in this chapter, you can preview and print the document, use all the parts of the Page Setup dialog box to control what appears on the printed page, and manage how multi-page worksheets are printed. Now it's time to use the PinPoint software and see what you can do. Remember, whenever you are unsure of what to do, you can reread that portion of the chapter or you can click Show Me for a live demonstration. Check out these skills in PinPoint:

• Change page orientation
• Change zoom setting
• Display formulas
• Header and footer
• Insert a page break
• Page margins
• Page titles
• Print a selection
• Print a worksheet
• Print a workbook
• Set the print area

Key Terms

You can find definitions for these words in this chapter:

Footer

Header

Landscape

Margins

Page break

Portrait

Print area

Print titles

Scaling

Review Questions

You can use the following review questions to test your knowledge and skills. Answers are given in Appendix D, "Answers to Review Questions."

True/False

Indicate whether each statement is true (T) or false (F).

___ 1. To print only a portion of the worksheet, select the cells and then click the Print button.

___ 2. To access Print Preview, click the Print button or choose File|Print.

___ 3. Print Preview is nice because you can view several pages at a time.

___ 4. You can always tell which part of a worksheet is the print area because it is surrounded by a thin blue border.

___ 5. Scaling lets you enlarge or reduce the printed worksheet by a certain percent.

___ 6. You can add page numbers, the file name, or the date to a header or footer by clicking a button in the Custom Header dialog box.

___ 7. When you print a page, it automatically shows fine gridlines delineating the rows and columns.

___ 8. Setting print titles is the printed version of freezing panes.

___ 9. When a dialog box is in the way, you can click a Collapse Dialog button so you can select cells on the worksheet.

___ 10. To print formulas instead of the number results of the calculations, click the button in the Page Setup dialog box.

Multiple Choice

Select the letter that best completes the statement.

___ 1. Print Preview is handy because it lets you:
   a. See how the worksheet appears on the page.
   b. Change the margins and column width.
   c. Switch to Page Break Preview.
   d. See the headers and footers in place.
   e. All of the above.

___ 2. When you want to define a particular portion of the worksheet to print, it's called the:
   a. Header.
   b. Margin.
   c. Page break.
   d. Print area.
   e. Selection.

___ 3. When you have a wide worksheet you want to print with the paper sideways, choose _____ orientation.
   a. AutoFit.
   b. Horizontal.
   c. Landscape.
   d. Portrait.
   e. Straight.

___ 4. In Print Preview when you click the Margins button, you can:
   a. Drag dashed lines to change the margin settings.
   b. Drag handles to adjust column widths.
   c. Drag blue lines to adjust page breaks.
   d. All of the above.
   e. Both a and b.

___ 5. Text that appears on the top of every printed page within the top margin is called a:
   a. Banner.
   b. Heading.
   c. Header.
   d. Title.
   e. Topper.

___ 6. Setting print titles means you show on every printed page:
   a. The column ABCs and row 123s.
   b. The same text, such as the page number at the top of every page.
   c. The contents of a certain row or column.
   d. The formulas found on the worksheet rather than the results.
   e. All of the above.

___ 7. The measurements you enter on the Margins tab are:
   a. The distance between the left and right margin, and top and bottom margin.
   b. The distance between the header and the footer.
   c. The distance between the edge of the page and the printed area.
   d. The size of the paper you are printing on.
   e. The size of the worksheet you want to print.

___ 8. To place your name or the page number in the top margin of every page, choose:
   a. Insert|Margin.
   b. Insert|Comment.
   c. View|Header.
   d. File|Page Setup.
   e. File|Print Preview.

9. Page Break Preview can be
used to see:
a. The print area.
b. Manual and automatic page
breaks.
c. The number of pages.
d. All the pages at once.
e. All of the above.

____ 10. In Page Break Preview, to add
another page break:
a. Drag the blue line to the
location.
b. Double-click the location.
c. Right-click and choose
Insert Page Break.
d. Click the Insert Page Break
button.
e. All of the above.

Screen Review

Match the letters in Figure 5.14 with the correct items in the list.

Figure 5.14

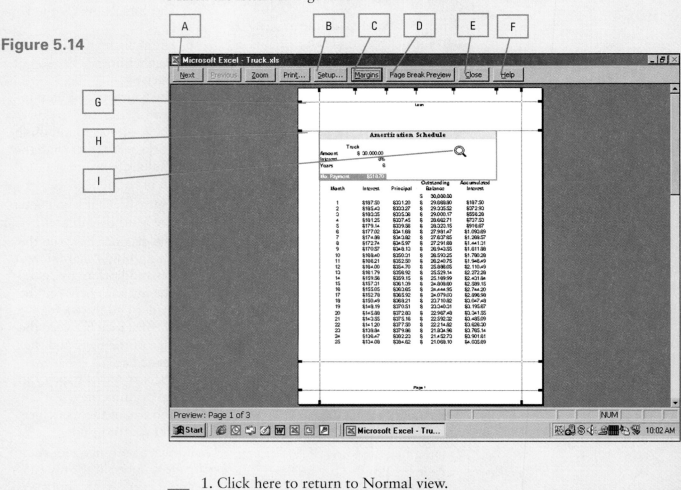

____ 1. Click here to return to Normal view.

____ 2. Click here to see the page breaks.

____ 3. Click here to see more pages.

____ 4. Drag here to change a column width.

____ 5. Drag here to change a margin.

____ 6. Click here to change the location of the header.

____ 7. This button has been clicked.

____ 8. Click here to see a close-up view.

____ 9. Click here to change to landscape orientation.

Exercise and Project

Follow these step-by-step instructions to create a worksheet. If you are working in a computer lab, ask your instructor where you should save and print your file.

Exercise

1. Open **Truck.xls** from the *Student\Chapter 5* folder on your PinPoint CD.
2. Click to view the contents of the three worksheets, *Deprec*, *Loan*, and *Expenses*, and then return to **Loan**.
3. In column E, add a formula to calculate a running sum of the interest paid month by month. Fill it down the column.
4. Access Print Preview. Notice the current header and footer on each page. Click **Next** to see how many pages there are.
5. Access the Page Setup dialog box, and click the **Header/Footer** tab. Create a custom header with these guidelines:
   - Delete the Tab label.
   - On the left side, type your name and class.
   - Beneath that, use the buttons to enter the current date and time. Remember to press Spacebar between the date and time.
6. Center the worksheet both horizontally and vertically.
7. In Page Break Preview, drag the page break to row 38 on page 1. Go to the next page and drag the page break to row 82. Does the worksheet now fit on two pages? If not, reset the margins.
8. Print both pages of the worksheet.
9. Set the print area from the top down through month 12. Print.
10. Access the **Deprec** worksheet.
11. Print Preview the pages. Change the orientation to landscape, and force it to fit on a single page.
12. Center the data on the page and change the header or footer to show your name. Print the sheet.
13. Finally, access the **Expenses** sheet. Select the check boxes to show gridlines as well as row and column labels.
14. View the formulas, and resize the columns to fit. Save the workbook and print the sheet.

Project

Open **Travel.xls** from the *Student\Chapter 5* folder on your PinPoint CD. This is the long-term projection that the company gives to potential investors. Decide the best way to print this worksheet so that it is professional, attractive, and easy to read. Add your name to the header and print.

Chapter 6

Format Worksheets

So far, you've learned a lot about putting together complex worksheets and printing them. Of course, the most important aspect of Excel is getting the formulas and numbers correct, so you are right to concentrate on that first. To put the finishing touches on a worksheet, you have to change the formatting. When you enhance the appearance of your worksheet with the appropriate number format, color, contrasting fonts, and borders, your worksheet is much more attractive and easier to read.

At the end of this chapter, you will be able to:

C	E	
❑	❑	Choose the appropriate number format
☑	☑	Apply number formats (accounting, currency, number)
❑	☑	Create custom number formats
☑	❑	Apply font styles (typeface, size, color and styles)
❑	❑	Apply various types of underlining
☑	❑	Modify horizontal and vertical alignment of cell content
☑	❑	Merge cells
☑	❑	Rotate text and change indents
❑	❑	Wrap long text within cells
☑	❑	Apply cell borders and shading
☑	❑	Apply an AutoFormat
☑	❑	Clear cell formats
❑	❑	Use the Repeat command
☑	❑	Use the Format Painter
☑	❑	Define, apply, and remove a style
❑	☑	Use Goal Seek

EXPERT OBJECTIVE: **Apply number formats (accounting, currency, number)**

What: As you learned in Chapter 2, "Edit Worksheet Contents," you can change the appearance of numbers by changing the format, for example by adding dollar signs and commas. You can do this several ways:

- ○ You can type dollar signs, commas, or percent signs as you enter the number in the cell. Excel automatically applies the correct formatting. This is also the case when you type dates or times.
- ○ You can select existing numbers and apply the appropriate formatting to them.

Excel makes it easy to apply typical number formats by providing several buttons on the Formatting toolbar. However, Excel offers even more choices for number formatting in the Format Cells dialog box. Here you can specify the symbol, the number of decimal places, and the way negative numbers should appear, as well as other choices.

Remember that Excel stores only the raw number in the contents of the cell. The format exists separately from the contents, so you can't click in the formula bar to remove commas or a percent sign, for example, even if you typed them when you entered the number in the cell.

Why: A number's format helps communicate meaning. Symbols, such as a dollar sign or percent sign, the number of decimal points, and even such items as hyphens in a social security number make the number not only more exact, but also easier to understand.

USE THE BUTTONS

How: Let's review the buttons you can use to format numbers. Here's what'll happen when you click each button.

$ Click the **Currency Style** button to show money. This adds several items to the number's appearance:

- ○ A dollar sign at the left edge of the cell
- ○ A decimal point
- ○ Commas, if the number is larger than 1,000
- ○ Two decimal places
- ○ Parentheses around negative numbers
- ○ Space between the number and the right edge of the cell (to make room for the parentheses in negative numbers)

%   Click the **Percent Style** button for percentage amounts. This changes the number's appearance these ways:

- ○ A percent sign appears at the right edge of the cell.
- ○ The raw number is multiplied by 100 (because decimals and percents are mathematically equivalent).
- ○ Percent signs appear in the formula bar (to indicate that the raw number has been multiplied by 100).

Click the **Comma Style** button for money amounts that don't need a dollar sign or other numbers greater than 1,000. (You'll use this for the second item in a list of money amounts.) This adds several items to the number's appearance:

○ Commas, if the number is larger than 1,000
○ A decimal point
○ Two decimal places
○ Parentheses around negative numbers
○ Space between the number and the right edge of the cell (to make room for the parentheses in negative numbers)

Click the **Increase Decimal** or **Decrease Decimal** button to control the number of decimal places displayed in the cell. You can click repeatedly to add or remove decimal places from the appearance, but the number in the formula bar will not change. If the number of decimals is reduced, the displayed amounts are rounded off.

Result: Suppose you have the raw number 1280.6 entered in a cell. Figure 6.1 summarizes the effect of each button on the number.

Figure 6.1 How number formatting buttons affect 1280.6

	A	B	C	D
1	Number	Toolbar button clicked	Result if positive	Result if negative
2	1280.6	None	1280.6	-1280.6
3		Currency Style	$ 1,280.60	$ (1,280.60)
4		Percent Style	128060%	-128060%
5		Comma Style	1,280.60	(1,280.60)
6		Increase Decimal	1280.60	-1280.60
7		Decrease Decimal	1281	-1281

USE THE DIALOG BOX

How: To access more choices for number formatting, select the cell or cells. Then choose **Format|Cells** (or press the shortcut key **Ctrl+1**, or right-click and choose **Format Cells**) and click the **Number** tab. This dialog box presents 12 categories of number format, each one with specific options. Here's a summary of the uses and options for each type of number format.

General. This is the raw number. Use General format when you want to remove all formatting from a number and just show the digits in the cell.

Number. Use this for typical, non-money numbers. Specify the number of decimal places, whether you want to use a comma to separate the thousands, and how you want the negative numbers to appear, as you see in Figure 6.2a.

Currency. Use this format to show money. Specify the symbol, decimal places, thousands separator, and appearance of negative number, as you see in Figure 6.2b. This format differs from Accounting in that it places the $ right next to the number.

Accounting. Use this format to show money. Specify the symbol and decimal places. This format differs from Currency in that it places the $ away from the number, at the left edge of the cell. This is good because all the $ symbols in a column of numbers line up.

TIPS FROM A PRO: Interestingly, when you type $ when you are entering your number, Excel applies Currency formatting, where the $ sits next to the number. If you click the $ button (called Currency Style in the ScreenTip), Excel actually applies Accounting formatting, where the $ sits at the left edge of the cell. Clicking the Comma Style button also applies Accounting formatting, but eliminates the $ symbol.

Date. Choose how to show the year (two digits or four), the month (text or numbers), and the day (before or after the month), any symbols (slashes or dashes), and whether or not you want to include the time as well (Figure 6.2c). Remember: Dates are actually a serial number counting up since January 1, 1900, so if you reformat it with General number format, Excel displays the serial number in the cell. Dates must always have a Date format to make sense.

Time. Specify whether to show the time with a 12-hour or 24-hour clock, whether you want to show seconds, and whether to include AM or PM. Time is a decimal number from 0 to 0.99999999, representing the times from 0:00:00 (midnight) to 23:59:59 (11:59:59 P.M.).

Percentage. Specify the number of decimal places. All percents are multiplied by 100 and displayed with a % symbol.

Figure 6.2 Four number formatting categories

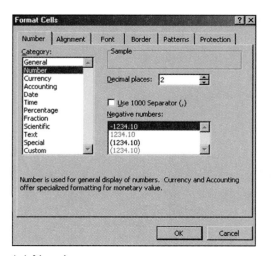

(a) Number

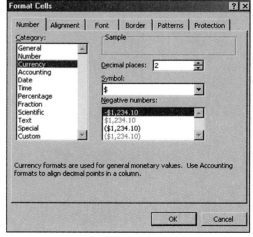

(b) Currency

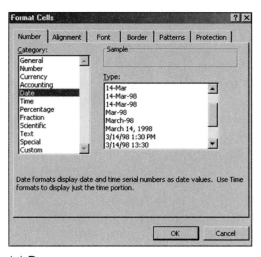

(c) Date

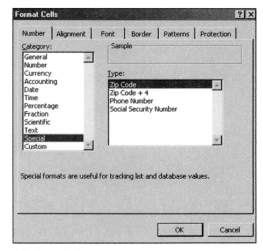

(d) Special

Fraction. Used often for stock prices, this converts decimals into fractions.

Scientific. Used for very large or very small numbers. The number after the E represents the number of places to move the decimal. Excel automatically formats a large number this way.

Text. Transforms digits into text, so that they are displayed exactly as entered (even if they begin with zeros). You might use this for social security numbers, telephone numbers, ZIP codes, and other numbers that are not used in calculations. As text, the numbers are left aligned.

Special. Provides the unique number formats used for telephone numbers (parentheses and hyphen), social security numbers (hyphens), and ZIP+4 (hyphen), as seen in Figure 6.2d.

Custom. Create your own number format based on one of the previously mentioned types. You'll learn how to do this in Task 2.

Result: When you click OK, the format you specified is applied to the active cell or all selected cells. To remove the number formatting, choose **Format|Cells**, click the **Number** tab, and choose **General**.

TASK 2   *Create Custom Number Formats*

EXPERT OBJECTIVE: *Create custom number formats*

What: Excel lets you create your own, custom number format. You can define these aspects:

- ○ The number of digits to show
- ○ The number of decimal places to show
- ○ What symbols and spacing to include
- ○ How negative numbers, zeros, or text should appear
- ○ What text should appear in the cell along with the number

The dialog box you use contains up to four sections of codes, each separated by a semicolon. The sections define the appearance of positive numbers, negative numbers, zero values, and text.

Why: Sometimes, none of the number formats supplied by Excel is exactly what you want. For example, suppose you regularly type a 16-digit credit card number, but you want the number formatted with spaces placed every four digits to make it easier to read. None of the existing number formats does this, so you can make a custom number format that does exactly what you want. Or, suppose you like the Accounting format, but you want the negative numbers to appear in red. This choice doesn't exist, so you'll have to create it yourself.

How: Here's the general approach to take when creating a custom number format.

1. Select the cell or cells that will have the new number format.
2. Choose **Format|Cells** and choose a type that's close to what you want, and then choose **Custom**. (In the case of our credit card number, there isn't one close.)

3. Click in the **Type** box and modify or enter the code for the number format.

- Use # for digits or decimals that are optional, or use 0 for required digits or decimals; for example to require two decimal places, use 0.00.
- Add symbols such as dollar signs, percents, or commas, if you want them displayed, for example $#,##0.00
- Add _) at the end of a code to allow an extra space on the right side of the number so that positive numbers line up with the negative numbers that are surrounded by parentheses, for example #,###_)
- Add [**Red**] to the beginning of the second section (after the semicolon) to make negative numbers appear in red. You'll need to do this to change Accounting format to show negative numbers in red.
- For the 16-digit credit card number example, type the code like this: 0000 0000 0000 0000 because we want to require all 16 digits and show spaces between them (Figure 6.3).

4. When the code for the custom format is correct, click **OK**.

Figure 6.3 Custom format applied to credit card number

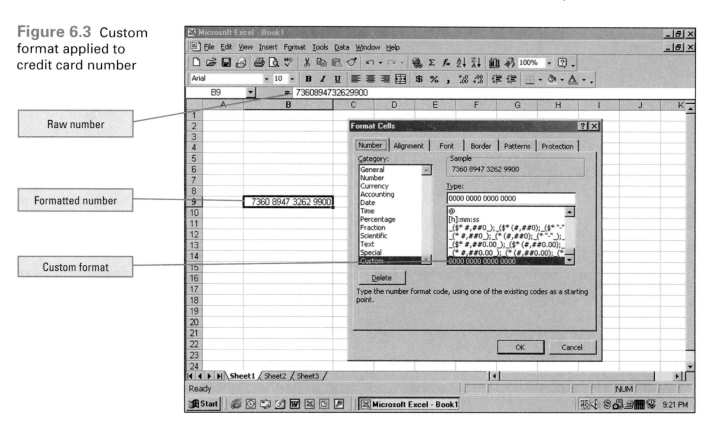

Raw number

Formatted number

Custom format

Result: After you create a custom format, it is listed as a Custom type in the dialog box, and you can apply it to other cells. To remove a custom format, highlight its name in the dialog box and click **Delete**.

THOUGHT QUESTION: What types of numbers would require a custom format? When would you want to include some text as part of the custom number format?

C   *CORE OBJECTIVE:* **Apply font styles (typeface, size, color, and styles)**

What: You can change the shape of the characters (their *font*, or typeface), the size (in points), the color, and whether the text is bold, italic, underlined, or a combination of the three.

Why: Although font formatting is not nearly as important in Excel as in Word or PowerPoint, you can still enhance the appearance and readability of a worksheet by choosing the best font.

FONT FORMATTING BUTTONS

How: Use buttons on the Formatting toolbar to change the appearance of the text and numbers.

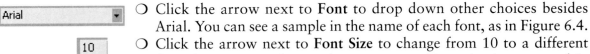

○ Click the arrow next to **Font** to drop down other choices besides Arial. You can see a sample in the name of each font, as in Figure 6.4.

○ Click the arrow next to **Font Size** to change from 10 to a different font size, or type the number you want. Font size is measured in *points*, with 72 points to the inch. The larger the number, the larger the size.

○ Click the **Bold**, **Italic**, or **Underline** button to add these special emphases to the cell contents. You can add one or several of these to a cell. You can tell which are in effect because the buttons appear pushed in.

○ Click the arrow next to **Font Color** to drop down a menu of colors, as you see in Figure 6.5, and click your choice. The font color you choose appears on the button face, so the next time you want to apply that color, you only need to click the button.

Figure 6.4 Font

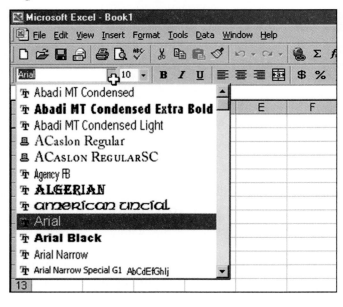

Figure 6.5 Font colors

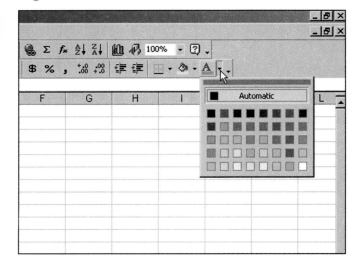

TIPS FROM A PRO: You can also use shortcut keys to apply font formatting. Press **Ctrl+B** for bold, **Ctrl+I** for italic, and **Ctrl+U** for underline.

 TIPS FROM A PRO: When you use colors in a worksheet, you need a color printer to see the results on paper. If you print colors to a black-and-white printer, you'll have to be careful that the colors you choose on the worksheet are legible.

Result: The letters and numbers in the selected cells show the new font format. Sample font formats are shown in Figure 6.6.

Figure 6.6 Sample font formatting

	A	B	C	D	E	F	G
1	Arial	10	Black	**Bold**	*Italic*	Underline	***Bold Italic Underline***
2	Arial	12	Brown	**Bold**	*Italic*	Underline	***Bold Italic Underline***
3	Times New Roman	14	Light Orange	**Bold**	*Italic*	Underline	***Bold Italic Underline***
4	Comic Sans	16	Dark Blue	**Bold**	*Italic*	Underline	***Bold Italic Underline***
5							

FONT DIALOG BOX

How: The Font dialog box shows other choices for underline styles and gives a preview of the format before you apply it.

1. Select the cell or cells to receive the format.
2. Choose **Format|Cells** (or press **Ctrl+1**). Click the **Font** tab to see the dialog box in Figure 6.7.
3. Click **Underline** to see a list of underline styles. Choose the one you want.
4. Make other font formatting choices.
5. Preview the effect in the dialog box, and click **OK** if you like it.

Figure 6.7 Font tab of the Format Cells dialog box

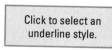
Click to select an underline style.

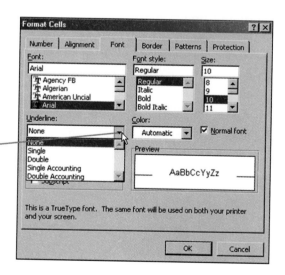

Result: When you click OK, the font effects are applied to the selected cells.

 TIPS FROM A PRO: You'll enjoy using double underlines to designate the "bottom line" of your worksheets. You can choose from two types of double underlines. **Double** places the underlines beneath the cell contents only, no matter how wide the cell is. **Double Accounting** underlines always extend nearly to the edges of the cell, no matter how wide the contents are.

TASK 4 *Format Alignment*

C CORE OBJECTIVE: *Modify alignment of cell content*

What: Entries in a cell, typically text or dates, can be shown with a variety of alignments. You can specify which edge of the cell to place the text against. Three buttons on the Formatting toolbar change the alignment of the selected cell or cells: Align Left, Center, and Align Right.

In addition, you can change the vertical alignment, wrap the text within the cell, or place text at an angle or up and down. Further, you can merge adjacent cells so they become one unit. These choices are found in the Alignment tab of the Format Cells dialog box.

Why: You'll want to change the horizontal alignment to align the column headings over a column. You'll change vertical alignment when the rows are taller than a single row of text and you want the column headings placed along the bottom edge of the cell. You'll often want to place a single heading centered across several columns, so for this you'll merge cells into a single unit.

CHANGE HORIZONTAL ALIGNMENT

 CORE OBJECTIVE: *Change indents*

How: Click buttons on the Formatting toolbar to change the horizontal alignment within the cells (Table 6.1).

Table 6.1 Alignment Choices

Button	Format	When to use this option
	Align Left	The default for text; keeps text against the left edge of the cell
	Center	Center column headings or titles above the column
	Align Right	Place short headings above the right-aligned numbers in the column
	Increase Indent	Indent subheadings from left edge of cell; click repeatedly for more indentation
	Decrease Indent	Reduce the amount of indentation

Result: Although you can use these alignments on any cell, numbers you use in calculations are nearly always right aligned. Figure 6.8 shows a sample

Figure 6.8
Horizontal alignment choices

	A	B	C
1	**Merge and Center**		
2	This text is left aligned	This text is left aligned	
3	Centered text	Indented text	
4	Right aligned	Indented more	
5			
6			

of the various horizontal alignments, including Merge and Center, which you learn about next.

MERGE AND CENTER

 CORE OBJECTIVE: *Merging cells*

How: You can merge adjacent cells to place a single heading above several columns.

1. Select the cells. They can be empty or contain text.
2. Click the **Merge and Center** button.

Result: The cells become a single unit, and the entry is centered horizontally.

TIPS FROM A PRO: You can also use the Merge and Center button to merge cells vertically, down a column. You have to adjust the vertical centering, though, because the button applies only horizontal centering.

VERTICAL ALIGNMENT

How: You most often use vertical alignment when you have tall cells where text can appear along the top edge, center, or bottom edge of a cell.

1. Select the cell or cells containing the text.
2. Choose **Format|Cells** and click the **Alignment** tab.
3. Drop down the **Vertical** list, choose **Top, Center, Bottom,** or **Justify,** and click **OK** (Figure 6.9).

Result: You can see sample vertical alignments in Figure 6.10.

Figure 6.9 Alignment tab of the Format Cells dialog box

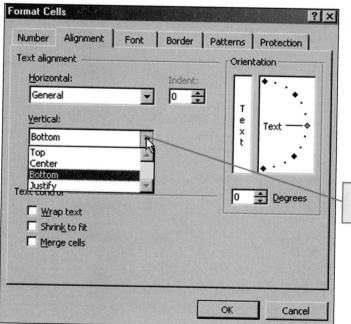

Figure 6.10 Sample vertical alignments

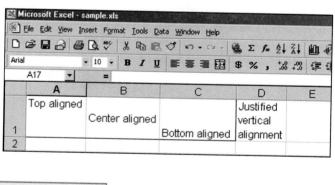

CORE OBJECTIVE: *Rotate text*

How: You can change the rotation of the text at an angle, up-and-down, or sideways like the title on the spine of a book. *Wrapping* text, on the other hand, forces long text to additional lines within the cell, rather than spilling over to adjacent blank cells or appearing cut off.

1. Select the cell containing the text.
2. Choose **Format|Cells** and click the **Alignment** tab (Figure 6.11). Choose one or more of the following options:
   - Drag the red handle in the **Orientation** box to angle the text.
   - Click **Wrap Text** to force long text to wrap within the cells.
   - Click **Shrink to Fit** to squeeze long text within the cell.

Result: The text appears within the cell with the orientation and wrapping you chose. If necessary, you can merge cells to give more room for the rotated, wrapped, or shrink-to-fit text.

TIPS FROM A PRO: Vertical text with the letters right side up but stacked vertically is impossible to read. Don't use this option. If you need vertical text, change the angle to 90 or –90 so you have to tip your head sideways to read it.

TIPS FROM A PRO: Combine bottom vertical alignment with text wrapping for column headings. This way, the shorter, single-line headings are aligned with the bottom row of multiline headings, as in Figure 6.12.

Figure 6.11 Changing rotation

Figure 6.12 Sample rotation, wrapping, and shrink to fit

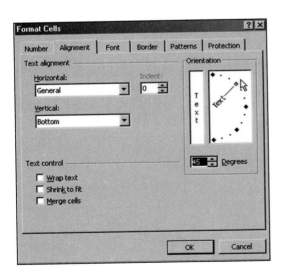

CORE OBJECTIVE: *Apply cell borders and shading*

What: When you print a worksheet, as you know, no lines appear on the printed page unless you click the Gridlines option in the Page Setup dialog box. Then you get lines between every row and column. Excel gives you more choices than that, however.

Excel supplies a variety of lines and shades you can use to format the edges of a cell. Lines can vary in thickness and line style, as well as color. Shading behind a cell can vary from light shades to black. Excel gives you several methods for adding and controlling borders and shading: buttons, and two tabs in the Format Cells dialog box.

Why: Adding shading or lines on the edges or a box around a cell or cells draws attention to the contents and adds a nice accent to the page. In some cases, you use borders between cells to make the contents more meaningful or easier to read.

USE THE BORDER BUTTONS

How: To add borders to the edges of cells, select the cell or cells and use the **Borders** button. You can click the button to add the border shown on it, or click the arrow to show all the choices for borders (Figure 6.13).

TIPS FROM A PRO: If you'll be applying a variety of borders to the cells, you can "tear off" the Borders menu to make it float on the page, as you see in Figure 6.14. To do this, drag the dark line at the top of the selections.

Figure 6.13 Borders button and menu   **Figure 6.14** Floating Borders toolbar

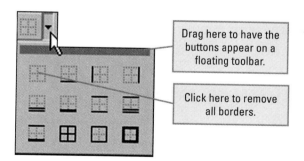

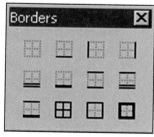

Result: Using the Borders button, you add a box around the selection or lines to one or more sides. Examine Figure 6.15 to see samples of paragraphs with borders on various sides.

TIPS FROM A PRO: Although they look as if they might be the same, applying borders has a different effect on the cell than underlining. A bottom border on the cell always extends completely across the cell, and when adjacent cells have the same border, the lines meet and continue across them all. Underlining, on the other hand, affects only the contents of the cell. Although Accounting underlining extends nearly from edge to edge, a little space is always left between the cells. You can see this in Figure 6.15.

Figure 6.15 Sample borders

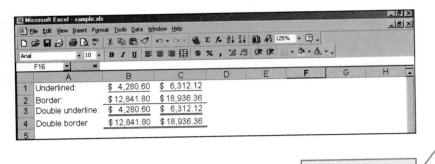

Figure 6.16 Borders tab of the Format Cells dialog box

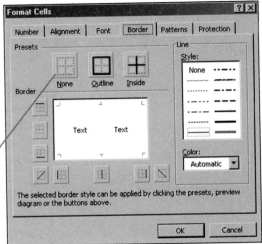

Click **None** to remove all borders.

USE THE BORDER DIALOG BOX

How: As usual, you get more options in the dialog box. Here you can specify the color and line style, as well as various locations.

1. Choose **Format|Cells** and click the **Border** tab, shown in Figure 6.16.
2. Specify the line style and color.
3. Click to set the location. To do this, click the buttons or click the preview area.
4. Repeat for additional line styles on the same selected cells. Click **OK**.

Result: The borders appear on the selected cells.

TIPS FROM A PRO: Whether you used the button or the dialog box to add a border, the quickest way to remove a border is by using the **No Border** button on the toolbar.

APPLY CELL SHADING AND PATTERNS

How: You can change the background color (called *fill* or *shading*) of selected cells. Use one of these methods:

○ Click the **Fill Color button** to apply the most recently used fill color, or click the down arrow to see 40 choices.
○ Choose **Format|Cells** and click the **Patterns** tab (Figure 6.17). Click a background color in the Cell Shading area. You can also click the **Pattern** arrow to see a menu of lines, dots, or shading you can add to the background color. (You won't use this much.)

Result: If you choose a light color, the shading appears behind the text. If you choose a dark color, you'll also have to change the color of the font so it will show up.

Figure 6.17 Patterns tab of the Format Cells dialog box

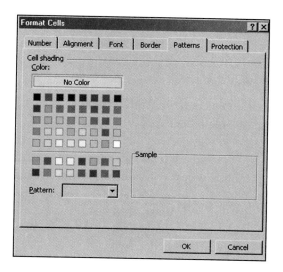

TASK 6 **Use AutoFormat**

CORE OBJECTIVE: *Apply AutoFormat*

What: It takes a bit of time to add all the font, color, borders, and shading formatting to a worksheet. Excel eases the process by grouping together a number of attractive formats that you can add all at one time. To do this, use the *AutoFormat* feature.

Why: With a single command, you can apply attractive number formatting, borders, font formatting, shading alignment, and cell height and width.

How: Follow these steps to use AutoFormatting.

1. Select the cells and choose **Format|AutoFormat**.
2. Scroll through the list to choose a predesigned format.
3. Click **Options** to see Figure 6.18. Select or clear the check boxes to use the AutoFormat's number format, border, font, shading, align-

Figure 6.18 AutoFormat dialog box

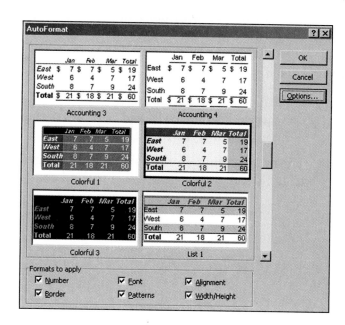

ment, and width/height feature. (Clear the check box if you've already specified one of these the way you want it.)

4. Click **OK** to apply the format. If you don't like the results, click **Undo** and start over.

Result: The worksheet is formatted with font effects, borders, shading, and colors, just as you specified.

TIPS FROM A PRO: Formatting a worksheet appropriately makes it easier to read. Follow these guidelines when considering which format to apply to a worksheet.

- For a worksheet you will read horizontally, place borders on top and bottom, but omit vertical lines. Add horizontal borders or use shading on alternate rows to lead the eye across the rows.
- For a worksheet you will read vertically, place a box around the outside. Use vertical borders between the columns or alternating strips of shading to lead the eye down the columns.
- To emphasize headings or totals, format the font as bold, or use bold borders or shading to contrast with the rest of the worksheet. For maximum emphasis, reverse the text (white text on dark shading).

TASK **7**	*Remove Cell Formatting*

CORE OBJECTIVE: *Clear cell formats*

What: Sometimes you get the format wrong and want to remove it completely before you start over. If you press Delete, the contents will be cleared, but the formats remain. Instead, you can clear just the formatting and leave the contents in place.

Why: Sometimes you get a format applied to the wrong cell, and it shows. This is the case with borders and shading, for instance. You can clear several types of formatting at once instead of having to remove each one individually.

How: Use either of the following methods after selecting cells.

○ Choose **Edit|Clear|Formats**.
○ Choose **Format|Style** and choose **Normal**. Click **OK**. (You'll learn more about styles in Task 8.)

Result: The number, font, border, shading, and alignment formatting is removed from the cell, leaving the cell entry and comments in their plain, original state.

What: When you have a cell with the correct formatting, you may want to copy the formatting to another, unformatted cell. You can do this three ways.

      ○ Use the Repeat command, if it was the last action you did.
      ○ Use the Format Painter.
      ○ Define a style.

      The Format Painter copies the formatting, but not the contents, of a given cell. You "paint" the format for the number, font, borders, shading, and so on, simply by swiping the mouse.

      The most sophisticated way to apply the same format to cells is to create a style. A *style* is a set of formats that have been grouped together and given a name. Excel has a number of styles already defined—you've used some already: Currency style and Comma style. You can create and apply your own styles.

Why: Applying number and font formatting, borders, shading, and so on might require several steps. Copying the cell formatting saves you time. Applying styles is not only a quick way to apply combinations of formatting, but it keeps the formatting consistent.

USE THE REPEAT COMMAND

How: If you've just formatted something, you can use the Repeat command to duplicate that action. You can use the menu or a shortcut key:

      ○ Choose **Edit|Repeat** (the menu's wording changes to match the action you just performed).
      ○ Press **Ctrl+Y**.

Result: The command repeats only the operation you just performed. If you click the Bold button and then click the Center button, for instance, it repeats only the Center action, not both. However, if you use the Format Cells dialog box to apply both formats and then click OK, the Repeat command repeats all the formatting choices you made in the dialog box.

 TIPS FROM A PRO: You can use the Repeat command to duplicate any operation you just used. It's useful for repeating the typing, inserting items, editing, and other operations.

USE FORMAT PAINTER

 CORE OBJECTIVE: Use the Format Painter

How: Unlike the Repeat command that only repeats the last action, the Format Painter copies formatting you have made at any time.

      1. Select the cell that has the formatting that you want to duplicate.

2. Click the **Format Painter** button.
3. Drag with the special Format Painter mouse pointer to highlight the text you want to receive the formatting, as you see in Figure 6.19.
4. To repeat the formatting several times, double-click the Format Painter button in Step 2, and when you're done, click the button to turn it off.

Result: The formatting of one cell is duplicated on other cells. This includes number and font formatting, borders, shading, and alignment options.

TIPS FROM A PRO: Here's a way to remember the steps:

1. Specify the "color" of the paint (select text with formatting that you want to copy).
2. Dip the paintbrush (click the **Format Painter** button).
3. Paint (drag mouse pointer across text to receive formatting).

Figure 6.19 Painting a format

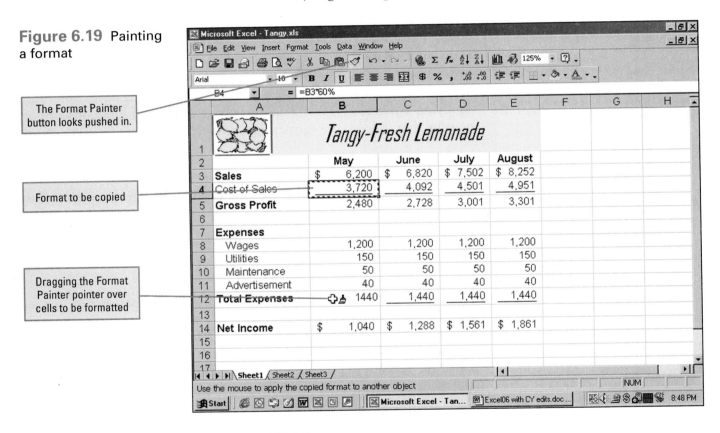

The Format Painter button looks pushed in.

Format to be copied

Dragging the Format Painter pointer over cells to be formatted

CREATE A STYLE

CORE OBJECTIVE: *Define a style*

How: You can define a style two ways: use the format of an existing cell, or start from scratch.

To use an existing cell as the basis of a style:

1. Select an existing cell with the formatting you want.
2. Choose **Format|Style** to see the dialog box in Figure 6.20.
3. Type a name for the new style.
4. Specify what the style includes, and click **Add**.

Figure 6.20 Create a style

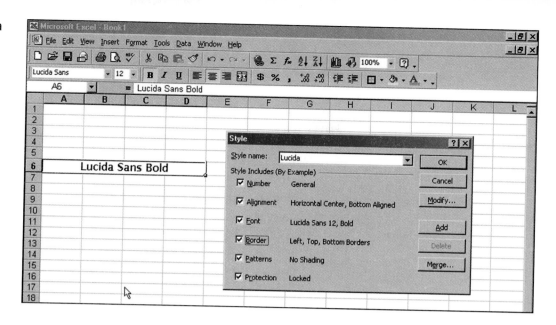

To create a style from scratch:

1. Select a cell you want to format with the style.
2. Choose **Format|Style**.
3. Type a name for the new style and specify what the style includes.
4. Click **Modify** to access the Format Cells dialog box. Here you set all your formatting choices. Click **OK** twice.

Result: The combination of formatting is saved under a single name. Now you can apply it easily wherever you want it.

USE A STYLE

CORE OBJECTIVE: *Apply a style*

How: Select the cells, and choose **Format|Style**. Choose the name of the style, specify which elements you want to include, and click **OK**.

Result: The combination of formatting is applied to the selection. If you modify the style with different formatting attributes, every cell using that style is immediately changed. This keeps your formatting consistent throughout the workbook and saves you the trouble of having to reapply the format here and there.

REMOVE A STYLE

CORE OBJECTIVE: *Remove a style*

How: You can remove a style's effect from the cell, or you can remove the style completely from the workbook.

○ To remove a style's effect on certain cells, choose **Edit|Clear|Formats** or choose **Format|Style** and choose **Normal**.
○ To remove a style from the workbook, choose **Format|Style**, choose the style name, and click **Delete**. Click **OK**.

Result: The cells are restored to the plain, unadorned contents.

E   *EXPERT OBJECTIVE: Use Goal Seek*

What: When you've built a worksheet that uses formulas or functions to calculate a result, you may have a result in mind but not know what number will get you there. Excel's Goal Seek feature automatically finds the value that gets the results you want.

Why: In a typical income statement, you may want to find the *breakeven point*, the place where the income equals the expenses, and net income equals zero. You may not know what amount of sales is required to reach breakeven. You could use the trial-and-error method to type in different numbers in the Sales cell until you see 0 in the Net Income cell. This would be time consuming, as you can imagine. Goal Seek does this for you, almost instantly.

How: To demonstrate how to use Goal Seek, let's see what level of sales are required to reach breakeven.

1. Click to make Net Income the active cell.
2. Choose **Tools|Goal Seek**. As you see in Figure 6.21, Set Cell contains the address for the active cell.
3. Type the goal in the **To Value** box. In this example, type **0**.
4. In **By Changing Cell**, click the cell or type the cell address where you want Excel to find the value that reaches the goal. In this case, click the Sales cell. Click **OK**.

Figure 6.21 Goal Seek dialog box

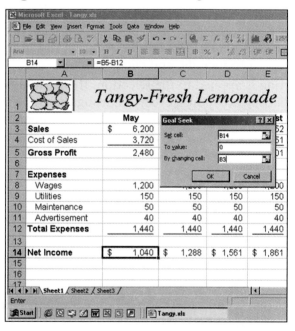

Figure 6.22 Results of Goal Seek

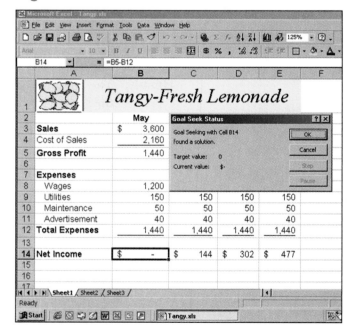

TIPS FROM A PRO. If the dialog box is in the way of the cell you want to click, drag its title bar to move it aside or click the **Collapse Dialog** button.

Result: Excel calculates the number that gives the desired result and displays it in the Goal Seek dialog box and in the worksheet (refer to Figure 6.22). To keep the answer, click **OK**, or you can just jot down the number and then click Cancel to return to your original figures.

Use PinPoint

After gaining the skills in this chapter, you can apply the correct number formatting to the cells and create a custom number format. You can format fonts, alignment, borders, and shading. You can duplicate formats with Format Painter and styles, and you can remove formats.

Now it's time to use the PinPoint software and see what you can do. Remember, whenever you are unsure of how to do something, you can reread that portion of the chapter or you can click Show Me for an explanation and demonstration. Check out these skills in PinPoint:

- Add a cell border
- Apply number formats
- AutoFormat
- Clear cell formats
- Custom format
- Define, apply, and remove styles
- Format a collection
- Format Painter
- Indent cell text
- Merge and center cells
- Modify alignment
- Use Goal Seek

Key Terms

You can find definitions for these words in this chapter:

AutoFormat

Fill

Font

Point

Style

Wrap text

Review Questions

You can use the following review questions to test your knowledge and skills. Answers are given in Appendix D, "Answers to Review Questions."

True/False

Indicate whether each statement is true (T) or false (F).

____ 1. When you change the format of the number, additional symbols such as dollar signs and commas appear in the formula bar as well as in the cell.

____ 2. When you click the Currency Style button, the number is automatically formatted with two decimal places as well.

____ 3. If you want to format a nine-digit number so that it looks like a telephone number with parentheses around the area code and a hyphen in the middle, you must set up a custom number format.

____ 4. To change the font color, you must choose Format Cells and click the Font tab.

____ 5. To add double accounting underline to the contents of a cell, you must access the Format Cells dialog box.

____ 6. You can change both the horizontal and vertical alignment of the contents of a cell.

____ 7. To add a double line beneath the last entry in a worksheet, it's easiest to choose Format Cells and click the Border tab to select the double-line style.

____ 8. When you want to add font, number, alignment, fill, and border formatting in one easy step, use AutoFormat.

____ 9. To remove formatting from a cell, select the cell and press Delete.

____ 10. To calculate the breakeven point, use Goal Seek and set Sales equal to 0.

Multiple Choice

Select the letter that best completes the statement.

____ 1. To format the number 4286.5 so that it appears as $4,286.50:
   a. Click the Currency Style button.
   b. Click the Comma Style button.
   c. Click the Increase Decimals button.
   d. All of the above.
   e. Both a and c.

____ 2. To remove the number formatting from a number but leave the font format as is:
   a. Change the style to Normal.
   b. Change the style to Plain.
   c. Change the number formatting to General.
   d. Change the number formatting to None.
   e. Choose Edit|Clear|Formats.

___ 3. To make a title much larger and bolder than the other text on the worksheet:
   a. Change the font size to 6 and click the Bold button.
   b. Change the font to Arial Bold.
   c. Change the font size to 24 and click the Bold button.
   d. Click the Create Title button.
   e. Choose Format|AutoFormat.

___ 4. The type of horizontal alignment appropriate for numbers you total is:
   a. Left-align.
   b. Center.
   c. Right-align.
   d. Justify.
   e. All of the above.

___ 5. The Alignment tab of the Format Cells dialog box enables you to:
   a. Wrap text so that it appears sideways in the cell.
   b. Rotate the text so that it is at an angle.
   c. Change the vertical alignment so that it is centered between the left and right edges.
   d. Merge cells so that long text overlaps blank cells to the left.
   e. All of the above.

___ 6. Click the Border button on the Formatting toolbar to:
   a. Apply a box around the selected cell or cells.
   b. Apply a line under the cell or cells.
   c. Apply a double line under the cell or cells.
   d. Remove all borders from the cell.
   e. All of the above.

___ 7. To format parts of your worksheet with a different color background, change its:
   a. Fill.
   b. Hue.
   c. Font color.
   d. AutoColor.
   e. Border.

___ 8. The Repeat command can be used to repeat:
   a. The last formatting applied.
   b. The action you just used Undo on.
   c. The cell entry.
   d. The last action, whatever it was.
   e. Both a and b.

___ 9. To create a style, select _____ and choose Format|Style.
   a. A cell that is formatted the way you want it.
   b. The cell or cells you want to receive the new format.
   c. Any cell containing text.
   d. Any blank cell.
   e. Either a or b.

___ 10. The advantage of using styles is that:
   a. You can apply font, number, alignment, border, and fill formatting in one step.
   b. All the cells with that style are consistently formatted.
   c. If you modify the style, all the cells with that style are automatically changed.
   d. The style is continually updated, depending on how the worksheet is calculated.
   e. Either a, b, or c.

Match the letters in Figure 6.23 with the correct items in the list.

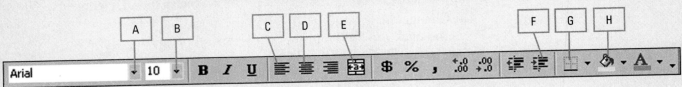

Figure 6.23

___ 1. Click here to change the color of the cells.

___ 2. Click here to center a title above several columns.

___ 3. Click here to change the shape of the letters to a script.

___ 4. Click here to make the size of the cell entry larger or smaller.

___ 5. Click here to center a heading within the cell.

___ 6. Click here to indent a subheading from the left edge of a cell.

___ 7. Click here to place a line along the bottom edge of the cell.

___ 8. Look here to see the default alignment for text.

Exercise and Project

Follow these step-by-step instructions to create the worksheet shown in Figure 6.24. If you are working in a computer lab, ask your instructor where you should save and print your document.

Exercise

1. Open **Wilderness.xls** from the *Student\Chapter 6* folder of the PinPoint CD.
2. Place a title in A1 called **Wilderness Rescue**. Format it as bold and change the font to Elephant or some other bold font.
3. Merge and center this and the *Pro Forma* heading in A2 across the quarters.
4. Fill the merged and centered cells green and make the font color white.
5. Center the quarter headings in row 4 and format them as bold.
6. Format the main headings in column A as bold, and indent the other headings in the column.
7. Place a heavy dashed green line as a border around the assumptions area, G2:J11.
8. Make the label **Assumptions** all caps, delete the colon, and rotate it vertically in the cell. Set the appropriate width for the cell. Use merge-and-center to place the heading along the left edge of the assumptions area. Change the vertical alignment for the cell to Center and the horizontal alignment to Right.
9. Build formulas for the worksheet using cell references to the percents in the assumptions area. (Remember to use absolute values.)
10. Format all percents with a % sign and 2 decimal places.
11. Format dollar values on the first and last rows to have $ signs, 2 decimals, and turn red if the value is negative.

Figure 6.24
Completed exercise worksheet

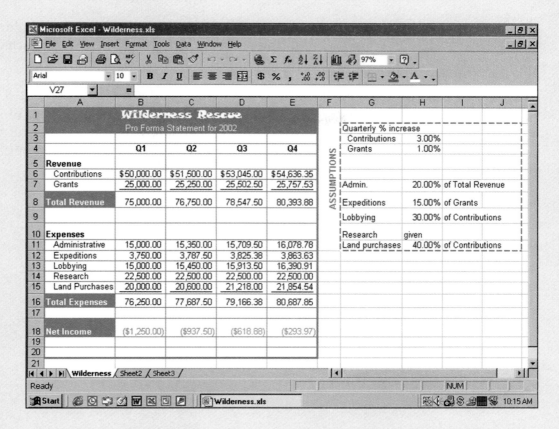

12. Format all other values in the statement area in Comma style. Add underlines above the subtotals.

13. Widen the row height and column width for Total Revenue and fill it with green and change the text to white. Use Format Painter to do the same for Total Expenses and Net Income.

14. Place a heavy green border around cells A1:E20 and a thin green gridline inside the area.

15. Save the file and use Print Preview. Place a page break between the assumptions area and the rest of the worksheet. Center it horizontally and vertically on the page. Place your name and class time in a header. Print the worksheet.

16. Use Goal Seek to find the value for Contributions that would yield a Net Income of 0. (This is the breakeven point.)

17. Highlight A1:E20 and choose Format|AutoFormat. Try various styles and then pick your favorite. Did it re-format the values? Fix any formatting errors.

18. Save and print the worksheet.

Project

As the director for Daisyland Daycare, you need to design a sample spreadsheet that you can give to the parents to show the status of their account each month.

Create a worksheet and place in the corner such things as the center's name and address, and your name as director. Then create a section for the child's name, class, and the parents' name, address and telephone number. Place borders around it.

For the account information, enter the number of children, whether the client pays weekly, bimonthly, or monthly. List the rate for each child, the amount paid, and the amount due. (Use formulas, where necessary).

Enter some sample information for one family with two children

Format the worksheet so that it communicates the type of image you want to project. For instance, you may choose a colorful and playful font at the top with the daycare name and perhaps a clip art image, if you know how to insert one (you'll learn how in Chapter 9). Print in color, if you can.

Chapter 7

Use Functions

Although Excel is easy to learn and use, it offers more than just speed and accuracy for crunching numbers. In fact, one of the features that makes Excel so powerful is the way it simplifies complex calculations through the use of functions. With functions, you don't have to be a math, statistics, or finance genius, or an experienced computer programmer to find the answers you're seeking.

At the end of this chapter, you will be able to:

C E

C	E	
☑	❑	Use basic functions (Average, Sum, Count, Min, Max)
☑	❑	Enter a range by dragging
☑	❑	Use date functions (Now, Date, and Today)
☑	❑	Revise formulas and functions
❑	☑	Use Lookup functions (Hlookup or Vlookup)
☑	❑	Use Paste Function to insert a function
☑	❑	Enter functions using the Formula Palette
☑	❑	Use logical functions (If)
❑	☑	Use conditional formatting
❑	❑	Nest functions inside other functions
❑	❑	Use the Round function

CORE OBJECTIVE: Use basic functions (Average, Sum, Count, Min, Max)

CORE OBJECTIVE: Enter a range by dragging

What: Excel provides a number of *functions* you can use to help you set up routine calculations quickly. These predefined formulas are set up so all you have to do is input the values needed for the calculation. As you know, functions contain an equal sign, the function name, a pair of parentheses, and (nearly always) *arguments* inside the parentheses providing the information needed for the calculation.

You've used the Sum and Average functions before. These simple functions have for their arguments only a range of cells. Several statistical functions work the same way:

- ○ **Sum** adds the contents of cells.
- ○ **Average** finds the average of cells containing values, ignoring cells containing text or blank cells.
- ○ **Count** finds the number of cells containing values, ignoring cells containing text or blank cells.
- ○ **Counta** counts the number of cells containing either text or values, ignoring blank cells.
- ○ **Min** finds the smallest value among the cells.
- ○ **Max** finds the largest value among the cells.

Why: True, you can count the number of cells yourself or search for the largest or smallest by eye, but using functions is easier, especially when you are working with a large number of items.

How: There's the AutoSum button for Sum, and the others are easy to type.

1. Make the active cell where you want the result to be.
2. Begin to type the function entry you want (capitals don't matter):
   =average(
   =count(
   =counta(
   =min(
   =max(
3. Click and drag to select the cells you want to use. (If they are not all adjacent, hold down the **Ctrl** key while you click or drag).
4. Press **Enter**.

Result: Excel puts on the final parenthesis, capitalizes the function name, and places the result in the cell, as you see in Figure 7.1.

Figure 7.1
Functions and their results

	A	B	C	D	E	F	G	H	
1	Sample	Function	Result						
2	5	=SUM(A2:A6)	30						
3	10	=AVERAGE(A2:A6)	10						
4	15	=COUNT(A2:A6)	3						
5	Text	=COUNTA(A2:A6)	4						
6		=MIN(A2:A6)	5						
7		=MAX(A2:A6)	15						
8									

TASK 2 *Use Date Functions*

CORE OBJECTIVE: *Use date functions (Now and Date)*

What: Excel uses functions to perform calculations involving dates. As you know, when you input dates, they are actually serial numbers formatted with a special Date format. The serial number represents the number of days since January 1, 1900. Excel provides three date functions to make it even easier to do calculations, as you see in Table 7.1.

These functions are different from the statistical functions you used in Task 1. Two of them (Today and Now) have no arguments at all—you don't even need to leave a space between the two parentheses. The others have three different arguments, rather than a range of cells. For Date and Time, you have to type specific numbers between the parentheses, separated by commas.

Table 7.1 Date Functions

Use this function	To do this calculation
=Today( )	Place the current date in the cell
=Now( )	Place the current date and time in the cell
=Date(year, month, day)	Place a particular date in the cell
=Time(hour, minute, second)	Place a particular time in the cell

TIPS FROM A PRO: The Today function and the Now function have no arguments, meaning nothing is required to calculate them. Even so, you have to type the parentheses, because all functions have them.

Why: When you want the current date or time every time you open the worksheet, use the Today or Now functions. That's a little different from using Ctrl+; to enter today's date, which is entered automatically but never changes.

When you want to determine how long until you have to start repaying your student loans, or how long it's been since you called your mother, use the Date or Time function to do calculations with dates.

Figure 7.2 Date functions and their results

	A	B
1	Function	Result
2	=TODAY()	4/20/01
3	=NOW()	4/20/01 9:19
4	=DATE(2000,1,1)	1/1/00
5	=TODAY()-DATE(2000,1,1)	475
6	=TIME(12,1,0)	12:01 PM
7	=TIME(12,1,0)-TIME(10,0,0)	2:01 AM
8		

The Now function includes the current time.

Reformat to omit AM or PM

How: You can use the functions to place a certain date or time on the sheet. You can also combine them in calculations. Here are some examples:

○ To find out the number of days between dates (say, the number of shopping days until Christmas), always take the later date and subtract the earlier date: =date(2001,12,25)–today()

○ To find out the amount of time between times (say, the time you began and the time you finished), always take the later time and subtract the earlier time: =time(15,30,00)–time(13,12,00)

Result: The calculations are easy to understand, but the format of the cell varies.

○ If you use the function to display a date in the cell, it is automatically formatted with a Date format.

○ If you use the date functions in a calculation, though, the result has a General format, so you can see how many days between.

○ If you use the time functions in a calculation, the result shows AM or PM, which is misleading. You should reformat the result to General format to show only the number of hours and minutes.

 TIPS FROM A PRO: You can enter dates in different cells and subtract them with a little formula, such as =A1-A2. If you do this, though, the results are something illogical, like March 3, 1900. That's because the answer also has a Date format. Change the format back to General (or click the Comma Style button) so the correct number of days appears.

TASK **3**   *Use the Formula Palette*

C   *CORE OBJECTIVE: Use Paste Function to insert a function*

C   *CORE OBJECTIVE: Enter functions using the Formula Palette*

C   *CORE OBJECTIVE: Revise formulas*

What: So far you've typed all the functions when you wanted them, and that's no problem with Min and Max and so on because they're easy to remember. Excel provides the *Formula Palette* that contains information about the function and each of the arguments required to calculate it. You can access the Formula Palette three ways:

○ Click the **Paste Function** button and choose the function.

○ Click the **Edit Formula** button on the formula bar and choose the function.

○ Type the function name (such as **=Date**) and then press **Ctrl+A(** for Alignment.

Why: When you're using a function you don't often use, particularly if it has several arguments, you'll want to use the Formula Palette to help you remember what to use for the arguments.

USE THE PASTE FUNCTION BUTTON

How: Using the Paste Function button, you can quickly access the Formula Palette.

1. Click the **Paste Function** button. This reveals the dialog box shown in Figure 7.3.
2. Click the category on the left so you can see the list of functions in alphabetical order on the right. Choose **Most Recently Used**, if you know you've used the function recently, or click another category.
3. Click the name of a function to see the arguments it requires and read a description of what the function does.
4. Double-click the function name or click **OK** to see the Formula Palette. Figure 7.4 shows the Formula Palette for the Date function.
5. Type the numbers in the boxes for each argument, or click a cell on the worksheet that contains the numbers. When you are finished, click **OK**.

Figure 7.3 Paste Function dialog box

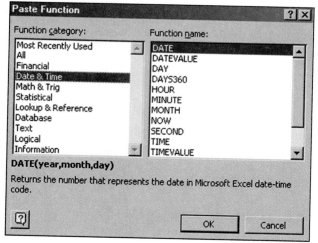

Figure 7.4 Formula Palette

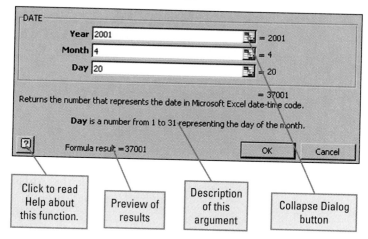

 TIPS FROM A PRO: Remember, you can click the Collapse Dialog button to see the worksheet without the dialog box in the way.

Result: You can use the Formula Palette to help you remember what the arguments are and what order to put them in. This also saves you the trouble of typing the function name, the parentheses, the commas, and everything.

By the way, when you finish with the Date function, the cell entry is properly formatted to show a date, not the serial number result shown in the Formula Palette.

Task 3: Use the Formula Palette **171**

USE THE FORMULA BAR

How: This technique is particularly handy for accessing the Formula Palette for functions you've used recently.

1. Click the **Edit Formula** button on the formula bar. This displays the last function you used, in this case, Date (Figure 7.5).
2. Click the function, if that's the one you want, to access the Formula Palette, or click the down arrow to see more functions, as in Figure 7.6.
3. Click the function name to access the Formula Palette, or choose **More Functions** if you still don't see the function you want. That action opens the Paste Function dialog box that was shown in Figure 7.3.

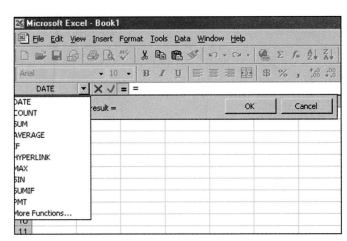

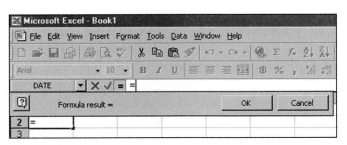

Figure 7.5 Accessing recently used functions

Figure 7.6 Accessing more functions

Result: You can use the Formula Palette to help you remember what the arguments are and what order to put them in. This also saves you the trouble of typing everything.

REVISE A FUNCTION

How: If you're really lazy, like me, you don't even want to type the Average function, though it's easy to remember. Instead, you can click the AutoSum button to enter the Sum function, and then edit it.

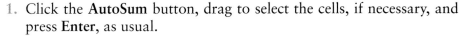

1. Click the **AutoSum** button, drag to select the cells, if necessary, and press **Enter**, as usual.
2. Click the formula bar, and delete the letters **SUM**.
3. In its place, type Average, Max, Min, Count, or Counta. Press **Enter**.

Result: Excel calculates the results of the new formula. You just saved yourself the trouble of typing the equal sign, parentheses, and range address.

E *EXPERT OBJECTIVE: Use lookup functions (Hlookup or Vlookup)*

What: You'll use the lookup functions when you want to look up an answer in a table of some sort. For example, if you have a list of products, you might want to look up the price for each one on the price list stored elsewhere in the workbook.

The Hlookup and Vlookup functions are used to look things up in a horizontal or vertical list, called a ***table array***. Hlookup requires that the list of items be stored in a row, and you'll look up the answer in a row beneath it. Vlookup, on the other hand, has the list of items down a column, and you'll look in another column to the right to see the answer.

Why: Don't look things up in a list if you can have Excel do it for you more quickly and more accurately.

How: Both the Vlookup and Hlookup functions require a list. For example, you might have a price list, like the one shown in Figure 7.7.

You can also use Vlookup for items within a range, rather than an exact match. For example, you might have a list of scores on a test and want to have Excel return a letter grade automatically, as in Figure 7.8. In this case, you must sort the list to start with the *lowest* number. Work your way through, giving the *lowest* possible number for each answer.

This is how you would set up the table array:

1. Create or find the list that contains the information you need.
2. Sort the list in ascending (smallest-to-largest) order. You can do this easily for a vertical list. (To sort a horizontal list, use the Data Sort

Figure 7.7 Sample price list

	A	B
1	**Item**	**Price**
2	Bacon ult cb	3.49
3	Ultimate cb	2.98
4	Jumbo cb	1.39
5	1/4lb burger	0.99
6	Double cb	1.79
7	Jr cheese	0.95
8	Jr hb	0.85
9		

Figure 7.8 Sample grade list

	A	B
1	0	F
2	60	D
3	70	C
4	80	B
5	90	A
6		

command. You'll learn about this in Chapter 13, "Manage Data and Lists.")

- Click anywhere in the first column. (Do *not* select the entire column.)
- Click the **Sort Ascending** button.

The following steps explain how to use Vlookup, but Hlookup is similar.

1. Make the active cell where you want the answer to appear (the answer that you'll look up in the list).

2. Click the **Paste Function** button, select the **Lookup & Reference** category, and choose the **Vlookup** function. The Formula Palette appears, as in Figure 7.9. Fill in the arguments using these guidelines.

   - **Lookup_value.** This refers to the text or number you'll use to look up the answer in the table, for example the cell containing **Jr hb**.
   - **Table_array.** This refers to the range of cells containing the list you'll use to look up the answer, for example the price list.
   - **Col_index_num.** This refers to which column of the table array the answer is in, in this case, Column 2.
   - **Range_lookup.** Because this is optional, the argument name is not shown in bold. You can leave it blank.

Figure 7.9 Vlookup Formula Palette

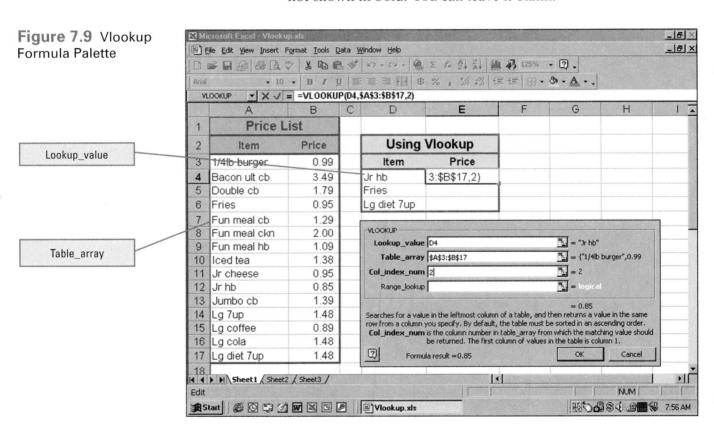

TIPS FROM A PRO: If you're going to copy or fill the formula containing the Vlookup function, be sure to use absolute cell references for the Table_array argument (type $ or press F4).

3. Fill in each of the arguments by typing or selecting cells on the worksheet. When you are finished, click **OK**.

Figure 7.10 Using Vlookup to find an answer

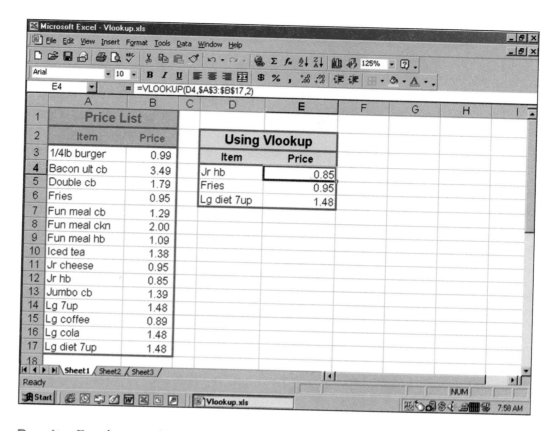

Result: Excel sees what you want to look up, goes down the list and finds a match, and jumps over to the column you specify to find the answer. Then it displays the answer in the cell (Figure 7.10).

Tɪᴘs ꜰʀᴏᴍ ᴀ Pʀᴏ: What are some other places you can imagine using Vlookup or Hlookup?

TASK **5**   *Create Conditional Formulas and Formatting*

What: Sometimes you want one result in a cell under certain conditions, and a different result in the cell if conditions are otherwise. For example, if the sales reps meet their goal, they earn a bonus; otherwise, they get only the regular commission. When you want the formula to change results under certain conditions, use an If function.

Other times you just want to highlight differences by formatting the cell a different way, although the calculation doesn't change. For example, you might want to make the numbers bright orange when values reach the danger zone, but make them green for a safe level. For this, use conditional formatting.

Why: Under certain conditions, the formula may change. You have to use an If function in this case.

IF FUNCTION

CORE OBJECTIVE: *Use logical functions (If)*

How: Here's a typical example of using an If function, and then how to create one.

To calculate the amount of income tax a company owes, you could multiply net income by the tax rate. But what if the company has a bad year and winds up *in the red*, with a negative amount for net income? The formula, shown in Figure 7.11, calculates a *negative* income tax!

Figure 7.11
Negative income tax worksheet

	A	B	C
1		Example 1: Profit	Example 2: Loss
2	Income	$15,528	$11,204
3	Expenses	11,414	14,846
4	Net income	$4,114	($3,642)
5	Tax rate	35%	35%
6	Income tax	$1,440	($1,275)
7			

C6 = =C4*C5

What's a negative income tax—do you think the U.S. Treasury pays the company instead of the other way around? Not likely! Instead, you have to use an If function to determine if a profit was made and therefore if any tax is owed.

1. Click the **Paste Function** button, select the **Logical** category, and click **If**. An If function has three arguments, as you see in the Formula Palette in Figure 7.12.
2. Fill in each of the arguments by typing or selecting cells on the worksheet. In our example, you can see =IF(B4>0,B4*B5,0) in the formula bar. Fill in the appropriate text or formula for each argument as follows:
   - **Logical_test.** This asks you to define what the conditions are. You can use any of the comparisons shown in Table 7.2 for the logical test. For the income tax example, you enter B4>0 (referring to the cell that contains net income).
   - **Value_if_true.** If the result of the logical test is true, which formula calculates the answer? In our example, if net income is greater than zero, the formula is B4*B5.
   - **Value_if_false.** If the result of the logical test is false, which formula gives the correct answer? In our example, if net income is *not* greater than zero, the value is 0.
3. When you are finished, click **OK**.

Table 7.2
Comparison Operators

Operator	Comparison
=	Equal to
<>	Not equal to
>	Greater than
>=	Greater than or equal to
<	Less than
<=	Less than or equal to

Result: The results of the If function change, depending on the conditions. In our income tax example, unprofitable years show $0 owed for income taxes, but profitable years show how much income tax is due.

Figure 7.12 If function's Formula Palette

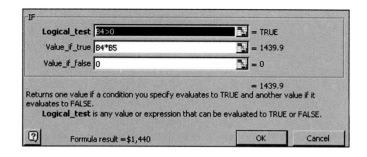

TIPS FROM A PRO: You can use text as one of the arguments of an If function. For example, you might want to display the word *Profit* if the net income is positive, and *Loss* if it is negative. To use text as an argument, you have to put quotation marks around it with the commas outside them, like this: =IF(B4>0, "Profit", "Loss"). If you use the Formula Palette to build the If function, though, Excel automatically supplies the quotation marks for you.

CONDITIONAL FORMATTING

EXPERT OBJECTIVE: Use conditional formatting

How: Use conditional formatting rather than an If function when you want the cell to have a certain appearance, depending on the results of the formula. For the example of student grades, you might want all the scores below 70 to show one color shading, and all the scores above 90 another color, as in Figure 7.13.

1. Select the cell or cells, and choose Format|Conditional Formatting to see the dialog box in Figure 7.14.
2. Specify the comparison: between, not between, equal, not equal, greater than, less than, greater than or equal to, or less than or equal to.
3. Specify a value or click a cell for what you will compare the cell to.
4. Click **Format** to see the Format Cells dialog box. This is the same dialog box you used in Chapter 6, "Format Worksheets," with tabs that enable you to define the format of the font, border, and/or shading for the cell. Set the formats and click **OK** to return to the Conditional Formatting dialog box.
5. Click **Add** to add another condition—you can have up to three, say for high, medium, and low. Click **Delete** to remove one or more of the conditions.
6. Click **OK** when finish, and test it by putting different values in the cell.

Result: The cell shows different formatting, depending on the amount in the cell. To copy the conditional formatting to other cells, use the Format Painter.

	A	B
1	**Test 1 scores**	
2	87	
3	66	
4	94	
5	82	
6	77	
7	74	
8	93	
9	69	
10	84	
11	86	

Figure 7.13 Conditional formatting

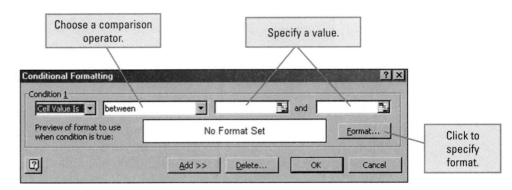

Figure 7.14 Conditional Formatting dialog box

TASK **6**   *Use Nested Functions*

What: You can use a function as an argument in another function, if you need to. When one function appears inside another one, this is called ***nesting***. An example of this is the way you might use the Round function.

The Round function is used to round a number up or down. It has two arguments: the value it's supposed to round, and the number of decimals. The Round function is different from reducing the number of decimals that are visible. Instead, it actually changes the number to eliminate the extra decimal places.

In this example, you can use the Round function to change the value of an Average to eliminate unneeded decimals.

Why: You nest functions when you want to use one inside another one. For example, you nest If statements when you have three or more conditions, such as the traffic signal. See if you can decode this nested If example: =IF(stoplight = green, Go, IF(stoplight = yellow, Proceed with caution, Stop)).

How: You can type the function, if it's a simple one, or use the Formula Palette. Here's an example using the Round function.

1. Click the **Paste Function** button and choose **Round** from the **Math & Trig** category to see the Formula Palette (Figure 7.15).
2. Starting from the bottom argument, enter the number of decimal places. (Set Num_digits to 0 if you want to round to an integer, or whole number.)
3. For the Number argument, use the Average of a series of numbers. Type the formula, or click the down arrow on the formula bar to see

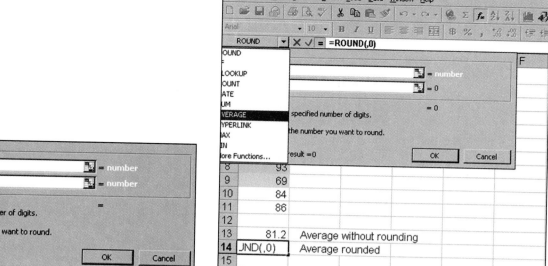

Figure 7.15 Round Formula Palette

Figure 7.16 Choosing a function to use in another function

a list of functions, as in Figure 7.16. Choose Average, and the Formula Palette changes from Round to show the information for the Average function.

4. Select the cells you want to average. Click the formula in the formula bar to return to the Round function, if necessary, or click **OK** to finish the nested function.

Result: You can see the nested function completed in the formula bar in Figure 7.17.

Figure 7.17 Nested functions

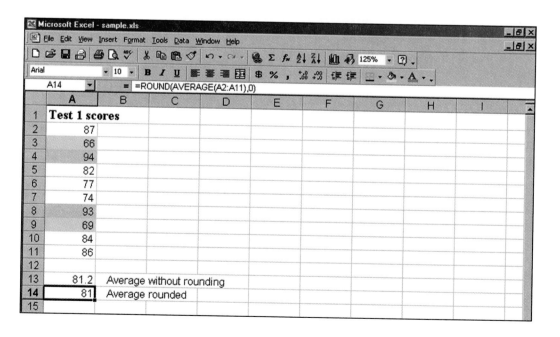

Use PinPoint

After gaining the skills in this chapter, you can create functions by typing, using the Paste Function button, and by using the Formula Palette. You've learned how to use all sorts of functions, including statistical, date, and lookup functions, and you can create conditional functions and formatting, as well as nested functions. Now it's time to try your hand with the PinPoint software and test your skills. Remember, whenever you are unsure of what to do, either reread that portion of the chapter or click Show Me for a demonstration. Check out these skills in PinPoint:

- Conditional formats
- Drag to fill a formula range
- Enter a function
- Nested functions
- Revise formulas
- Use a date function
- Use the Formula Palette
- Use the If function

Key Terms

You can find definitions for these words in this chapter:

Arguments
Formula Palette
Functions
In the red
Nesting
Table array

Review Questions

You can use the following review questions to test your knowledge and skills. Answers are given in Appendix D.

True/False

Indicate whether each statement is true (T) or false (F).

____ 1. Certain pieces of information that functions require to do their calculation are called arguments.

____ 2. The Counta function counts the number of cells in a range that are not blank, whether they contain text, numbers, or formulas.

____ 3. The function you can use to find the smallest number among a range of cells is Least.

____ 4. Use the Present( ) function to insert the current day and time into a cell.

____ 5. You can subtract one date function from another to find out how many days are between them.

____ 6. The trouble with using arithmetic to find out the number of days between two dates is that you may get an answer like March 3, 1900, which doesn't make sense.

____ 7. You can access recently used functions by clicking the check mark on the formula bar.

____ 8. To revise a function, click in the formula bar and retype.

____ 9. The Vlookup function is used to look up the number of days between two dates.

____ 10. Use conditional formatting if you want to calculate tax only if there is a profit, otherwise show 0 for income tax owed.

Multiple Choice

Select the letter that best completes the statement.

____ 1. The function that you can use to find the average of the numbers in a range of cells is:
   a. Average.
   b. Ave.
   c. Avg.
   d. Mean.
   e. =Sum/Count.

____ 2. The easiest way to calculate the average of a range of cells is to:
   a. Click the Average button.
   b. Type =Avg, drag to select the cells, and press Enter.
   c. Type =Average(and then select the cells and press Enter.
   d. Select the cells, right-click, choose Avg, and press Enter.
   e. Click the Paste Function button, scroll to find the Ave function, and click OK.

____ 3. Riding behind any date function is a serial number that counts the number of days since:
   a. You got your computer.
   b. January 1, 1900.
   c. January 1, 2000.
   d. Personal computers were invented.
   e. Excel was invented.

____ 4. The dialog box that Excel provides to help you remember what arguments to use for each function is called:
   a. Argument Wizard.
   b. AutoFormula.
   c. Formula Palette.
   d. Formula Wizard.
   e. Function Wizard.

____ 5. When you have a list of parts and their prices in two columns, you can use a function to refer to it and have Excel find the price for you. When you do this, be sure that you:
   a. Have the list of parts sorted in ascending order.
   b. Have the prices sorted in ascending order.
   c. Apply conditional formatting.
   d. Use all the arguments for the If statement.
   e. All of the above.

____ 6. When you want a formula to display different results, depending on certain conditions, use:
   a. An If function.
   b. Conditional formatting.
   c. A When function.
   d. The Condition Wizard.
   e. A nested function.

7. The correct formula to calculate a bonus of 25% if a sales representative's total orders in cell D2 are greater than $10,000 is:
   a. =IF(D2>10000,D2*25%,0).
   b. =D2>10000(D2*25%,0).
   c. =D2(10000>D2*25%,0).
   d. =WHEN(D2>10000, D2*25%,0).
   e. =D2*25%(IF D2>10000).

8. When you want the results to have a different appearance, depending on the results of a formula, use:
   a. An If function.
   b. Conditional formatting.
   c. A When function.
   d. The Condition Wizard.
   e. A nested function.

9. The function you can use to permanently eliminate unneeded decimals in a number is:
   a. Count.
   b. Decimal.
   c. Max.
   d. Min.
   e. Round.

10. When you use a function as the argument for another function, this is called a(n):
    a. Conditional function.
    b. Double function.
    c. Inner function.
    d. Layered function.
    e. Nested function.

Screen Review

Match the letters in Figure 7.18 with the correct items in the list.

Figure 7.18

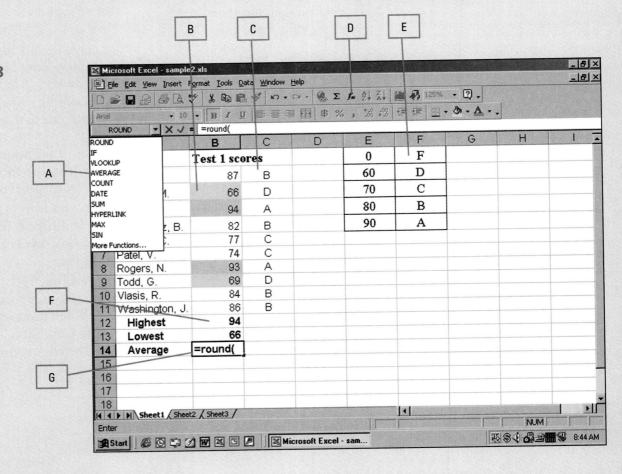

____ 1. Look here to see where a nested function will appear.

____ 2. Click here to access the Formula Palette.

____ 3. Look here to see where conditional formatting has been applied.

____ 4. Look here to see the results of the Vlookup function.

____ 5. Look here to see the results of the Max function.

____ 6. This range is an argument for the Vlookup function.

____ 7. Click here to access the entire list of functions.

Exercise and Project

Follow these step-by-step instructions to create a worksheet. If you are working in a computer lab, ask your instructor where you should save and print your file.

Exercise

1. Open **Sales Quota.xls** from the *Student\Chapter* 7 folder of your PinPoint CD.
2. Calculate the % Quota by dividing Sales by Quota. AutoFill the remaining cells in the column. Format the calculated values with percent signs and two decimals.
3. Sort the rating table in cells J2:K6 in ascending order on the entries in column J.
4. Use VLookup to determine the store's rating based on the % Quota. Center the rating, and fill the formula down.
5. Create an If statement in the Bonus column that will place "Yes" if the rating equals "A" and "No" if it is not. (*Hint*: Remember to use quotation marks around the text arguments.) Center the results and fill down.
6. In cell E13, calculate the average sales. Label it **Average Sales**.
7. In cell E14, find the lowest sales value and label it.
8. In cell E15, find the highest sales value and label it.
9. In cell E16, find the total number of sales made and label this.
10. Create conditional formatting for the rating cells that contain "A" so the cell has a navy blue pattern with a red and bold font.
11. Use Print Preview to change the orientation to landscape and center the sheet on the page. Under Setup, also click the header and place your name at the top left side.
12. Finally, set the print area so that the rating table is *not* included. Print the sheet.

Project

Open the file called **Designs.xls** from the *Student\Chapter* 7 folder of the PinPoint CD. Sort the data by Salesperson. Then use the proper function to find the price per hour for each product, referring to the table in columns H and I. In column E use the Round function to calculate the Total Price rounded to 2 decimals.

Insert 3 rows below the last row for each salesperson. In column D of the first new row for each salesperson, type **Max** and below that type, **Average**, and then **Total.** For example, cells D9, D10, and D11 will have labels for Max, Average, and Total respectively and column E will contain the functions. Nest the Round function and the Average value to round the answer to two decimal places.

In column F next to each person's total, calculate the commission (put a heading in row 2). This is a calculated value using a nested If. The conditions are these:

- If the Total Sales per person is less than 10,000, no commission is given.
- If the Total Sales per person is between 10,000 and 15,000, the commission is 15% of the Total.
- If the Total Sales per person is over 15,000, the commission is 20% of the Total.

Place a currency format on all of the cells where it is appropriate. Apply conditional formatting to highlight the three separate conditions. Place your name and class information in the header and print the worksheet only, without including the table array.

Use Financial Functions

Excel has a set of functions particularly for use in financial calculations. You don't need a special financial calculator to find the payment on a loan, the value of an investment, or the depreciation of an asset. You'll learn how to do all of these calculations in this chapter.

At the end of this chapter, you will be able to:

C E

☑	❏	Calculate the payment on a loan (Pmt)
☑	❏	Calculate the amount to save (Pmt)
❏	❏	Create an amortization table
❏	❏	Use Ipmt and Ppmt functions
❏	❏	Set up a running balance
☑	❏	Find present and future values (Pv and Fv)
❏	❏	Depreciate an asset (Sln, Ddb, Syd)
❏	❏	Calculate book value after depreciation

TASK 1   *Use the Pmt Function*

C   CORE OBJECTIVE: *Use financial functions (Pmt)*

What: The Pmt function calculates the payment on a loan. Pmt, like all of the financial functions, takes into account the ***time value of money***, the fact that money earns interest over time. That is, you can't take out a $12,000 loan for 10 years and expect to pay it back at $100 per month ($100*12*10). No, the bank charges a fee for you to use its money, ***interest***. The amount of interest depends on how much you owe and what the interest rate is, so it's not so easy to figure out how to calculate what the monthly payment will be—unless you use Excel's Pmt function.

Pmt requires three pieces of information to make its calculation:

- ❍ The amount of the loan (**Pv**, the ***present value*** of the loan, or what it's worth today)
- ❍ The interest rate (**Rate**, often expressed as an annual percentage rate or **APR**). The trick with the rate is that you must use the rate *for a single payment*. Thus for a monthly payment, you only pay 1/12 of the annual interest.
- ❍ The length of the loan (the total number of payment periods, **Nper**)

Two other arguments are optional:

- ❍ The ***future value*** of the loan (**Fv**, the amount it'll be worth at the end of the loan)
- ❍ The **Type**, whether you'll pay it at the end of the month (type 0) or beginning (type 1)

Why: You can use Pmt not only to calculate the payment on a loan, but to figure how much money to stash away into savings each month to reach a future goal.

CALCULATE A PAYMENT ON A LOAN

How: First set up the worksheet so you can see the amounts to use to calculate the payment.

1. In the worksheet, type the text shown in Figure 8.1 and fill in appropriate numbers. The example is for a car loan of $17,700, at 10.5% interest for 5 years.

Figure 8.1 Setting up the Pmt function

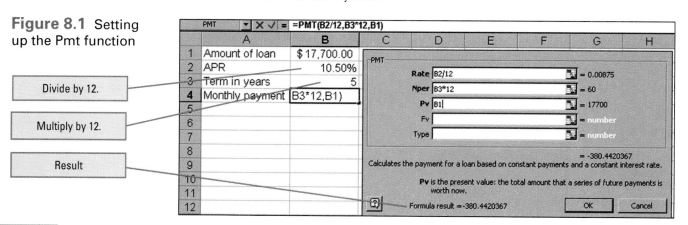

2. Click the **Paste Function** button or click the **Edit Formula** button on the formula bar to access the formula palette for **Pmt** in the Financial category (also shown in Figure 8.1).

  - For **Rate**, click B2 and divide it by 12. Why? B2 holds the *annual* interest rate, but you are looking for a *monthly* payment. You only have to pay 1/12 of the annual interest each month.
  - For **Nper**, click B3 and multiply by 12. Why? Because it's a monthly payment, you'll make 12 payments each year.
  - For **Pv**, click B1. This is how much the loan is worth today, its present value.

3. Click **OK** to finish.

Result: The monthly payment is calculated for the given loan. The payment is negative, meaning the money is going away from you (to the bank).

It's a good idea to set up the Pmt function referring to cells, rather than just typing the loan amount, interest rate, and number of payments in the palette (although you could). This way you can change the amount of the loan, the interest rate, or the length of the loan and see the effect each time on the monthly payment.

 TIPS FROM A PRO: If you don't want to bother with red numbers and parentheses indicating negative values, edit the formula to place a minus sign after the equal: = –**Pmt**.

CALCULATE THE AMOUNT TO SAVE

How: The Pmt function also calculates how much money to sock away into savings to have it grow to a certain future amount. For example, you can use Pmt to find how much to save every month at 5% for 2 years to have $4,000 (in the future) for a trip to Europe. You'll make the deposit at the beginning of every month.

1. In the worksheet, type the text shown in Figure 8.2 and fill in appropriate numbers.
2. Click the **Paste Function** button or click the **Edit Formula** button on the formula bar to access the formula palette for **Pmt** in the Financial category.

  - For **Rate**, click B2 and divide it by 12. Again, you only earn 1/12 of the annual interest each month.
  - For **Nper**, click B3 and multiply by 12. Why? Because it's a monthly payment, you'll make 12 deposits to savings each year.

Figure 8.2 Setting up the Pmt function

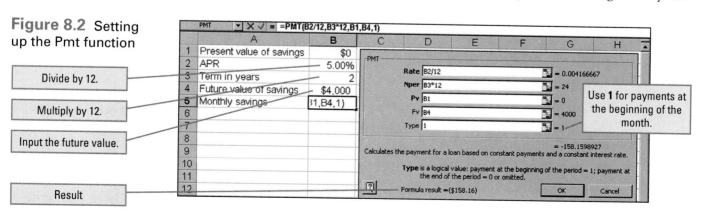

Divide by 12.

Multiply by 12.

Input the future value.

Result

- For **Pv**, click B1. This example shows that you've got nothing to start with, although perhaps you could start by depositing your birthday money, if you had any.
- For **Fv**, click B4. This is the future value, how much you want it to be worth at the end of the 2 years.
- For **Type**, enter 1, meaning you're depositing at the beginning of the month, rather than the end.

3. Click **OK** to finish.

Result: Excel uses Pmt to calculate how much you will save each month to reach the future desired amount.

 THOUGHT QUESTION: Just for grins, find out how much interest your savings earns over the two years. Multiply the monthly savings by 24, and compare it to $4,000. What does the difference represent?

 TIPS FROM A PRO: In Chapter 6, you used Goal Seek to find the breakeven point in an income statement. Goal Seek is also handy with financial functions. For example, in the payment on a loan you calculated in Task 1, you may know how much you can afford as a monthly payment, but not know how much you can borrow. Use Goal Seek to calculate the amount of the loan you can get for a given monthly payment, such as $250, as shown in Figure 8.3.

Warning: You have to set To Value to a negative number if the payment shows a negative result (that is, if you didn't change the function to = –PMT).

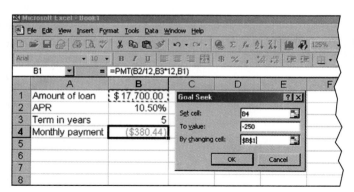 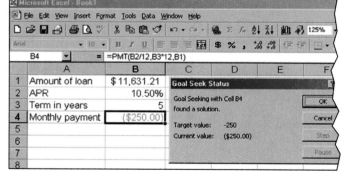

Figure 8.3 Using Goal Seek with financial functions

TASK 2 *Create an Amortization Table*

What: Whether you're a borrower trying to pay off a loan or a tycoon lending money to your less successful brother, you'll like using Excel to create an ***amortization table***. This worksheet shows the progress, payment by payment, toward paying off a loan.

Creating an amortization table requires two new financial functions, Ipmt and Ppmt. Each loan payment you make—each check you write to the bank to repay your car loan or **mortgage** (house loan)—consists of two parts: a fee you pay to the bank (the interest), and part of what you owe on the loan (the **principal**). Here it is in mathematical terms:

$$\frac{\text{Interest}}{\text{+ Principal}} \qquad \frac{\text{Ipmt}}{\text{+ Ppmt}}$$
$$\text{Monthly payment} \qquad \text{Pmt}$$

As you've discovered from any credit card bills you've run up, the first money you pay goes toward interest, and the rest toward the amount you owe (the principal). Because you owe a great deal on the loan at the beginning, most of the payment goes toward interest. As you gradually pay back the loan, you owe less and less interest, and more goes toward principal. For this reason, when you use the Ipmt or Ppmt functions, you have to specify which payment you're talking about. (There's an extra argument, **Per**, the payment number.) However, each month, the amount of the check you write, the Pmt, stays the same.

Why: When you have an amortization table, you can see how much interest and principal you are paying each month. Further, as you pay month by month, you can watch your loan gradually die, the Latin root *mort* (for *die)* being part of *amortization.*

USE IPMT AND PPMT

How: Set up your amortization schedule as in Figure 8.4 to see the interest, principal, and balance for each payment throughout the life of the loan.

1. Set up separate columns for Payment Number, Interest Paid, Principal Paid, and the Balance on the loan after each payment.
2. For the Payment Number (cells A8 and A9), type in numbers 1 and 2, and then select them both. Fill down the column from 1 through 60 (12*5 for this example) or even farther for a longer loan such as a mortgage (12*however many years the loan lasts).
3. For Interest Paid (cell B8), use the Ipmt function.
   - For **Rate**, click B2 and divide it by 12. Again, you only pay 1/12 of the annual interest each month.
   - For **Per**, click A8, the payment number. Remember, the interest changes each month, depending on how much you still owe on the loan.

Figure 8.4 Setting up an amortization table

	A	B	C	D
1	Amount of loan	$17,700.00		
2	APR	10.50%		
3	Term in years	5		
4	Monthly payment	(PMT funct)		
5				
6	Payment Number	Interest Paid	Principal Paid	Balance
7				
8	1			
9	2			

- For **Nper**, click B3 and multiply by 12. Why? Because it's a monthly payment, you'll make 12 payments each year.
- For **Pv**, click B1. This example shows the present value, or the amount of the loan, at the beginning of the loan.

4. Don't click OK yet to finish the function. Plan ahead. You're going to fill this formula down the column, right? So you must use absolute values for the entries for Rate, Nper, and Pv. Press **F4** to change the cell references to absolute. Leave Per relative, though, because you want it to refer to the different payment numbers each time. Click **OK** when you're finished.

 TIPS FROM A PRO: Instead of pressing F4 to make these cells absolute, you can use named ranges. Select the cells and the labels to the left and choose **Insert| Name|Create**. Then build the formula using words instead of $B$1, and so on.

5. Go back and add a minus sign between the = and the Ipmt to eliminate the red numbers and parentheses, so the formula looks like this: = –Ipmt.
6. Fill the formula five or six cells down the column. Does it get less and less each time? Then you've done it correctly. Do you see #NUM! and #VALUE!? If so, you need to go back to cell B8 and add $ to the cell references to make them absolute, as in Step 3.
7. Calculate Principal Paid by taking Pmt and subtracting the current month's Ipmt. Make the reference to Pmt absolute. (Alternatively, you can use the Ppmt function, which has the exact same arguments as Ipmt. Both methods work out the same.)
8. Fill both Ipmt and Ppmt values down the columns.

Result: If you've set up the Interest Paid and Principal Paid columns correctly, the amounts add up to the monthly payment, as you see in Figure 8.5.

 THOUGHT QUESTION: Why is the interest portion higher at the beginning than at the end?

Figure 8.5 Interest and principal payment

	A	B	C	D	E	F	G
		=-IPMT($B$2/12,A8,$B$3*12,$B$1)					
1	Amount of loan	$ 17,700.00					
2	APR	10.50%					
3	Term in years	5					
4	Monthly payment	$380.44					
5							
6	Payment Number	Interest Paid	Principal Paid	Balance			
7							
8	1	$154.88	$225.57				
9	2	$152.90	$227.54				
10	3	$150.91	$229.53				
11	4	$148.90	$231.54				
12	5	$146.88	$233.57				
13	6	$144.83	$235.61				
14	7	$142.77	$237.67				
15	8	$140.69	$239.75				

CREATE A RUNNING BALANCE

How: To complete the amortization table, you need to create a *running balance*. Similar to a running total, it shows the amount in an account after each addition or subtraction. You use a running balance in your checkbook register, for example, where you add each deposit and subtract each check to keep an eye on how much is currently in your account. The amortization table uses a running balance to see how much is left on your loan after each payment.

1. Click the cell in the Balance column *above* Payment 1 to make it the active cell (cell D7 in the example).
2. For the first time only, the balance equals the amount of the loan (=B1, in the example).
3. Click the balance for Payment Number 1 (see Figure 8.6). Enter the formula that takes the previous balance and subtracts the Principal Paid for this payment. In the example, this will be =D7–C8.
4. Drag to fill the formula down the column.

TIPS FROM A PRO: Why do you only subtract the Principal Paid from the previous balance? Because the interest is a fee you pay to the bank for the privilege of using its money. Only the principal you pay reduces what you owe on the loan.

Result: The balance on the loan grows less and less until it equals 0 at Payment Number 60. This means the loan is completely paid off.

THOUGHT QUESTION: What do you find out when you sum the Interest Paid column? Shocking how much interest you pay on a loan, isn't it? What could you change that would reduce the amount of interest you have to pay?

Figure 8.6 Balance on the loan

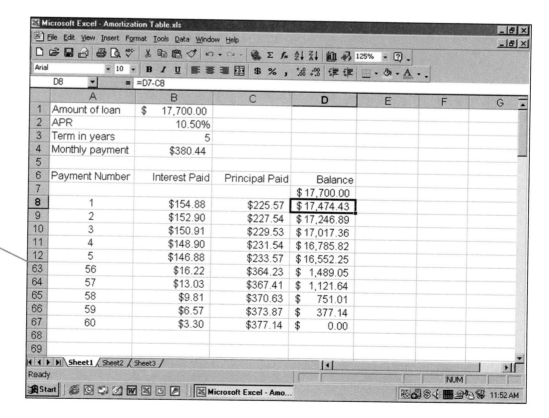

Rows 13-62 are hidden.

CORE OBJECTIVE: Use financial functions (Fv)

What: Because of the way money earns interest, it's hard to tell at a glance the value of a series of payments, month after month or year after year, is worth. When you're saving money, the interest is ***compounded***, that is, the interest itself earns interest. To find out what a series of payments is worth, either today (its present value) or in the future (its future value), use this formula:

$$pv*(1+r)^n + \frac{pmt*(1+r)^n-1}{r} + fv = 0$$

Oh, forget it—you don't have to use that complicated formula! You simply use one of Excel's financial functions, Pv or Fv. (I threw that in there so you can appreciate how wonderful these functions are, and how easy they are to use, compared to the alternative!)

Why: Just as you can't compare the happiness of a long marriage to a single date, you can't compare a series of payments to a single value because of the interest. You have to convert the series of payments to a present value or a future value.

Suppose you save just $10 a month for retirement for the next 40 years. You deposit your savings in a money market account earning 10%. At the end of the time, you would have deposited $4,800. But you know what your account will be worth? Over $63,000! But you don't know that until you find its future value with the Fv function.

Or suppose you win the $20 million lottery. You receive $1 million each year for the next 20 years. What is that $20 million worth today? Some lesser amount because if you had money today, you could put in an account earning 10% interest. You can find out exactly how much by using the PV function to find its present value.

USE FV

How: Let's use the retirement savings example for Fv. This time you'll input the numbers directly into the Formula Palette.

1. Click the **Paste Function** button and choose **Fv** in the Financial category.
2. Enter these figures for the arguments:
   - For **Rate**, enter **10%** and divide it by **12** (you earn 1/12 of the annual interest each month).
   - For **Nper**, enter **40*12**. (Instead of 40, type the number of years you have until you retire).
   - For **Pmt**, enter **10** (or whatever amount you think you can save each month).
   - The Fv and Type arguments are optional, so leave them blank.
3. Click **OK** to see the result.

Figure 8.7 Future value

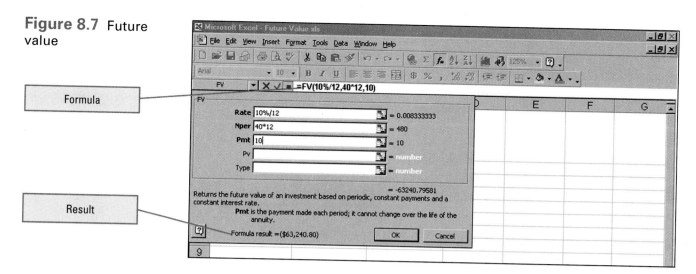

Formula

Result

Result: Your little monthly deposit grows amazingly high, as you see in Figure 8.7. (If you want to get rid of the red numbers and parentheses of the negative formatting, place a minus sign between = and Fv.)

USE PV

How: Let's use the lottery winnings example for Pv. This time you'll input the numbers directly into the formula palette.

1. Click the **Paste Function** button and choose **Pv** in the Financial category.
2. Enter these figures for the arguments:
   - For **Rate**, enter 10%. Do *not* divide by 12, because the $1 million payment only happens once a year.
   - For **Nper**, enter 20. Do *not* multiply by 12, because you only get 20 payments total.
   - For **Pmt**, enter 1000000. Do *not* use commas! If you do, Excel thinks you are separating the arguments.
   - The Pv and Type arguments are optional, so leave them blank.

Result: The amount today that is equal to the $20 million over the next 20 years is much lower than the advertised prize, as you see in Figure 8.8. (If you want to get rid of the red numbers and parentheses of the negative formatting, place a minus sign between = and Pv.)

Figure 8.8 Present value

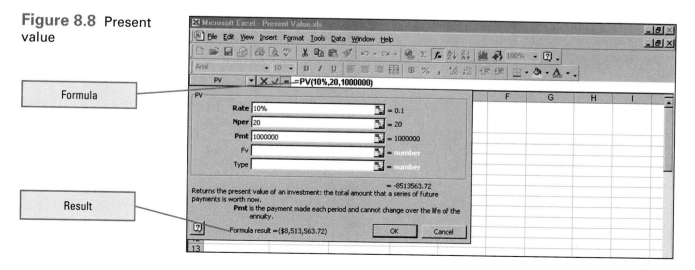

Formula

Result

What: Investments are not the only thing that changes over time. When you purchase any big item, an *asset* such as a building, a vehicle, or some equipment, its value gradually goes down over the years, which is called *depreciation.*

Excel has several functions that calculate depreciation, each using a slightly different calculation. Sln, Ddb, and Syd all use these three arguments:

- ○ *Cost,* what you paid for the asset.
- ○ *Salvage,* what it's worth at the end (such as when you sell it for scrap).
- ○ *Life,* how many years the asset will be used. The number you use here comes from the Internal Revenue Service.

The amount the asset is worth each year after you subtract the depreciation is its *book value.* You may actually be able to sell it for more, but this is its value according to your accounting records, or books—hence the name.

Why: A business uses depreciation to show the way the value of an asset goes down over time. Because it appears on a company's income statement as an expense, it helps reduce the income tax, and that's good.

USE SLN

How: The Sln function calculates depreciation using the *straight-line* method.

1. Begin by setting up the worksheet to show the information about the asset. The numbers are for the example of a computer used for a business (Figure 8.9).

Figure 8.9
Depreciation
worksheet

	A	B	C
1	Cost	$ 2,450.00	
2	Salvage	$ 500.00	
3	Life	5	
4			
5	Year	Sln	Book value
6			
7	1		
8	2		
9	3		
10	4		
11	5		

2. Click the **Paste Function** button and choose **Sln** in the Financial category to access the Formula Palette.
3. Fill in the arguments for the Sln function:
   - For **Cost**, click cell B1. Press **F4** to make it absolute.
   - For **Salvage**, click cell B2. Press **F4** to make it absolute.
   - For **Life**, click cell B3. Press **F4** to make it absolute.
4. Click **OK** to complete the formula, and fill down the column.

Result: As you can see in Figure 8.10, straight-line depreciation calculates the same value for each year.

Figure 8.10
Straight-line depreciation

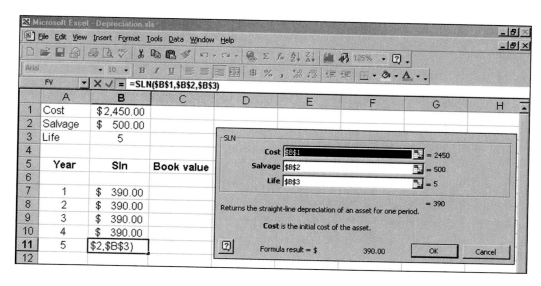

CALCULATE THE BOOK VALUE

How: Book value is a simple running balance, where you subtract this year's depreciation from the previous book value.
1. Click the Book Value cell above year 1, cell C6 in the example. Enter a formula referring to the original cost of the asset, in this case =B1.
2. For the book value in year 1, take the previous book value and subtract the current year's depreciation, in this case =C6–B7.
3. Fill the formula down the column.

Result: If you've calculated the book value correctly, at the end of the life, the book value equals the salvage value.

USE DDB AND SYD

How: Use Ddb to use the *double-declining-balance* method of depreciation, and Syd to use the *sum-of-the-years'-digits* method of depreciation. These functions require one additional argument, **Per**, referring to which year or period. This is because unlike straight-line depreciation, which calculates the same amount each year, Ddb and Syd accelerate the depreciation, allowing more the first year and less in later years.

1. Click the **Paste Function** button and choose **Ddb** or **Syd** in the Financial category to access the Formula Palette.

Figure 8.11 Syd and Ddb depreciation

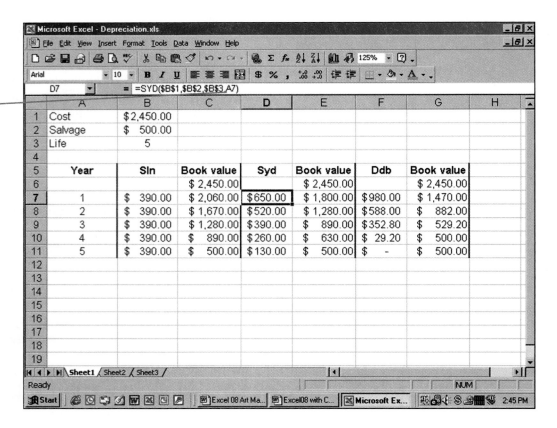

Per

2. Using the computer example shown earlier, enter the arguments for the Ddb or Syd function:
   - For **Cost**, click cell B1. Press F4 to make it absolute.
   - For **Salvage**, click cell B2. Press F4 to make it absolute.
   - For **Life**, click cell B3. Press F4 to make it absolute.
   - For **Per**, click cell A7 to refer to the year number. Do *not* make it absolute, as you want this to change as you fill the formula down the column.
3. Click **OK** to complete the formula, and fill down the column.

Result: As you can see in Figure 8.11, these methods of depreciation calculate a different value for each year, larger at first, smaller later.

Use PinPoint

After gaining the skills in this chapter, you can use several important financial functions to find the value of investments, loans, and assets. You can set up an amortization table and a depreciation table, and you can calculate a running balance. Now it's time to use the PinPoint software and see what you can do. Remember, whenever you are unsure of how to do something, you can reread that portion of the chapter or you can click Show Me for an explanation and demonstration. Check out these skills in PinPoint:

- Use a financial function
- Use Goal Seek

Key Terms

You can find definitions for these words in this chapter:

Amortization table   APR
Asset   Book value
Compound interest   Depreciation
Double-declining-balance depreciation   Future value
Interest   Life
Mortgage   Present value
Principal   Running balance
Salvage   Straight-line depreciation
Sum-of-the-years'-digits depreciation   Time value of money

Review Questions

You can use the following review questions to test your knowledge and skills. Answers are given in Appendix D.

True/False

Indicate whether each statement is true (T) or false (F).

____ 1. You use the Pmt function to calculate the amount of money to borrow.

____ 2. The interest rate is always expressed in annual terms.

____ 3. To access the Formula Palette, click the Paste Function button or click the Edit Formula button on the formula bar.

____ 4. For a monthly payment on a loan, in the Pmt function, always divide the rate by 12.

____ 5. An amortization table is used to show how a loan is gradually paid off.

____ 6. In a monthly payment, Ipmt is always more than Ppmt.

____ 7. A running balance in your checkbook is the amount you have after each deposit and check.

____ 8. To calculate a running balance, you must use absolute cell references.

____ 9. To find out what your monthly savings will be worth in the future, use the Fv function.

____ 10. Depreciation is the way that the value of an asset decreases over the years.

Multiple Choice

Select the letter that best completes the statement.

___ 1. The fee a bank charges to borrow money is:
   a. Amortization.
   b. Compounding.
   c. Depreciation.
   d. Interest.
   e. Principal.

___ 2. In the Pmt function, the amount of the loan will be put in this argument:
   a. Pv.
   b. Rate.
   c. Fv.
   d. Int.
   e. Nper.

___ 3. You would use the _____ function to calculate the amount of monthly savings to reach a future goal.
   a. Ddb.
   b. Fv.
   c. Pmt.
   d. Ppmt.
   e. Pv.

___ 4. When you know how much you can afford for a monthly payment and want to find out how big a loan you can get, use:
   a. An amortization table.
   b. A depreciation table.
   c. Goal Seek.
   d. Pmt.
   e. A running balance.

___ 5. To find out how much of a single monthly payment is interest, use:
   a. APR.
   b. Fv.
   c. Int.
   d. Ipmt.
   e. Ppmt.

___ 6. The amount your monthly savings will grow to over the years is worth:
   a. Less than the total deposited.
   b. The same as the total deposited.
   c. More than the total deposited.
   d. The total deposited times the interest rate.
   e. An unknown amount.

___ 7. To calculate a monthly payment, the Rate argument should be:
   a. The APR divided by 12.
   b. The APR times 12.
   c. The Nper divided by 12.
   d. The Nper times 12.
   e. None of the above.

___ 8. The function that shows the same amount of depreciation each year is:
   a. Ddb.
   b. Int.
   c. Pv.
   d. Sln.
   e. Syd.

___ 9. The function that shows different amounts of depreciation each year is:
   a. Ddb.
   b. Int.
   c. Pv.
   d. Sln.
   e. Both a and d.

___ 10. The amount that an asset is worth at the end of its life is its:
   a. Amortization.
   b. Book value.
   c. Current value.
   d. Present value.
   e. Salvage value.

Screen Review

Match the letters in Figure 8.12 with the correct items in the list.

Figure 8.12

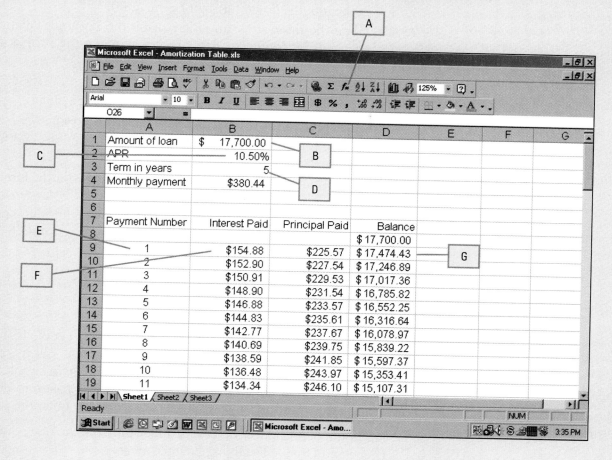

_____ 1. Look here to see a running balance.

_____ 2. This number is calculated by the Pmt function.

_____ 3. Click here for the Rate argument and divide by 12.

_____ 4. Click here for the Pv argument.

_____ 5. Click here for the Nper argument and multiply by 12.

_____ 6. This number is calculated by the Ipmt function.

_____ 7. Click here to access the Formula Palette.

Exercise and Project

These exercises will have you work through various tabs of the file called **Fin Functions.xls** in the *Student\Chapter 8* folder of the PinPoint CD.

Exercise 1

Assume you have a 1997 Chevrolet with a trade-in value of $4,000. You have just fallen in love with a 2000 new Jeep Grand Cherokee with a sticker price of $29,000 and want to determine your monthly payment. After shopping around for the best financing deal, you end up with a 5-year loan at 6.5% annual interest. Use this information to fill in the **Amortization** tab of the **Fin Functions** workbook, and calculate your monthly payment. Format the cells appropriately then follow these steps:

1. Fill in the months down through Payment 60.
2. Calculate the Interest for month 1 using the Formula Palette. Assume the formula will be copied so don't forget to make the proper cell references absolute.
3. Calculate the Principal for month 1.
4. Calculate the Outstanding Balance after the first payment.
5. Start the formula for the running sum on the Interest.
6. Format the top row of calculations. Copy the functions and formulas down through the last payment.
7. Freeze the panes beneath the column headings: Month, Interest, Principal, and so on. Scroll down to row 70.
8. Review using Goal Seek: Play "what if" by changing the payment to $280 per month and determine how high the loan amount could be.
9. Make the worksheet fit on one page and print the cells.
10. Save the file to your disk.

Exercise 2

You just started a new company that rents bicycles to people in a city park. The bikes cost you $6,000 and, after being ridden hard for 3 years, can be sold for $800. Use the **Depreciation** tab of the **Fin Functions** workbook, and fill in the three different depreciation tables on the worksheet. Be sure to use absolute cell references in the appropriate places before copying the functions and formulas.

1. Fill in the depreciation functions under the Straight Line, Sum of the Years' Digits and Double Declining Balance areas.
2. Find the Book Value in all three scenarios.
3. Note which method depreciates the bicycles the fastest and the slowest.
4. Print the cells and use landscape orientation if it suits the data better.
5. Show the formulas and print again. Toggle the formulas off and save.

Exercise 3

For this exercise, use the **Investments** tab of the **Fin Functions** workbook. For each problem, enter the numbers directly into the Formula Palette, if you want, rather than referring to cells on the worksheet.

1. Assume you have landed your first job after graduation. You are planning for the future and the taxes you will have to pay this year on your income so you decide to put $1,000 a year away in an IRA account. The account will earn 8% annual interest and you plan to leave the money there for 25 years. How much money will you have when you are ready to retire in 25 years? (Hint: What will it be worth in the future?)
2. Suppose you have a goal to accumulate a million dollars by the time you retire. How much money do you need to put in every year for 25 years at 8% annual interest to acquire this? (*Hint*: What payment will you make to your savings account to accumulate a certain value in the future?)

3. What if you just inherited $50,000 and could earn 7% annual interest for 4 years in a Certificate of Deposit? How much money will you have accumulated at the end of 4 years? (*Hint*: The $50,000 is a lump sum or present value and there are 0 payments being made to the account.)

4. How much money would you have to place in an interest-bearing account today in order to have $6,000 for a down payment on a new car in 4 years? Assume you can earn 6% interest on your money. (*Hint*: This is a lump sum you are placing in the account.)

5. Print the worksheet. View the formulas and print again. Toggle off the formulas and save.

Projects

Set up a worksheet like Figure 8.13.

Figure 8.13

Make & Model	Car 1:	Car 2:	Car 3:
Loan Value			
Annual Interest			
Years			
Monthly Payment			
Affordable?			
Goal Seek Value		Make & Model	

Search the Web or use the Sunday newspaper to find three cars you could feasibly own. If you have a car you can trade in, determine a reasonable amount for it and then calculate the loan value needed for each car you find. Next, call at least two lending institutions or car dealers in your area to find the interest rate for a five-year loan. Calculate the payment, and then use an If function to place "Yes" in the cell if the payment is under $300 and "No" if not. If none of the cars you picked were affordable, use the Goal Seek method to find the loan value that would be acceptable. Then find the make and model of that car and place it in the last cell of the table.

Determine how much you would need to start putting in a savings account today until you graduate in order to place a down payment that is equal to 1/3 of the cost of the car. Assume a 4% interest rate.

Work with
Pictures and Objects

Live it up! Illustrations, decorative graphics, and clip art all add pizzazz to a worksheet.

At the end of this chapter, you will be able to:

C   **E**

❏	❏	List various sources for pictures
☑	❏	Insert, move, and delete a picture
❏	❏	Size and crop pictures
❏	❏	Change image control settings
☑	❏	Create shapes, lines, and other objects
❏	❏	Insert a text box
☑	❏	Modify lines and objects
❏	❏	Use WordArt

TASK **1**   *Insert Pictures*

Core Objective: Insert, move, and delete an object (picture)

What: To illustrate, decorate, or enhance a worksheet, add pictures. You can get pictures from a number of sources:

- ○ Thousands of images come with Office 2000 in the Clip Gallery, and many more are available through Clips Online.
- ○ Nearly any image you see on the Web can be yours by right-clicking it and choosing Save Image As or Save Picture As. (Of course, you've got to pay attention to copyright issues before you use it.)
- ○ You can scan any picture, if you have access to a scanner, or take photographs with a digital camera, if you have one.
- ○ You can draw your own illustration using the Paint accessory or other drawing software.
- ○ You can create simple images and diagrams with the drawing features in Excel. You'll learn about this in Task 3.
- ○ You can illustrate with decorative text, as you'll see in Task 5.
- ○ Any picture you can copy to the Clipboard can be pasted into Excel.

Why: Get your message across by including an illustration or diagram. Break up long rows and columns of numbers with white space and colorful images. Jazz up a worksheet by giving your readers something to look at. They will thank you.

USE THE CLIP GALLERY

How: The Microsoft Clip Gallery is a nice little program that organizes the thousands of professionally drawn *clip art* images that accompany the Office programs. (The Clip Gallery also contains sounds and motion clips, but they are not useful in printed worksheets.) Place the insertion point where you want to insert a picture.

1. Choose **Insert|Picture|Clip Art**. This opens the Insert ClipArt window, shown in Figure 9.1.

Tips from a Pro: You might have to insert the Office 2000 CD-ROM into the drive before you access the Clip Gallery with the Insert|Picture command.

2. Click a category to browse through the collection of small versions or *thumbnails* of the pictures.
3. If you prefer, type a keyword in the **Search for Clips** box to search for pictures that fit your description from all the categories.
4. Place the mouse pointer over an image and pause to see a short description, file size, and file type.
5. Click the image you want to insert, and a pop-up menu appears, as you see in Figure 9.2.
6. Click the top button to insert the image into your worksheet.
7. Close the Clip Gallery to return to the worksheet and see the picture inserted.

Task 1: Insert Pictures   **203**

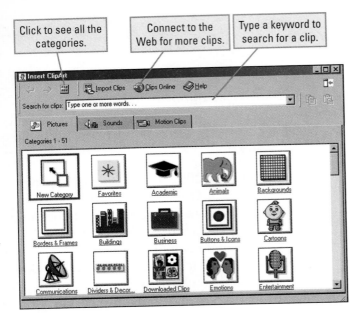

Click to see all the categories.

Connect to the Web for more clips.

Type a keyword to search for a clip.

Figure 9.1 Clip Gallery

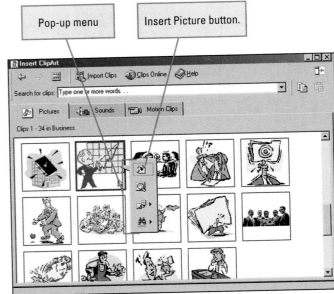

Pop-up menu

Insert Picture button.

Figure 9.2 Inserting clip art

Result: The picture appears in the worksheet, aligned with the top-left corner of the active cell and overlapping the cells beneath it. It is surrounded by eight boxes, called *sizing handles*, which you use to change the size of the picture.

TIPS FROM A PRO: If you are going to insert several pictures throughout the worksheet, minimize the Clip Gallery instead of closing it. That way you can quickly return and insert more pictures when you're ready.

INSERT A PICTURE FROM A FILE

How: If you have a picture of your own, whether it's from a scanner, another clip art collection, or from the Web, you can insert it into a document.

1. Choose **Insert|Picture|From File**.
2. Navigate using the dialog box until you see the file name. The dialog box resembles the Open dialog box, as you see in Figure 9.3. You may have to change folders or drives to the location where the file is stored.
3. Click the file name to preview the image, and double-click to insert it.

TIPS FROM A PRO: You can add your own scanned pictures or downloaded images to the Gallery. The Clip Gallery has its own Help system and you can learn details there.

Result: The picture is inserted into the worksheet aligned with the top-left corner of the active cell and overlapping the cells beneath it and surrounded by sizing handles.

Whenever you insert a picture, the size of the file also increases dramatically. If storage space is limited, such as on a floppy disk, you might have to omit some of the pictures.

TIPS FROM A PRO: Various types of files can be used as images in Excel workbooks. We typically refer to the file type by its three-letter file extension. Table 9.1 shows a few of the commonly used file types and their features.

Table 9.1 Some Graphics File Types Excel Can Use

Image file type	File extension	Features
Bitmap	.bmp	Graphics format used by Microsoft Paint and other programs
TIFF	.tif	Graphics format often used by scanner software
GIF (pronounced "jif")	.gif	Graphics format used for small clip art files found on the Web
JPEG (pronounced "jay-peg")	.jpg	Compressed image format used for photographs on the Web
Windows Metafile	.wmf	Format used for many images in the Clip Gallery; may be converted to drawing objects and modified

 THOUGHT QUESTION: Why should you not use the File|Open command for a picture file?

MOVE (POSITION) A PICTURE

How: A picture appears in a layer above the worksheet and can be placed anywhere on the sheet by dragging it.

1. Click the picture to select it (you'll see the sizing handles appear).
2. Place the mouse pointer on the picture, and it will turn into a four-headed arrow.
3. Drag.

Result: The picture is moved to a new location.

 TIPS FROM A PRO: You can specify what happens to the picture when you rearrange the cells in the worksheet. To do this, choose Format|Picture and click the Properties tab (Figure 9.4).

Figure 9.3 Insert Picture dialog box

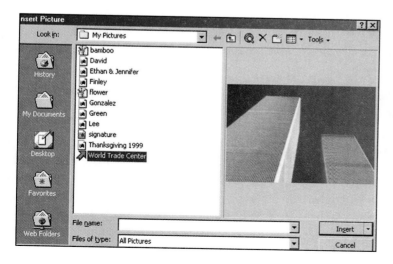

Figure 9.4 Picture positioning

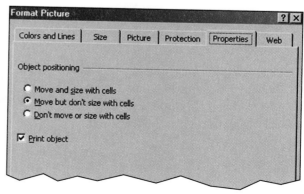

Task 1: Insert Pictures

DELETE A PICTURE

How: To delete a picture, click to select it and then press **Delete** or **Backspace**.

Result: The picture is removed, and the size of the file will be smaller when you save it.

TASK 2   *Modify Pictures*

What: When you've inserted a picture into a document, you can modify the picture to fit your needs. Some of the ways you can change a picture include these:

○ Size it larger or smaller.

○ *Crop* or trim off one or more edges.

○ Change it to black and white or *grayscale* (shades of gray) instead of color.

○ Increase or reduce contrast and brightness, just like a television screen.

The first step in modifying is to click the picture to select it. When you do this, the Picture toolbar appears, offering a number of buttons for modifying the picture. You can see this in Figure 9.5.

Figure 9.5 Selected picture

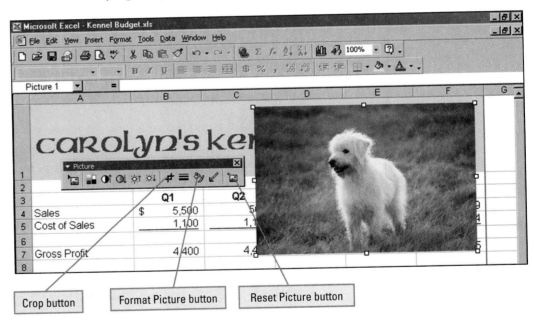

Crop button   Format Picture button   Reset Picture button

 TIPS FROM A PRO: If the Picture toolbar doesn't appear automatically, right-click the picture and choose **Show Picture Toolbar** from the shortcut menu.

Why: A picture has to fit the worksheet, not only in the choice of image, but also in its size and appearance. To focus in on a portion of the image and trim off extraneous parts of the picture, you can crop it. If you're printing on a black-and-white printer or duplicating on a regular copier, you'll want to use pictures that look good in black and white. You can apply these effects and see how they improve your document.

SIZE A PICTURE

How: You can change the size of a picture by using the mouse or by accessing the Format Picture dialog box.

1. To use the mouse, click the picture to reveal the sizing handles.
2. Place the pointer over a corner sizing handle until it turns into a diagonal two-headed arrow. Drag in or out, and the picture changes size but stays in proportion.
3. Place the mouse pointer over an edge sizing handle and drag. This distorts the picture by squashing or stretching it. If you don't like the result, click the **Reset Picture** button on the Picture toolbar to restore the original proportions.

The Format Picture dialog box offers other options.

1. Click the picture to select it.
2. Open the Format Picture dialog box by clicking the Format Picture button on the Picture toolbar, choosing Format|Picture from the menu, or right-clicking and choosing Format Picture from the shortcut menu.
3. Click the **Size** tab to see the dialog box shown in Figure 9.6.
4. Type the exact measurements for height and width, or specify a percent to increase or reduce the picture. If you made a mistake and want to return to the original picture settings, click **Reset**.

Result: Changing the size of the picture alone does not affect the file size, so you won't save disk space by making a picture smaller.

CROP A PICTURE

How: To crop a picture, you can use the mouse or the dialog box.

1. To use the mouse, click to select the picture.
2. Click the **Crop** button on the Picture toolbar, and the mouse pointer changes to indicate cropping.
3. Drag a corner or edge sizing handle toward the center of the picture. You can see cropping in Figure 9.7.

Figure 9.6 Size tab of the Format Picture dialog box

Figure 9.7 Cropping a picture

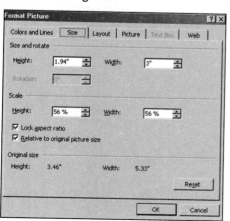

Figure 9.8 Picture tab of the Format Picture dialog box

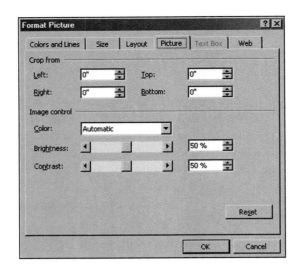

Result: The edge of the picture is trimmed, changing the overall dimensions of the picture, but the size of the image remains unchanged. (You can see how to set cropping measurements in the Picture tab of the Format Picture dialog box in Figure 9.8.)

TIPS FROM A PRO: After you've cropped a picture, the edges you trimmed aren't gone. You can use the Crop tool and drag outward to restore them.

CHANGE IMAGE CONTROL SETTINGS

How: When you have a picture selected, you can change it from color to black and white and adjust the contrast and brightness.

- ❍ Click the **Image Control** button and choose **Grayscale, Black & White,** or **Watermark** from the list.
- ❍ Repeatedly click one of the **Contrast** buttons to increase or decrease the contrast.
- ❍ Repeatedly click one of the **Brightness** buttons to increase or decrease the brightness.
- ❍ Click the **Format Picture** button and click the **Picture** tab to use the dialog box shown in Figure 9.8. Here you specify in inches the amount to crop off each edge, as well as indicate the image control, contrast, and brightness settings you prefer.
- ❍ Click **Reset** in the dialog box to return the picture to its original form.

Result: The picture is modified in the worksheet.

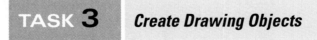

TASK **3**   *Create Drawing Objects*

C   CORE OBJECTIVE: *Create and modify lines and objects*

What: Click the **Drawing** button on the Standard toolbar, and a new toolbar, shown in Figure 9.9, appears at the bottom of the window.

Figure 9.9 Drawing toolbar

The buttons on the Drawing toolbar have useful tools for—what else?—drawing objects, such as shapes and lines. Not only can you make simple squares, circles, ovals, and lines, but Excel provides *AutoShapes*, a gallery of typical shapes such as stars, pentagons, block arrows, and so forth. You can also use a *text box* to position a block of text independent from the cells.

Other buttons on the Drawing toolbar are useful for modifying these objects, such as changing their fill color, borders, line style, rotation, shadow, or 3-D effect.

Figure 9.10 The AutoShapes menu

Why: You can't always find clip art to express your ideas; sometimes you need to draw a quick diagram. You might also want to use an arrow to draw attention to a particular component of your worksheet, but you can't just scrawl something by hand; that wouldn't look professional. The drawing tools make it easy to draw, modify, and position objects such as these.

DRAW SHAPES AND LINES

How: Use the buttons shown in Table 9.2 to draw various drawing objects. Use AutoShapes to draw certain preset shapes. You can see the menu selections and some basic shapes in Figure 9.10.

Table 9.2 Shape- and Line-Drawing Buttons on the Drawing Toolbar

Button name	Button	Drawing method
Line		• Drag on the page to draw a straight line. • Ctrl+drag on the page to draw a line extending both directions from a center point. • Shift+drag to constrain the line to 15-degree angles.
Arrow		• Drag from the tail to the head of the arrow. • Shift+drag to constrain the line to 15-degree angles.
Rectangle		• Drag from corner to corner to draw a rectangle. • Click once to draw a one-inch square. • Shift+drag to draw a perfect square of any size. • Ctrl+drag to draw a rectangle outward from a center point.
Oval		• Drag to draw an oval. • Click once to draw a one-inch circle. • Shift+drag to draw a perfect circle of any size. • Ctrl+drag to draw an oval outward from a center point.
AutoShapes		• Click once to draw the shape a preset size (usually about an inch). • Drag to draw the shape any size. • Shift+drag to keep height and width in proportion. • Ctrl+drag to draw outward from a center point.

Result: When you draw an object, whether it's a shape or a line, the item appears as a floating object above the text, surrounded by sizing handles. Just as with pictures, you can drag it to position it on the page or use the sizing handles to size the object.

TIPS FROM A PRO: To keep an object in proportion while resizing it, press **Shift** as you drag a corner sizing handle.

TIPS FROM A PRO: To draw curved lines, arcs, or irregular objects, use AutoShapes.

TIPS FROM A PRO: You can add text inside a shape, as well. For example, you might want a burst shape containing the words "New and Improved." To do this, right-click and choose **Add Text**.

INSERT A TEXT BOX

How: Draw the text box and then type the text inside it.

1. Click the **Drawing** button to display the Drawing toolbar, if necessary.
2. Click the **Text Box** button.
3. Perform one of the following actions:
   - Drag anywhere on the worksheet to define the size the box so text wraps within it.
   - Click the page to make a text box that automatically widens to contain the text in a single line.

Result: An empty text box appears, surrounded by a thick border with eight sizing handles (Figure 9.11).

Figure 9.11 A sample text box

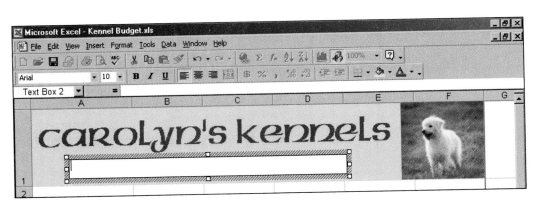

TASK **4**   *Modify Drawing Objects*

What: You can change the color of an object's fill and line, control its line style, add shadows and 3-D effects, and control the way it appears relative to other objects.

Why: Use the colors and effects that best communicate your message.

Figure 9.12 Fill
Color menu

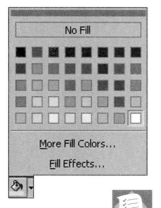

CHANGE FILL

How: When you first draw a shape, it is filled in white with a thin black border. You can add color, shading, and fill effects to a selected shape by using the Fill Color button, or remove the color so that it is transparent so the underlying cell contents appears.

This is the same button that appears on the Formatting toolbar, but when you have an object selected before you click it, you get more choices than just the colors.

Click the **Fill Color** button to see the menu shown in Figure 9.12. Here you can click a color to fill the shape, or click **More Fill Colors** to open a dialog box offering even more colors.

TIPS FROM A PRO: Don't see the color you want on the color palette? You can customize the palette to include different colors. You'll find out how in Chapter 16 "Work with Templates and Macros."

After you select a color, you can add fill effects. Click the **Fill Effects** button on the Fill Color menu to see the Fill Effects dialog box.

❍ On the **Gradient** tab, shown in Figure 9.13, you can choose to shade from one color to another.
❍ The **Texture** tab, shown in Figure 9.14, offers a selection of realistic textures you can give to the object, such as paper, marble, and wood. Two little-used options are those to apply a colored pattern or picture to fill an object.
❍ The **Pattern** tab enables you to add black lines or dots on top of the fill color is shown in Figure 9.15.
❍ Click the **Picture** tab to insert a picture inside the shape.

Figure 9.13 Gradient Fill Effects

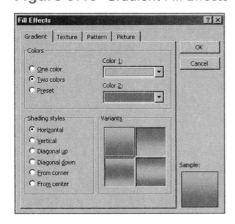

Figure 9.14 Texture Fill Effects

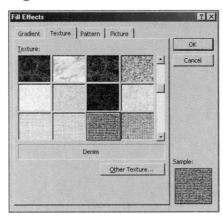

Figure 9.15 Pattern Fill Effects

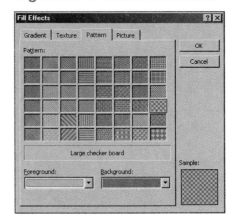

Result: Samples of each of the fill options are shown in Figure 9.16. To remove the fill, click the **Fill Color** button and choose **No Fill**.

TIPS FROM A PRO: Check out the preset gradient color schemes such as Early Sunset and Rainbow for some extra-fancy fills.

Figure 9.16 Sample fills

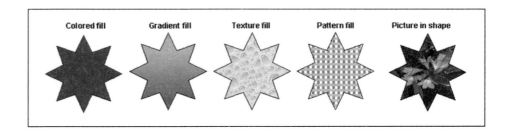

Colored fill   Gradient fill   Texture fill   Pattern fill   Picture in shape

LINE COLOR, DASH STYLE, AND ARROW STYLE

How: First click the object to select it. You can then modify the lines of an object to a different color, thickness, or line style.

❍ The choices you get when you click the **Line Color** button are similar to those for the Fill Color button.
❍ When you click the **Line Style** button, you see the variety you can apply to the shapes and lines you've drawn (Figure 9.17).
❍ If you want, you can change any of these to dotted or dashed lines by clicking the **Dash Style** button (Figure 9.18).
❍ The **Arrow Style** button works only on lines, not shapes. Some arrow choices are shown in Figure 9.19.

Figure 9.17 Line Style choices

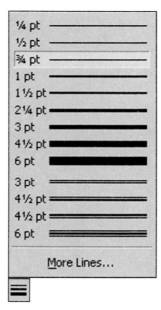

Figure 9.18 Dash Style choices

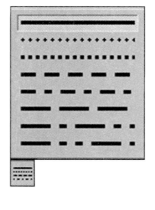

Figure 9.19 Arrow Style

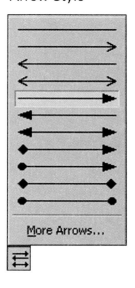

Result: As with fill color, if you want a shape to have no line at all, click the **Line Color** button and choose **No Line**. You can combine these effects to good effect. Sample line styles are shown in Figure 9.20.

TIPS FROM A PRO: The currently selected fill color and line color are shown on the Fill Color and Line Color button. If you want to repeat the color on another object, you can simply click the button. You don't have to display the menu to find the color you want.

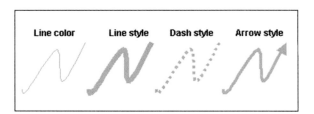

Figure 9.20 Sample line styles

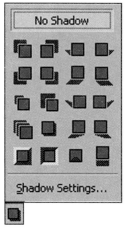

Figure 9.21
Shadow effects

Figure 9.22 Shadow Settings
toolbar

SHADOW AND 3-D EFFECTS

How: Two of the most amazing modifications you can make are with the Shadow and 3-D buttons. Using these buttons give your flat shapes a three-dimensional appearance.

Shadows behind an object make it appear as if it were floating above the paper. They come in a variety of presets that you can access by clicking the **Shadow** button, as you see in Figure 9.21. If you want even more choices for a shadow's color and offset, choose **Shadow Settings** to see the Shadow Settings toolbar, shown in Figure 9.22. To remove a shadow, click the **Shadow** button and choose **No Shadow**.

3-D effects add a three-dimensional effect to a shape or line to give some depth to the object. When you click the 3-D button, you're offered a variety of 3-D effects (Figure 9.23). Choose **3-D Settings** to see the 3-D Settings toolbar, shown in Figure 9.24, which allows you to customize the color, rotation, depth, lighting, and surface texture.

Figure 9.23 3-D effects   **Figure 9.24** 3-D Settings toolbar

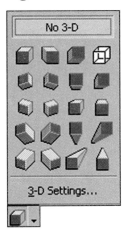

Result: You can see some sample 3-D and shadow effects applied to various shapes in Figure 9.25.

Figure 9.25 Sample 3-D and shadow effects

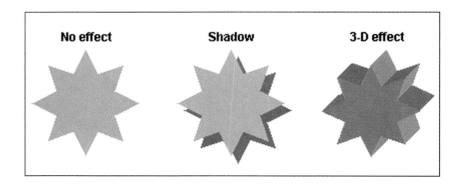

No effect   Shadow   3-D effect

ROTATE AND FLIP AN OBJECT

How: When an object is not going the right direction, you can flip or rotate it to your preference. When you want to pivot the object so that it is at a different angle, you can change its rotation. If you want a mirror image of the object, you can flip it.

To rotate an object:

1. Select the object so that sizing handles surround it.
2. Click the Free Rotate button. This changes the sizing handles to green circles and changes the mouse pointer as well.
3. Drag any of the green handles to pivot the object, as you see in Figure 9.26.
4. When you are finished, click away from the shape to return to the normal mouse pointer.

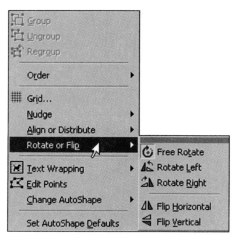

Figure 9.26 Rotating an object

Other times you need to rotate an object exactly 90 degrees or flip it around completely so that it faces the other direction. A menu choice does this for you. Click the **Draw** button on the Drawing toolbar and click **Rotate or Flip** to see the menu in Figure 9.27.

Result: You can see samples of the effects of rotating and flipping an object vertically and horizontally in Figure 9.28.

Figure 9.27 Draw|Rotate or Flip menu

Figure 9.28 Sample objects rotated and flipped

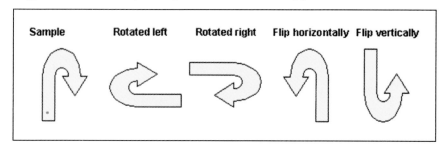

Sample   Rotated left   Rotated right   Flip horizontally   Flip vertically

TIPS FROM A PRO: Rotation and flipping work only on drawing objects, not on pictures or clip art. However, if the clip art image is a Windows Metafile (wmf), you can ungroup it (as explained in the section titled "Align, Stack, and Group Objects") to change it into drawing objects. Then you can modify it in parts or as a whole.

SELECT MULTIPLE OBJECTS

Figure 9.29 Multiple objects selected

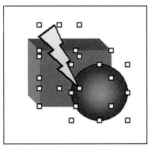

How: When you want to apply the same effect to several objects, it's easiest to select the objects first and then apply the formatting. You can select objects in two ways:

- ○ Click the **Select Objects** button on the Drawing toolbar and drag to surround all the objects with a dotted line. When you finish selecting, click the **Select Objects** button again to restore the normal mouse pointer.
- ○ Click the first object, hold down the **Shift** key, and select additional objects. If you want to eliminate one selected item while keeping the others, hold down the **Ctrl** key and click the one to omit.

Result: Sizing handles surround the selected objects, as you see in Figure 9.29.

TIPS FROM A PRO: To add the same format to several objects, select them all or group them before you apply the effect.

ALIGN, STACK, AND GROUP OBJECTS

How: When you have created several drawing objects that together make up the diagram or art for your document, you might want to align them precisely, arrange them in various layers on top of one another, or group them to be a single unit. The choices on the Draw menu of the Drawing toolbar make this a breeze.

- ○ To align several objects, select them, choose **Draw|Align or Distribute**, and specify an alignment (Figure 9.30).
- ○ To make the object jump to the edge of a cell as you move it, choose **Draw|Snap|To Grid**.
- ○ Objects that overlap each other are stacked in several layers. To change the stack order, first click to select just one of the objects. Choose **Draw|Order** and specify one of the options shown in Figure 9.31.
- ○ To change the separate objects into a single unit, group them. Select the objects and choose **Draw|Group**.

Result: After objects are grouped, they no longer have individual sizing handles, but a single set. This means that you can size, position, and modify them all at once. The results of several alignment, stacking, and grouping choices are shown in Figure 9.32.

TIPS FROM A PRO: Changing the stack order is particularly helpful when you are trying to select a specific shape but can't because it is behind another object.

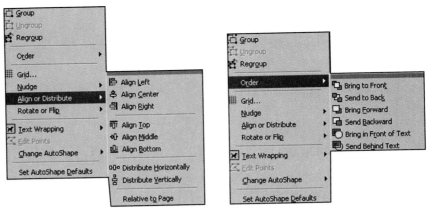

Figure 9.30 Alignment options

Figure 9.31 Stacking order options

Figure 9.32 Sample objects aligned, stacked, and grouped

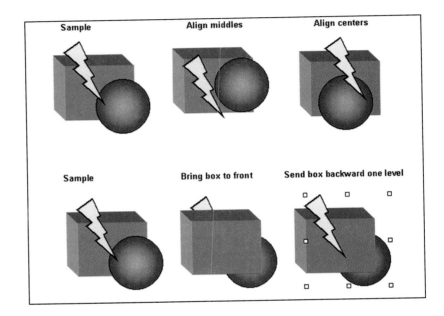

 TIPS FROM A PRO: Want to make changes to clip art? If the clip art you chose is a Windows Metafile (wmf), you can convert it to a drawing object so you can modify its color, line style, shadow, rotation, and so on. To convert it, select the picture and choose **Draw|Ungroup**, using the menu on the Drawing toolbar.

TASK 5   *Use WordArt*

What: *WordArt* is an element of Microsoft Office that enables you to define the shape, fill, and text of decorative text—everything from rainbow-colored and shaped words to the gleam of chrome on 3-D block letters.

Why: Sometimes you need interesting lettering that goes beyond just changing the font and size.

CREATE WORDART

How: WordArt is available from the Drawing toolbar or by choosing **Insert|Picture|WordArt**.

 1. From the Drawing toolbar, click the **Insert WordArt** button to see the WordArt Gallery, shown in Figure 9.33. This is a selection of predefined WordArt from which you can choose.

Figure 9.33
WordArt Gallery

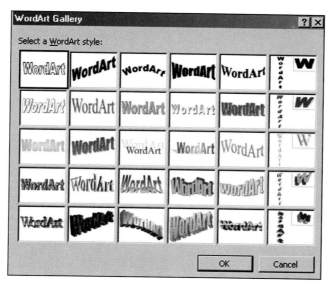

2. Click the choice that most nearly matches your preference and click **OK**. You can change the shape, color, and other properties later.
3. In the Edit WordArt Text dialog box that appears, type your text (to replace *Your Text Here*) and click **OK**.

Result: WordArt appears on screen as a floating object with sizing handles, as you see in Figure 9.34.

Figure 9.34
WordArt

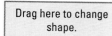

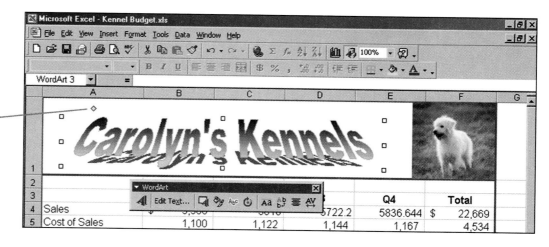

MODIFY WORDART

How: You can change the WordArt using these techniques:

○ Drag the yellow adjustment handle to exaggerate or minimize the shape effect of the WordArt.

○ Size and position the WordArt as you do with floating pictures.
○ Use buttons on the Drawing toolbar to change the shadow, fill, line, and 3-D effect, just as you do with any drawing object.

The WordArt toolbar also appears on screen, giving you buttons to modify the WordArt in the following ways:

○ Edit the text or return to the WordArt Gallery.
○ Choose from a different selection of WordArt shapes.
○ Adjust the rotation and text wrapping.
○ Change the text letter height, alignment, and character spacing.

Result: WordArt is customized to fit your preference.

Use PinPoint

After gaining the skills in this chapter, you can insert clip art and pictures from various sources and position them on the page. You can also create all sorts of drawing objects, including text boxes, shapes, and lines. You learned how to modify pictures and objects by sizing, cropping, changing the fill and line style, and adding 3-D and shadow effects. You can also create decorative text out of WordArt.

Now it's time to use the PinPoint software and see what you can do. Remember, whenever you are unsure of what to do, you can reread that portion of the chapter or you can click Show Me for a live demonstration. Check out these skills in PinPoint:

• Add a text box
• Draw an object
• Insert a picture

Key Terms

You can find definitions for these words in this chapter:

Clip art	Thumbnail
Sizing handles	Crop
Grayscale	AutoFormat
AutoShapes	Text box
WordArt	

Review Questions

You can use the following review questions to test your knowledge and skills. Answers are given in Appendix D.

True/False

Indicate whether each statement is true (T) or false (F).

_____ 1. Excel provides about a hundred professionally drawn clip art images in the Image Gallery.

_____ 2. To insert a picture you have stored on a disk, use the File|Open command.

_____ 3. To move a picture on the page, you must drag with the right mouse button.

_____ 4. To delete a picture, select the cell at the picture's top-left corner and choose Edit|Clear.

_____ 5. When you crop a picture, you trim off one or more edges without affecting the size of the image.

_____ 6. To make a picture larger and keep it in proportion, drag the corner sizing handles.

_____ 7. The Picture toolbar contains a button to change a picture to black and white.

_____ 8. To create WordArt, begin by placing text inside a text box.

_____ 9. You can add realistic textures to a drawing object instead of filling with a color.

_____ 10. To draw a perfect square, click the Rectangle button, and hold down the Alt key while dragging.

Multiple Choice

Select the letter that best completes the statement.

_____ 1. When you choose Insert|Picture, the first thing you see is:
   a. A selection of photographs.
   b. A selection of metafiles.
   c. A random assortment of clip art images.
   d. Several categories.
   e. A list of file names.

_____ 2. In addition to the Clip Gallery, Excel can handle pictures from this source:
   a. Digital camera.
   b. Scanner.
   c. Web.
   d. Any image you can copy and paste.
   e. All of the above.

_____ 3. The type of graphics image that you can ungroup and then modify is:
   a. bmp.
   b. gif.
   c. jpg.
   d. tif.
   e. wmf.

_____ 4. In the Clip Gallery, when you see a picture you like and then click it:
   a. A pop-up menu appears with an Insert button.
   b. A dialog box appears, asking you whether you want to insert it.
   c. The picture is immediately inserted into the document and Clip Gallery closes.
   d. The picture is immediately inserted into the document, but Clip Gallery remains open.
   e. You get a description of the file name and file type.

_____ 5. You can tell if a picture is selected because:
   a. It is shaded.
   b. It has a hatched border around it.
   c. The Drawing toolbar appears.
   d. Sizing handles appear.
   e. The status bar says PIC.

____ 6. To insert a perfect circle, click the Oval button and:
   a. Hold down the Shift key and drag.
   b. Click once on the worksheet.
   c. Use an AutoShape.
   d. All of the above.
   e. Both a and b.

____ 7. To make a mirror image of an arrow, so that it's facing the opposite direction,
   a. Use the Flip command.
   b. Use the Rotate command.
   c. Use the Rotate button.
   d. Click the Mirror button.
   e. Delete the current arrow and start over.

____ 8. When you want to combine several objects into a single unit, click the Draw menu and choose:
   a. Combine.
   b. Group.
   c. Join.
   d. Merge.
   e. Unite.

____ 9. When you drag the yellow handle on WordArt, it changes:
   a. The height.
   b. The shape effect.
   c. The font size.
   d. The width.
   e. All of the above.

____ 10. To add explanatory text on top of the cells in a worksheet, use a(n):
   a. Text box.
   b. Caption box.
   c. AutoText.
   d. WordBox.
   e. WordArt.

Screen Review

Match the letters in Figure 9.35 with the correct items in the list.

____ 1. Click here to make artsy text with rainbow colors.

____ 2. Click here to remove the outline from a shape.

____ 3. Click here to make the Drawing toolbar disappear.

____ 4. Drag here to make the picture smaller or larger.

____ 5. Click here to change the color of an object to dark blue.

____ 6. Click here to add a shadow to an object.

____ 7. Click here to angle an object.

____ 8. Click here to create a text box.

____ 9. Click here to see a menu to allow you to flip, group, or align drawing objects.

Figure 9.35

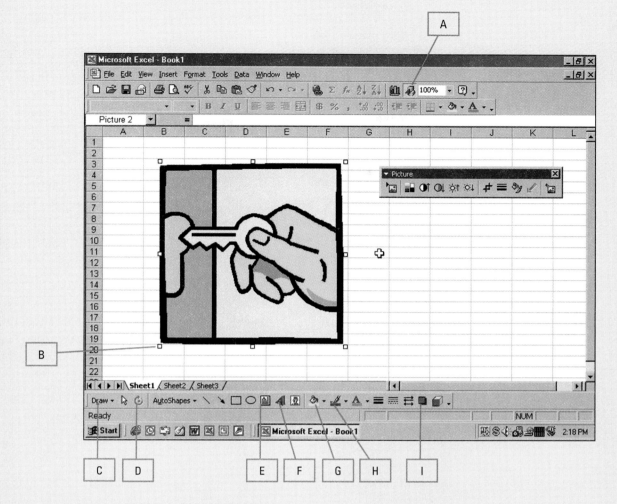

Exercise and Project

Follow these step-by-step instructions to create a worksheet. If you are working in a computer lab, ask your instructor where you should save and print your file.

Exercise

1. Open the file called **Loans R Us.xls** from the *Student\Chapter 9* folder of the PinPoint CD.
2. Calculate the monthly payment for each of the three loans.
3. Insert five rows at the top of the sheet. Click the WordArt button and create the title **Loans R Us** (or rename the company and use the new name). Make it colorful.
4. Insert a clip art image of a car in the Car Loan area of the worksheet.
5. Reposition the picture and size it to fit in the area.
6. Recolor the car. Recolor the lines of the car.
7. Draw your own picture of a house using the tools on the Drawing toolbar. Color it with multiple colors and group the parts.
8. Place the house in the Home Loan area of the worksheet.
9. In the same area, insert a text box with the words **Home Sweet Home**. Format the text white and add a gradient fill effect for the background.

10. Insert a picture or photograph of a boat. Position it beside the Boat Loan worksheet cells.

11. Flip the picture, if possible. Crop it closely to show mainly the boat.

12. Insert an Explosion AutoShape and apply a thick, colorful line style and a shadow. Size it large enough to contain the boat picture, and send it to the back, behind the boat picture.

13. Insert a piece of clip art or picture of some type of money: coins, dollar bills, money bag, or so on.

14. Size the money picture to cover most of the page.

15. View the Picture toolbar. Click Image Control and change the money to a watermark. Send the picture behind the text. (*Hint*: You might have to choose this command twice.)

16. Save the file. Preview the worksheet and make sure it fits on one page. Print the worksheet, using a color printer if you have access to one.

Project

Create a logo for the Loans R Us Company (or make up a new name for the company). You can use the drawing toolbar strictly, or use WordArt and/or pictures for this. Make sure it is grouped together to be used on letterhead and in spreadsheets. At the top of a worksheet, use WordArt to create a heading for Loans R Us. Place the logo in the top left corner. Print the worksheet. Save the workbook and store it for use in later chapters.

Chapter 10

Create Charts

Some numeric data may be more easily understood by displaying it in charts. Excel can take the numbers you have so carefully entered, calculated, and formatted in a worksheet and depict them so that you can see at a glance how they compare and what direction they are headed.

At the end of this chapter, you will be able to:

C	E	
❏	❏	Create an automatic chart
❏	❏	Name the elements of a chart
✔	❏	Use the Chart Wizard to create a chart
❏	❏	Size and move charts
❏	✔	Display and hide the Chart toolbar
❏	❏	Choose the appropriate type of chart for the data
✔	❏	Modify the legend, data labels, data series, and values
❏	❏	Format the, plot area, fill, gridlines, legend, axes, and 3-D view
❏	❏	Use pictures in charts
✔	❏	Preview and print charts

TASK 1   *Create an Automatic Chart*

What: Only a single keystroke is needed to create a chart of data on a worksheet.

Why: This feature is handy for a quick view of your data.

How: Here's the procedure:

1. Select a range of cells, including both the numbers and corresponding labels, as you see in Figure 10.1. To do this, drag with the mouse, or hold down the **Shift** key and press the arrow keys.
2. Press **F11**.

Result: Excel creates a column chart on a new sheet of your workbook, as you see in Figure 10.2. Of course, you'll want to go back and format it, change the chart type, and add titles, and so on. Excel makes it easy to modify charts by replacing the Data menu with a Chart menu on the menu bar when a chart is selected. You'll learn how to modify charts in later tasks in this chapter.

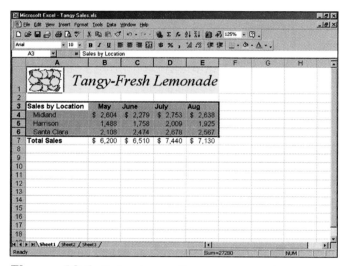

Figure 10.1 Selecting cells to create a chart

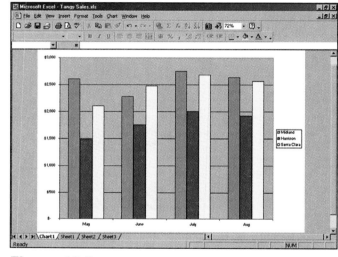

Figure 10.2 Chart of sales

TIPS FROM A PRO: Never, never include the totals when you're selecting the cells you want to chart. Totals throw the rest of the numbers out of proportion because they are so much larger than the others as you see in Figure 10.3. That is, chart either the totals only or the numbers only; never both together in the same chart.

Figure 10.3 Chart should not include totals

TASK 2   *Learn About Charts*

What: Before you learn more about creating and modifying charts, you need to learn the terminology.

Why: When you know the terminology, you'll be able to set up the various chart options the way you want them.

How: Examine the chart and underlying data in Figure 10.4.

Figure 10.4 Sample chart

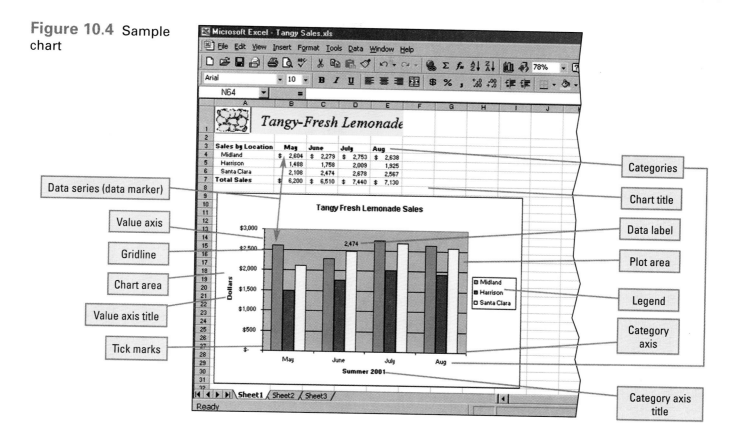

Result: The sample chart represents the numbers in the worksheet by the height of the columns. You'll learn in the coming tasks how to add all these elements to a chart and format them.

TASK 3 Create Charts Using the Wizard

CORE OBJECTIVE: *Use Chart Wizard to create a chart*

What: For more control over the chart as it is being created, use the Chart Wizard. A *wizard* guides you through a series of steps to create a sophisticated product, in this case a chart.

Why: Use the Chart Wizard to create an *embedded chart*, one that acts like a picture that you can move around on the worksheet. When you use the wizard, you make many of the formatting decisions so you have a finished product right away.

How: The following steps create a chart of the sales data for Tangy-Fresh Lemonade.

1. Select the text and numbers that will form the basis for the chart.

TIPS FROM A PRO: You can create a chart from non-adjacent cells. To do this, hold down the **Ctrl** key while you drag the various ranges. The only trick is that the overall shape of the highlighted cells must be a rectangle, so you may have to include blank cells. An example is shown in Figure 10.5.

Figure 10.5
Selecting non-adjacent cells to create a chart

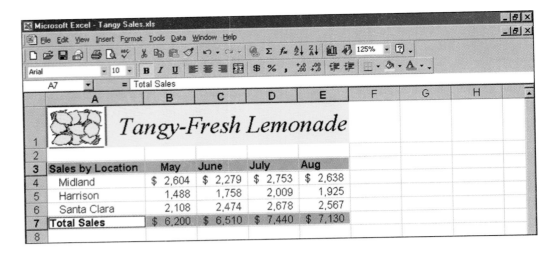

2. Click the **Chart Wizard** button. This opens the dialog box shown in Figure 10.6.
3. Select the chart type and subtype. Click and hold the button to preview how your data will appear in that type of chart. (You learn to choose the best chart type for your data in Task 6.)
4. Click **Next** to see Step 2 (Figure 10.7). Choose Rows or Columns and preview the difference. (Since you selected the cells for the chart before you began, the data range is already filled in.)

Figure 10.6 Chart Wizard: chart type

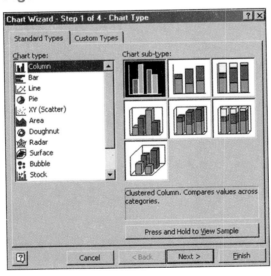

Figure 10.7 Chart Wizard: data series

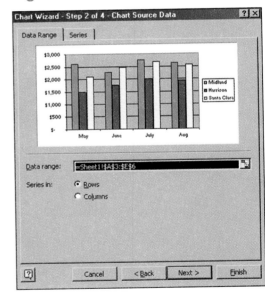

5. Click **Next** to see Step 3 (Figure 10.8). Type the title and axis labels. Click through the other tabs in the dialog box to change other options. (You learn how to use each of these in Task 7.)
6. Click **Next** to see Step 4 (Figure 10.9). Choose whether you want the chart on its own chart sheet (like the automatic chart you created in Task 1), or on top of the current worksheet containing the data.
7. Click **Back** to back up and change any of the choices, or click **Finish** to view the completed chart.

Result: The chart appears on the worksheet (assuming you picked that option), using the choices you made. You can see a sample chart in Figure 10.10.

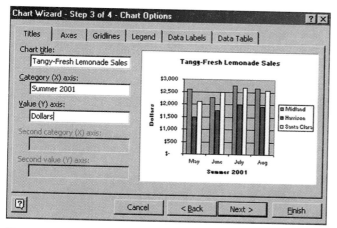

Figure 10.8 Chart Wizard: chart options

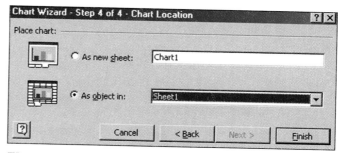

Figure 10.9 Chart Wizard: chart location

Figure 10.10
Embedded chart

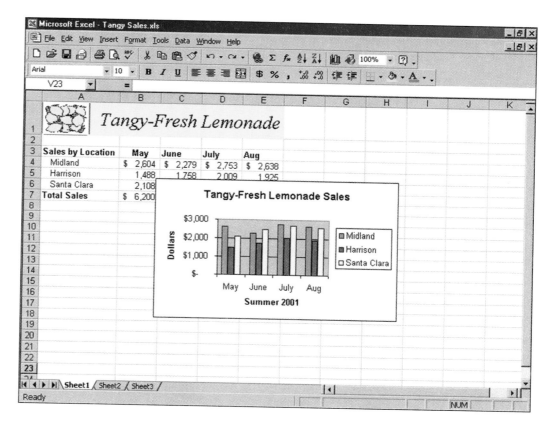

| TASK **4** | *Size and Move an Embedded Chart* |

What: Embedded charts appear on the worksheet, sometimes right on top of your data. The first thing you'll want to do is place them where they belong. You can also change the size of the chart.

Why: The size of the default chart might be so small that the plot area is smaller than the legend. That's no good. The plot area has to be large enough so the reader can see the data easily.

How: Like pictures, you drag a chart to move and drag sizing handles to size it.

- ❍ To move a chart, place the mouse pointer on the outer edge of the chart and drag. (The Name box in the formula bar will say *Chart Area* if you're dragging the right place.)
- ❍ To size a chart, click to see the sizing handles around the outer edge, and drag one of the handles.

Result: When you enlarge the size of a chart, the font size enlarges to stay in proportion (Figure 10.11). The larger the chart, the larger the font size—sometimes alarmingly large. When you have the overall size of the chart the way you want it, you can go back and specify an appropriate font size for the chart's text. You learn how to do that in Task 8.

Figure 10.11 The chart enlarged

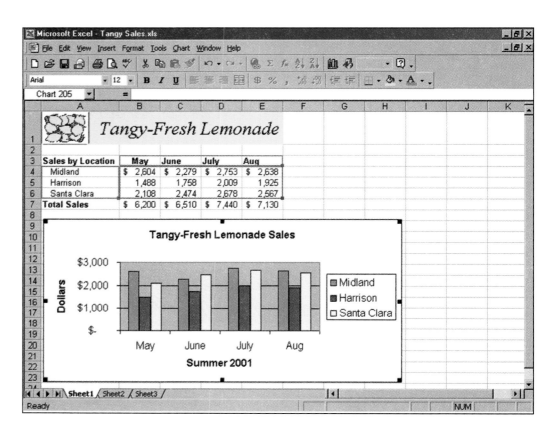

 TIPS FROM A PRO: To prevent the font from automatically changing as you size the chart, turn off the AutoScale feature. To do this, click to select the chart. Choose **Format|Selected Chart Area**. Select the **Font** tab, and click to clear the **AutoScale** check box. This sets all the fonts at Arial 10.

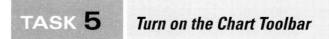

TASK **5**   *Turn on the Chart Toolbar*

E

EXPERT OBJECTIVE: *Hide and display toolbars*

What: When modifying an existing chart, you can use either menu selections or the Chart toolbar.

Figure 10.12 Chart toolbar

(a) Docked

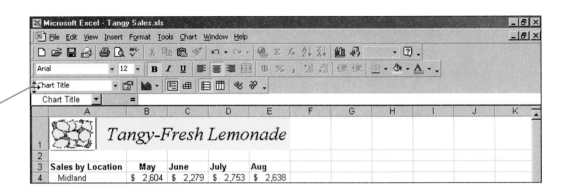

Drag here.

(b) Floating

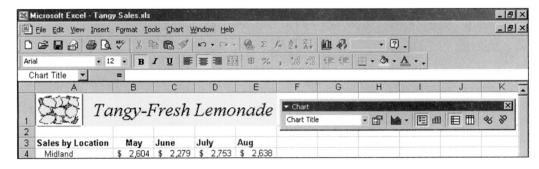

Why: If the Chart toolbar does not appear when you click to select the chart, you must turn it on.

How: Choose **View|Toolbars|Chart**.

Result: The Chart toolbar most often appears as a *floating toolbar* in the middle of the screen somewhere. Here are some things you can do with a toolbar:

- To move it, drag its title bar.
- To move it to the top of the screen along with the other toolbars, double-click its title bar. This changes it into a *docked toolbar*, and its title bar no longer shows.
- To change a docked toolbar back into a floating toolbar, drag the vertical line at its left edge down into the middle of the screen. (The pointer changes to a four-headed arrow, as shown in Figure 10.12.)
- To get rid of the floating toolbar, click its Close button, or choose **View|Toolbars|Chart** again.

TASK 6 *Choose the Chart Type*

What: Excel offers 14 major types of charts and many more subtypes. The one you should use depends on the purpose of your chart and the data you will depict. You choose the chart type if you use the Chart Wizard, but you can always change it later.

Table 10.1 shows a sample of each chart type and the purpose for using it. You can read more about the various chart types in Excel's Help. Search for the topic "Examples of Chart Types."

Table 10.1 Chart Types

Chart Type	Sample	Use This Type To
Column		Compare values by category or across time
Bar		Compare values by category but *not* over time
Line		Display trends over time
Pie		Show each item's contribution to the total
XY (scatter)		Show relationships between two aspects
Area		Display trend of totals over time
Doughnut		Show proportions, like several pie charts
Radar		Plot points on two intersecting axes
Surface		Display trends in three dimensions
Bubble		Show relationship, like scatter; includes a third factor
Stock		Record stock prices (high, low, close)
Cylinder		Same as column, using a unique shape
Cone		Same as column, using a unique shape
Pyramid		Same as column, using a unique shape

Two important chart subtypes have specific uses:

Stacked column		Compare totals by category or over time
100% stacked column		Compare proportions of a whole over time, like a series of pie charts

 TIPS FROM A PRO: Hard to remember which is the column chart and which is the bar chart? Column charts, like columns on a building, run vertically. Bar charts, like the bar in your local pub, are horizontal.

Why: You must carefully determine which type of chart to use to depict your data accurately, and so as not to mislead or confuse the reader. For example, column charts and bar charts might seem to be used the same way because they look similar. However, column charts can be used to compare data over time, with the years represented by the horizontal axis.

Bar charts, in contrast, are *not* appropriate for comparing data over time, as the time would appear on the vertical axis. In our Western culture, time is always depicted from left to right, never from top to bottom.

CHOOSE THE CHART TYPE

How: You can click the **Chart Type** button on the Chart toolbar to choose a type of chart from the drop-down list, but this limits your choices. Instead, follow these steps.

 1. Choose **Chart|Chart Type**. This opens the dialog box shown in Figure 10.13. You may recall this from the Chart Wizard.

2. Designate the major chart type on the left side of the dialog box, and then click the subtype on the right side of the dialog box.
3. Click and hold the button to preview your data with that chart type.
4. Click the **Custom Type** tab (Figure 10.14) to use one of the jazzy, preformatted charts.

Result: The figures are appropriately represented on the chart. Several most common types of charts are discussed in the next sections.

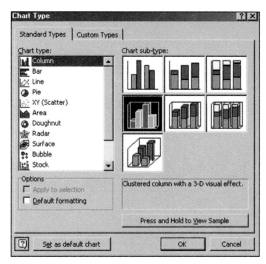
Figure 10.13 Chart Type dialog box

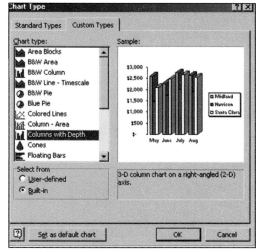
Figure 10.14 Custom Types tab

USE STACKED COLUMN AND STACKED BAR CHARTS

How: A specific subtype of chart you will find handy is the stacked column chart.

1. Select the numbers and their accompanying labels.
2. Choose **Chart|Chart Type** and click the **Column** or **Bar** type.
3. Choose the **Stacked** subtype, as in Figure 10.15.

Figure 10.15 Stacked column choices

Figure 10.16 Sample stacked column chart

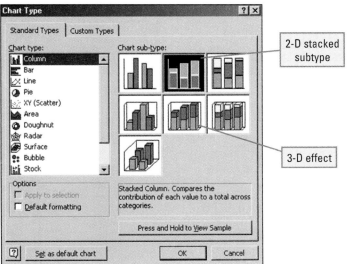

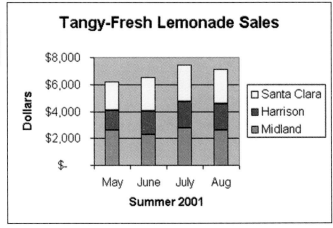

Task 6: Choose the Chart Type **231**

Result: With a stacked chart, you can see at a glance the total for each category, as shown in the sample in Figure 10.16. It also shows the contribution of each *data series* (the set of numbers represented by each color), which is what makes this type of chart so valuable.

USE PIE CHARTS

How: When you want to see the proportion to a whole, use a pie chart. For example, when you want to see which location had the greatest percent of sales, or which expense was the largest percent of all, use a pie chart. Pie charts are unique in that they depict only one set of numbers.

1. Select a single set of numbers (one data series) and the accompanying labels.
2. Choose **Chart|Chart Type** and choose **Pie**.

Result: The numbers are automatically transformed into percents, as in the sample in Figure 10.17. You can even display the percents if you want—read the section later in this chapter about data labels.

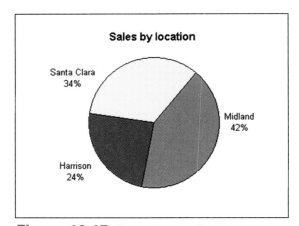

Figure 10.17 Sample pie chart

USE 100% STACKED COLUMN CHARTS

How: When you want to depict the percents for several months in succession, you can't use a pie chart, because pie charts depict only a single data series. You could create a sequence of pie charts, but that's too much trouble. Instead, use a 100% stacked column chart.

1. Select the numbers (data series) and their accompanying labels.
2. Choose **Chart|Chart Type** and click the **Column** or **Bar** type.
3. Choose the **100% Stacked** subtype, as in Figure 10.18.

Result: Notice on the sample in Figure 10.19 that the numbers on the vertical axis have been changed to percents. What this type of chart shows is how much each item contributes, like a pie, but how the contributions change over time.

 TIPS FROM A PRO: Doughnut charts are used for the same purpose as 100% stacked column charts. Most people find them difficult to decipher, but they are also correct to use if you prefer them.

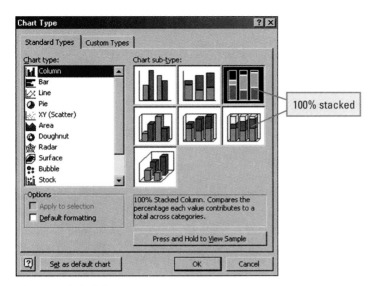

Figure 10.18 Stacked column choices

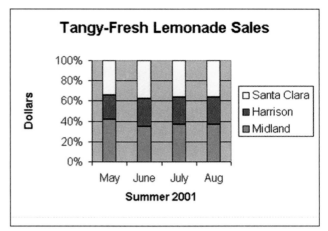

Figure 10.19 Sample 100% stacked column chart

TASK **7**   *Modify the Chart*

 C   CORE OBJECTIVE: *Modify charts*

What: After you create a chart, either with the wizard or by pressing F11, you can always modify it. You can control how the data appears in the chart, and you can add either a legend or data labels to show what the various colored data series represent. (Column and bar charts most often use a legend, whereas pie charts most often use data labels.) Instead, you might want to show a table of all the numbers, or include an additional series of numbers.

Why: You may be completely satisfied with the appearance and the way your figures are represented, but more often, you'll see some refinements you'd like to make. Excel gives you control over the location of the legend and the colors of the lines or bars; it allows you to add gridlines and labels and to format the text and numbers appropriately.

MANAGE HOW THE CHART PLOTS THE DATA

How: You can choose how to display the data in the chart, not only when you create one using the Chart Wizard, but also for an existing chart. To do this, click the **By Row** and **By Column** buttons on the Chart toolbar to change the way the data is compared.

Result: The way the chart compares the numbers changes if by row or by column. In column charts, both may make sense, as you see in Figure 10.20. Other times, you get funny-looking charts, such as those shown in Figure 10.21.

Figure 10.20 Chart by row or by column

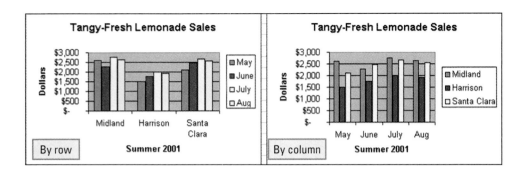

Figure 10.21 Wrong choice of By Row or By Column

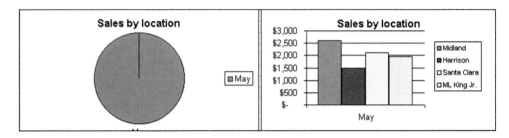

 TIPS FROM A PRO: You can also rearrange the order in which the items are depicted. Use one of these methods:

- Rearrange rows or columns of the numbers on the worksheet.
- Click to select a data series and then double-click it to access the **Format Data Series** dialog box. Choose the **Series Order** tab, and click the **Move Up** or **Move Down** button to adjust the order of the data series (Figure 10.22).

Figure 10.22 Changing the series order

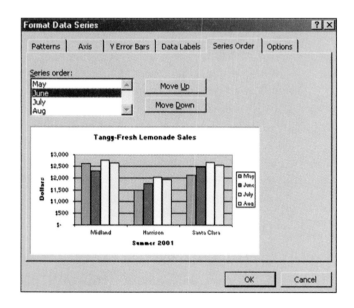

DISPLAY THE LEGEND OR NOT

 How: Click the **Legend** button on the Chart toolbar to turn the legend off and on.

Result: The legend (or key) labels the various colors of the data series. It appears on the right side of the chart when you turn it on.

ADD DATA LABELS

How: When you want to see the actual numbers next to the columns or pie slices, for example, add *data labels*.

1. Click to select a data series and, if you want, click again to select a single *data marker*, such as a single column, bar, or pie slice.
2. Double-click to access the Format Data Series dialog box and choose the **Data Labels** tab (Figure 10.23).
3. The choices available depend on what type of chart it is. For a column chart, choose **Show Value** to see a number, as in Figure 10.4 on page 185. For a pie chart, choose **Show Label and Percent**, and omit the legend.

Result: Pie charts especially are improved by using data labels rather than a legend, as you see in Figure 10.24. You can even drag the data labels on top of the wedges, if the colors are light enough. Column charts, though, usually appear too cluttered with data labels on all the columns.

Figure 10.23 Data labels tab

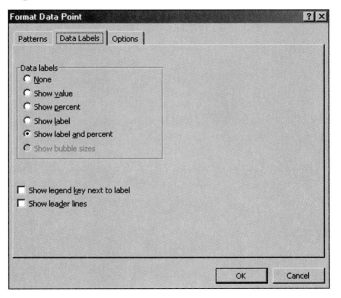

Figure 10.24 Use data labels and not a legend

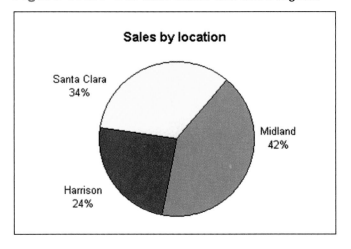

ADD A DATA TABLE

How: To show the actual numbers being depicted on the chart, you can either add data labels or show the data table. To do this, click the **Data Table** button on the Chart toolbar.

Result: Figure 10.25 shows the data table that is added to the chart display. This feature is particularly helpful with charts displayed on a separate chart sheet, where the chart cannot be shown next to the figures.

ADD DATA SERIES

How: You can add new data to an existing chart, or delete an unwanted series. To add new data, follow the steps to copy and paste.

1. Select the data on the worksheet (include both the label and the numbers).
2. Copy it.

Figure 10.25 Data
table

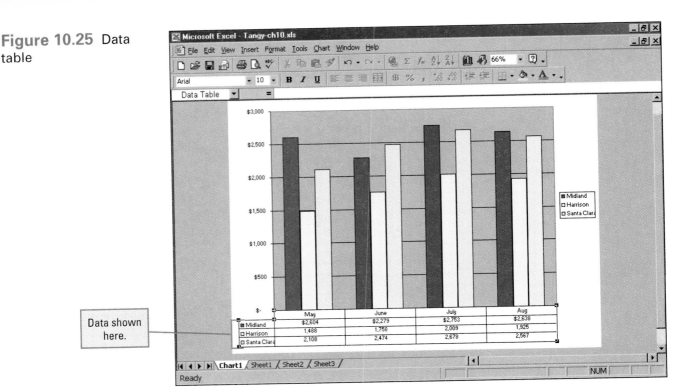

Data shown
here.

3. Click the chart to select it.
4. Paste.

Result: Like magic, the chart adjusts to include the new numbers (Figure 10.26).
To delete a data series, click to select it and press **Delete**. The chart
immediately adjusts the rest of the data.

Figure 10.26 Chart
with data added

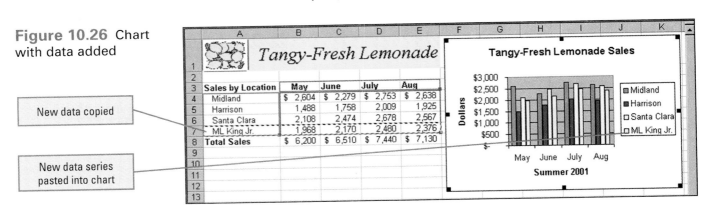

New data copied

New data series
pasted into chart

CHANGE VALUES

How: When you change the numbers on the worksheet, the chart changes
instantly. You know that. Did you also know you can drag the chart to
change the worksheet?

1. Click a column to select the data series.
2. Click a single column a second time to select just that column. The
handles appear on the selected column only.
3. Place the mouse pointer over the top sizing handle until it turns into
a two-headed arrow and drag up or down to change its size (Figure
10.27).

Figure 10.27 Drag
to change the chart
value

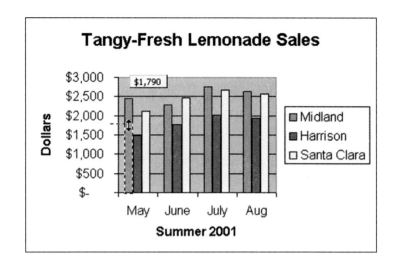

Result: The column size changes, but the number on the worksheet also changes to match the chart. If the cell underlying that column is a formula, the Goal Seek dialog box appears, asking which precedent cell you want to change so that the formula reaches that value.

TASK 8   *Format Chart Components*

What: Although the Chart Wizard does a pretty nice job of making an attractive chart, you can refine the appearance of the chart. Excel automatically adjusts the size of the text, plot area, and the various elements as you modify the chart, and sometimes the results are not very good.

Why: You may prefer different colors, or you might want to improve the way a chart element communicates the data. For example, the horizontal axis might not have room to display all the category names. In that case, Excel drops every other name, as you see in Figure 10.28. You can change the way the text appears so that all the categories are labeled.

Figure 10.28
Category labels
omitted

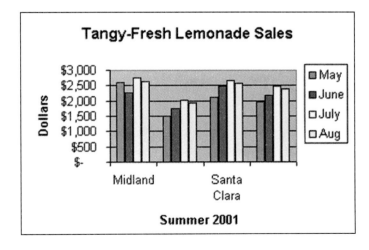

SELECT CHART COMPONENTS

How: As with everything else you format, the first step is to select it. You can use one of two methods:

1. Click the item. This is often not as easy as it may seem.
2. Drop down the **Chart Objects** list on the Chart toolbar and select the item you want (Figure 10.29).

Result: Excel places handles on or around the item you selected.

 TIPS FROM A PRO: When you right-click a chart element, the shortcut menu offers options for modifying and formatting that item.

FORMAT AND ROTATE TEXT

How: As always, you can change the font, size, and style of selected text. More importantly, you can force the category labels to fit by changing their size or rotation.

1. Click the horizontal axis to select it, as the categories are part of the axis.
2. Click one of the buttons to angle the text upward or downward.
3. Alternatively, reduce the font size or enlarge the plot area so that all the text can fit.

Result: Instead of seeing only every other category, one of these methods enables you to display all of them (Figure 10.30). Of course, if you can enlarge the chart as a whole, the axis might have enough room to display all the category labels.

Figure 10.29 Choosing chart elements

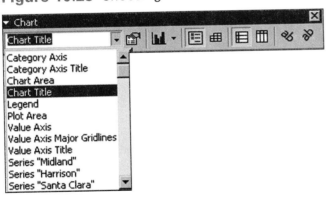

Figure 10.30 Angled category labels

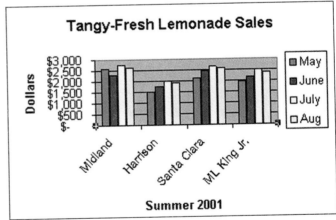

CHANGE SIZE OF PLOT AREA

How: You know how to change the size of the chart overall, but when you add or delete legends, the plot area may not be the correct size or proportion to display the chart.

1. Select the plot area by clicking it or from the Chart toolbar.

2. Drag one of the sizing handles to enlarge it, or drag the center to move it.

Result: You control the size and proportion of the plot area, instead letting Excel adjust it. Watch out, though. You can drag it so that it overlaps the titles by mistake.

 TIPS FROM A PRO: Double-click the data series of the chart and access the Options tab. When you're working with column and bar charts, you can modify the width of the bars (if they seem too fat or thin), or how far apart they are (if they seem too crowded or sparse). For pie charts, the Options tab lets you modify the angle of the first slice.

CHANGE COLOR OF FILL, BORDER, AND LINES

How: You can change the color of the fill and border of every chart element, and for line charts, you can change the color and thickness of the lines and add markers for the data points.

1. Select the element, either by clicking once or by choosing it from the list on the Chart toolbar.
2. Double-click the element and click the Patterns tab, as you see in Figure 10.31. Make your choice here. Figure 10.32 shows a sample.

Figure 10.31 Change colors on the Patterns tab

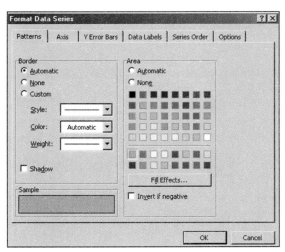

Figure 10.32 Color changes

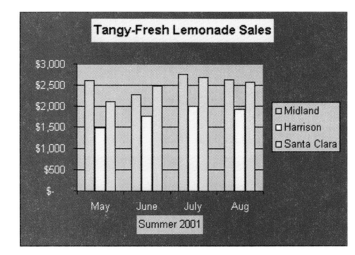

 TIPS FROM A PRO: You can use other colors besides the ones offered on the color palette. See Chapter 16 "Work with Templates and Macros," to learn to customize the color palette.

Result: As you learned in Chapter 9, "Work with Pictures and Objects," you can also choose fill and line colors by clicking buttons on the Drawing toolbar.

For a sophisticated, 3-D look, choose Fill Effects and add a gradient fill to the columns as you see in Figure 10.33. (You have to repeat the effect for each of the data series.)

Figure 10.33
Columns have a
gradient fill

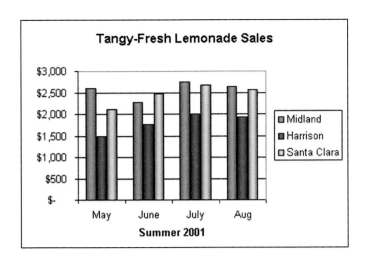

 TIPS FROM A PRO: To format an individual data marker, such as a single bar, column, or pie wedge, click it to select the data series, and then click it again to select the individual point.

ADD GRIDLINES

How: Click to select the chart. Choose **Chart|Chart Options**, and click the **Gridlines** tab, shown in Figure 10.34. Choose the gridlines you want to display.

Result: If the chart is cluttered, remove the gridlines from the display. If they are needed for the reader to make comparisons, insert gridlines.

CONTROL THE LEGEND

How: To change where the legend is located, double-click it and choose the **Placement** tab (Figure 10.35).

Figure 10.34 Gridlines tab

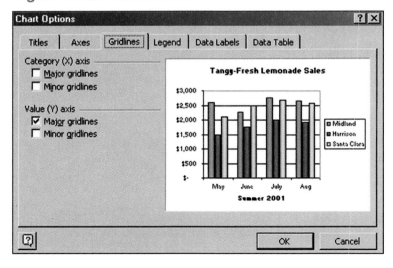

Figure 10.35 Legend placement

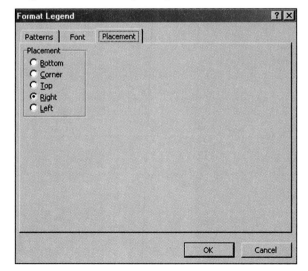

Result: When you use the dialog box to change the location of the legend, the chart adjusts to create room for it. You can also drag the legend to move it, but then the chart doesn't adjust automatically.

CONTROL THE AXES

How: Double-click the axis and click the various tabs on the dialog box to see the choices for modifying its appearance. The examples here are for the value (vertical) axis.

1. Click the **Patterns** tab to display more or fewer tick marks (Figure 10.36).
2. Click the **Number** tab to increase or decrease the number of decimals or to add or remove $ symbols to the numbers given on the chart.
3. Click the **Scale** tab to see the options in Figure 10.37.

Figure 10.36 Modifying tick marks

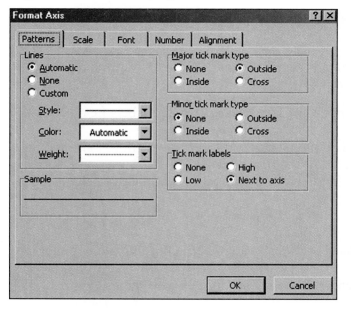

Figure 10.37 Modifying the axis scale

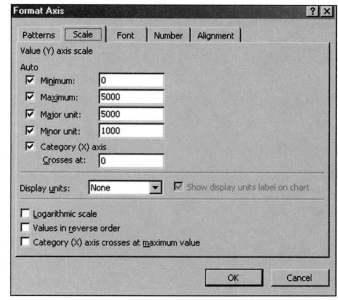

- Specify the minimum and maximum numbers you want to display on the chart's axis.
- Specify how often tick marks are displayed and labeled. For example, you can specify to show hundreds, rather than five hundreds.
- Change the display units if the numbers are large, as in Figure 10.38. For example, instead of showing the label $10,000,000 and so on along the vertical axis, you can choose Millions to so that the chart shows $10 along with the label "Millions."
- Designate where you want the x-axis to cross the vertical axis, either at 0 or the maximum value, or anywhere you choose.
- Choose **Values in Reverse Order** to make the items go from low to high instead of the reverse. You'll use the same feature with bar charts, **Categories in Reverse Order**, because bar charts may awkwardly plot the categories from bottom to top. (You'll probably combine this with moving the x-axis to cross at the maximum value.)

Figure 10.38
Display units changed

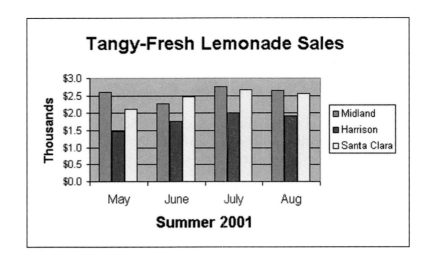

Result: The chart is plotted with the axis you designed. If you want to use Excel's automatic settings instead, all you have to do is click the check boxes for Auto.

FORMAT 3-D CHARTS

How: Charts with 3-D appearance have special formatting requirements to make them easier to read.

1. Change the font size or plot size so that the labels fit on the third axis.
2. Remove the legend (if you have the labels on the third axis) and readjust the plot size, if necessary.
3. Reorder the data series so that the taller columns are behind shorter ones.
4. Change the elevation and rotation of the 3-D view. You can do this two ways:
   - Choose **Chart|3-D View** and click the buttons in the dialog box (Figure 10.39a).
   - Select the chart corners, and drag, as you see in Figure 10.39b. You can drag up or down to view it through the roof or floor, or turn it completely around to see it from the rear. This ability to rearrange 3-D chart is one of the most amazing things you can do with Excel.

Figure 10.39 (a) 3-D View dialog box

(b) Drag the corners to change the 3-D view

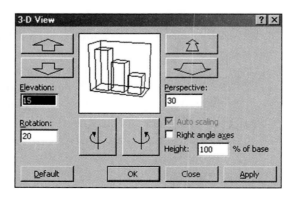

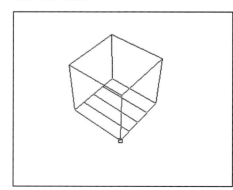

Result: The 3-D chart appears at the angle and elevation that best depicts your data.

 TIPS FROM A PRO: Although they look stylish, 3-D charts make your charts harder to read and may even distort the numbers. Examine the two sets of charts in Figure 10.40. Notice how the 3-D chart distorts the size of the wedges so it's impossible to judge the percentages. And in the column chart, we can't tell exactly what number is represented. Therefore, for the most accurate charts, stick with 2-D charts.

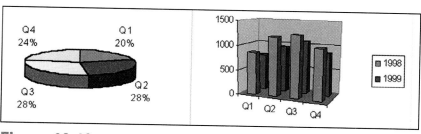

Figure 10.40 3-D charts may mislead

Figure 10.41 Exploded pie

FORMAT PIE CHARTS

How: Pie charts have specific formatting requirements.

○ Display data labels (percents and labels) and eliminate the legend.
○ Draw attention to a single item by *exploding* the wedge, drawing it out from the rest of the pie, as you see in Figure 10.41. Here's how:
  • Click once to select the pie.
  • Click a second time to select a single wedge.
  • Drag outward.

Result: The pie's appearance is enhanced.

TASK 9   *Use Pictures in Charts*

What: For something very different, combine pictures with charts. You can add pictures to the background of the chart, or you can create a *pictograph*, where pictures are used instead of bars or columns to indicate the numbers.

Why: Sometimes a clever picture attracts attention to the data and makes it more interesting to look at.

PLACE A PICTURE IN THE BACKGROUND

How: To add a picture to the background of a chart, you have to know the file name and location of the picture you want to use. You can't just use the Clip Gallery to insert the picture in the background.

1. Select the chart area.
2. Double-click to access the **Patterns** tab of the Format Chart Area dialog box.
3. Click **Fill Effects** and choose the **Picture** tab.
4. Browse to find the file name of the picture, and click **OK** several times.

Result: As you can see in Figure 10.42, when you put a picture in the background, the text and chart elements must be quite bold to show up well.

Figure 10.42
Picture in the background

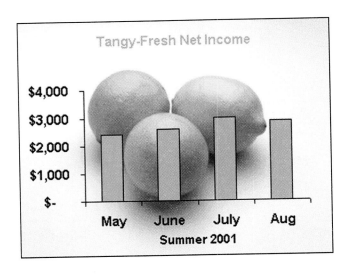

 TIPS FROM A PRO: You can also put pictures in the background of your worksheet, but if you do, make sure you have enough contrast so that the text is easy to read.

CREATE PICTOGRAPHS

How: Use copy and paste to create a pictograph:

1. Insert a picture into the worksheet, if necessary, and copy it.
2. Click the chart to select it, and then select the data series.
3. Paste.

Result: The pictures are inserted in place of the standard column or points along a line chart (Figure 10.43). You can control whether the pictures are stacked or stretched by double-clicking the columns and choosing **Fill Effects** to see the dialog box in Figure 10.44.

Figure 10.43
Pictographs

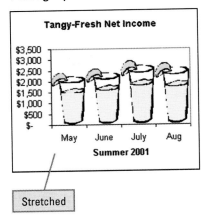

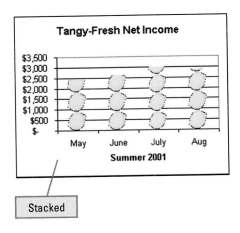

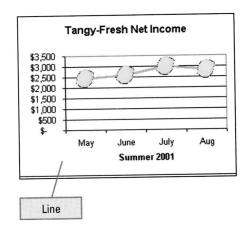

Figure 10.44 Fill effects of a pictograph

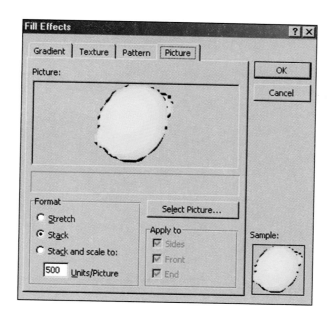

TASK 10 *Print Charts*

C   CORE OBJECTIVE: *Preview and print charts*

What: When you're ready to get a printed copy of the chart on the page, what you see on paper depends both on the chart and how you handle it.

○ Charts embedded on a worksheet print along with the worksheet if you first select a cell in the worksheet.

○ Embedded charts print alone on a page if you first click to select them.

○ Charts on a separate chart sheet print alone on a page.

When you want to see how the chart will appear when printed, use the Print Preview feature.

Why: You may want to see how the chart will appear in black and white, or how it fits on a page.

How: Follow these steps to control how your charts are printed.

1. To print a chart alone on the page, click to select it and click the Print Preview button. Close Print Preview when you are finished.

2. To control how large a chart appears on the page, click to select the chart, choose **File|Page Setup**, and click the **Chart** tab. Figure 10.45 shows three choices:

   • **Use Full Page** maximizes both the height and width of the chart to fill the page between the margins. This may change the proportion of the chart from the way it appears on screen.

   • **Scale to Fit Page** expands the chart keeping it in the current proportions, until it is as large as it can be. Either the height or width is maximized, but not both, so the appearance on the printed page is the same as the way you set it up on screen.

   • **Custom** leaves the chart at the size you created it on screen.

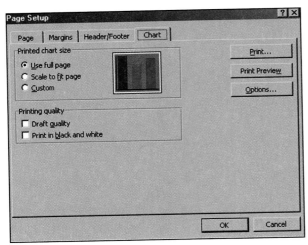

Figure 10.45 Chart tab of the Page Setup dialog box

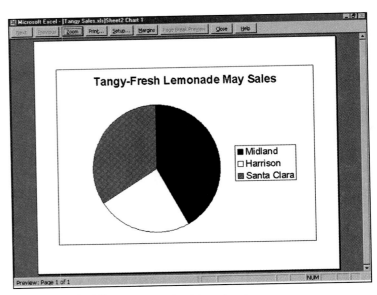

Figure 10.46 Black and white chart

3. The Chart tab of the Page Setup dialog box also offers you a way to see how the chart appears when printed in black and white. Choosing this option changes the colors to various patterns so the data series are easy to distinguish (Figure 10.46).

4. When you're printing an embedded chart along with the worksheet, choose **Page Break Preview** to position the chart so that it fits on the page the way you want.

5. Click **Print**.

Result: When you preview the chart and use the Chart tab, you can control how the chart appears on the printed page.

Use PinPoint

After gaining the skills in this chapter, you can create a chart the fast way and by using the Chart Wizard. You can change the chart type, how the data is displayed, and the appearance of the various elements of the chart. You also learned how to handle 3-D charts and pictographs. Now it's time to use the PinPoint software and see what you can do. Anytime you are unsure of what to do, reread that portion of the chapter or click Show Me for a live demonstration. Check out these skills in PinPoint:

- Create a chart
- Modify a chart
- Preview chart
- Print a chart
- Rotate text in a chart

Key Terms

You can find definitions for these words in this chapter:

Data marker

Wizard

Data Series

Docked toolbar

Embedded chart

Exploding

Floating toolbar

Pictograph

Review Questions

You can use the following review questions to test your knowledge and skills. Answers are given in Appendix D, "Answers to Review Questions."

True/False

Indicate whether each statement is true (T) or false (F).

____ 1. When you create an automatic chart with a single keystroke, it appears on a separate chart sheet in the workbook.

____ 2. The feature that takes you through the four-step process of creating a chart is called the Chart Wizard.

____ 3. To move a chart around on the worksheet, click to select it and then drag the sizing handles.

____ 4. When you enlarge the chart, the text size is automatically enlarged also.

____ 5. The best type of chart to show proportions of a whole is a bar chart.

____ 6. For a pie chart, it's usually better to use a legend than data labels.

____ 7. To add new data to a chart, you can simply copy it and click the chart and paste.

____ 8. One reason to rotate text is that the categories are too long to fit along the horizontal axis.

____ 9. To change the color of a chart element, click the element and click the Fill button on the Drawing toolbar

____ 10. When you drag a pie wedge out from the pie chart to draw attention to it, that's called "embedding."

Multiple Choice

Select the letter that best completes the statement.

___ 1. To create a chart, the quickest way is to select the numbers and labels and then:
   a. Choose Insert|AutoChart.
   b. Right-click and choose ChartIt.
   c. Press Ctrl+C.
   d. Press F11.
   e. Use the Chart Wizard.

___ 2. Charts that appear on the worksheet are called:
   a. Embedded.
   b. Entrenched.
   c. Implanted.
   d. Sizable.
   e. Sheet charts.

___ 3. Use the View|Toolbar command to:
   a. Display a toolbar.
   b. Move a toolbar around on screen.
   c. Make a toolbar docked.
   d. Make a toolbar floating.
   e. All of the above.

___ 4. The best type of chart to show the total amount along with each component of the total is:
   a. Column.
   b. Stacked column.
   c. 100% stacked column.
   d. Bar.
   e. Never depict the totals.

___ 5. When you have several data series depicted in a column chart, you can tell what each color represents by looking at the:
   a. Category axis.
   b. Data labels.
   c. Legend.
   d. Tick marks.
   e. Value axis.

___ 6. You can use pictures in a chart for the:
   a. Background.
   b. Columns.
   c. Plot area.
   d. Data labels.
   e. Both a and b.

___ 7. Before you print, to position the chart correctly on the printed worksheet, use:
   a. Print Preview.
   b. Chart view.
   c. Page Break Preview
   d. The Chart tab of the Page Setup dialog box.
   e. All of the above.

___ 8. The Chart tab of the Page Setup dialog box enables you to:
   a. Fill the page with the chart from margin to margin.
   b. Enlarge the chart but keep it in the same proportion it currently has.
   c. Change the chart to print patterns in black and white.
   d. All of the above.
   e. None of the above.

___ 9. To change large numbers (such as 10,000,000) to small ones (10), the best thing to do is:
   a. Change the axis scale for a maximum of 10 rather than automatic.
   b. Change the display units.
   c. Divide the cells by 1,000,000 in the worksheet.
   d. Click the axis labels and retype them.
   e. All of the above.

___ 10. When you create a pictograph, you can format the picture so that it:
   a. Stretches the length of the column.
   b. Stacks pictures along the column.
   c. Represents data points in a line chart.
   d. All of the above.
   e. None of the above.

Match the letters in Figure 10.47 with the correct items in the list.

Figure 10.47

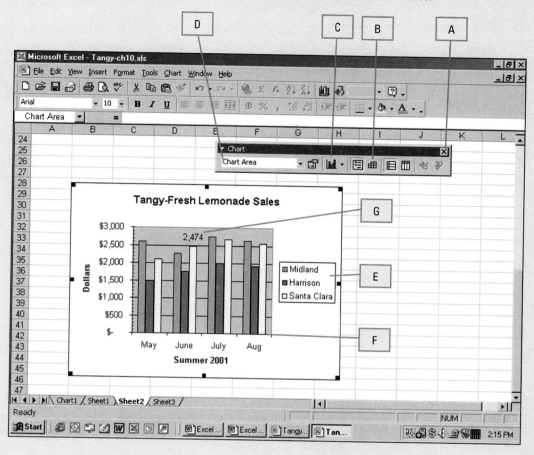

_____ 1. Click here to display all the numbers corresponding to the chart's data series.

_____ 2. Click here to change the chart type.

_____ 3. Click here to select the various parts of the chart by name.

_____ 4. Click here to hide the Chart toolbar.

_____ 5. Look here to see a data label.

_____ 6. Look here to see a data series.

_____ 7. Look here to see the legend.

Exercise and Project

Follow these step-by-step instructions to create some charts. If you are working in a computer lab, ask your instructor where you should save and print your file.

Exercise

Open **Dept Store.xls** from the _Student\Chapter 10_ folder of the PinPoint CD. Suppose that Macy's and Dillard's have merged to form a new chain of department stores called Mallard's. Use the worksheet to create the following four charts. As you go, save your work.

CHART I

1. Select A3:E3 (don't include the Total column) and hold down Ctrl and select A9:E9.
2. Create an automatic chart. Add an appropriate title. Print the chart.

CHART II

1. Return to the Mallard's worksheet. Select A3:E3 to include the X-axis labels. Hold down Ctrl and select the quarterly Sales values for Men's, Women's, Children's, and Gifts (A5:E8).
2. Use the Chart Wizard to create a stacked column chart.
3. Make sure the legend displays the department names. If it doesn't, you need to make the data series in rows.
4. Enter these titles:
   Chart: **Mallard's Departmental Sales**
   X axis: **Quarters**
   Y axis: **Sales**
5. Position the chart below the data. Insert blank rows, if necessary, so it doesn't overlap the numbers.
6. Use primary colors for the columns.
7. Delete the gridlines.
8. Print the data and the chart on one page. (Use Print Preview to make sure it fits on one page and the data is at the top.)

CHART III

1. Select the Expense labels and the values for Quarter 1 only.
2. Use the Chart Wizard to create a 3-D pie chart.
3. Title the chart **Quarter 1 Expenses**.
4. Use data labels and percents rather than a legend.
5. Place the chart in a new sheet.
6. Change the font size to 24 for the title and to 16 Bold Italic for the labels.
7. Recolor the Travel Expenses wedge and then explode it.
8. Print the chart.

CHART IV

1. Select the Quarters, Gross Profit, Total Expenses, and Number of Employees. (Don't include the totals column.)
2. Use the Chart Wizard, and choose the Custom Type tab and scroll down to Line–Column on 2 axes.
3. Add these titles:
   Chart Title: **Mallard's Dept. Store**
   Category (X) axis: **Quarter**
   Value (Y) axis: **$100,000s**
   Second category (X) axis: blank
   Second value (Y) axis: **No. Employees**
4. In the completed chart, recolor the line to dark blue and make it a heavier weight.
5. Print the chart using the Custom option under File|Page Setup.

Project

Create a worksheet like Figure 10.48 to use as the basis for two charts:

Figure 10.48

	A	B	C	D
1	Finals Study Hours			
2		Friday	Saturday	Sunday
3	Morning	3	4	3
4	Lunch Break	2	2	1
5	Afternoon	3	2	3
6	Study Break	2	3	1
7	Evening	4	4	6

Chart I. Create a bar chart for the data in the figure. Make sure the data series is in columns. Apply data labels, include the data table, and delete the gridlines. Title the x-axis **Time Frame** and y-axis **Hours of Study**. Use WordArt to create a title for the entire chart. Print the chart only.

Chart II. Calculate the total hours studied each day, not including the breaks. Create a column chart depicting the day and total hours. Title it **Finals Mania**. Delete the legend. Insert an appropriate picture for the chart, such as books, and scale it down so that it is fairly small. Replace the columns with the picture. Make sure the picture is stacked, not stretched. Print the chart along with the worksheet.

Handle Multiple Worksheets

When a project requires several worksheets, you may want to keep them together in a single workbook. For example, you may have data from various months on separate worksheets, or sales reports from several stores, or budgets from several departments. You can copy and move these worksheets, arrange them in the order you prefer, and create formulas that refer to the other sheets, or even to separate workbooks. The best thing is the ability to consolidate the information from several sheets onto a single, summary sheet.

At the end of this chapter, you will be able to:

C	E	
☑	❑	Insert and delete worksheets
☑	❑	Move between worksheets in a workbook
☑	❑	Rename a worksheet
❑	❑	Select sheets
☑	❑	Move and copy worksheets
☑	❑	Link worksheets
❑	☑	Link workbooks
❑	❑	Edit several worksheets at once
☑	❑	Consolidate data using 3-D references
❑	❑	Use the Data Consolidate command
❑	❑	Link and consolidate
❑	☑	Use grouping and outlines
❑	☑	Print and preview multiple worksheets

CORE OBJECTIVE: Insert and delete worksheets

What: When you create a new workbook in Excel, it comes with three work-sheets. You can add new sheets or remove unwanted sheets, as needed.

Why: When you are creating several worksheets that you want to keep together in a single workbook, you'll use several sheets, and you may need more than the standard three. On the other hand, if your information only requires a single sheet, you can streamline your file and keep others from being confused by removing unused sheets. (It saves a little space on disk, but not much.)

INSERT SHEETS

How: You can insert a new sheet three ways:

   ❍ Choose **Insert|Worksheet**.
   ❍ Right-click the **Sheet** tab and choose **Insert** (Figure 11.1).
   ❍ Copy a sheet from another Excel file. (You'll learn about this in Task 3.)

Result: A new blank sheet is inserted to the left of the active sheet. The new sheet becomes the current sheet, and it's typically named Sheet4 (assuming the workbook has three existing sheets), as you see in Figure 11.2.

When you use the shortcut menu, the Insert dialog box opens, giving you the option of using a template on the new worksheet. Click **OK** to insert a blank worksheet. You'll learn about templates in Chapter 16, "Work with Templates and Macros."

Figure 11.1 Shortcut menu

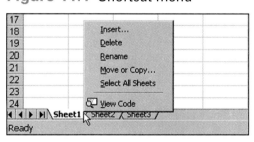

Figure 11.2 New sheet

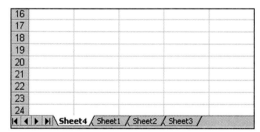

DELETE SHEETS

How: Click the tab of the sheet you want to delete and choose one of these methods:

   ❍ Choose **Edit|Delete Sheet**.
   ❍ Right-click and choose **Delete**.

Result: Excel prompts you to be sure because this deletion is permanent. Click **OK** to complete the process.

Warning: You can't use Undo to restore a deleted sheet, so think carefully before you do this.

Core Objective: Move between worksheets in a workbook

Core Objective: Rename a worksheet

What: Way back in Chapter 1, "Get Started with Excel," you learned how to navigate in Excel. Because we haven't used multiple sheets since then, here's a review of those techniques. They're more important as you use more than the three sheets in a workbook.

Why: When you have several sheets that relate to the same project, you can keep them in a single file by using different worksheets within a workbook. This is especially handy when you keep monthly reports and want to total them at the end of the quarter or year, for instance.

RENAME SHEETS

How: Double-click the sheet tab. Type the new name and press **Enter** (Figure 11.3). Repeat for the other sheets in the workbook.

Result: Your worksheet has a more meaningful name than Sheet1.

VIEW VARIOUS SHEETS

How: Use the sheet tabs and the tab scrolling buttons at the bottom of the workbook.

    ❍ Click a sheet tab at the bottom of the screen to bring that sheet to the top and make it the current sheet.

    ❍ Click the tab scrolling buttons to view more sheet tabs.

    ❍ Right-click the tab scrolling buttons to see a list of sheets by name (Figure 11.4). Choose one to jump immediately to that sheet.

Result: The tab you choose becomes the active sheet.

Figure 11.3 Renaming a sheet   **Figure 11.4** Choosing another sheet

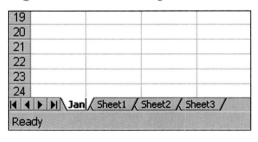
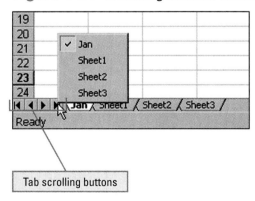

TIPS FROM A PRO: You can change the amount of space used to display sheet tabs versus the horizontal scroll bar. To do this, place the mouse over the tab split box (the vertical line on the left of the horizontal scroll bar) and drag left or right.

TASK 3 Move and Copy Sheets

C CORE OBJECTIVE: *Move and copy worksheets*

What: You may want to arrange your sheets in a different order, or even make a copy of a sheet and modify it. Whether you're working within a single workbook or among several, the techniques are simple.

Why: When you create chart sheets or insert a new sheet, the sheet may be out of order. Or you may want to include a sheet from a different workbook.

SELECTING SHEETS

How: Before you can copy and move them, you have to select them, of course.

- ❍ To select a single sheet, click its tab.
- ❍ To select several adjacent sheets, click the first tab, hold down the **Shift** key, and click the last tab.
- ❍ To select several non-adjacent sheets, hold down the **Ctrl** key while you click each tab.
- ❍ To select all the sheets, right-click the sheet tab and choose **Select All Sheets**.

Result: The sheet tabs turn white, indicating that the sheet or sheets are selected. When several sheets are selected, you see the label "(Group)" on the title bar, as in Figure 11.5.

Figure 11.5 Multiple sheets selected

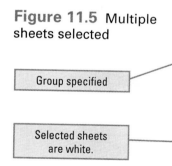

Group specified

Selected sheets are white.

 TIPS FROM A PRO: To ungroup sheets again so that only one sheet is selected, right-click and choose **Ungroup Sheets** from the shortcut menu.

MOVE AND COPY WITHIN A SINGLE WORKBOOK

How: Drag the sheet tabs to arrange or copy sheets.

- ❍ To move a sheet, drag the sheet tab left or right.
- ❍ To copy a sheet, hold down the **Ctrl** key and drag left or right.

Result: As you drag, the pointer displays a small worksheet icon, and a black arrowhead shows you where the sheet will be placed.

When you hold down the Ctrl key as you drag the sheet tab, a small plus sign indicates that you're making a copy, not just rearranging (Figure 11.6). When you copy a sheet within a workbook like this, Excel gives the copy the same name as the original, followed by a parenthetical number, like **Sheet1 (2)**.

MOVE AND COPY AMONG SEPARATE FILES

How: To copy or move sheets between files, have both of them open.

Warning: Be careful when moving or copying sheets. They may contain charts or formulas that depend on other sheets in the original workbook, or other items in the original may depend on them. It's a good idea to use Excel's auditing tools to trace the precedents and dependents to ensure that nothing will be wrecked if you move or copy the sheets.

---

1. Open both workbooks, both the source and the destination.
2. Select the sheets you want to copy or move.
3. Right-click the sheet tab and choose **Move or Copy**. This opens the dialog box shown in Figure 11.7.
4. Drop down the **To Book** list to specify which workbook to insert the sheets into. Choose **New Book** if you want to place them in a new file.
5. Specify which sheet you want to insert them before.
6. Click to select **Create a Copy** or leave the check box empty to move the sheets. Click **OK**.

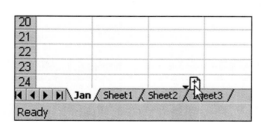

Figure 11.6 Copying a sheet by dragging

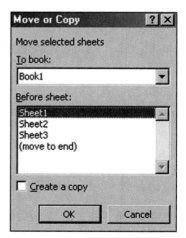

Figure 11.7 Move or Copy dialog box

Result: The selected sheets are moved or copied to the destination workbook.

What: Just as you can use formulas to refer to other cells in the worksheet, you can refer to cells on other worksheets or even other Excel files. You can use the pointing method or use the Paste Special command.

Why: You may have information from several departments, each on a separate worksheet within a file. Or if the worksheets are very large or complex, you may have several separate files. You could copy the data onto one huge worksheet, but very large files take a long time to open, save, and catch up with recalculating after every change. Instead, you can use links to refer to data kept in its original location.

THOUGHT QUESTION: What are some examples that use multiple sheets within a book or multiple files that you would want to combine into a summary worksheet?

LINK WORKSHEETS WITH THE POINTING METHOD

CORE OBJECTIVE: Link worksheets

How: Begin in the active cell by pressing =. Build the formula as usual, but when referring to a cell on another sheet, click the sheet tab first, and then click the cell. As you continue with the formula or press **Enter**, the formula is deposited in the active cell.

Result: The formula contains a cell reference that includes the name of the sheet. The reference contains the sheet name and the cell reference separated by an exclamation point (!), like this: **=Sheet1!B3.**

LINK WORKSHEETS USING PASTE SPECIAL

CORE OBJECTIVE: Cut, copy, paste, Paste Special, and move selected cells

How: If you want merely to display the contents of cells on another sheet, and not include them in a formula, you can use this method instead.

1. Select the cells or range you want to show and copy.
2. Move to the destination worksheet.
3. Choose **Edit|Paste Special**, and click the **Paste Link** button.

Result: As with the pointing method, the sheet name precedes the cell references (Figure 11.8). The difference is that with this method, the cell references are always absolute. Therefore, the formula looks like this: **=Sheet1!$B$3.**

Figure 11.8
Consolidating
worksheets

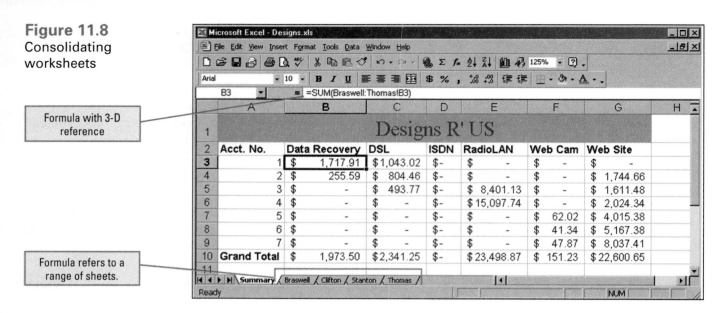

Formula with 3-D reference

Formula refers to a range of sheets.

LINK WORKBOOKS

E

EXPERT OBJECTIVE: Link workbooks

How: Before you begin, open both files—the one containing the data you want to link, and the destination where you want it to appear. Use either of the methods you used to link worksheets: use the pointing method or use Paste Special, Paste Link.

Result: The result refers to the name of the workbook [in brackets], the worksheet (followed by !), and the cell reference. If the worksheet is stored in a different drive or folder, the path or address of the file are also given. For example, ='[Bookname]Sheet1'!B3.

TASK 5   *Consolidate Worksheets*

C

CORE OBJECTIVE: Consolidate data using 3-D references

What: You can enter information on several sheets at once. This is called working in 3-D, because in addition to rows and columns, you have sheets stacked one on the other, giving your work a third dimension.

When you have the same information on several separate sheets, you can easily **consolidate** or combine them using **3-D references**, where the formulas refer to a range of worksheets followed by a cell address. The functions that you can use for consolidation include Sum, Average, Count, Counta, Min, Max, and others.

Consolidate worksheets using any of these techniques:

❍ Use 3-D references
❍ Use the **Data|Consolidate** command
❍ Link and consolidate

Why: Sometimes you want to total up the information for several months or for several individuals or departments. Don't retype or copy and paste. Instead, work efficiently by inputting the information on several sheets at a time. Consolidate information by referring to the various sheets. When the information is updated often, you may want to create links, or you may want to create a static, unlinked summary of the information at a given time.

EDIT SEVERAL WORKSHEETS AT ONCE

How: To create similar or identical worksheets at one time, follow these steps:

1. Click the tabs to select several sheets. The word "(Group)" appears on the title bar.
2. Enter text, formulas, and formatting on the top sheet.
3. Click the various sheets to check the results.

Result: All the selected sheets contain the same text, formulas, and formatting. They are all ready for you to enter separate numbers for each individual, department, or time period.

CONSOLIDATE WORKSHEETS WITH 3-D REFERENCES

How: Use the pointing technique you used to link cells in other worksheets—with a twist.

1. Insert a new sheet that will contain the consolidated information, or copy a sheet so that labels are already in place.
2. Copy and paste the labels to match (or, if you copied a sheet, erase the numbers).
3. Begin the function by typing **=** and then the name of the function and the opening parenthesis, for example: **=sum(**
4. Select the sheets containing the data you want to consolidate. (Click the first tab, hold down the **Shift** key, and click the last tab, as you learned in Task 3.)
5. Click to select the cell on one of the sheets and then complete the formula.

Result: The formula looks something like this: **=SUM(Sheet1:Sheet3!D2)**. You can then format the cell and fill it down for other cells in the column. Because the information is linked, when numbers change on any of the component worksheets, the consolidated worksheet reflects the update. Figure 11.8 shows a 3-D reference.

TIPS FROM A PRO: If the worksheets you want to consolidate do not have the cells in the exact same position each time, you can still consolidate them by using one of these methods:

- Refer to named ranges.
- Use linked formulas, as you learned in Task 4.

USE THE DATA|CONSOLIDATE COMMAND

How: The nice feature about the Consolidate command is that it enables you to use information in separate files, not just sheets within a single workbook. You can also do the entire range at once:

1. Select the range on the consolidation sheet where you want the results.
2. Choose **Data|Consolidate**, and you see the dialog box shown in Figure 11.9.

Figure 11.9
Consolidate dialog box

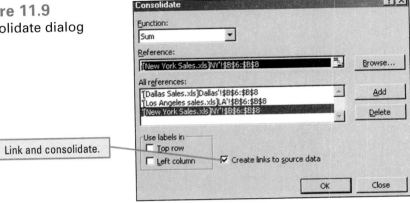

Link and consolidate.

3. Specify what function you want to perform, typically Sum or Average.
4. Click the **Collapse Dialog** button next to Reference and click the first tab. Select the range you want to refer to, and click **Add**.
5. Click another sheet tab. Excel automatically inserts the same range reference. Click **Add**. Repeat for all the sheets.
6. To refer to other files, click **Browse**. Specify the file, the sheet tab, and the range.
7. When you are finished adding references, click **OK**.

Result: Excel sums (or averages) the contents of the cells on each of the sheets and inserts numbers, not formulas referring to the original cells.

TIPS FROM A PRO: The Data|Consolidate command has another handy feature. When the worksheets are not in the exact same order but have the same labels, you can select the Use Labels in Top Row or Use Labels in Left Column check box. Excel picks up the correct information and consolidates it correctly.

LINK AND CONSOLIDATE

How: In the Data|Consolidate dialog box, choose **Create Links to Source Data** before you click OK (Figure 11.9).

Result: As you see in Figure 11.10, a formula appears, in this case =SUM(B6:B8). It seems curious because the formula doesn't refer to other sheets. But as you see in the figure, two changes have been made on screen:

○ The row numbers have changed, because hidden rows have been inserted.
○ Outlining symbols appear on the left edge of the screen.

Figure 11.10
Results of link and
consolidate

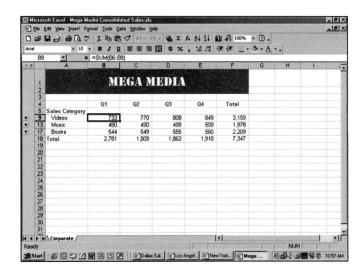

Excel has, behind the scenes, created rows containing links to the other
sheets, created a formula to sum (or average) them, and then hidden the
new rows, displaying only the summary information. Learn about outlining in the next section.

USE OUTLINING

EXPERT OBJECTIVE: Use grouping and outlines

How: The outlining symbols enable you to display or hide the detail rows, as
shown in Figure 11.11.

❍ To *expand* or show the detail on the hidden rows, click the small 2 at
the top of the outlining area.

Figure 11.11 Group
with outlines

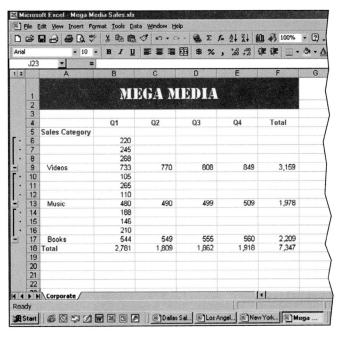

○ To *collapse* or hide the detail again, click the small 1.
○ To show the detail for a single row, click the + symbol.
○ To hide the detail for a single row, click the – symbol.

Result: As you expand the outline to show the detail, you see that a new row has been added to contain the data from each of the other sheets. The cell contains a link to each cell, and the summary row totals the values of the linked references.

To remove the outlining symbols from the screen and show all the hidden rows, choose **Data|Group and Outline|Clear Outline**. You'll use outlining again in Chapter 13, "Manage Data and Lists."

TIPS FROM A PRO: You've learned three different methods for consolidating data on different sheets or workbooks. To determine which one is best for a certain situation, read Table 11.1.

Table 11.1 Consolidation Methods and Results

Method	Use	Result
3-D references Consolidate command (not linked)	Worksheets in one file • Worksheets in one or several files • Sheets that have the same labels, but may not be exactly the same order	Linked references Numbers, not links
Link and consolidate	Worksheets in one or several files	• Linked references • Outline of details

TASK **6**   *Preview and Print Multiple Worksheets*

E

EXPERT OBJECTIVE: *Print and preview multiple worksheets*

What: When you have a workbook with multiple sheets, you'll probably want to print them. To do this efficiently, you need to specify what you want to print in the dialog box. You learned how to do this in Chapter 5, "Manage Pages and Printing," but here you'll learn specific techniques for handling multiple sheets.

Why: When you click the Print Preview button or Print button, the current sheet is previewed or printed. You probably don't want to repeat that process for each tab—you may forget one. Use these techniques to preview and print them all at once.

TIPS FROM A PRO: It's a good idea to include headers or footers that identify the sheet, especially if the worksheets are otherwise identical.

PREVIEW MULTIPLE SHEETS

How: First select several sheets, and then click the **Print Preview** button.

Result: In Print Preview, when you click the Next button, you see the contents of the next sheet.

PRINT MULTIPLE SHEETS

How: You can print multiple sheets.

○ Select the sheets and click the **Print** button.
○ Choose **File|Print** and under **Print What** choose **Active Sheet(s)** or **Entire Workbook**

Result: All the selected worksheets or the sheets in the entire workbook come rolling out of the printer.

Use PinPoint

After gaining the skills in this chapter, you can manage multiple worksheets, as well as copy and move them within a workbook or between separate files. You've created links between various sheets and consolidated the data. Now it's time to use the PinPoint software and see what you can do. Remember, whenever you are unsure of what to do, you can reread that portion of the chapter or you can click Show Me for a live demonstration. Check out these skills in PinPoint:

- Insert and name a sheet
- Link workbooks
- Link worksheets
- Move between sheets
- Move or copy sheets
- Print a workbook

Key Terms

You can find definitions for these words in this chapter:

3-D references
Collapse
Consolidate
Expand

Review Questions

You can use the following review questions to test your knowledge and skills. Answers are given in Appendix D.

True/False

Indicate whether each statement is true (T) or false (F).

___ 1. By default, each Excel workbook contains five worksheets.

___ 2. When you click the sheet tab, a shortcut menu appears.

___ 3. If you delete a sheet by mistake, don't worry because you can use Undo to restore it.

___ 4. To move a sheet within a workbook, hold down the Ctrl key and drag its tab left or right.

___ 5. When several sheets are selected, what you type appears on every sheet.

___ 6. To use 3-D references, build the formula as usual, but select all the sheets before completing the formula.

___ 7. You can use 3-D references to consolidate data or create several worksheets at once.

___ 8. When you use the Data| Consolidate command, you must use the Outline command to see the results.

___ 9. When several sheets are selected, you can preview the contents in Print Preview by clicking Next.

___ 10. When you click the Print button, Excel prints a page for every non-empty sheet in the workbook.

Multiple Choice

Select the letter that best completes the statement.

___ 1. To insert a worksheet:
   a. Choose Insert|Worksheet.
   b. Right-click the sheet tab and choose Insert.
   c. Copy a sheet from another Excel file.
   d. Move a sheet from another Excel file.
   e. All of the above.

___ 2. When you use the Move or Copy worksheet command, the new worksheet is inserted:
   a. As the first worksheet in the workbook.
   b. As the last worksheet in the workbook.
   c. Just before the active workbook.
   d. At the location it appeared in the original workbook.
   e. Wherever you specify in the dialog box.

___ 3. To rename a sheet:
   a. Double-click the sheet tab and type the new name.
   b. Choose Edit|Rename.
   c. Choose File|Save As and type the new name.
   d. Choose Edit|Replace and type the old name and the new name.
   e. All of the above.

___ 4. The tab scrolling buttons are used to navigate quickly to:
   a. The first or last sheet.
   b. The next or previous sheet.
   c. Any sheet by name.
   d. All of the above
   e. Only a and b.

___ 5. A cell reference that looks like this: =’[Sales]Sheet1’!B2:
   a. Refers to a cell in a worksheet in another file.
   b. Refers to a cell in another worksheet in the same file.
   c. Refers to a cell in the same worksheet in the same file.
   d. Is absolute.
   e. Is consolidated.

___ 6. An example of a 3-D reference is:
   a. =SUM(Sheet1:Sheet3!D2).
   b. =SUM(‘ [Book1]Sheet1’! D2:D5).
   c. =SUM(Sheet1!D2:D5).
   d. =3DSUM(Sheet1:Sheet3).
   e. All of the above.

___ 7. To consolidate data found in separate workbooks, use:
   a. A template.
   b. Paste Special.
   c. Data|Consolidate.
   d. The outlining feature.
   e. All of the above.

___ 8. When you use the Data| Consolidate command and create links, what you get is:
   a. An outline with the details hidden.
   b. Linked 3-D references in the Sum formula.
   c. Linked references, but not 3-D formulas.
   d. Numbers, not formulas.
   e. None of the above.

___ 9. To expand the results of the Consolidate command to see all the details:
   a. Click the + symbol.
   b. Click the – symbol.
   c. Click the 1 button.
   d. Click the 2 button.
   e. Choose View|Outline Details.

___ 10. To print all the sheets within a workbook:
   a. Click the sheet and click the Print button and repeat for each worksheet.
   b. Choose File|Print and choose Entire Workbook.
   c. Right-click the sheet tab and choose Print All Worksheets.
   d. Double-click the Print button and choose All Worksheets.
   e. Select all the sheets and choose File|Set Print Area.

Screen Review

Match the letters in Figure 11.12 with the correct items in the list.

Figure 11.12

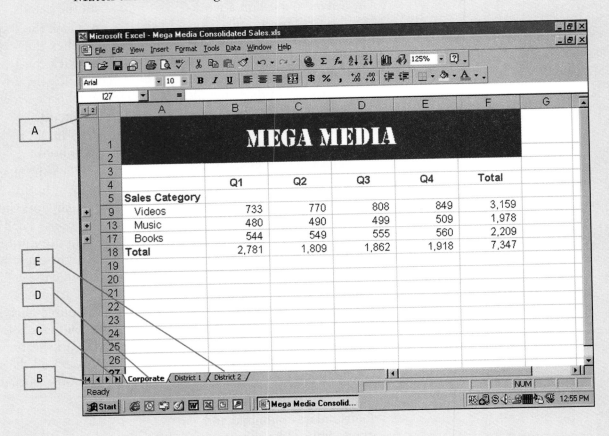

_____ 1. Click here to go to the last sheet in the workbook.

_____ 2. Double-click here to rename a worksheet.

_____ 3. Right-click here to move this sheet to a different workbook.

_____ 4. Click here to see cells with links to other worksheets.

_____ 5. Hold down the Shift key and click here to work in 3-D.

Exercise and Project

Follow these step-by-step instructions to create a workbook. If you are working in a computer lab, ask your instructor where you should save and print your document.

Exercise

1. Open **Multiple Sheets.xls** from the _Student\Chapter 11_ folder of your PinPoint CD.
2. Insert two new worksheets.
3. Rename the five sheets **Corporate, Dallas, LA, NY,** and **Houston.**
4. In cell C6, enter a formula to make the video sales grow by 5% each quarter. In cell C7, enter a formula to make music sales increase by 2% each quarter.

In cell C8, enter a formula to make book sales increase by 1% each quarter. Copy the formulas through Q4.

5. In row 9, enter a formula to sum rows 6 through 8 for each of the four quarters. In column F, enter a formula to sum columns B through E for each sales category.

6. Format cells B6:F9 as Number, with no decimal places.

7. Highlight A1:F9 in the Corporate sheet and click the Copy button. Now click the Dallas Sheet to make it active and click in cell A1. Next hold down Shift and click the Houston sheet tab.

8. With all of the worksheets selected, click the Paste button. You have copied the formulas and labels to the four sheets. Save the workbook.

9. The Houston store closed last quarter. Delete its sheet.

10. Fill the title headings with different colors for each city. Change the titles to **Dallas Stores, LA Stores,** and **NY Stores.**

11. Enter the following data on the individual sheets:

Dallas	Q1		LA	Q1		NY	Q1
Videos	220		**Videos**	245		**Videos**	268
Music	105		**Music**	265		**Music**	110
Books	188		**Books**	146		**Books**	210

12. Go to the Corporate sheet and create a 3-D reference. To do so, go to the Total for Q1 and type the following: **=SUM(** to begin the formula. Now click the **Dallas** sheet tab, hold down **Shift** and click the **NY** sheet tab; then click cell **B9** and type the closing parenthesis. The function should read =SUM(Dallas:NY!B9).

13. Copy the formula down to rows 7 and 8.

14. Add your name and the date to the Corporate sheet and print it once with values and once with formulas.

Project

Open the workbooks you created for the Exercise and Project in Chapter 8, where you created a depreciation table and amortization schedule. Start a new workbook. Tile the workbooks so you can see them all. Copy the sheets with the amortization table and the depreciation schedule to the new workbook.

On the new workbook, enter the following headings down Column A: Car payment, Outstanding balance, Depreciation, Current book value.

Next to each of these labels, link or copy the amounts for the 12th payment (or end of year 1) from the inserted sheets.

Enter a new label below the rest: **Current Status.** Create an If statement to determine whether you owe more than the car is currently worth. (*Hint*: If the Outstanding Balance is less than the Book Value, you are "OK," otherwise, you are "Upside Down" in your loan.)

Save the new workbook as **Car Finances.** Name each of the sheets appropriately, and make sure both your name and the sheet name appear in the header. Preview and print all the sheets.

Chapter 12

Import and Export

W hen data already exists electronically, you don't have to retype it to use Excel to format, analyze, or manage it. You can import it into Excel and put it in worksheet form so you can use all of Excel's familiar and powerful features. In the same sense, you can take existing Excel worksheets and charts and export them to other applications, including Word, PowerPoint, Access, and others.

At the end of this chapter, you will be able to:

C **E**

C	E	
❏	☑	Import data from text files (insert, drag and drop)
❏	☑	Create a link with an external data file
❏	☑	Use drag-and-drop to open a text file
❏	☑	Import from other applications
❏	☑	Import from other spreadsheet programs
❏	☑	Paste a Word table
❏	☑	Link a Word table
❏	☑	Use data from Access
☑	❏	Convert an imported file to Excel
❏	☑	Embed Excel into Word or PowerPoint
❏	☑	Link Excel into Word or PowerPoint
❏	☑	Export to Microsoft Access
❏	☑	Export to other applications

E

EXPERT OBJECTIVE: Import data from text files (insert, drag and drop)

What: When the information you want to use already exists in electronic format, you can *import* it to bring in into Excel. A *text file* is a very simple document containing only numbers and letters, but no formatting or formulas. Although text files are not pretty, they are handy because many programs can make use of the information stored in them. The items in a text file are either *delimited* (separated by tabs or commas) or of *fixed width*, meaning the same number of characters is used for any given item on every line.

You import text files into Excel three ways:

- ❍ Use the File|Open command to copy the data into Excel, without maintaining a link to the original file.
- ❍ Use the Data|Get External Data command to establish a link between the Excel file and the source file.
- ❍ Drag and drop the file name into an open Excel workbook to work directly with the text file itself.

Linking sets up a link between the worksheet cells and the original source of the data. Because of the link, any changes in the original are automatically reflected in the Excel worksheet.

Why: Now that you're skilled in using the various features of Excel, you'll want to use all the powerful and familiar features to manage the data and do calculations using the data. In Chapter 13, "Manage Data and Lists," you learn commands for manipulating and managing collections of data like this. But first, you have to bring the data into Excel.

OPEN THE TEXT FILE IN EXCEL

How: Text files are stored on disk with the extension *.txt*.

1. Click the **Open** button or choose **File|Open**.
2. In the Open dialog box, change **Files of Type** to **Text Files,** as you see in Figure 12.1.

Figure 12.1
Opening a text file

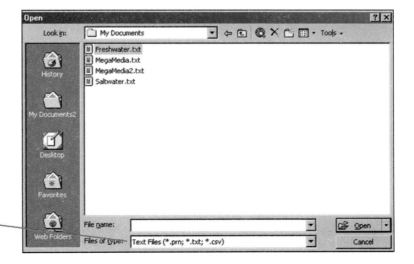

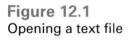

Change file type to Text.

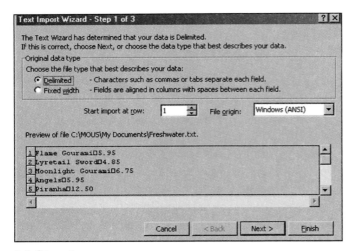

(a) Step 1

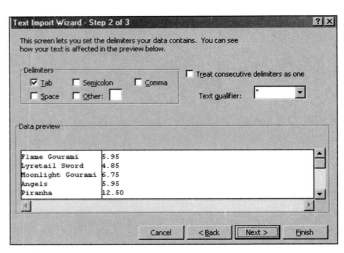

(b) Step 2

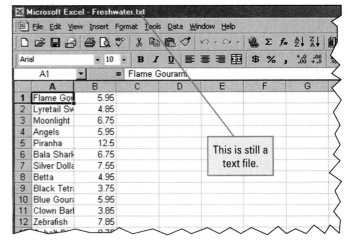

(c) Step 3

(d) Imported text file

Figure 12.2 Using the Text Import Wizard with a Delimited File

3. Browse to the correct drive and folder to see the file name and double-click it. This starts the Text Import Wizard, as you see in Figure 12.2a.

4. Specify whether the text file is delimited or fixed width. (Excel usually picks the correct one for you. For an example of fixed width, see the next section on using External Data.)

5. Click **Next** to see Step 2 of the wizard. Figure 12.2b shows how Excel guesses at how you want to separate the data into columns.

6. Click **Next** to see Step 3 of the wizard, as in Figure 12.2c. Here you specify what format to use for each column of the data. **General** is a good choice in most cases. To change it, click the column and choose General, Text, Date, or Skip.

TIPS FROM A PRO: When the data you are importing contains social security numbers or other numeric information that is used only as an ID, don't use **General** format for that column. Instead, choose **Text** for social security numbers. If you use General rather than Text by mistake, any leading zeros in the social security number are dropped.

Result: Click **Finish**, and the data is placed into columns and rows of an Excel worksheet (Figure 12.2d). This is not an Excel file, though, just a text file, as you can see in the title bar. To convert it permanently into an Excel file, choose **Save As** and change **Save as Type** to **Microsoft Excel Workbook,** as you'll see in Task 3.

MAINTAIN A LINK TO EXTERNAL DATA

How: Use this approach to establish a link to the original text file.

1. In Excel, click the cell where you want the data inserted.
2. Choose **Data|Get External Data|Import Text File.**
3. Step through the three steps of the Text Import Wizard. You learned how to use a delimited file; here are instructions for a fixed-width file. (Use either approach when importing a text file, whether or not you create a link.) When you choose Fixed Width, Step 1 of the wizard looks like Figure 12.3a.
4. Click **Next** to see Step 2 of the wizard. As you see in Figure 12.3b, here you use lines to specify where to divide the data into columns.
5. Click **Next** to see Step 3 of the wizard, as in Figure 12.3c. Here you specify what format to use for each column of the data. **General** is a good choice in most cases. To change it, click the column and choose General, Text, Date, or Skip.
6. Click **Finish,** and the Import Data dialog box appears (Figure 12.3d).
7. Specify where you want the data placed, either where you started the process or in a new sheet of the active file.
8. Click **Properties** to specify the column width, the formatting, and how often to refresh the data (Figure 12.3e). Click **OK** twice to complete the process.

Result: The text is brought into the rows and columns of Excel (Figure 12.3f). Later, if the text file changes, you can refresh it.

To refresh a file, choose **Data|Refresh Data** or click the **Refresh Data** button on the External Data toolbar. The new information is automatically brought into the Excel file, and old information is removed.

 TIPS FROM A PRO: In the Properties dialog box, check the box next to Fill Down Formulas in Columns Adjacent to Data. When you refresh the data, Excel looks for new rows and automatically fills any formulas down next to them. Pretty smart!

DRAG AND DROP

How: You don't have to use the Text Import Wizard if you want to let Excel handle how the text and columns are brought in.

1. Start Excel.
2. Open My Computer or Windows Explorer and browse until you see the name of the text file.
3. Drag the icon of the text file down onto the Excel button on the taskbar and pause. (Don't release the mouse button.) When the Excel window opens, drag and drop onto the sheet.

Result: The text file opens in Excel, with the data in rows and columns. This is not an Excel file, though, just a text file, as you can see in the title bar. To convert it permanently into an Excel file, choose **Save As** and change **Save as Type** to **Microsoft Excel Workbook,** as you'll see in Task 3.

Figure 12.3 Using the Text Import Wizard with a Fixed Width File

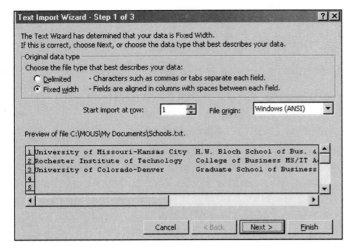

(a) Step 1

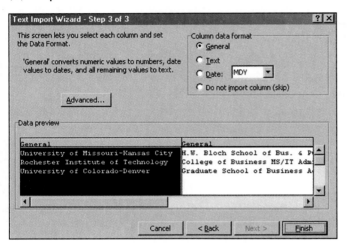

(c) Step 3

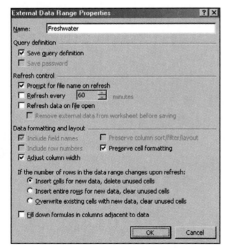

(e) External Data Range
Properties dialog box

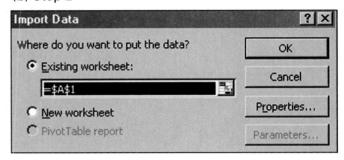

(d) Import Data dialog box

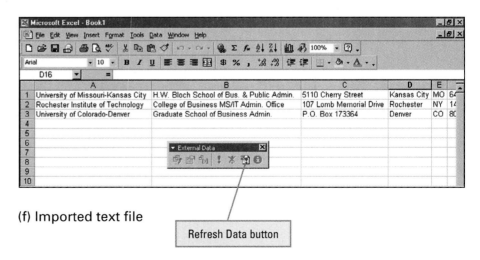

(f) Imported text file

Refresh Data button

E

Expert Objective: Import from other applications

What: Besides text files and other external data sources, Excel can make use of information from other spreadsheets, such as Lotus 1-2-3 and Works, or other Microsoft Office programs such as Word and Access.

Why: If you're sharing files with others who use different spreadsheet programs, you'll need to import them. In other cases, you might have a table in Word and need more formulas than Word provides. These are all reasons for importing.

IMPORT FROM OTHER SPREADSHEET PROGRAMS

How: Use the same technique you used for opening a text file.

1. Click the **Open** button or choose **File|Open**.
2. In the Open dialog box, change the **Files of Type** to the appropriate choice (various versions of Lotus 1-2-3, Works, Quattro Pro, and so on).
3. Browse to find the correct file, and double-click to open it.

Result: The file opens in Excel, with the formulas intact. To convert it permanently into an Excel file, choose **Save As** and change **Save as Type** to **Microsoft Excel Workbook**, as you'll see in Task 3.

Tips from a Pro: If you don't see the correct file type listed in the Open dialog box, you have to install the correct converter. If no converter is available, you might be able to save the other file in a format Excel can read, such as a text file, and then import it.

PASTE FROM WORD

How: You can't use File|Open with a Word file, but you can copy and paste from Word into Excel (Figure 12.4).

1. Select a short bit of text or a table in Word and copy it.
2. Change to Excel, click the cell where you want to insert the information, and paste.

Result: Each paragraph of text is inserted into a cell. (That's why this is not really appropriate for long paragraphs of text.) Word tables work beautifully, because the merged cells, font formatting, and contents are brought into the Excel worksheet. (You have to adjust the column width and row height, though.) The table in Word and the Excel worksheet are not linked when you simply paste.

Figure 12.4 Text and table pasted from Word
(a) In Word

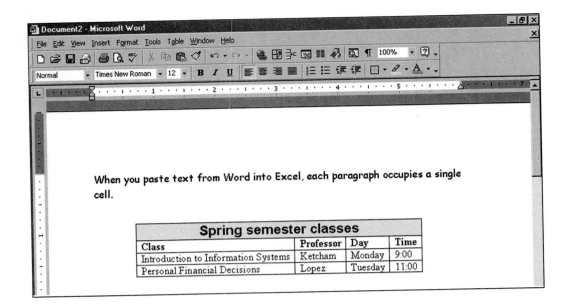

(b) In Excel after adjusting column width and row height

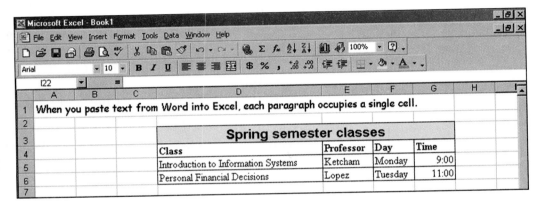

PASTE LINK FROM WORD

How: Establish a link from a Word table to an Excel worksheet with the Paste Special command.

1. Highlight the text or table in Word and copy it.
2. Change to Excel and click the cell that is at the top-left corner of where you want to insert the information.
3. Choose **Edit|Paste Special** to see the dialog box in Figure 12.5.
4. Click the option for **Paste Link**. In the As section, choose **Text** or **HTML**.

Figure 12.5 Paste Special, Paste Link dialog box

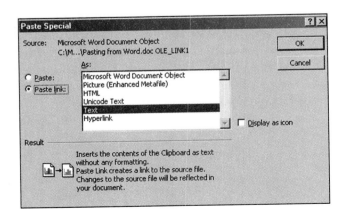

Figure 12.6 Cells linked to a Word table

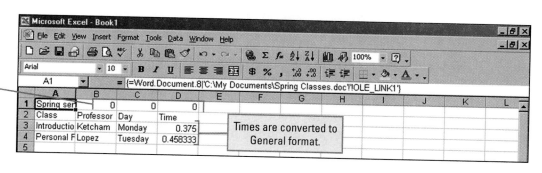

Formerly merged cells show 0.

Times are converted to General format.

Result: The table is inserted with the cells arranged the same as the Word table. However, the formatting is not brought in. Instead, Excel's default format is applied to the text and numbers (Arial 10, black, with left-aligned text and right-aligned numbers). If you look in the formula bar, you won't see the numbers in the cells. Instead, you see a curious reference to the Word document (Figure 12.6).

You can't change the information in Excel (you get an error message if you try), but you can build formulas that refer to the cells. To change the information, you have to edit the table in Word, and the information in Excel immediately changes to show the new information.

USE DATA FROM MICROSOFT ACCESS

How: You can copy and paste information from an Access table, query, or form into Excel.

1. In Access, change to Datasheet View, and select the columns and rows. Copy.
2. In Excel, click the cell that is at the top-left corner of where you want the data inserted. Paste.

Alternatively, you can create an Excel worksheet from an Access table, query, form, or report. In Access, choose **Tools|Office Links|Analyze It With MS Excel**.

Result: The data appears in rows and columns, with the field names as the top row of each column. This technique is good for analyzing small amounts of data in Excel that will not change. To analyze large amounts of data or to maintain a refreshable link between Excel and Access, you should use other techniques. For additional information, search Excel's Help for the topic "Exchange Data between Microsoft Excel and Microsoft Access."

TASK 3   *Convert an Imported File to Excel*

C

CORE OBJECTIVE: *Use Save As (different name, location, format)*

What: You import a text file or some other type of file into Excel so you can use all of the powerful features to build formulas and add formatting. When you save the file, however, some of these Excel features might be lost. To keep the features, the file must be converted to an Excel worksheet.

Why: If you've gone to the trouble of using the Import Wizard, adding formulas and formatting, you probably want to save these additions to the file so you can use them again. To do this, you must convert the file to an Excel worksheet.

How: Begin the process with the imported file open in Excel.

1. Choose **File|Save As**.
2. Click **Save as Type** and choose **Microsoft Excel Workbook (*.xls)**, the top choice on the list.
3. Rename the file if you want, and click **Save** to complete the process.

Result: The file is saved with *.xls* as its extension, and the formatting and formulas are preserved.

TASK 4   *Export a Worksheet or Chart*

EXPERT OBJECTIVE: **Export to other applications**

What: The programs in the Office suite are built to be *integrated,* to work together, so you can seamlessly bring your work from Excel into Word or PowerPoint. When you have an Excel worksheet with the information you need to use in another program, you can copy and paste it there. There are three approaches you can use when sharing Excel with Word or PowerPoint:

❍ Paste the information, so that it becomes data in the document or presentation.
❍ *Embed* the information, so that it retains Excel's formulas and functionality.
❍ Link the information, so that it stays connected to the original Excel worksheet. Any changes in Excel are automatically reflected in the destination.

Why: You've done your analysis in Excel and created charts, but now you need to write up a report or make a presentation. To create documents, you need Word, and to make great visual aids, rely on PowerPoint. You'll want to take the worksheet or chart you created in Excel and use it in these other programs.

EMBED EXCEL SHEETS AND CHARTS IN WORD OR POWERPOINT

How: To do this, open both the Excel workbook that contains the information and the Word or PowerPoint file where you want to place it.

1. In Excel, select the cells or chart. Copy.
2. In Word or PowerPoint, place the insertion point where you want the information to be placed.
3. Choose **Edit|Paste Special**. The Paste Special dialog box appears, as shown in Figure 12.7.

Figure 12.7 Paste Special dialog box

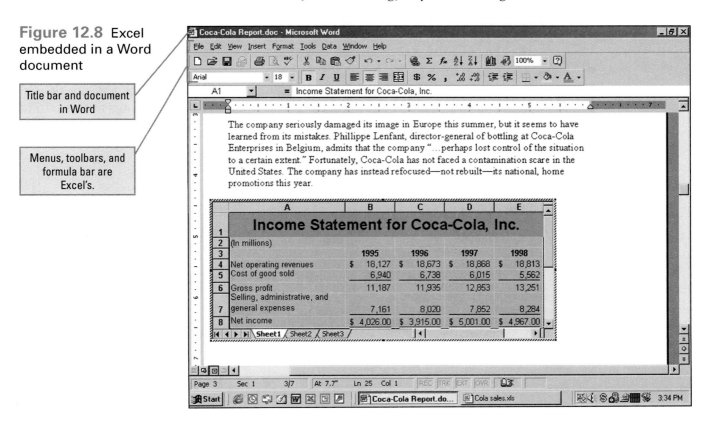

Choose these options to embed.

4. If necessary, click the **Paste** option on the left side of the dialog box.
5. In the As section, click **Microsoft Excel Worksheet Object**. (The other choices simply insert the cells as picture, text, or HTML, without retaining Excel's formulas.)
6. Click **OK**.

Result: The selected worksheet cells appear in the document surrounded by sizing handles, like a picture. The formulas and formatting are the same as in the original Excel worksheet.

Although only the selected cells are displayed, a copy of the complete Excel workbook is contained within the Word or PowerPoint file. Changes in the original Excel file do not affect the copy contained in the document.

Embedding means that when you want to make changes, you double-click the "picture" of the Excel chart or cells. Immediately, the Excel menus and toolbars appear for you to use to modify the information, formulas, or formatting, as you see in Figure 12.8.

Figure 12.8 Excel embedded in a Word document

Title bar and document in Word

Menus, toolbars, and formula bar are Excel's.

LINK SHEETS AND CHARTS INTO WORD OR POWERPOINT

How: Before you can establish a link between Excel and the other program, the original Excel workbook must be saved, and you must have both files open.

1. Copy the Excel cells or chart as usual.
2. Switch to Word or PowerPoint, and place the insertion point where you want to place the Excel information.
3. Choose **Edit|Paste Special**.
4. Click the **Paste Link** option on the left side of the dialog box, shown in Figure 12.9.
5. In the As section, click **Microsoft Excel Worksheet Object**. Click **OK**.

Result: The cells of the worksheet appear in the destination surrounded by sizing handles, like a picture. If the Excel sheet changes, the new numbers are automatically updated in the Word document or PowerPoint presentation. When you double-click a linked object, the original file opens in a separate Excel window for you to make changes.

Figure 12.9 Paste
Special dialog box

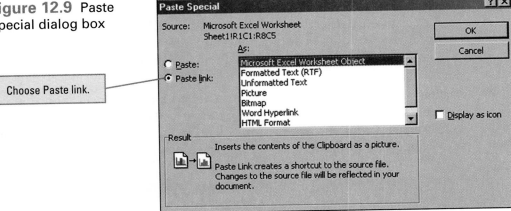

Choose Paste link.

 TIPS FROM A PRO: After you insert the chart or cells into PowerPoint, use the sizing handles to make the item much larger. To project well, the fonts must be 16 to 20 points at a minimum (the bigger the better).

EXPORT TO MICROSOFT ACCESS

How: Data in Excel can be copied and pasted in Access, but only if you have already created a table with the exact same column headings and data types (dates, numbers, text, and so on). Instead, you can use Excel's automatic converter.

1. In Excel, click anywhere within a data list. (You learn about this in Chapter 13.)
2. Choose **Data|Convert to MS Access**.
3. Choose one of the following options:
   - New database, to create a brand new Access database from the Excel data.
   - Existing database. You need to browse to specify which Access file to use.

Result: From there, Access takes over and provides a wizard to help you permanently convert the worksheet.

TIPS FROM A PRO: If the Convert to MS Access command isn't on the Data menu, you need to install the AccessLinks add-in program.

EXPORT TO OTHER SPREADSHEET PROGRAMS

How: Begin the process with the worksheet open in Excel.

1. Choose **File|Save As**.
2. Click **Save as Type** and choose the appropriate file type on the list.
3. Rename the file if you want, and click **Save** to complete the process.

Result: The file is saved with a new extension. Some of the formatting and formulas may be lost, but Excel does a pretty good job at substituting the equivalent formulas and functions so the other program can read it.

Use PinPoint

After gaining the skills in this chapter, you can import data from text files, create links with other files, import and export to and from Excel, and integrate Excel with other programs in the Microsoft Office suite. Now it's time to use the PinPoint software and see what you can do. Remember, whenever you are unsure of what to do, you can reread that portion of the chapter or you can click Show Me for a live demonstration. Check out these skills in PinPoint:

- Export data
- Import a text file

Key Terms

You can find definitions for these words in this chapter:

Delimited
Embed
Fixed width
Import
Integrated
Link
Text file

Review Questions

You can use the following review questions to test your knowledge and skills. Answers are given in Appendix D.

True/False

Indicate whether each statement is true (T) or false (F).

___ 1. A simple document containing numbers and text that you can use in Excel is called a text file.

___ 2. When you use the File|Open command to open a text file, you establish a link with the original file.

___ 3. You can use drag-and-drop to place a text file in Excel without even opening the text file.

___ 4. When you want the information you brought from another file to change when the original changes, you must link it.

___ 5. When you open a text file, Excel automatically starts the Text Import Wizard.

___ 6. To link an imported Excel worksheet with its original file, choose Text|Import Wizard.

___ 7. To link a Word table with an Excel worksheet, use the Edit|Paste Special|Paste Link command.

___ 8. To embed a chart or worksheet into Word or PowerPoint, use the Paste Special command.

___ 9. To change an Excel chart or worksheet embedded in Word or PowerPoint, double-click it to use Excel's menus and toolbars.

___ 10. To paste a chart or worksheet into Word or PowerPoint, you must use the Paste Special command.

Multiple Choice

Select the letter that best completes the statement.

___ 1. When importing data from a text file, you have to specify whether the data is:
   a. Delimited with commas.
   b. Demarcated by commas.
   c. Defined by commas.
   d. Derived with commas.
   e. Defamed by commas.

___ 2. When you copy a table in Word and switch to Excel and click the Paste button, what appears is:
   a. Cells with the same formatting as in Word.
   b. Cells without any formatting at all.
   c. An embedded Word object.
   d. A linked Excel worksheet.
   e. A chart.

___ 3. When you copy a table in Word and use Paste Special to create a link to it, what appears in Excel is:
   a. Cells with the same formatting as in Word.
   b. Cells without any formatting at all.
   c. A picture of the Word table with sizing handles.
   d. A text file.
   e. A chart.

___ 4. After you open a text file in Excel, to keep the formulas and formatting you added, choose:
   a. File|Convert.
   b. File|Export.
   c. File|Import.
   d. File|Save.
   e. File|Save As.

_____ 5. The Text Import Wizard is used to:
   a. Define how a text file will be placed into Excel's columns.
   b. Permanently convert a text file into Excel.
   c. Make a text file readable to Excel.
   d. Convert an Excel file into a text file.
   e. Set up a refreshable link between the Excel worksheet and the text file.

_____ 6. Excel can handle data and information from:
   a. Text files.
   b. Word tables.
   c. Other spreadsheet programs such as Lotus 1-2-3 or Works.
   d. All of the above.
   e. Both a and b.

_____ 7. Importing and exporting among Word, Excel, and PowerPoint is easy, but you can't:
   a. Bring Excel worksheets into Word and PowerPoint.
   b. Bring Excel charts into Word and PowerPoint.
   c. Bring Word text into an Excel worksheet.
   d. Bring Word tables into an Excel worksheet.
   e. All of the above are things you can do.

_____ 8. When an Excel chart is embedded into Word or PowerPoint:
   a. It will not change if the Excel worksheet changes.
   b. You can double-click to modify it using Excel's menus and toolbars.
   c. It has sizing handles so you can enlarge it.
   d. The chart looks the same as it does in Excel.
   e. All of the above.

_____ 9. The best way to take data from Excel into Microsoft Access is to:
   a. Copy and paste it into any datasheet if both are open.
   b. Use a special command to convert it into an Access database.
   c. Export the data to a text file and then import the text file into Access.
   d. Bring the worksheet into a Word table, and from there, export it to Access.
   e. None of the above. You can't bring Excel into Access.

_____ 10. Word and Excel can work together to bring charts into a document because they are:
   a. Interpolated.
   b. Interrelated.
   c. Integrated.
   d. Interactive.
   e. Intelligent.

Screen Review

Match the letters in Figure 12.10 with the correct items in the list.

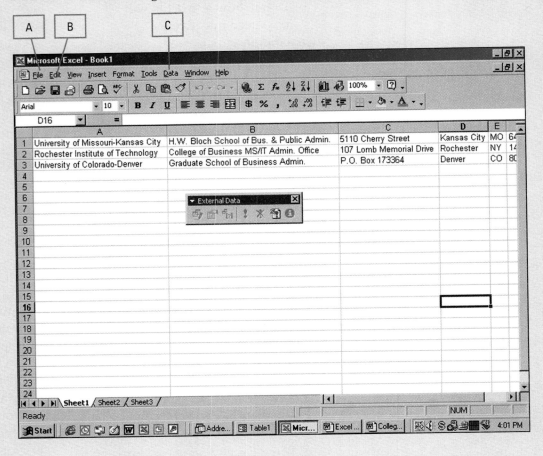

Figure 12.10

___ 1. Click here to open a text file in Excel.

___ 2. Click here to import data from an external database.

___ 3. Click here to link a Word table into Excel.

___ 4. Click here to convert an imported file to Excel file format.

___ 5. Click here to convert an Excel database into an Access table.

Exercise and Project

Follow these step-by-step instructions to import and export worksheets. If you are working in a computer lab, ask your instructor where you should save and print your file.

Exercise

1. In Excel, open **Freshwater.txt** from the *Student\Chapter 12* folder of your PinPoint CD. The text is tab delimited and needs a General format.

2. Name the sheet **Freshwater**. Save the file as an Excel workbook named **Sea Reef** (with the extension **.xls**). Place your name and class time in the header.

3. On Sheet 2, use the command **Data|Get External Data|Import Text File** to import **Saltwater.txt** from the PinPoint CD. The file is tab delimited and

needs a General format. When you get to the Finish button, click **Properties** and choose **Refresh data on file open.**

4. Name the sheet **Saltwater** and save the file again.

5. Print both sheets. Close the workbook. Minimize Excel.

6. Go to Windows Explorer and locate **Saltwater.txt** in the *Student\Chapter 12* folder of the PinPoint CD. Drag this file to the Excel button on the taskbar. Wait, and when Excel opens, drop it into the worksheet. Close without saving.

7. In Word, open the document **Schedule.doc** from your PinPoint CD. Select the table data and copy it. Now start a new file in Excel, choose Edit|Paste Special, and paste link as an HTML file.

8. Change the exam time on Wednesday from 8:00 to 2:00 in the Word document.

9. In Excel, widen the columns, place an AutoFormat on the table, and title it **Finals Schedule.** Print the worksheet.

10. Reopen **Sea Reef.xls** and insert a new worksheet.

11. Start the program Microsoft Access, and open the database called **Sea Reef.mdb** from the *Student\Chapter 12* folder of your PinPoint CD.

12. On the left side of the window, click **Tables,** and on the right side, double-click **Inventory Table.** Highlight the column headings and data and copy.

13. Go back to the Excel file and paste the data into the new worksheet. Name the sheet **Equipment.** Print the sheet and save the file.

14. Open the file called **Expense Chart.xls** from the PinPoint CD. Select the chart and copy it.

15. Start a new file in Word and type your name and class heading on it. Embed the chart in the document. Print the document.

16. Close all open files and exit Access, Word, and Excel.

Project

Create a table in Notepad (using tabs) with a list of your monthly expenses and save it as a text file. Link this to an Excel file using Data|Get External Data. (Don't forget to click Properties in the wizard to refresh the data every minute or on File Open.) Now create a 3-D pie chart in Excel of those expenses. Link this to a Word document and print it. Make a change in the Notepad table for one of the expenses. Go back to Excel and explode the pie portion representing the changed expense. Return to Word and print the document with the updated chart.

Manage Data and Lists

What's the difference between data and information? Information is data that has been collected and organized so that you can use it as the basis for decision making. Databases are collections of organized data, and they're found everywhere, from the telephone book to the receipt from the grocery store, as well as in electronic form. Excel has a powerful data management capability that lets you add and edit items in a database, sort data, query it, and summarize it.

At the end of this chapter, you will be able to:

C **E**

- ☐ ☐ Create an Excel list and add and edit data
- ☐ ☑ Use a data form
- ☐ ☑ Use data validation
- ☐ ☑ Perform single and multilevel sorts
- ☐ ☐ Create and use a custom list for sorting
- ☐ ☑ Use subtotaling
- ☐ ☑ Use grouping and outlines
- ☐ ☑ Apply AutoFilters and advanced filters
- ☐ ☑ Extract data
- ☐ ☑ Query an external database
- ☐ ☑ Use PivotTables
- ☐ ☑ AutoFormat a PivotTable
- ☐ ☑ Create a PivotChart

What: The first step in creating a database is to plan its components. You want to keep the information in a form you can use easily. What is it you want to know, and how will you use it? Individuals keep a list of names and addresses for their class reunions, or for Christmas card lists, or for wedding invitations, for example.

Collections of information use certain terms. Using a dictionary as an example of a database, the *fields* or categories include the word, its part of speech, pronunciation, definition, and synonyms. The *records* are all the information about a single word. A dictionary might have several *lists* or tables of information: the main part to define standard English words, another section in the back with geographical names, or a section explaining foreign words and phrases.

Why: When you set up the database correctly, you can either type directly in the worksheet or use a data form to add and edit the contents of the database.

How: In Excel, you must set up a database this way:

○ In the top row, type the *field names*, or categories for each column of information.

○ Format the field names differently from the records (for instance, in bold), so that Excel recognizes this information as a *header row*, not part of the subsequent rows of data.

○ In each subsequent row, place a single record, a collection of information about one individual.

○ For each record, type the contents of each field, or column. Make sure to put similar items in the same field for each record.

○ Keep at least one blank row and column between an Excel list (called a "table" in Access) and any other information on the worksheet.

Result: A sample database of employees for Mallard's Department Store is shown in Figure 13.1. Notice the blank line between the heading and the field names at the top of the list.

Figure 13.1 Sample database

E   EXPERT OBJECTIVE: *Use data forms*

What: After creating the database, you can type the data directly in the worksheet, or you can use a *data form*, a special dialog box used for managing entries in the database.

Why: The data form offers a nice view of all the fields for a single record. When you're using the worksheet to enter your data, you often have to scroll left or right to see the various fields, and if your database gets large, the field names may scroll off the screen. The data form keeps them together in a single dialog box.

ADD DATA

How: Click anywhere within the database and choose **Data|Form.**

1. Click **New** to get a blank form, ready for you to type in the information for a new record. As you see in Figure 13.2, field names are listed down the left side.
2. Type in the information for the first field. Press **Tab** to move to the next field text box, or press **Shift+Tab** to move to the previous text box (or click with the mouse).

Figure 13.2 Data form

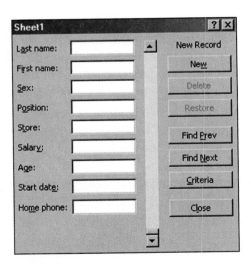

 TIPS FROM A PRO: If you press Enter by mistake, you'll find yourself with a new blank record when you hadn't finished the other one. Click the **Find Prev** button to back up to the unfinished record.

3. To undo all the changes, click **Restore**, or if all is correct press **Enter** or click **New**. A blank form appears, ready for you to type the next record.
4. When you have entered all the records, click **Close** to return to the worksheet.

Result: The information you enter using the data form is added to the worksheet. New records appear on the bottom row.

DELETE A RECORD

How: Use one of these methods to delete a record, either on the worksheet or in the data form:

- On the worksheet, select the row and choose **Edit|Delete**.
- In the data form, click **Find Next** or **Find Prev** until you see the record you want to delete. Click **Delete**.

Result: The current record (row) is removed from the worksheet. You'll learn more about using the data form for searching for specific records in Task 7.

| TASK **3** | *Validate Data* |

EXPERT OBJECTIVE: Use data validation

What: When others are entering data into the database, you may want to place restrictions or give instructions on how the data is entered.

Warning: Data validation doesn't work when entering data using the data form.

Why: Validation enables you to restrict the data in our example database the following ways:

- Allow management employees only age 21 or older.
- Require start date to be entered as numbers (10/1), rather than text (Oct. 1).
- Provide instructions on how to enter the data: "Enter telephone number with area code first."
- Restrict entries to those on a list. For example, you don't want varied entries for a single position, such as "assistant manager," "asst. manager," "asst. mgr," and so on.

RESTRICT THE TYPE AND AMOUNT OF DATA ENTERED

How: Use the Settings tab of the Validation dialog box.

1. Select the column you want restricted by the data validation.
2. Choose **Data|Validation**, and click the **Settings** tab (Figure 13.3).
3. Click **Allow** to specify how you want to restrict the cell entry. Choose from the drop-down list to set the requirements for the data:
   - Whole number
   - Decimal
   - List (you'll learn about this in the next section)
   - Date
   - Time
   - Text length
   - Custom (to have it based on a formula or an entry in another cell)

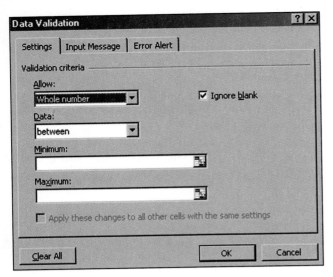

Figure 13.3 Validating data

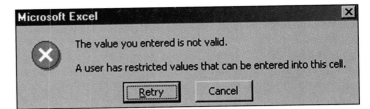

Figure 13.4 Invalid data gets an error message

4. Specify the boundaries. In our example, for Age you would choose **Whole Number**, and then specify **Greater than or equal to 21**.
5. Click **OK**.

Result: When someone tries to enter an incorrect item in those cells, an error message appears, as you see in Figure 13.4.

 THOUGHT QUESTION: What examples can you give where you would use data validation to restrict the type of data entered?

OFFER A LIST OF ITEMS TO CHOOSE FROM

How: To keep data consistent, set up a list of items to choose from.

1. Type the list of valid entries somewhere on the same worksheet. Do not include blank cells in the list. (If it's a short list, you can skip this step.)
2. Select the cells that you want to restrict.
3. Choose **Data|Validation**, and choose the **Settings** tab.
4. Drop down the **Allow** list box and click **List** (Figure 13.5).
5. In the **Source** box, refer to cells containing the list of possible entries, or simply type the list here with the items separated by commas. Click **OK**.

Result: A drop-down arrow appears on the worksheet next to the cell. When you click the arrow, the list of possible entries is shown for you to choose from (Figure 13.6). If you try to type another entry into it, an error message appears.

CUSTOMIZE THE ERROR MESSAGE

How: Use the Error Alert tab of the Validation dialog box.

1. Select the column you want restricted by the data validation.
2. Choose **Data|Validation** and click the **Error Alert** tab (Figure 13.7).
3. Choose the style of the icon (Stop, Warning, or Information), and type the title and text of the error message. A Stop message won't let

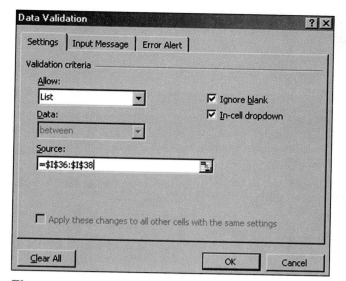

Figure 13.5 List settings

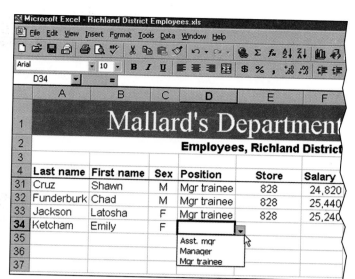

Figure 13.6 Drop-down list for data entry

you continue (*Retry, Cancel*). A Warning message lets you go ahead if you want to (*Continue? Yes, No, Cancel*), and an Information message simply makes you confirm the entry. Click **OK**.

Result: If you do this right, you can offer a more friendly and helpful error message than the default one that appears (Figure 13.8).

Figure 13.7 Error Alert tab

Figure 13.8 Sample error message

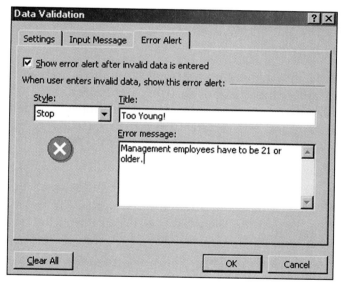

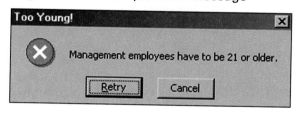

OFFER AN INPUT MESSAGE

How: Use the Input Message tab of the Validation dialog box to offer a hint as to what to type.

1. Select the column you want restricted by the data validation.
2. Choose **DataValidation** and choose the **Input Message** tab (Figure 13.9).
3. Type the title and the text for the message and click **OK**.

Result: As soon as a user clicks the cell, the Input Message appears (Figure 13.10).

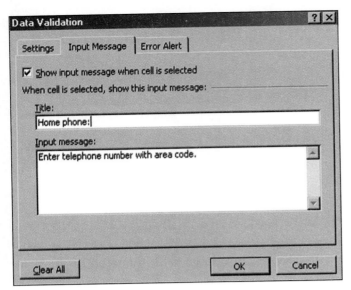

Figure 13.9 Input Message tab

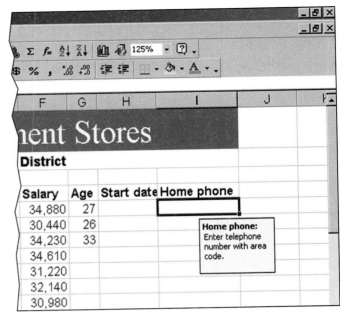

Figure 13.10 A sample input message

TASK 4   *Sort*

E

EXPERT OBJECTIVE: *Perform single and multilevel sorts*

What: Sort the data to organize the information the way you want. You can order the data in one of two ways:

- ○ **Sort ascending.** This alphabetizes text, arranges numbers from lowest to highest, and orders times and dates from first to last.
- ○ **Sort descending.** This arranges text from Z to A, arranges numbers from highest to lowest, and orders dates and times from most recent to earliest.

You can sort a database according to the information in a single column, or sort on several columns if there is a tie in the first field. For example, you can sort on last name and then on first name. All the last names are alphabetized, but all the Johnsons are further sorted by first name. You can also sort on a third field.

Why: Of course you want to alphabetize names. You might want to arrange the database by department. On the other hand, you might want to arrange a database with the highest number on top, such as students' test grades, or the number of widgets sold.

DO A SINGLE SORT

How: Use the buttons to sort on a single field.

1. Click anywhere within the field you want to use as the basis of the sort.

 2. Click the **Sort Ascending** or **Sort Descending** button.

Result: The entire database is rearranged so the data is in the order you specified.

Warning: Do *not* highlight a column before sorting. If you do, the only thing that will be sorted is that column, independent of the rest of the database. Imagine doing this when sorting the Sex column and finding the names separated from their respective M or F! Your employees won't like that!

MULTILEVEL SORT

How: You can sort on several fields using either the buttons or the dialog box.

1. Click anywhere in the database.
2. Choose **Data|Sort**. The dialog box shown in Figure 13.11 appears.
3. Choose the field you want to sort first (the field names are shown in the drop-down list box) and designate whether to sort ascending or descending.
4. Specify the second and third sort, as needed. Click **OK**.

Result: The database is sorted based on information in more than one column. In the example in Figure 13.12, you can see the men listed first, and then they are sorted alphabetically by last and first name.

TIPS FROM A PRO: You can also use the buttons for a multilevel sort, but you have to keep your wits about you. Start by sorting on the *least* important field. Then sort on the second most important field, and finish by sorting on the *most* important field. You see, each sort supersedes the last, but it doesn't rearrange more than it has to.

Figure 13.11 Sort dialog box

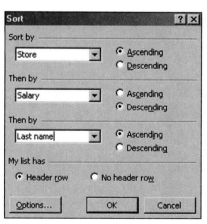

Figure 13.12 A sorted database

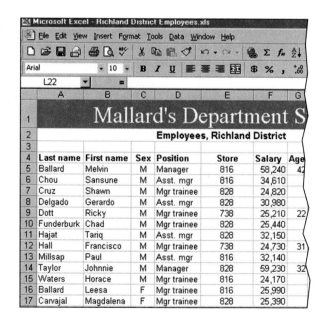

What: Have you wanted to sort items in a different order than ascending or descending? Create a custom data list and use it as the basis for your sort.

Why: High, Medium, and Low should be sorted in a logical order, not alphabetical. Same thing with Spring, Summer, Autumn, and Winter; Monday, Tuesday, Wednesday; and January, February, March. You might have special department names or categories that you want sorted in a certain, logical order.

 TIPS FROM A PRO: When you create a custom list, you can also use it with AutoFill. Just type in the first one of the series, and when you drag the fill handle, AutoFill supplies the next ones in the sequence.

CREATE A CUSTOM LIST

How: Follow these steps to set up your custom list.

1. Select cells in the worksheet that contain the sequence, if any. (This step is optional.)
2. Choose **Tools|Options** and click the **Custom Lists** tab.
3. Type the sequence in the List Entries box, or click **Import List From Cells** to specify which cells contain the list. (If you selected cells first, their cell references appear here.) Click **Add** (Figure 13.13).

Result: Your custom list is added to the ones that Excel provides for you (days of the week, months of the year, and so on). Click OK, and use the custom list for filling or for sorting.

Figure 13.13
Creating a custom list

Your custom list added here.

Type your list here.

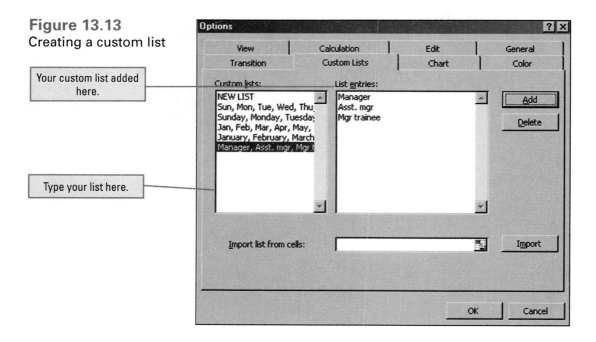

SORT USING A CUSTOM LIST

How: It's easy to sort in logical order when you've created a custom list.

1. Click somewhere in the database, preferably the field you want to sort using the custom sort order.
2. Choose **DatalSort**.
3. In the dialog box, specify the field and click the **Options** button to see the Sort Options dialog box (Figure 13.14).
4. Choose the custom sort order from the drop-down list, and click **OK** twice.

Result: The database is sorted in logical order, according to your custom list (Figure 13.15).

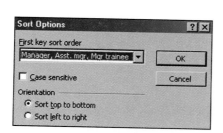

Figure 13.14 Sort Options dialog box

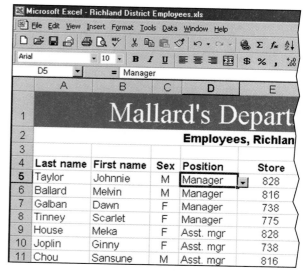

Figure 13.15 A database sorted in logical order

 TIPS FROM A PRO: You can also use the Sort Options dialog box to sort columns. To do this, choose **Sort Left to Right**.

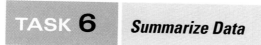

TASK 6   *Summarize Data*

What: Sure, you know how to calculate a sum. The Subtotals feature lets you quickly find totals for a subgroup of data, say, the total payroll for each store. You can use the Subtotals command to summarize the data using the Sum, Average, Min, Max, and Count functions, as well as several others.

Why: When working with a large database, imagine how much trouble it would be to sort the database, insert a blank row, and create a function to sum, average, or count the data for each department or other category. The Subtotals command does it for you automatically, and lets you view the summary information several ways.

SUBTOTAL THE DATA

EXPERT OBJECTIVE: Use subtotaling

How: This works great not only on a database, but on any worksheet where you want to create subtotals or averages automatically.

1. Sort the database into groups. Don't forget this crucial first step! If you want to subtotal the salaries for each store, for example, you have to sort by the store column first. If you want to average the salary for each position, you have to sort by the position first.
2. Choose **Data|Subtotals** to open the dialog box shown in Figure 13.16.
3. For **At Each Change In**, specify the column you want the subtotals grouped by (the one you sorted on in Step 1).
4. Choose the function you want to use (typically Sum, Average, Min, or Max for numbers, or Count for text fields).
5. For **Add Subtotal To**, click to choose the columns on which you want the function performed. You can choose one field or several, but the same function is used on all of them.
6. Click **OK** to apply the subtotals.

Result: Excel automatically inserts rows and headings and calculates the subtotal, whether sum or average or another function. It also inserts the outline symbols on the left edge of the screen (Figure 13.17). You'll learn how to use these in the next section.

Figure 13.16 Subtotals dialog box

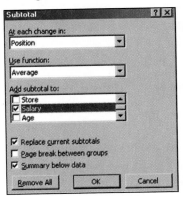

Figure 13.17 Subtotals added to a database

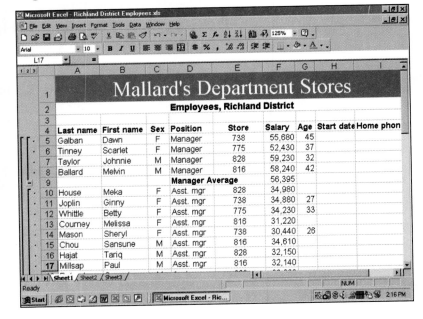

TIPS FROM A PRO: What happens if you forget to sort before you apply subtotals? Your database gets to be a mess, as you see in Figure 13.18. The Subtotals command works by adding the sum or average every time there is a change in a certain field. If the field is unsorted, too many subtotals are added, rather than a single one.

Figure 13.18
Subtotals added to an
unsorted database

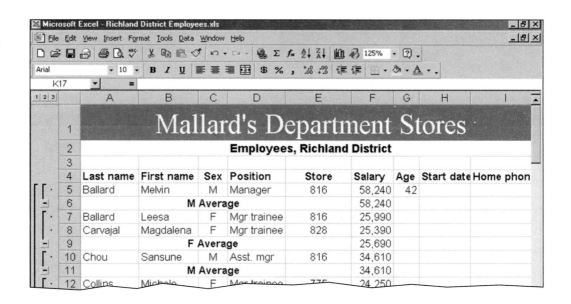

USE GROUP AND OUTLINE

 E

EXPERT OBJECTIVE: Use grouping and outlines

How: After you apply subtotals, you can use the group and outline feature.

❍ Click the **2** button in the Outline symbols to collapse the outline to see the subtotals only and hide the rows of data (Figure 13.19).

❍ Click the **1** button in the Outline symbols to collapse it even further and show only the Grand total.

❍ Click the **+** buttons to expand a single group of records.

❍ Click the **–** button to collapse a single group and hide the detail.

❍ Click the **3** button to expand all the groups to show all the records again.

❍ Choose **Data|Group and Outline|Clear Outline** to remove the outlining symbols, or choose **Data|Subtotals** and click **Remove All** to remove both the outlining symbols and the subtotals as well. (Press **Ctrl+Shift+8** to hide or display the outline border along the left side of the worksheet.)

Result: You can use the outlining symbols to see the best view of your data.

Figure 13.19 Detail
hidden, subtotals
visible

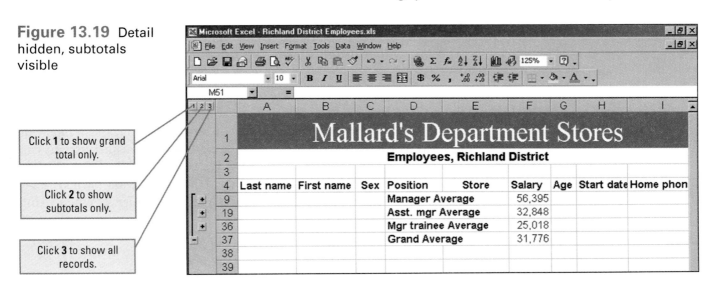

Click **1** to show grand total only.

Click **2** to show subtotals only.

Click **3** to show all records.

TIPS FROM A PRO: You can apply the Group and Outline feature to any worksheet that has averages or totals in it, even when you created them yourself. You can see in Figure 13.20 that you even get outlining symbols to collapse the columns if you have a total in the right-hand column.

Figure 13.20 Group and Outline applied to a worksheet

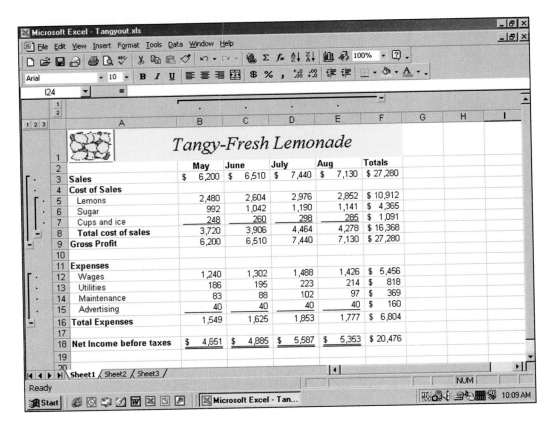

 TIPS FROM A PRO: You can also do averages and sums and so on for a certain subset of your database and use the results in a formula. To do this, use the *database functions*, also called Dfunctions (Dsum, Daverage, and so on). For details, see Excel Help on "Database functions."

 TIPS FROM A PRO: When you want to do subtotals based on two fields at once, use a PivotTable. You'll learn about this in Task 10.

TASK 7   Find a Record Using a Data Form

What: Having the data organized into a database enables you to use several Excel features to find records that match certain criteria. Use a *query* or question to *filter* the records according to the criteria, just as you can use a sieve on the beach to keep the shells but let the sand go through. (Although they are synonyms, Excel uses the term "filter" when referring to information in an Excel worksheet and "query" when using external databases, as in Task 9.)

○ Use a data form to jump from record to record that meet the requirements.
○ Use AutoFilters to show all the records that match the criteria.
○ Use advanced filters to set up complex criteria and show records that meet them.

Why: Collecting information in a database becomes particularly useful when you can ask questions and find an answer. You can see what items match the conditions you set up.

How: This shows each record that meets the conditions one at a time.

Figure 13.21
Setting criteria in a data form

1. Click anywhere in the database and choose **Data|Form**.
2. Click the **Criteria** button.
3. Type the condition you want to match in one or more of the boxes. Here are some examples (Figure 13.21):
   • Type the characters to match all records with information beginning with those characters. For example, typing "Will" in the last name field finds records having "Willis," "Willem," and "Williams."
   • Type a comparison operator and a number (or text), such as >=1000. Use any of these comparison operators: equal to =, greater than >, greater than or equal to >=, less than <, less than or equal to <=, or not equal to < >. (These comparison operators are summarized in Table 7.2 of Chapter 7, "Use Functions.")
4. Click **Find Next** or **Find Prev** multiple times.
5. To remove the criteria and see all the records, click the **Criteria** button and then click the **Clear** button.

Result: As you click Find Next or Find Prev, you see all the records that match your criteria one at a time. If only one record matches, the contents of the dialog box remain the same. If no matches are found, the form shows the next record—watch out, Excel doesn't warn you that it's not a match.

TASK 8   *Use an AutoFilter to Find Certain Records*

E *EXPERT OBJECTIVE: Apply data filters*

E *EXPERT OBJECTIVE: Extract data*

What: An AutoFilter offers the simplest way to specify certain criteria and see all the records that meet the criteria at one time. Use AutoFilters to see records that match these sorts of criteria:

○ Exact match for one field
○ Exact match for more than one field
○ Exact match for two items on a single field (use Custom)
○ Comparisons (use Custom)
○ Top 10 (top 10 values, top 10 percent, and so on)

Additionally, you can set up an AutoFilter to use comparisons in English (rather than the > and < symbols that you used in the data form), including these:

○ Equals	○ Is less than or equal to
○ Does not equal	○ Begins with
○ Is greater than	○ Does not begin with
○ Is greater than or equal to	○ Ends with
○ Is less than	○ Does not end with

Why: AutoFilters are simpler to set up than advanced filters and have the advantage of showing all the records that satisfy the conditions you specify.

TURN ON THE AUTOFILTER

How: Click anywhere inside the database and choose **Data|Filter|AutoFilter**.

Result: As soon as you do that, drop-down arrows are added to the field names, as you see in Figure 13.22. To remove them when you are through, choose **Data|Filter|AutoFilter** again.

Figure 13.22
Starting AutoFilter

Arrows added to field names.

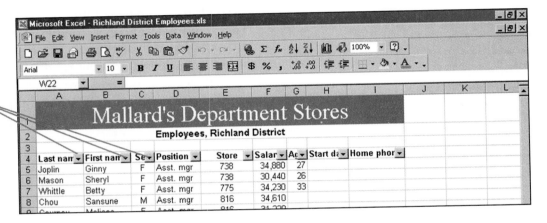

FIND A MATCH ON ONE OR MORE FIELDS

How: Use the drop-down arrows to find a match.

1. Click one of the arrows to drop down the list and choose one of the items, as shown in Figure 13.23. The items listed here are all the various entries in that column of the database.
2. Repeat for other columns if you want to see items that match several conditions.

Result: Immediately, Excel hides all the rows except the ones that match the items you chose. Figure 13.24 shows that the row numbers turn blue, signifying that these are a subset of the database. You can tell which fields were used to set a condition, because those drop-down arrows have turned blue.

You can print the worksheet, or you can *extract* the subset of the data by copying and pasting to a new worksheet. To remove the effects of the AutoFilter and see all the records again, perform one of these actions:

○ Drop down the blue arrows and choose (**All**) to remove the conditions one at a time.

○ Choose **Data|Filter|Show All**.

Figure 13.23
Choosing an item to match

Figure 13.24
Applying an AutoFilter

Arrows turn blue.

Rows are hidden.

Row numbers turn blue.

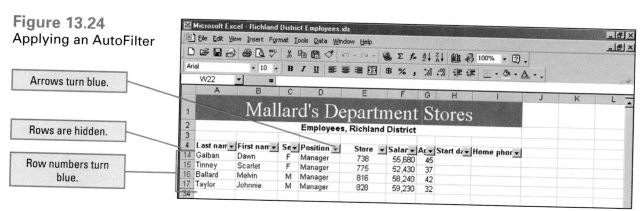

CREATE CUSTOM AUTOFILTERS

How: AutoFilters also work when you don't have an exact match (for example, when you want to use comparisons, such as greater than). You also use a custom AutoFilter when you want to set up an either/or condition.

1. Click the drop-down arrow for a certain field and choose Custom. The dialog box shown in Figure 13.25 opens.
2. Choose the comparison operator from the drop-down list on the left, and type or choose in the list on the right. For example, set Salary greater than or equal to 35,000.
3. Choose a second item if you want to. For example, you want the text in the Position field to be either Manager or Asst. Manager, or you want a number, such as Salary, to be between $25,000 and $30,000.

Figure 13.25
Custom AutoFilter

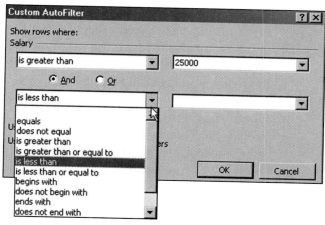

Result: Excel hides all the rows except the ones that meet the criteria you set.

TASK 9 — Use Advanced Filters

 EXPERT OBJECTIVE: Apply data filters

 EXPERT OBJECTIVE: Extract data

What: Use an advanced filter rather than an AutoFilter under any of these conditions:

○ You want to set three or more conditions on a single column.
○ You want to set up either/or conditions on two or more columns.
○ You want to display the criteria next to the results.
○ You want to automatically extract or copy the data to another location.
○ You want to use a calculation as the basis for the criteria.

Why: Advanced Filters offer more functionality than AutoFilters, but setting them up requires a little bit of effort.

How: Remove the AutoFilter before beginning this process.

1. Insert at least three blank rows above the list.
2. In the first blank row, type or copy the field names that you want to use in the criteria.
3. In the row (or rows) below the field names, set up the criteria as follows:
   - For a single condition, type the match or comparison immediately below the field name.
   - For several conditions to be true, type all of them on the same row, immediately below the field name. Be sure you leave at least one blank row between the criteria and the database.
     Example: All employees whose Sex is F, whose Position is Manager, **and** whose Salary is >55,000.
   - For either/or conditions, where only one must be true, type the conditions on separate rows below the field name.
     Example: All employees whose Store is 818 **or** all employees whose Position is Manager.
4. If you plan to extract the results of the filter to a new location, select a separate area on the worksheet (or on a different sheet) with plenty of blank rows to display the results. If you want the filter to show only part of the fields in the original list, copy those field names on the first row of the new location. (If you want the filter to show all the fields, you don't have to do this.)
5. Click anywhere in the database and choose **Data|Filter|Advanced Filter**. The dialog box shown in Figure 13.26 opens.
6. Specify these items in the dialog box:
   - Choose **Copy to Another Location** if you want to extract the results to a new location.
   - **List Range** is already specified because you clicked in the database before you started.
   - For **Criteria Range**, select the cells containing the field names and criteria you set up in Step 2.
   - For **Copy To** range (available only if you chose Copy to Another Location), select the top-left corner of the area where you want to display the subset, or, if you copied field names in Step 3, select only those field names.
   - Use **Unique Records Only** if you only want to see a single instance of the data that matches the criteria. For example, if you have a list of orders that have been placed, and you want to see which companies have placed orders over $1,000, you only want to see each company name listed a single time, not each one over and over again.

Figure 13.26
Setting up an
advanced filter

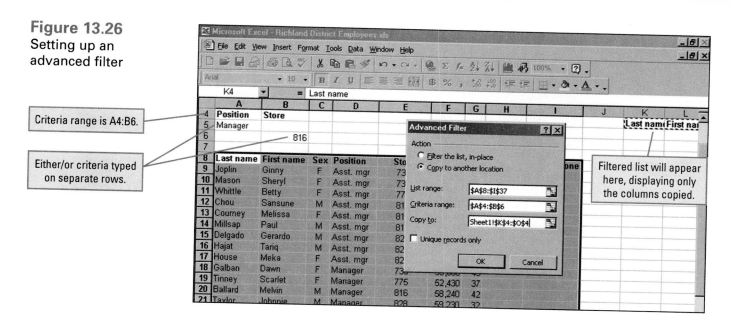

Criteria range is A4:B6.

Either/or criteria typed
on separate rows.

Result: The subset of the database that meets the criteria you set up in the criteria range is displayed in place or copied to the new location.

TASK 10   *Query an External Database*

EXPERT OBJECTIVE: *Query databases*

What: Excel (as well as Word and Access) works with Microsoft Query to make it easy to get a subset of information from an external database. If you want to use this feature, you must first install it. (A prompt appears when you begin the process, but you need to have your Office 2000 CD available.)

Why: Although you learned how to bring an external data into Excel in Chapter 12, "Import and Export," a database might be too large to fit in a single worksheet. You might only need part of the data, rather than all of it. Using Microsoft Query enables you to keep the data in its original source but still use Excel to analyze a subset of the information.

How: This three-phase process requires you to do these tasks:

   O Install Microsoft Query, if necessary.
   O Create a data source, a file that contains connection information to the external database.
   O Define the query using the Query Wizard.

1. Click the cell where you want the data placed.
2. Choose **Data|Get External Data|New Database Query**.
3. If necessary, insert the Office 2000 disc and install Microsoft Query when prompted.
4. Choose **New data source** in the Choose Data Source dialog box (Figure 13.27.) Be sure the box is checked to use the Query Wizard and click **OK**.

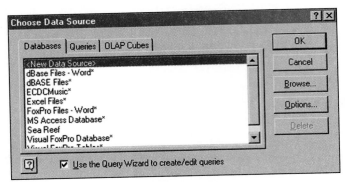

Figure 13.27 Choose Data Source dialog box

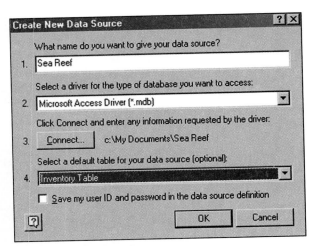

Figure 13.28 Create New Data Source dialog box

5. Provide the needed information in the Create New Data Source dialog box that opens (shown in Figure 13.28):
   - In box 1, enter a name for the data source you are creating.
   - In box 2, choose the type of database you are accessing.
   - Click **Connect**, and the ODBC Setup dialog box opens. Specify the information about the name and location of the external database and return to the Create New Data Source dialog box.
   - In box 4, choose an individual table if the external database has more than one. Click **OK** to return to the Choose Data Source dialog box where the new data source is now listed, and click **OK** again to start the Query Wizard.

6. Provide the information requested in the Query Wizard's four screens:
   - In the **Choose Columns** screen, specify the columns you want to add to your query and click **Next**.
   - In the **Filter Data** screen, set up a filter to show only a subset of the data, if you want, and click **Next**.
   - In the **Sort Order** screen, choose up to three ways to sort the data, if you want, and click **Next**.
   - In the **Finish** screen, choose the option to Return Data to Microsoft Excel and click **Finish** to close the wizard.

Figure 13.29 Query of an external database

	A	B	C	D
1	Item	Stock No	Quantity	Cost/Item
2	air hose	2312	20	5.85
3	air pump	3543	10	12.2
4	air stones	5578	20	2.5
5	chlorine drops	1121	15	5.55
6	decorative rocks	8733	50	8.75
7	gravel	7645	8	16.25
8	plants	6342	22	2.5
9	salt	3423	10	12.8
10	tubes	1123	10	1.85
11				

7. In the Returning External Data to Microsoft Excel dialog box, which opens, specify the location for the data and click **OK**.

Result: The subset of the data appears in the Excel worksheet, along with the External Data toolbar (refer to Figure 13.29). Now you can use it as you do any other Excel list, and you can click the Refresh button to get new data from the external database if it changes.

TASK **11**   *Use PivotTable and PivotChart Reports*

EXPERT OBJECTIVE: Use data analysis and PivotTables

What: You've already learned to use Data|Subtotals to find out the sum, count, or average for a set of data. For example, you can find the average salary for each position, or you can find the average salary for men and for women. But what if you want to find out both at one time? The average salary for men and women in each store? Subtotals won't work for this; you have to create a special summary table called a *PivotTable*. Further, you can chart the data from the PivotTable with a PivotChart to get a visual illustration of the data.

After you create a PivotTable, you can manipulate how the information appears, and you can format it with the AutoFormat command. Using AutoFormat, you can easily give the same appearance to all your PivotTables.

Why: Using the PivotTable and PivotChart Wizard simplifies the process of summarizing your data. With a PivotTable or PivotChart report you only have to drag and drop the fields, and Excel does the work—it would be terribly time consuming to create these by hand.

CREATE A PIVOTTABLE

How: Click anywhere in the database before starting the wizard.

1. Choose **Data|PivotTable and PivotChart Report**.
2. In the PivotTable and PivotChart Wizard, provide the information needed, as shown in the three parts of Figures 13.30:
   * In Step 1 of 3, specify the source for the data, and choose whether to create a PivotTable or PivotChart. Click **Next**.
   * In Step 2 of 3, select the data you want to include (Excel assumes the entire database). Click **Next**.
   * In Step 3 of 3, choose whether you want the item to appear on the same worksheet or on a different one, and click **Finish**.
3. The wizard creates a work area and offers the PivotTable toolbar, as you see in Figure 13.31. Decide how you want your database to appear. You can use two or three different sets of fields easily, plus one set of data to sum, average, or count. Typically you'll place the set with more items or longer names down the left side of the table, and the set with fewer items or shorter names in rows across the top.
4. Drag the field names from the PivotTable toolbar, and drop them in various locations. For our example, we want to compare average

Figure 13.30 The
PivotTable and
PivotChart Wizard

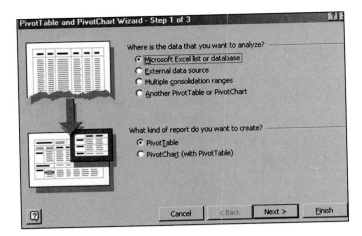

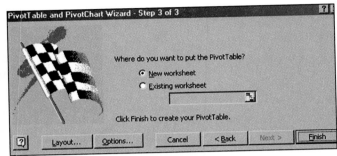

Figure 13.31
Setting up the
PivotTable

Work area

Drag field names from
the toolbar to the work
area.

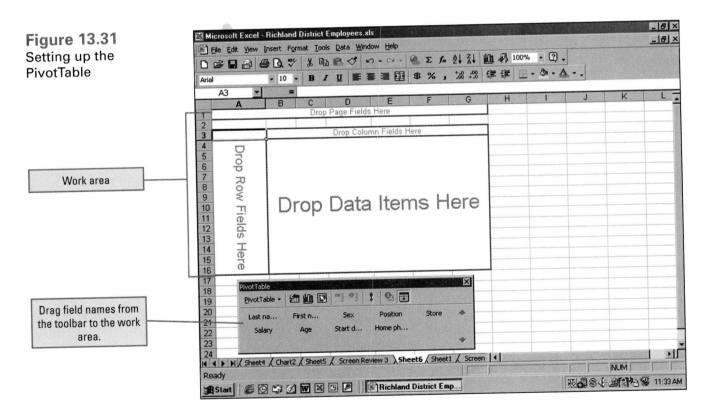

salaries for men and women in each position. Here's how you should
set it up:

- Drag Sex to where it says **Drop Column Fields Here**.
- Drag Position to where it says **Drop Row Fields Here**.
- Drag Salary to where it says **Drop Data Items Here**. Now the
  PivotTable displays the sum of the salaries (as in Figure 13.32).

Figure 13.32 Using the PivotTable Field
dialog box

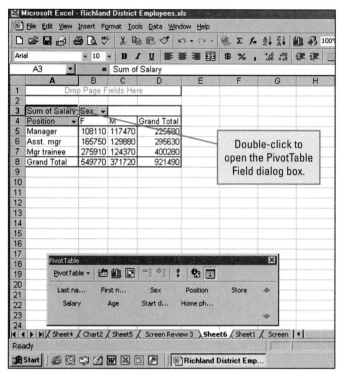

Double-click to open the PivotTable Field dialog box.

(a) PivotTable displaying Sum of Salary

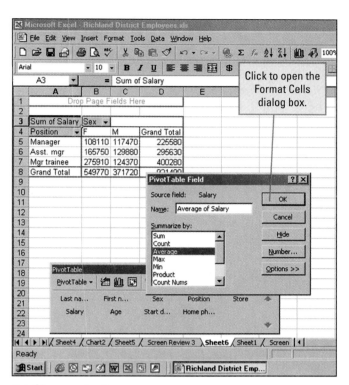

Click to open the Format Cells dialog box.

(b) Change to Average

5. To change from sum to the average salary, double-click **Sum of Salary** and choose **Average**, as you see in Figure 13.32b. Click **Number** to change the number formatting.

Result: Each time you drop a field, the PivotTable shows the items for each field. When the PivotTable is complete, you can use it to make good business decisions. Here are some ways to use PivotTable data:

○ Looking at the average salaries, we see that women managers get paid less than men, but women assistant managers and trainees are paid more (Figure 13.33a).
○ Drop Store next to Sex at the top of the table and see the breakdown that way (Figure 13.33b).
○ Drag Sex back to the toolbar, and see how the salaries are averaged by store alone.
○ Are there more men or women at each position? Double-click Average of Salaries and change to Count.
○ Drag Store to the page fields area. Now you can use a drop-down arrow to change from store to store, or to see all (Figure13.33c).
○ Show only certain items under each category. To do this, drop down the field names and click to specify which items to display. For example, drop down Sex and clear the mark from F to display only the men (Figure13.33d).

	A	B	C	D	E
1					
2					
3	Average of Salary	Sex			
4	Position	F	M	Grand Total	
5	Manager	$54,055	$58,735	$56,395	
6	Asst. mgr	$33,150	$32,470	$32,848	
7	Mgr trainee	$25,083	$24,874	$25,018	
8	Grand Total	$30,543	$33,793	$31,776	
9					
10					

(a) Average of salaries

	A	B	C	D	E	F	G	H	I	J
1										
2										
3	Average of Salary	Store	Sex							
4		738		738 Total	775	775 Total	816		816 Total	
5	Position	F	M		F		F	M		F
6	Manager	$55,680		$55,680	$52,430	$52,430		$58,240	$58,240	
7	Asst. mgr	$32,660		$32,660	$34,230	$34,230	$31,220	$33,375	$32,657	$34,9...
8	Mgr trainee	$24,680	$24,970	$24,825	$25,008	$25,008	$25,297	$24,170	$25,015	$25,3...
9	Grand Total	$34,072	$24,970	$31,471	$31,115	$31,115	$26,778	$37,290	$32,034	$28,53...
10										

(b) By Store and Sex

Figure 13.33
Completed
PivotTables

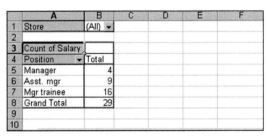

(c) With Store in the Page field

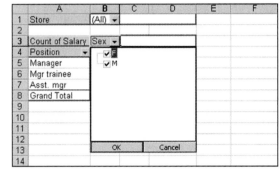

(d) Specifying items in a field

AUTOFORMAT A PIVOTTABLE

EXPERT OBJECTIVE: Use PivotTable AutoFormat

How: Click anywhere in the PivotTable and either click the **Format Report** button on the PivotTable toolbar or drop down the PivotTable menu on the same toolbar and click **Format Report**.

Result: In the AutoFormat dialog box, choose the format you prefer. They come in two main varieties: an indented format, with each category shown at a different level of indentation and a subtotal beneath each, or the cross-tabulated type, where the categories appear in the top row and left column. Figure 13.34 shows the dialog box, and 13.35 shows a formatted PivotTable report.

CREATE A PIVOTCHART

EXPERT OBJECTIVE: Create PivotChart reports

How: You can begin PivotCharts two ways:

- ❍ Start from scratch. Choose **Data|PivotTable** and **PivotChart Report**, and in the first step choose **PivotChart**.
- ❍ Click anywhere in an existing PivotTable and click the **Chart** button on the PivotTable toolbar or drop down the PivotTable menu on the same toolbar and choose **PivotChart**. Build the chart as you did the table: drop fields in the category axis, the data area, and the legend. Add a page category if you want.

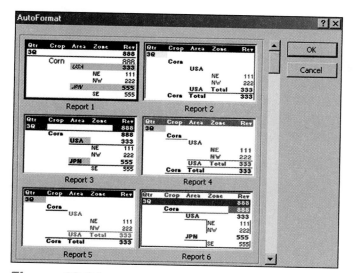

Figure 13.34 PivotTable AutoFormat dialog box

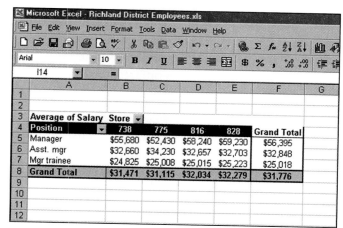

Figure 13.35 AutoFormatted PivotTable

Result: The PivotChart shows the data in chart form, for easy comparison. Format the chart as you would any regular chart. The sample in Figure 13.36 has been changed to show columns side by side rather than stacked.

Figure 13.36
Sample PivotChart

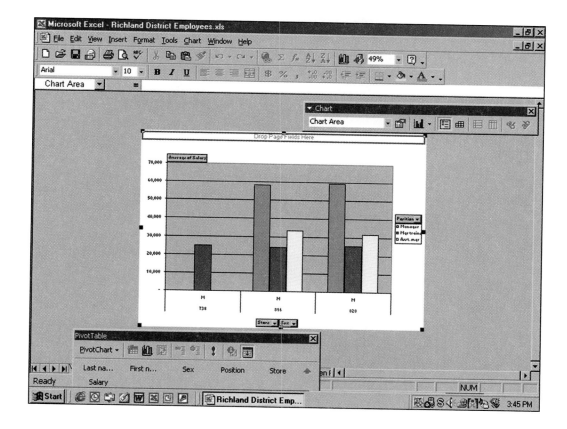

 TIPS FROM A PRO: Notice the drop-down arrows next to field names in the legend and category axis? Drop that down and you can click to specify which items to display. For example, drop down Sex and clear the check from F to display only the men, as you see in the sample.

Use PinPoint

After gaining the skills in this chapter, you can use Excel to manage data in lists. You can create the database, add and edit records, find certain records, and sort them various ways. You can also subtotal the data and use PivotTables. Now it's time to use the PinPoint software and see what you can do. Remember, whenever you are unsure of what to do, you can reread that portion of the chapter or you can click Show Me for a live demonstration. Check out these skills in PinPoint:

- Apply an outline
- Create a custom list
- Create a database
- Data validation
- Extract data
- Filter a database
- Query a database
- Query a list
- Sort data
- Use data forms
- Create a PivotTable chart
- PivotTable AutoFormat
- PivotTables

Key Terms

You can find definitions for these words in this chapter:

Data form
Extract
Field
Field names
Filter
Header row
List
PivotTable
Query
Record

Review Questions

You can use the following review questions to test your knowledge and skills. Answers are given in Appendix D.

True/False

Indicate whether each statement is true (T) or false (F).

____ 1. When you create a database, put a heading or title in row 1, and put the field names in row 2.

____ 2. When you delete a record using a data form, it automatically deletes the row from the worksheet.

____ 3. Data validation is used to restrict what can be entered into a cell.

____ 4. To alphabetize a database by last name and then by first name, use Data|Sort.

____ 5. A custom list can be used with sorting or AutoFill.

____ 6. When you use Data|Subtotals, the Outline symbols automatically appear.

____ 7. You can use the Sum, Average, and Count functions with Data|Subtotals.

____ 8. When you see drop-down arrows next to the field names, you know you have applied an Advanced Filter.

____ 9. Use Microsoft PivotTable to query an external database.

____ 10. PivotTables are easily set up by dropping field names onto the work area.

Multiple Choice

Select the letter that best completes the statement.

____ 1. You can use a data form to:
   a. Add records.
   b. Delete records.
   c. Find records that meet certain criteria.
   d. All of the above.
   e. Either a or b.

____ 2. Using a telephone book as an example of a database, a field would be:
   a. All the information on a single individual.
   b. All the people whose names start with J.
   c. All the listings in the business section.
   d. The phone number.
   e. All of the above.

____ 3. If you want to provide a drop-down list to select from when entering data, use:
   a. A data form.
   b. Data validation.
   c. A filter.
   d. A query.
   e. A PivotTable.

____ 4. In order to sort the data in a database:
   a. Click the column heading to select the column you want to use as the basis for the sort and then click one of the buttons.
   b. Click the Sort Ascending button to list Salaries from highest to lowest.
   c. Click the Sort Descending button to sort alphabetically by last name.
   d. Use Data|Sort to be able to use a custom sort order.
   e. All of the above.

____ 5. You must sort the data before you use:
   a. AutoFilter.
   b. PivotTables.
   c. Query.
   d. Subtotals.
   e. Validation.

____ 6. When you click the 2 row level symbol in an outlined worksheet, Excel:
   a. Collapses the worksheet to show only the subtotals and grand totals.
   b. Collapses the worksheet for a single subheading.
   c. Expands the worksheet to show all the rows.
   d. Inserts blank rows and calculates subtotals and grand totals.
   e. Applies a filter to hide all the records not containing a 2.

____ 7. To find a record that meets certain criteria, use:
   a. AutoFilter.
   b. A data form.
   c. A PivotTable.
   d. Subtotals.
   e. Both a and b.

____ 8. When you want to see all the records in a database where the salary is greater than 35,000, drop down the list next to the Salary field name and choose:
   a. 35,000.
   b. <35,000.
   c. Custom.
   d. Greater than 35,000.
   e. Top 10.

____ 9. To extract data, use:
   a. Advanced Filter with the Copy To Another Location option.
   b. PivotTable with the Place on New Worksheet option.
   c. AutoFilter, and then copy and paste to another location.
   d. Query, and then copy the results to Excel.
   e. Both a and c.

____ 10. To compare subtotals or averages broken down by several fields, use:
   a. An AutoFilter.
   b. An advanced filter.
   c. Data validation.
   d. A PivotTable report.
   e. Subtotals.

Screen Review 1

Match the letters in Figure 13.37 with the correct items in the list.

____ 1. Click here to sort the salaries from highest to lowest.

____ 2. Click here to see all the rows.

____ 3. Click here to display only the grand total.

____ 4. Click here to sort the stores in the usual order.

Screen Review 2

Suppose you want to view the average age of the men and women at each position. Match the letters in Figure 13.38 with the correct items in the list.

____ 1. Drop the Age field here.

____ 2. Drop the Sex field here.

____ 3. Drop the Position field here.

____ 4. Double-click here to change to Average (after the PivotTable has been created).

____ 5. Create a PivotChart.

____ 6. Apply an AutoFormat to the chart.

Figure 13.37

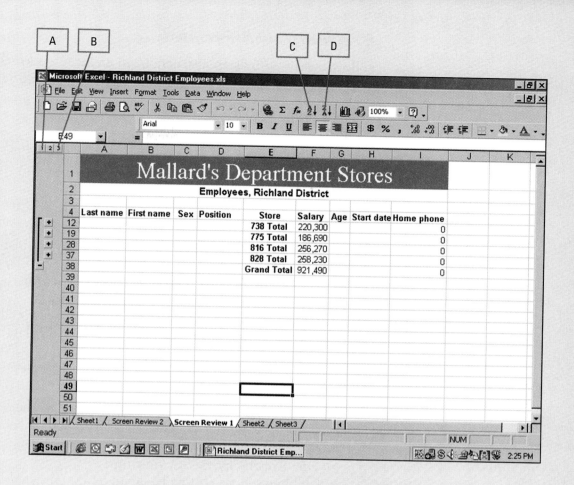

Figure 13.38

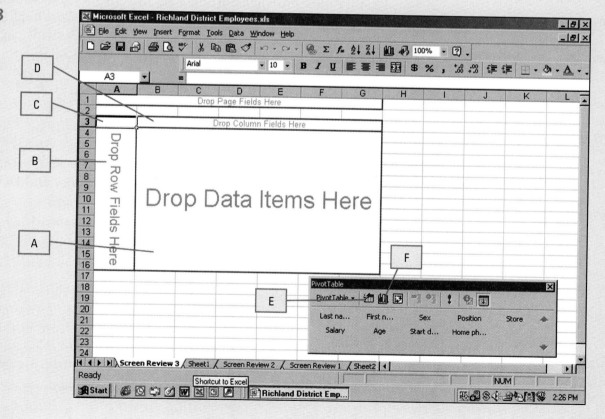

Exercise and Project

Follow these step-by-step instructions to create a worksheet. If you are working in a computer lab, ask your instructor where you should save and print your file.

Exercise

1. Open **MegaMedia.xls** from the *Student\Chapter 13* folder of your PinPoint CD.
2. Widen the columns and format the two cost fields with currency formats.
3. Create a header containing your name and class time.
4. Use a data form to add the following record:
   - Category: **B**
   - Title: **Bunny's Big Day**
   - Description: **Children**
   - Author: **Sarah Bancroft**
   - New Release: **Y**
   - In Store: **10**
   - On Order: (blank)
   - Cost/Item: **5.95**
   - Total: (calculation)
   - Sold: **0**
5. Sort the database by Description alphabetically, and, within each description, by Cost/Item from most to least. Print the database so that it fits on a single page.
6. Use the data form to find all items in the Children's section costing less than $15.00 per item.
7. Use AutoFilter to find the records that match the following criteria. Each time, copy the results to a new sheet and place a label above them. When you have copied all, print the resulting worksheet.
   - Julia Roberts movies on videotape
   - Children's items costing less than $15.00 per item
   - Items with a description of children's or Disney
   - The ten most expensive items in inventory
8. Remove the AutoFilter. Sort the data by Category, and within each category by Description, and within each description by Cost/Item from highest to lowest. Print the sorted database so that it fits on a single page.
9. Find the *average* cost per item in each category. Collapse the rows to show only the averages for the categories and the grand average. Widen Column A, and hide all the columns except columns A and H. Print.
11. Unhide all the columns and remove the subtotals.
12. Create a PivotTable on a new worksheet to show the Sum of Total Cost. To do so, drop Category in the column fields area, Description in the row fields area, and Total Cost in the data items area, Apply a Table (not Report) style AutoFormat. Enter the title **Total Cost by Category and Description** above the PivotTable.
13. Move the active cell four rows below the PivotTable. Click the PivotTable Wizard button on the toolbar to add a new PivotTable that shows the *maximum* Total Cost by Category and Description. Title it **Maximum Cost of Inventory**. Use the same AutoFormat for this table.
14. Move below the second table by four rows. Now make a three-way PivotTable to count new releases. Drop Category in the page fields area, Description in the row fields area, and New Release in the column fields area. Drop New Release in the data items area also. Now display a count of new video releases. To do so, click the down arrow for Category and choose

V for Video. Click the down arrow for New Releases and pick Y but not N. Title this PivotTable **New Video Releases by Description**. Apply the same AutoFormat.

15. Name the worksheet **PivotTables**. Print the sheet.

16. Select the first PivotTable and create a PivotChart out of it. After the chart appears, choose only the Video category by dropping down the list in the legend. Change the chart type to a 3-D column. Print the chart.

17. Save the file as **MM2**. (You use this file again in Chapter 15, "Work with Templates.")

Project

Suppose you want to start your own clothing consignment shop just off campus to allow fellow students to buy and sell gently used or vintage clothing. You plan to start with your own and your roommate's clothes from your overfilled closets.

1. Create a database in Excel like that shown in Figure 13.39. Place your name in the header of the worksheet. Create a drop-down list to use when entering the category, using very broad categories. Enter at least 15 more records from three or four different people's closets following the example in the figure.

2. In column F, place a formula for *Consignor amount* that equals 60% of the Price. Under *Sold*, type Y for the items that have sold, but leave the unsold items blank.

3. Sort the data by Category, then by Price from highest to lowest. Use subtotals to find the total potential amount of income from each category of clothing.

4. Filter the database to find all the items that have sold. Sort the results by Consignor ID and get subtotals on the Consignor Amount field at each change in Consignor ID. This shows how much you owe each person. Print.

5. Does the pricing affect whether the items sell? Find out by creating a PivotTable to compare the *average* Price broken down by Category and Sold. Format and title the table appropriately.

Figure 13.39

	A	B	C	D	E	F	G
1			Amy's Attic				
2							
3	Consignor ID	Category	Description	Size	Price	Consignor Amount	Sold
4	1305	Shorts	Abercrombie khaki	32	$14.99		
5							

Do What-If Analysis

Before we had computers, accountants used to spend hours with pencil and paper "running the numbers" to figure out what would happen if the price (or some other variable) was raised or lowered. Excel makes doing *what-if analysis* like this a snap because after the formulas are set up, you can change a number at the top, and the effects ripple through to the bottom line.

Doing what-if analysis, by substituting one or two numbers at a time, though, can get to be a mess. You can change so many factors that affect the bottom line that all the different variations are hard to keep straight and compare rationally. The analysis tools you learn about in this chapter keep you organized so you can make good decisions.

At the end of this chapter, you will be able to:

C E

C	E	
❑	❑	Set up data tables with one or two variables
❑	☑	Work with scenarios
❑	☑	Use the Report Manager
❑	☑	Use Solver

What: Sometimes you want to see the effect of using a variety of different numbers in a single formula. For example, when deciding on an investment, you might want to see the result of investing at a number of different interest rates. Alternatively, you might want to see how much your investment would grow by changing the term, the length of time for the investment, or even both the interest rate and term.

Data tables enable you to see the results of a formula using either one or two *variables*, numbers that you can change.

Why: You could change the numbers and print, and change the numbers and print, but imagine how much paper that would take, and how much trouble to spread them all out to compare the difference. Using data tables puts the results of all the variations on a single worksheet.

ONE-VARIABLE DATA TABLES

How: To use data tables, you have to set up an input zone that you refer to in your formula. We'll use the example here to find out the future value of an investment at various interest rates.

1. Begin by setting up an input area for the formula (cells A1:C4 in Figure 14.1a).
2. Insert the formula using the numbers in the input area. (The example shows the future value with the Fv function in cell C6. Remember to divide the interest rate by 12 and multiply the years by 12 for a monthly deposit.)
3. Type the numbers you will use as a variable down the left column (B7:B16 in the figure).
4. Select the range that contains the variable in the left column and the formula at the top of the next column, with blank cells below. These blank cells will contain the results. In the example this range is B6:C16.

Figure 14.1 Setting up a one-variable data table

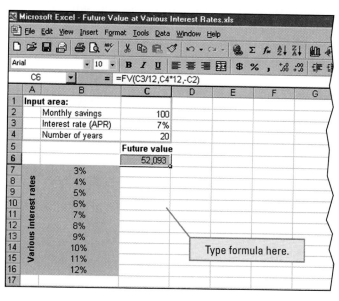

(a) Specifying the variable

(b) Table dialog box

5. Choose **Data|Table**. In the Table dialog box that opens (Figure 14.1b), specify which cell is being replaced by the numbers in the column. In our example, the numbers in the column will replace the interest rate originally given in cell C3.

Result: The data table substitutes the interest rates in the column and shows the future value (Figure 14.2). You have to format the numbers appropriately.

Use the data table to compare the results using a variety of interest rates. In our example, you can see that putting your money in stocks (average growth is 12%) is much better than keeping it in a credit union savings account (APR 3%).

Figure 14.2 A one-variable data table

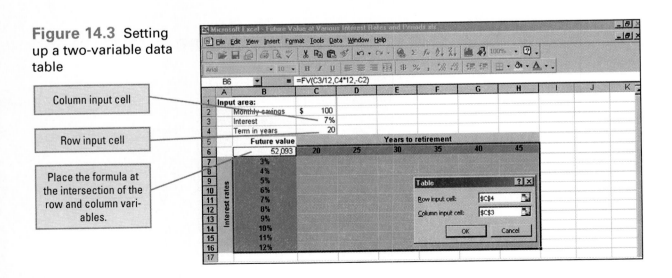

TWO-VARIABLE DATA TABLES

How: The two-variable data table lets you see the effect of changing two variables. In our example, we'll change not only the interest rates, but also the number of years to save before retirement.

1. Place the formula used in the data table just above the column of variables.
2. Enter the number of years until retirement across the same row, as you see in Figure 14.3.

Figure 14.3 Setting up a two-variable data table

Column input cell

Row input cell

Place the formula at the intersection of the row and column variables.

3. Select the range that contains the formula, the variables, and the blank cells for the results. In the example this range is B6:H16.3.

4. Choose **Data|Table**. For the Column variable, choose the cell in the input area that contains the interest rate (cell C3). For the Row variable, choose the cell in the input area that contains the number of years (cell C4).

Result: Excel substitutes values for the interest rates and the years and shows the future value (Figure 14.4). You have to format the numbers appropriately.

To use the data table, you look at the number of years to retirement and then choose a given interest rate. At the intersection of the row and column, you see the future value of your $100 monthly savings. In our example, you can see that starting to save in your twenties (where you have 45 years until retirement) offers much better prospects than starting in your mid-forties (with only 20 years until retirement), no matter what the interest rate!

Figure 14.4 A two-variable data table

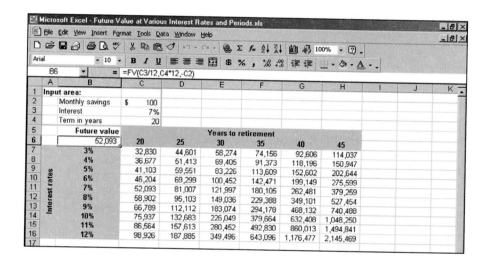

 TIPS FROM A PRO: You can't delete or change the entries in a data table individually. You have to delete them all and start over completely.

TASK **2** | **Use Scenarios**

 E | EXPERT OBJECTIVE: **Work with Scenarios**

What: What if we reduce the price? What if our costs increase? What if we pay a larger bonus? What if we give bigger discounts to those who pay their bills early? Use scenarios to manage all the changes you'd like to make when playing "what-if" with your worksheets in a single step. You can define several situations with a number of changes for each one and save them with a single name, for example, a set of conditions for an optimistic forecast, a pessimistic forecast, and an average forecast. Then you can apply each scenario with a single command to see what happens to the worksheet.

Why: It's so hard to remember all the changes needed each time. When you group them all together in a scenario, you can reuse these sets of conditions without having to figure them all out and enter them again. Scenarios are handy because you can specify the entire set of conditions by name and instantly see the results.

SET UP SCENARIOS

How: Begin in a worksheet with formulas.

1. Choose **Tools|Scenarios**. This opens the Scenario Manager (Figure 14.5).
2. Click **Add** to define a scenario in the Add Scenario dialog box (Figure 14.6).
   - Type a name. Use a descriptive name that will help you remember its use.
   - Select the cells that will change; collapse the dialog box if necessary, and hold down the Ctrl key to select cells that are not adjacent.
   - Click **OK**.

Figure 14.5 Scenario Manager

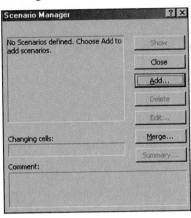

Figure 14.6 Using the Add Scenario dialog box

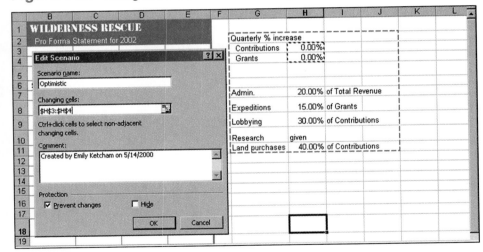

3. In the Scenario Values dialog box, which opens, enter the value for each cell that will be used in the calculations (Figure 14.7). Click **Add**.
4. Create additional scenarios for the worksheet by repeating steps 2 and 3.
5. When you are through creating scenarios, click **OK** in the Scenario Values dialog box and click **Close** in the Scenario Manager.

Result: The scenarios that you created are listed in the Scenario Manager, as you see in Figure 14.8.

USE THE SCENARIOS

How: Choose **Tools|Scenarios**. Choose the scenario you want to see, and click **Show**.

Result: The worksheet changes to show what happens with the different set of figures.

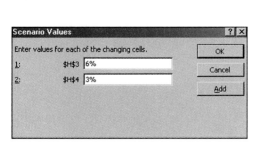

Figure 14.7 Scenario Values dialog box

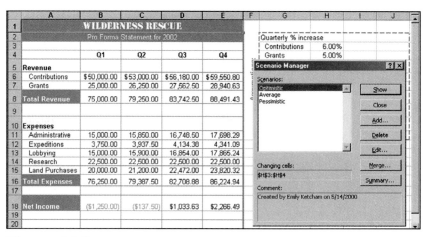

Figure 14.8 Using scenarios

SUMMARIZE VARIOUS SCENARIOS

How: To see the bottom-line results for all the scenarios at once, create a scenario summary.

1. Choose **Tools|Scenarios**, and click **Summary**.
2. In the dialog box, choose **Scenario Summary** (Figure 14.9).
3. Specify the **Result cells**, that is, the cell or range that changes under each scenario. Click **OK**.

Result: Excel creates a new worksheet to contain the summary information, as you see in Figure 14.10. Here you can see at a glance how each scenario compares, without having to print them out on separate sheets of paper and place them side by side to compare them.

Figure 14.9 Scenario Summary dialog box

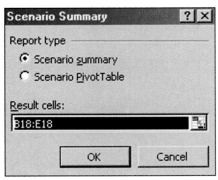

Figure 14.10 Scenario Summary

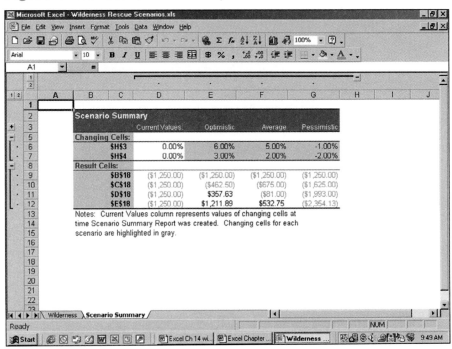

THOUGHT QUESTION: In a company, what persons would be most interested in seeing the results on the Scenario Summary?

<table>
<tr><td>TASK **3**</td><td>*Use Report Manager*</td></tr>
</table>

 E EXPERT OBJECTIVE: *Use the Report Manager*

What: The Report Manager add-in is used to create printed reports containing different print areas, custom views, and scenarios. You can also combine different items from various worksheets in a single report.

Why: Because you save the report with a name, it can be accessed with a single command. This saves you the trouble of setting the print area, hiding rows or columns, collapsing outlines, and choosing a scenario before you print.

 TIPS FROM A PRO: Before you can use Report Manager (or Solver for Task 4), you must have them installed. If you don't see the View|Report Manager or Tools| Solver commands, install them by following these steps: Choose **Tools|Add-Ins** and select them in the dialog box. Be sure to have the Office CD in the drive.

How: You can create one or more reports for each worksheet.

1. Set up the worksheet the way you want it to appear when it is printed. Hide the columns or rows, set the print area, or collapse an outline.
2. Choose **View|Report Manager**. Click **Add** to define a new report.
3. In the Add Report dialog box (Figure 14.11), name the report and specify the Sheet, View, and Scenario to use. Click **Add**.

Figure 14.11 Add Report dialog box

Figure 14.12 Report Manager dialog box

Click here.

Select this check box.

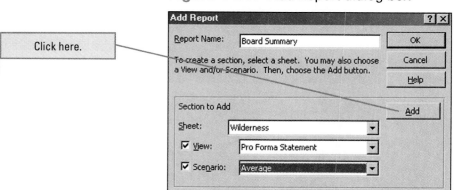

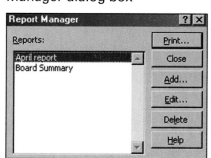

Tips from a Pro: Use *custom views* to define the way your worksheet appears so you can choose that appearance by name later. To do this, set up the worksheet to look the way you want it and choose **View|Custom Views**.

4. Repeat to add more worksheets, views, and scenarios. (If necessary, close the dialog box and return to the worksheet to make changes to the print area, hidden items, and so on). Arrange the sections in the appropriate order. Click to check **Use Continuous Page Numbers**. Click **OK** twice.

5. To print a given report, choose **View|Report Manager**, choose a report and click **Print** (refer to Figure 14.12).

Result: Report Manager collates the items you specified and prints a report in the order you specified.

TASK 4 — *Use Solver*

EXPERT OBJECTIVE: *Use Solver*

What: Solver, an Excel add-in program, can be used for what-if analysis when you have a problem with several variables and a number of constraints. Solver is similar to Goal Seek (another great tool for what-if analysis that you used in Chapters 6 and 8), where you have a solution for a formula in mind and want to see what inputs will provide that solution. Goal Seek enables you to change only one value to reach the desired goal; whereas Solver lets you change as many as you want.

You typically define the problem with constraints: budget constraints where the total spent must be less than a given amount, or time constraints, where you cannot exceed 24 hours in a day, for example.

Why: Solver helps you when you have several choices and must find the optimal combination. For example, suppose you are trying to decide what sorts of dates to plan. Your choices are between one where you grab fast food and go to a movie (which costs about $24) and a nice, romantic dinner and flowers (for about $85). You earn 5 "brownie points" for each cheap date, but you get 20 points for the lavish date. (Economists call these points "utility.") Your budget constrains you to spend less than $500 per month, and because of work, studies, or other commitments, your time is constrained to no more than 10 dates per month. How many dates of each type will earn you the most brownie points or happiness (utility)?

Businesses use the same approach in a number of decisions, such as choosing how much of each product to manufacture—many of a cheaper one or fewer of a more expensive one, given budget and time constraints.

How: The key to using Solver is to set up the worksheet correctly. Here we'll use the dating example (Figure 14.13).

○ Set up the worksheet with the two (or more) choices. In the example, you can see the two choices on different rows.

Figure 14.13
Setting Up Solver

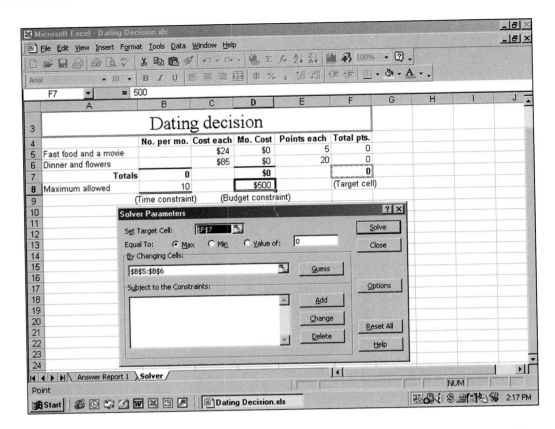

- Calculate totals of what all the choices require wherever you need to place a constraint. In our example, we constrain both time and budget on a monthly basis.
- Calculate the amount you want to optimize. For the dating example, we calculate the number of points times the number of dates each month, with more points earned for the lavish dates than the cheap one. We want to maximize the number of points, representing happiness or utility.
- Choose **Tools|Solver** and follow these steps to fill out the dialog box in Figure 14.14:
  1. Select the Target Cell, and specify whether you want to maximize, minimize, or set it equal to a certain value.
  2. Designate which cells will be changed to find the answer.
  3. Specify constraints. To do this, click **Add** and fill out the Add Constraint dialog box, shown in Figure 14.14. You can refer to numbers (as we did with the number of dates where B7 <= 10) or to cells (where we had the budget maximum D7 <= D8). Other constraints are these: the number of dates must be integers (whole numbers) because you can't go on a fraction of a date, and the number of dates must be greater than or equal to zero, because you can't have a negative number of dates. When you've added all of the constraints, click **OK** to return to the Solver Parameters dialog box (Figure 14.15).
  4. Click **Solve**.

TIPS FROM A PRO: It's a good idea to put your constraint minimum or maximum in a cell on the worksheet. It's easier to change that way than to edit the constraints.

Figure 14.14 Add Constraint dialog box

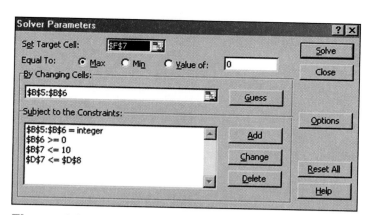

Figure 14.15 Solver Parameters dialog box

Result: Excel takes a few moments to calculate and then displays the Solver Results dialog box (Figure 14.16). Here you can choose whether to accept the results or restore the original values.

Figure 14.16 Solver Results dialog box

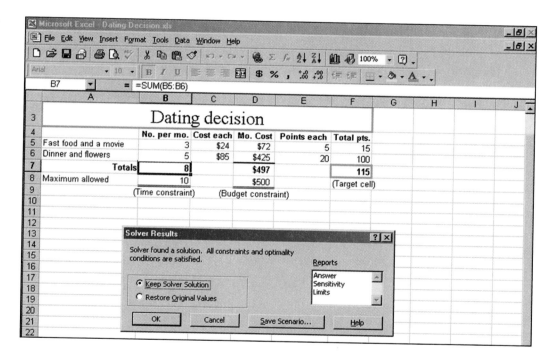

Click **Scenario** to save the results with the given conditions. For example, you might want to define dating scenarios where your budget is limited to $100 a month, where it is limited to $250 per month, and where you have as much as $500 to spend each month.

Click the name of a **Report** and click **OK** to generate a report of the conditions and answers used by Solver (Figure 14.17).

TIPS FROM A PRO: Sometimes Solver can't find an answer to the problem. Often this is because it runs out of tries before it hits the right answer. Other times the limits you've set make the answer impossible. If this happens, change the constraints slightly and try again, or click Options and change the amount of time it has to work. You can also look in Help under the topic "Troubleshoot Solver."

Figure 14.17
Sample answer report

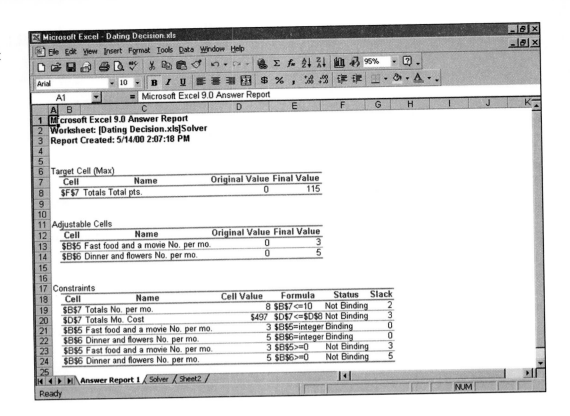

Use PinPoint

After gaining the skills in this chapter, you have the expertise to do what-if analysis using one- and two-variable data tables, set up and view different scenarios, and use the Solver and Report Manager add-ins. Now it's time to use the PinPoint software and see what you can do. Remember, whenever you are unsure of what to do, you can reread that portion of the chapter or you can click Show Me for a live demonstration. Check out these skills in PinPoint:

- Scenarios
- Use the Solver

Key Terms

You can find definitions for these words in this chapter:

Custom views
Variables
What-if analysis

Review Questions

You can use the following review questions to test your knowledge and skills. Answers are given in Appendix D.

True/False

Indicate whether each statement is true (T) or false (F).

_____ 1. To see the results of a formula for an entire series of numbers for one of the inputs, use a data table.

_____ 2. To use a data table, you have to create an input area for the values you will use in the formula.

_____ 3. For a one-variable data table, put the formula at the top of a column containing the various entries for the input.

_____ 4. You can make no more than three scenarios for each worksheet.

_____ 5. The Scenario Summary is used to automatically print a page for each set of conditions.

_____ 6. Report Manager is used to print a certain view and sheets of a single workbook only.

_____ 7. To create a report, choose Tools|Report Manager, and define the look of the worksheet.

_____ 8. The Report Manager can contain only one report for each worksheet.

_____ 9. Solver lets you find the inputs to reach a certain goal, such as a maximum or minimum.

_____ 10. You can combine Solver with scenarios and reports, but you have to set them up separately.

Multiple Choice

Select the letter that best completes the statement.

_____ 1. For a two-variable data table, put the formula:
  a. At the bottom of a column of variables.
  b. At the top of a column of variables.
  c. To the right of a row of variables.
  d. Below the entries in the input zone.
  e. In cell A1.

_____ 2. When you want to group a set of inputs or conditions together in a single name, use a:
  a. Data table.
  b. PivotTable.
  c. Scenario.
  d. Report.
  e. What-if statement.

_____ 3. When you choose Tools|Scenarios, you can:
  a. Add new scenarios.
  b. Edit current scenarios.
  c. Apply the results of a scenario.
  d. Create a summary of all the scenarios on a single worksheet.
  e. All of the above.

_____ 4. To specify the print range, custom view, scenarios, and worksheets you want printed with a single command, use:
  a. Data tables.
  b. Solver.
  c. Report Manager.
  d. Scenario Manager.
  e. All of the above.

_____ 5. Similar to Goal Seek, you can use this to change cells to get a certain result, but with more than one variable:
   a. Data table.
   b. PivotTable.
   c. Report Manager.
   d. Scenario.
   e. Solver.

_____ 6. When a number can change that affects the result of a formula in what-if analysis, this is called a:
   a. Budget.
   b. Condition.
   c. Constraint.
   d. Value.
   e. Variable.

_____ 7. If you don't see Report Manager or Solver as a choice in the menus, that means you must:
   a. Set up the worksheet correctly first.
   b. Save the workbook first.
   c. Install the add-ins.
   d. Remove the effect of the last scenario.
   e. Choose Tools|Options and check the box next to Use What-If Analysis.

_____ 8. To generate a report of the conditions and answers used by Solver for a given what-if situation:

   a. Choose a report name in the Solver Results dialog box and click OK.
   b. Choose View|Report Manager and specify Solver Report.
   c. Choose Tools|Scenario and click Show.
   d. Click File|Print and choose Solver Results.
   e. All of the above.

_____ 9. If you've used Solver to find the right combination of two choices to reach a certain budget maximum, you can save the name of these results (and the next results using a different budget constraint) by using:
   a. AutoWhat-If.
   b. Data tables.
   c. PivotTables.
   d. Reports.
   e. Scenarios.

_____ 10. To find the right combination of two or more choices subject to constraints, use:
   a. Data table.
   b. PivotTable.
   c. Report Manager.
   d. Scenario.
   e. Solver.

Screen Review

Match the letters in Figure 14.18 with the correct items in the list.

_____ 1. Where you'd begin to use Solver.

_____ 2. The target.

_____ 3. The changing cell(s).

_____ 4. The time constraint.

_____ 5. The budget constraint.

Figure 14.18

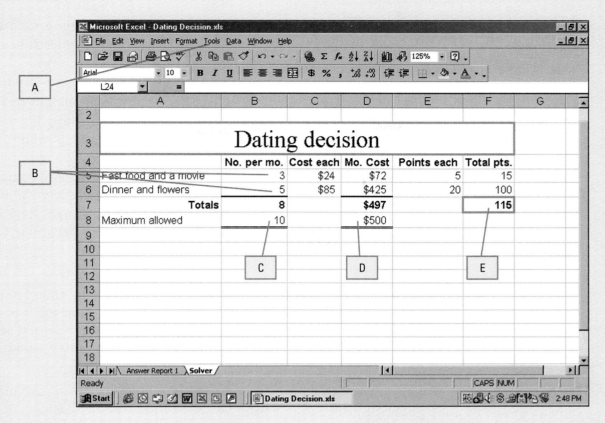

Exercise and Project

Follow these step-by-step instructions to create a worksheet. If you are working in a computer lab, ask your instructor where you should save and print your file.

Exercise

This exercise assumes you are the manager of a business where baseball players go to practice the batting skills. As manager, you need to know how many rounds at bat will cover the cost of doing business. The point at which you spend the same amount as you make is called Breakeven. Any amount of money over that is called Net Income.

Your job is to create an income statement in which you show a table with varying numbers of rounds from 10,000 to 20,000 increasing by 500 rounds on each row.

1. Open the **Batting Cage.xls** file from the *Student\Chapter 14* folder of the PinPoint CD. Fill in the Rounds from 10,000 to 20,000, increasing by 500 on each row.

2. Use cell references to copy the Total Revenue (=C6), Total Expenses (= B21) and Net Income (=B22) into cells F4, G4, and H4 respectively.

3. Select E4:H24 and choose Data|Table. Move to the text box for Column Input Cell and type **C4**.

4. Format the Net Income column using Currency style with 2 decimal places and negative numbers appearing in red.

5. Add your name and class time as a header and print the worksheet.

6. Continue using the *Batting Cage* file to create three scenarios. Start by choosing Tools|Scenarios and the Add button.

7. Name the first scenario **Pricing**, changing cell C5 (the price per round). Click OK to open the Scenario Values dialog box, and enter **2.30** as the value for the changing cell. Click OK.

8. Add another scenario called **Advertising**, changing cell C10 to $1800.

9. Add one more scenario called **Salaries**, changing cell C11 to $28000.

10. Click Summary. In the Scenario Summary dialog box, list the result cells as H4:H24 and click OK. Place your name at the bottom of the Scenario Summary sheet and print the sheet. Save the file.

11. Return to Sheet1 and use Solver to maximize Total Revenue by changing Price. Price is subject to the constraint that it must be <= $4.00.

12. Save the Solver results as a scenario named **Maximum Revenue** and restore the original values. Show this scenario and print the worksheet.

Project

If you haven't done the exercise for this chapter, do it now. Continue using the *Batting Cage* file in which you saved the scenarios. Your job is to create a report for the owners on a proposed advertising change. You believe it could help bring in more revenue if the owners were willing to spend more on advertising with a slight rise in prices to cover the cost.

Create a scenario in which you spend $2,000 on advertising and increase the price to $3.50. Create a view with custom formatting, the date and your name as the header. Now make a report entitled **Proposed Advertising and Pricing Change**. Print the report.

Use Excel with the Web

Typically, you use Excel to compute numbers for a particular project as you sit in your home or office, and you might even share the information with colleagues or team members across the hall. Yet thanks to the opportunities offered by the Internet, you can easily share your Excel data with people across the globe without even leaving your desk. Using Excel, you can email your work to others or publish it on the World Wide Web for public access.

At the end of this chapter, you will be able to:

C	E	
☑	❏	Send a workbook via email
☑	❏	Create hyperlinks
☑	❏	Save a worksheet/workbook as a Web Page
☑	❏	Use Web Page Preview
❏	☑	Import a table from an HTML file
❏	☑	Create interactive PivotTables for the Web
❏	☑	Add fields to a PivotTable using the Web browser

CORE OBJECTIVE: *Send a workbook via email*

What: When you want to share your Excel data with colleagues, whether they are in Asia or across the hall, there's no need to save your work on a disk and carry it or send it there. All you need is email capabilities to forward a workbook or worksheet without leaving your desk.

Why: Sending your work by email is free and fast. As you'll learn in Chapter 17 "Collaborate with Workgroups," Excel offers you the ability to send your data to a team member, for your collaborator to make comments or changes and return it to you in a flash, so you can review the work.

SEND A WORKSHEET

How: Use these steps to send a single worksheet:

1. Select the sheet and then choose either of these methods to open the email header shown in Figure 15.1.
   - Click the **E-Mail** button.
   - Choose **File|Send To|Mail** Recipient.
2. Complete the **To:** line like the example in Figure 15.1; the **Cc:** and **Bcc:** lines are optional. When you are sending to multiple recipients, separate their names with semicolons. If you have addresses saved in an address book, click **To:** or **Cc:** and select the recipients. By default, the sheet name is used in the Subject line, but you can enter something else if you want.
3. When you're ready to send the worksheet, click **Send this Sheet.**

Figure 15.1
Sending a worksheet
as email

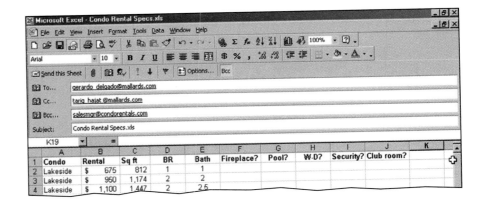

Result: The worksheet is immediately sent to the recipient, the email header closes, and you are returned to the regular Excel window.

TIPS FROM A PRO: Depending on your email configuration, a dialog box *may* appear when you click the E-mail button with the following options:

- Send the entire workbook as an attachment.
- Send the current sheet as the message body.

If this message doesn't appear, and you want to send another file as an attachment in addition to this worksheet, click the **Insert File** button.

SEND A WORKBOOK AS AN ATTACHMENT

How: When you want to send an entire workbook using email, it's more efficient to attach the file to an email message than to send it one worksheet at a time. You can send a saved workbook as an *attachment* without exiting Excel.

1. Open the workbook that you want to send and choose **File|Send To|Mail Recipient (as Attachment)**. A window similar to the one shown in Figure 15.2 appears.
2. Complete the To:, Cc:, and Subject lines, and add a message if you want.

3. Click the **Insert File** button or choose **Insert|File Attachment** to attach additional files to the email message.
4. Click **Send** when you are ready to transmit the email and attachments.

Figure 15.2
Sending a workbook as an email attachment

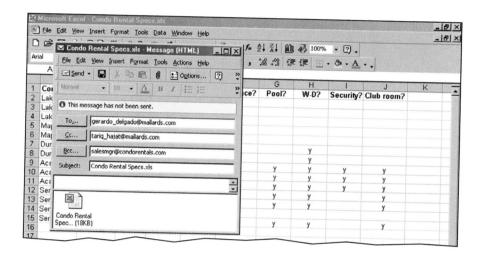

Result: The email message and its attachments begin transmitting to the recipient you have designated. The email window closes, leaving you staring at the Excel window and your active worksheet.

TIPS FROM A PRO: Before you can send email from within Excel you must have a network or modem connection to the Internet. In addition, you must have a recent e-mail program (older versions don't support this feature). See Excel Help if you have trouble.

TASK 2   *Use Hyperlinks*

C   CORE OBJECTIVE: *Create hyperlinks*

What: When you want to jump from one place to another on a worksheet, within a workbook, or to a location outside of the active file, insert a *hyperlink*, a connection between one location and another. To activate the link and jump to the new location, you click the linked element. Hyperlinks can be used to connect to these destinations:

- ○ A Web page anywhere in the world
- ○ Another file
- ○ Another location in this file
- ○ An email address

Why: Hyperlinks take you to a location via a single mouse click. This way you don't have to take the time to search for worksheets, files, or Web addresses. This is a particularly useful feature when you are working with an interactive worksheet on the Web (you learn about this in Task 3).

INSERT A HYPERLINK

How: Follow these general steps to insert a hyperlink to another file or Web page.

1. Select the cell or object that will contain the hyperlink.
2. Click the **Insert Hyperlink** button (or right-click and choose **Hyperlink**, or press **Ctrl+K**, or choose **Insert|Hyperlink**) to access the Insert Hyperlink dialog box, as in Figure 15.3.
3. Specify the destination.
   - To insert a hyperlink to another Web site, type the Web address (such as *www.jcrew.com*) in the Type the File or Web Page Name box, or click the **Browsed Pages** button and choose it from the list, if you've been there in the last month or so. Alternatively, you can click the **Web Page** button to start your browser and go out on the Web and find the page.
   - To insert a hyperlink to another file, such as an Excel file or a Word document, type the file name and address, click the **Recent Files** button to choose from the list, or click the **File** button to open a Link to File dialog box (like an Open dialog box).
   - To insert a hyperlink to an email address, click the **E-mail Address** button and type the address in the E-mail Address box (Figure 15.4). Type a Subject if you want. This allows users to send feedback to a certain email address when they click the link. When the link is activated, this email address automatically appears in the **To** line.

Figure 15.3 Insert Hyperlink dialog box

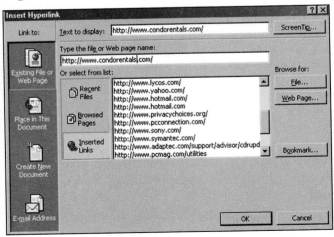

Figure 15.4 Inserting a hyperlink to an email address

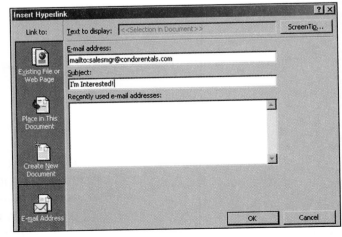

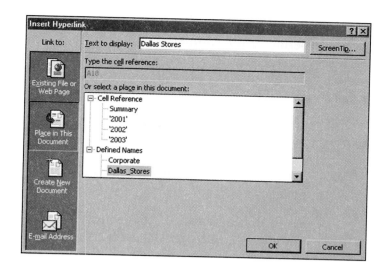

Figure 15.5
Inserting a hyperlink to a place in this file

- To insert a hyperlink to a specific location within the current file, click **Place in This Document** (Figure 15.5). Here you can specify a range name or a cell reference on a certain sheet.
- To insert a hyperlink to a file that doesn't yet exist, click **Create New Document.**
- To have custom text displayed in the cell, type it in the **Text to Display** box. To have a custom ScreenTip appear when you point to the hyperlink, click the **ScreenTip** button and enter the custom text.

4. Click **OK**.

Result: The content of the selected cell appears in blue and is underlined, indicating that it's a hyperlink (but graphic objects don't look any different). If the cells you selected were empty, they now contain the link-to address as shown in Figure 15.6.

When you move the mouse pointer over the cells or object containing a hyperlink, the mouse pointer changes to a pointing hand, and the destination address appears in a ScreenTip. Of course, if you added a ScreenTip yourself, the text you entered appears instead. Figure 15.6 provides examples of hyperlinks. To go to the destination, click the hyperlink.

TIPS FROM A PRO: The simplest way to create a hyperlink to another web page or email address is to type the address in the cell and press Enter. The format of the text changes to blue underlined, signifying that Excel automatically converted it into a hyperlink.

Figure 15.6
Hyperlinks in a worksheet

(a) Link to a cell in this sheet

	A	B	C	D	E	F
1	**Contents**					
2	Corporate					
3	Dallas Stores					
4	LA Stores					
5	NY Stores					
6	C:\My Documents\MegaMedia Results.xls - NY_Stores					
7	**MEGA MEDIA CORPORATE**					
8						

(b) Link to a Web page

16	
17	Visit our site:
18	http://www.condorentals.com/
19	http://www.condorentals.com/
20	

TIPS FROM A PRO: By default, the text that shows as you run the mouse pointer over a hyperlink is the address of the link-to site. However, if you are publishing your page on the Web, this may not offer meaningful information for the average viewer. Instead, consider replacing the address with a ScreenTip using regular English words.

MODIFY A HYPERLINK

How: After you insert a hyperlink, you can easily modify or remove it completely.

1. To edit a hyperlink, don't just click it, or you'll activate the hyperlink. Instead, right-click the cell and choose **Hyperlink** from the shortcut menu to edit it. Right-click the cell or object and choose **Hyperlink|Edit Hyperlink** to access the Edit Hyperlink dialog box.
2. To remove a link, click **Remove Link**.
3. To modify a link, change the fields in the dialog box as necessary and click **OK**.

Result: The hyperlink has been deleted or modified.

 TIPS FROM A PRO: If you want to modify the before and after hyperlink font colors, select the hyperlink and choose **Format|Styles**.

TASK 3 | *Save a Workbook as a Web Page*

 CORE OBJECTIVE: Save a worksheet/workbook as a Web page

What: You've learned many of the capabilities that Excel offers for creating spreadsheets and crunching complex numbers. Yet Excel is not limited to worksheets that you store on a disk, ready for you to use when you need them. Instead, you can place a workbook or worksheet on the Web so that it can be viewed—and even manipulated—by anyone with Web access, even those who do not have Excel installed on their computers. Here are the general steps for putting your Excel file on the Web:

1. Convert an existing Excel file into a Web page.
2. Preview it in the browser to be sure that it looks right and works correctly.
3. Publish it on a Web server to give the public access to it.

Why: The worksheets that you created so far were saved as typical Excel files. However, Web browsers can't read the same language as your personal computing software. Instead, they use their own special language called *hypertext markup language* or *HTML*. If you want people to have access your work on the Web, you must first translate it into HTML.

SAVE AS A NON-INTERACTIVE WEB PAGE

How: You can quickly convert an existing workbook or worksheet or cells into a Web page, or save a new Excel file in that format by using the following steps:

1. Open the workbook you want to create a Web page from, and select the sheet and cells, if you want only part of the file.
2. Choose **File|Save as Web page**. The Save As dialog box in Figure 15.7 appears.
3. Specify where you want to save it, and whether you want the entire workbook or the selection. (Don't choose interactivity yet—you'll learn about that in the next section.)
4. Enter the name of the file. Notice that the default extension is *.htm*.
5. Click **Change Title** and type the text that will appear on the title bar of the browser when your page is being viewed, as well as on the screen above the worksheet if you saved a selection.
6. Click **Save** to complete the process.

 TIPS FROM A PRO: It's a good idea to save the file as a regular *.xls* file as a backup before you convert it into a Web page.

Result: Your Excel workbook is now ready for viewing on the Web by anyone, even those who don't have Excel on their computers. You can click the tabs to view the various worksheets.

A couple of things happen behind the scenes when you save your workbook or worksheet as a Web page. First, your Excel file was copied and translated into HTML; it now has an *.htm* file extension. Additionally, if you had added any graphics or charts, a secondary folder now exists with a similar file name (Figure 15.8). This folder organizes and stores all of the supporting graphics files such as colored fonts, pictures, background colors or images, and so on.

The workbook or worksheet changes in other ways as well. Wrapped, rotated, and indented text now appears as plain, horizontal text. Some numbers may not be aligned correctly. Conditional formatting and named ranges are not retained. You can learn more about what happens

Figure 15.7 Saving a file as a Web page

Figure 15.8 Excel Web page and its supporting graphics folder

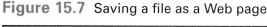

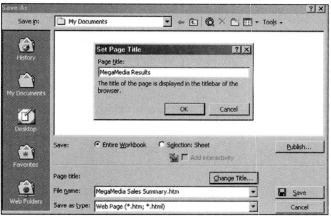

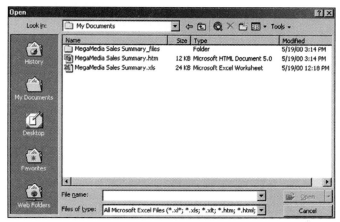

when you save a worksheet as a Web page by reading the Help topics "Put a worksheet on a Web page," "Ways to put Excel data on the Web," and "Troubleshoot publishing and saving Excel data as a Web page."

TIPS FROM A PRO: If your worksheet contains a chart, when you save the sheet as a Web page, the chart is automatically converted to a GIF file and stored in the folder along with other graphics found on the Web page.

TIPS FROM A PRO: To fine-tune the formatting of your workbook for the Web, choose **Tools|Options**, click the **General** tab, and click **Web Options**. The Web Options dialog box has five tabs with many items you can change. Here's an example: In the Compatibility section of the General tab, a check box lets you Save Any Additional Hidden Data Necessary to Maintain Formulas. This option, which is selected by default, saves all data used in the workbook, even if it isn't displayed on the Web page. This enables you to save an Excel workbook as a Web page and reopen it in Excel with no loss of function. (This is called HTML *round tripping*.) If you choose not to use this feature (which makes the file smaller if your work includes references), the relevant cells show calculated values—the underlying formulas are gone. For more detail on the Web Options dialog box, see *Prentice Hall's MOUS Test Preperation Guide for Power Point 2000*, by Colene Coldwell, a companion book in this series. You can also click the Web Options dialog box's Help button and click each item to see a description. The Excel Help page "Troubleshoot Web page options" also contains useful information.

USE WEB PAGE PREVIEW

CORE OBJECTIVE: Use Web page preview

How: Certain functions, graphics, and other characteristics might not translate correctly when you convert an Excel file to a Web page. By checking the page before it is published on the Internet, you can remove or correct any items that don't appear or function as you had intended.

1. Open the Excel file that you have saved as a Web page and click the worksheet that you want to view.
2. Choose **File|Web Page Preview**.

Result: The Web workbook opens in your default browser window. Although the workbook isn't interactive, each sheet is available for display. Viewers can click the tabs to view individual sheets, as shown in Figure 15.9. If you have saved a worksheet or range and have added interactivity (explained in the following section), you must use Internet Explorer (not another browser) to test the interaction.

THOUGHT QUESTION: Why do you suppose this feature works only in Internet Explorer and not in Netscape or other browsers?

Figure 15.9 Web Page Preview

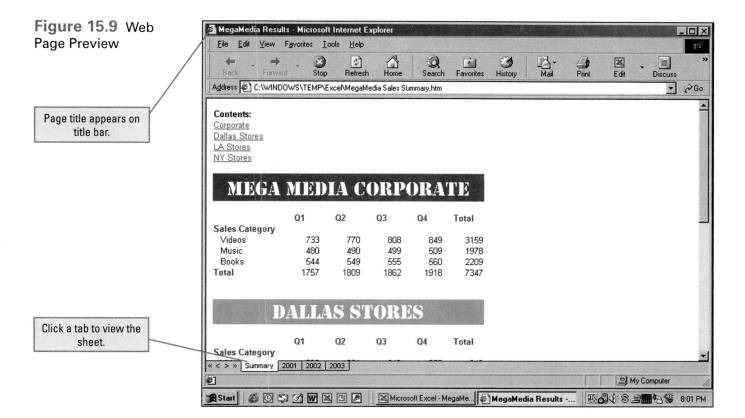

Page title appears on title bar.

Click a tab to view the sheet.

CREATE AN INTERACTIVE WEB PAGE

How: Create interactive Web pages from your Excel data to allow users not only to view the data, but also to enter numbers, sort, and calculate with the worksheet. For example, you can publish a real estate calculator that allows users to sort and filter a database to display information the way they want.

1. Open the worksheet you want to make interactive. (You can make an interactive Web page only from a single sheet or range of cells, not an entire workbook.)
2. Choose **File|Save As Web Page**.
3. Click **Selection** and **Add Interactivity**.
4. Title and save the worksheet as you learned in the previous section.

Result: The Web page and supporting folder are created just as before, but interactive Web pages have some new features, as you can see in Figure 15.10a. Using the buttons on the Interactive Worksheet toolbar, you can add subtotals, sort the data, or filter the data to match certain criteria (Figure 15.10b). When you click the Property Toolbox button, you can format various aspects of the worksheet (Figure 15.10c).

The great thing about interactive Excel Web pages is that users don't even have to have Excel to be able to use these features.

Remember that when users interact with the worksheet, their changes don't affect the original Web page, only the copy in their browser.

Figure 15.10 Web
Page Preview
(a) Interactive Excel
sheet as Web page

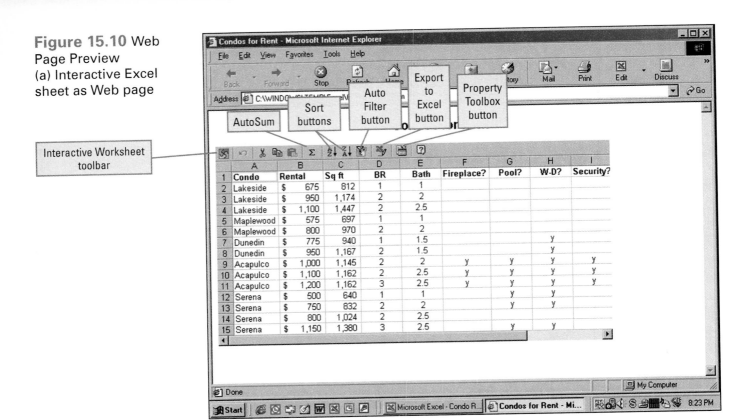

(b) Interacting with the Excel Web page

(c) Property Toolbox

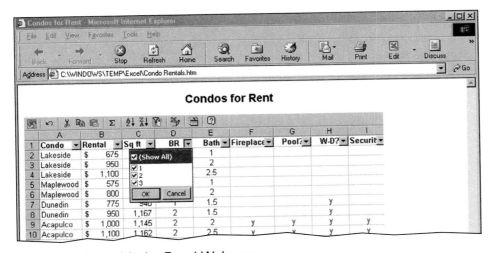

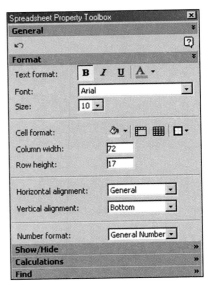

TASK **4**   *Save and Publish on the Web*

What: The final step in making your Excel data available on the Web is to *pub-lish* it, or save it on a Web server so that it's available to the public.

   TIPS FROM A PRO: To publish interactive Excel worksheets or PivotTables on the Web, you must have the Office 2000 Web Components installed on your computer. To view a Web PivotTable or use interactive Web worksheets, you must use Microsoft Internet Explorer version 4.01 or later. This feature doesn't work in other browsers.

Why: If you have access to a Web server, you can save and publish your Excel data on the Web in a single operation.

How: Open the file that you want to publish on the Internet or on an intranet network.

1. Choose **File|Save as Web Page** to access the dialog box that you saw previously in Figure 15.7.
2. Choose whether you want the entire workbook or a selection, and specify whether you want it to be interactive.
3. Click **Publish** to access the Publish as Web Page dialog box (Figure 15.11).
   - Select the cells or item that you want to publish if you forgot to make this selection earlier.
   - Add interactivity if you forgot to in the previous dialog box, and designate whether it will be used to change a spreadsheet or a PivotTable. (You'll learn more about this in Task 6).
   - Change the title of your Web page if you forgot in the previous dialog box.
   - Browse to find a Save To location. If you know the Web address, or *Uniform Resource Locator* (URL), of your Web space on the server, type it, plus your file name, into the **File name** box (for example, *http://www.servername/myname/home.htm*). You can also upload your page by saving it to a Web Folder or by sending it to an FTP Location. (If you need help with this aspect, contact your instructor or network administrator.)

Figure 15.11
Publishing a Web page

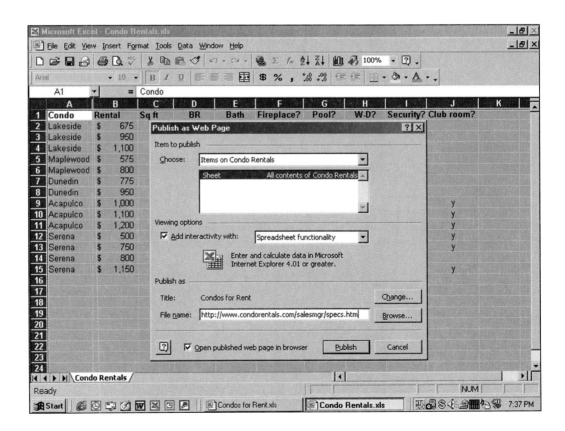

- Select **Open Published Web Page in Browser** to view the results as soon as it is published. This option is similar to Web Page Preview.
4. Click **Publish** to complete the process.

Result: As soon as you click Publish, Excel and the mechanism that you have chosen to upload your page immediately begin to transfer your work and all of its parts to the Web server that you have designated. (If you are uploading a large workbook and graphics, this process may take a few minutes.) When everything has been moved to the server, the Web page opens in your browser if you chose that option.

 TIPS FROM A PRO: Another way to publish your Web page is to save your Web page using either the Windows' Web Folders or Office's FTP Locations. Contact your network administrator for specific details on locations and software requirements.

| TASK **5** | *Edit an Excel Web Page* |

E

EXPERT OBJECTIVE: *Import a table from an HTML file (insert, drag and drop—including HTML round tripping)*

What: Excel can be used to open and edit an HTML file if Excel was the program that originally created it. This is known as round tripping. The way this happens depends on whether it was saved as an interactive file.

Why: Although it can be tricky to edit a Web page that contains a worksheet, text, graphics, and other elements, you can sometimes use Excel to edit Web pages that were originally created in Excel.

How: Follow any of these methods for opening an Excel Web page in Excel.

❍ **Use the Edit command.** If you have access to the HTML file, either on your own computer or a networked drive or in a Web folder, follow these steps:
1. In My Computer, browse to find the name of the file.
2. Right-click the file and choose **Edit**.

❍ **Drag and drop.** If you have access to the HTML file, you can use drag-and-drop to edit the file in Excel:
1. In My Computer, browse to find the name of the file.
2. If Excel is already open, drag the file's icon to the Excel button on the taskbar and pause. When the Excel window opens, drop the file into it. If Excel is not open yet, you can simply drag and drop the file onto the Excel icon in the Quick Launch area of the taskbar.

❍ **Use File|Open.** If you have access to the HTML file, you can simply open the file in Excel:
1. In Excel, choose **File|Open**.
2. If necessary, change the Files of Type to All Microsoft Excel Files to display HTML files.
3. Browse through the drives and folders to find the file name, and double-click to open it.

○ **Copy and paste from the browser to Excel.** Use these steps:
   1. In the browser, drag to select the items you want to copy.
   2. Choose **Edit|Copy** (for a non-interactive Web page) or click the **Copy** button on the Interactive Worksheet toolbar in Internet Explorer (for an interactive Web page).
   3. Paste in an Excel worksheet.

 ○ **Export from Internet Explorer.** If the file was saved as interactive, you can simply click the **Export to Excel** button on the Interactive Worksheet toolbar in Internet Explorer.

Result: Any of these methods creates a worksheet where you can change data, formulas, and formatting, and use all of Excel's features to analyze the data. (Note that if you used the Export button, however, the file opens as Read Only, which means you have to save it with a new name to keep any changes you make to it.) When you edit an Excel Web page, the changes you make have no effect on the original Web page.

If you, as the originator of the file, want to make changes to the file, you can edit it in Excel, save it, and republish it.

TASK 6   *Publish a PivotTable on the Web*

What: Just as you can turn any worksheet, workbook, or range of cells into a Web page, you can also publish a PivotTable. To make an interactive PivotTable, though, requires a couple of extra steps.

Why: When you want to display summary data, a PivotTable works great. When you publish the data on the Internet or an intranet, you allow others to view and manipulate the data to view the summary different ways.

PUBLISH A PIVOTTABLE

How: If you want to publish a PivotTable for display only, select the table and choose **File|Save As Web Page.** Use the procedures you learned in Task 3.

Result: The PivotTable is formatted appropriately for viewing in any Web browser.

CREATE AN INTERACTIVE WEB PIVOTTABLE

 EXPERT OBJECTIVE: Create interactive PivotTables for the Web

How: To create an interactive PivotTable so multiple users can add fields or rearrange the PivotTable, you can use an existing PivotTable Report or other Excel data.

   1. With the file open in Excel, build a PivotTable Report, just as you learned in Chapter 13, "Manage Data and Lists."
   2. Select the PivotTable and choose **File|Save As Web Page.** In the Save As dialog box, click **Selection: PivotTable** and **Add Interactivity.**

3. Change the title and file name if you like, and click **Publish** to access the Publish as Web Page dialog box (Figure 15.11). Choose **PivotTable** and under Viewing Options choose **PivotTable functionality.**

4. Specify where you want to save the file, and select the check box to open the published Web page in the browser. Click **Publish.**

Result: Internet Explorer opens and displays a PivotTable List, as you see in Figure 15.12.

Figure 15.12
PivotTable List

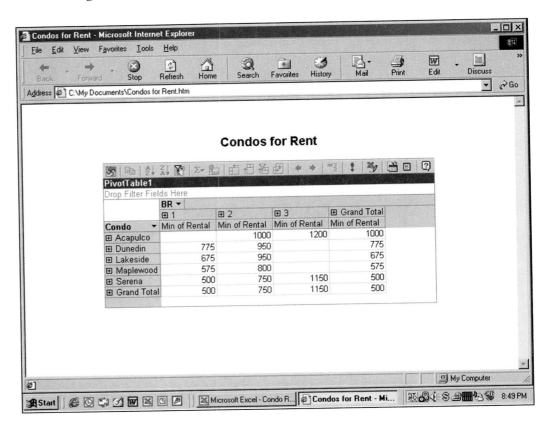

INTERACT WITH A WEB PIVOTTABLE

EXPERT OBJECTIVE: Add fields to a PivotTable using the Web browser

How: After a PivotTable has been published, you can interact by expanding or collapsing it, or you can add or rearrange the fields. Open the PivotTable List in Internet Explorer.

○ To add data fields, click the **Field List** button to display the list of fields. Choose each field you want to use in the PivotTable, and specify where you want to add it. For example, you might want to add a field to the Filter Area. You might want to see only those condos with a pool (Figure 15.13), or you might want to see the number of baths as well as bedrooms (Figure 15.14).

○ To rearrange data fields, place the mouse pointer over the field name until it turns to the four-headed pointer. Now you can use drag and drop to rearrange the field.

Figure 15.13
PivotTable Field list

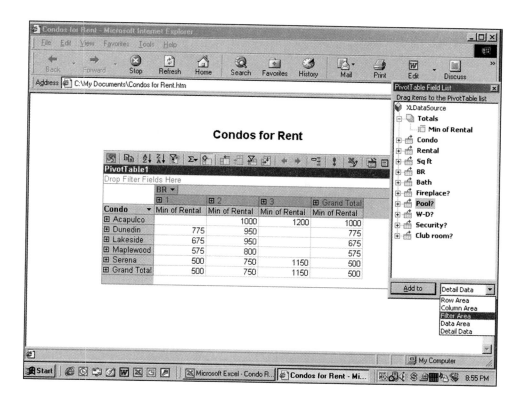

○ To delete data fields, select the field and press **Delete** or right-click, and choose **Remove Field** from the shortcut menu.
○ To expand to see details or collapse to see subtotals only, click the plus-sign or minus-sign icons (Figure 15.14).
○ To change the function to Sum, Count, Min, or Max, click the **AutoCalc** button.

Figure 15.14
Expanded PivotTable

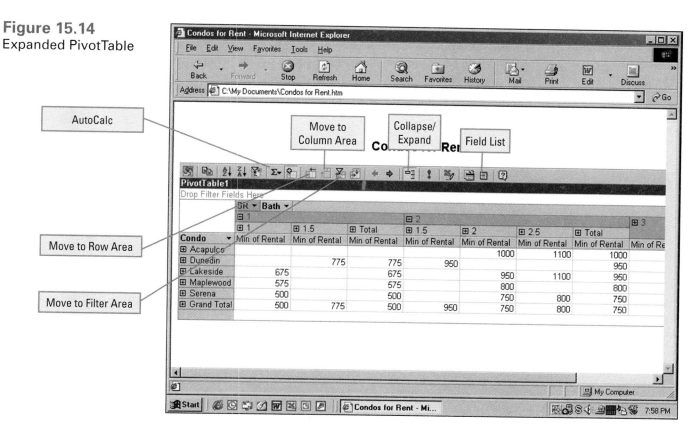

TIPS FROM A PRO: Another way to modify and manipulate published PivotTable data is to export the data to Excel by clicking the Export to Excel button on the toolbar. When you do this, an Excel workbook immediately opens—the PivotTable is included on one sheet and the data fields on another. This way you can create a table and save to a disk location. This method requires you to have Excel installed on your computer, though.

Result: As you rearrange, modify, or delete the fields, the PivotTable list is recalculated and the data is changed.

 ## Use PinPoint

After gaining the skills in this chapter, you can send Excel data via email, create a hyperlink; preview your work on the Web; save an Excel workbook, worksheet, or PivotTable as a Web page, and publish it. Now it's time to use the PinPoint software and see what you can do. Remember, whenever you are unsure of what to do, you can reread that portion of the chapter or you can click Show Me for a live demonstration. Check out these skills in PinPoint:

- Create a hyperlink
- Save a Web Page
- Web Page Preview
- Publish PivotTable

Key Terms

You can find definitions for these words in this chapter:

Attachment
Hyperlink
Hypertext markup language (HTML)
Round tripping
Uniform Resource Locator (URL)

Review Questions

You can use the following review questions to test your knowledge and skills. Answers are given in Appendix D.

True/False

Indicate whether each statement is true (T) or false(F).

____ 1. To publish a workbook on the Web, you must first save it as an HTML file.

____ 2. PivotTables can be published on the Web, but they don't allow for interactivity.

____ 3. Using Web Page Preview is a good way to see what the Excel data looks like in a browser before you publish it on the Web.

____ 4. Sending a file as an email attachment is the same as copying and pasting it into the message area.

___ 5. Interactive worksheets published on the Web come with a special toolbar.

___ 6. Interactive worksheets published on the Web must be viewed with Netscape Navigator.

___ 7. After you insert a hyperlink, you can't remove it.

___ 8. Hyperlinks enable you to jump quickly from one location to another.

___ 9. The small hand that appears when you run the mouse pointer over text indicates the presence of a hyperlink.

___ 10. The fastest, most efficient way to get an Excel workbook to your collaborator two floors up is to copy it onto a disk and run it up there.

Multiple Choice

Select the letter that best completes the statement.

___ 1. Hyperlinks can be used to:
   a. Jump to a cell location on the active worksheet or other worksheet in the workbook.
   b. Jump to another file.
   c. Jump to a Web site.
   d. Send email to a certain person.
   e. All of the above.

___ 2. To add a hyperlink within the active worksheet, select a cell and:
   a. Choose Tools|Hyperlink.
   b. Click the Insert Hyperlink button.
   c. Choose Insert|Hyperlink.
   d. Right-click and choose Hyperlink from the shortcut menu.
   e. b, c, and d.

___ 3. The best way to rush a workbook to a collaborator in Hawaii is:
   a. Package it up and send it through an express package delivery service.
   b. Save it on a drive on the local area network.
   c. Attach it to an email message.
   d. Print the sheet and fax it to him or her.
   e. Both a and b

___ 4. To begin the process of publishing Excel data as a Web page:
   a. Choose File|Save As Web Page.
   b. Choose File|Save And Publish.
   c. Right-click the active worksheet and choose Convert to HTML.
   d. Save the page as normal, and use the browser to open the file.
   e. Click the Insert Hyperlink button.

___ 5. To edit a hyperlink, select the item containing the hyperlink and:
   a. Right-click and choose Hyperlink from the shortcut menu.
   b. Click the Insert Hyperlink button on the Standard toolbar.
   c. Choose Insert|Hyperlink.
   d. Press Ctrl+K.
   e. All of the above.

___ 6. When you publish Excel data on the Web:
   a. You send the data to a Web server location.
   b. The data is stored on a Web server.
   c. Anyone with Internet access could theoretically view your data.
   d. The data is uploaded from your computer to a remote site on the Web.
   e. All of the above.

___ 7. To view an interactive PivotTable on the Web, you must:
   a. Use Internet Explorer 4.01 or later.
   b. Purchase special software.
   c. Have at least a Pentium III processor.
   d. Create a PivotTable in Excel first.
   e. All of the above.

___ 8. If you have added graphics to your workbook and save it as a Web page:
   a. The graphics are all deleted.
   b. Excel creates a backup copy of the file for you in case something goes wrong.
   c. Excel creates a secondary folder in the same location and stores the graphics inside.
   d. You receive a prompt asking whether you want to save the graphics too.
   e. You get an error message because you can't publish an Excel file that includes graphics.

___ 9. When an interactive PivotTable list is published on the Web, data fields can be:
   a. Added.
   b. Deleted.
   c. Moved.
   d. Collapsed.
   e. All of these are possible.

___ 10. One reason for publishing an Excel file on the Web is that:
   a. Others not only can view but also manipulate the data.
   b. The data is much easier to maintain than a typical workbook.
   c. It's an easy way to share your worksheet with others.
   d. People enjoy surfing the Web.
   e. Both a and c.

Screen Review

Match the letters in Figure 15.15 with the correct items in the list.

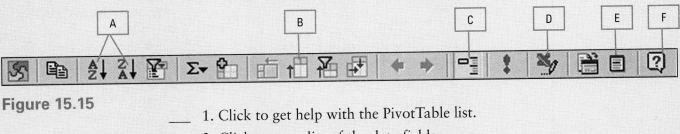

Figure 15.15

___ 1. Click to get help with the PivotTable list.

___ 2. Click to see a list of the data fields.

___ 3. Click to export the data to Excel.

___ 4. Click to sort the data.

___ 5. Click to add the selected field to the column area.

___ 6. Click to collapse the field.

Exercise and Project

Follow these step-by-step instructions to create a worksheet and Web page. If you are working in a computer lab, ask your instructor where you should save and print your file.

Exercise

Before you start this exercise, obtain the email address of one of your classmates.

1. Open the file called **Car Loan.xls** from the *Student\Chapter 15* folder of the PinPoint CD.
2. Beneath the title place the name of a lending institution such as Wells Fargo. Place a picture of a bank or the Wells Fargo logo beside the title. (*Hint*: If you want to capture a picture off the Internet, right-click the picture and click the Save Picture As or Save Image As command.)
3. Resize the picture to fit anywhere between C1 and H5. Select the picture and create a hyperlink to the Wells Fargo Web site, *http://www.wellsfargo.com/*.
4. Save the file. Send the file as an attachment to a classmate. In the subject line type **Exercise 15**. In the body of the email type **Exercise 15 is enclosed**.
5. Save the file as a Web page. First scan your Web settings to be sure the proper settings are selected. To do so, choose Tools|Options, click the General tab, and click the Web Options button. In the Web Options dialog box, click the General tab. All three options should be selected: Rely on CSS, Save Any Additional Hidden Data, and Load Pictures.
6. Use Web Page Preview. Is the picture in the correct location?
7. Make any adjustments that are needed and print the file.
8. If possible, publish your page on a Web server. Check with your instructor to get specific instructions on how and where to do this.

Project

Open the file called **MegaMedia.xls** from the *Student\Chapter 15* folder of the PinPoint CD and resize the columns. Create a PivotTable report from the database in Sheet1. Drag *Category* to the Row area, *Description* to the Column area, and *Total Cost* to the Data area for summing.

Select the PivotTable and publish it as an interactive Web page with PivotTable functionality. Add a descriptive title, such as **Total Cost by Category and Description**.

In Internet Explorer, drop down the Category and choose only Videos. Print the page. (*Hint*: Your Internet connection must be established for this to work; you cannot work offline.)

Work with Templates and Macros

Powerful features of Excel include those that help you automate your tasks. You can use Excel to create standard worksheets to use repeatedly. You can automate a series of commands and choices to run whenever you press a certain shortcut key or click a custom button. Further, you can customize Excel by adding buttons that help you get your work done efficiently.

At the end of this chapter, you will be able to:

C **E**

☐ ☑ Create templates
☑ ☐ Use templates to create a new workbook
☐ ☑ Apply templates
☐ ☑ Edit templates
☐ ☑ Record macros
☐ ☑ Run macros
☐ ☑ Edit macros
☐ ☑ Customize a toolbar
☐ ☑ Assign a macro to a command button
☐ ☐ Open a file automatically
☐ ☑ Create a workspace file
☐ ☐ Change colors in the color palette
☐ ☐ Manage default file settings

What: Excel supplies several ***templates*** containing the formulas, formatting, and settings that you can use for typical worksheets. For example, you can use one of Excel's templates to create an expense statement, an invoice, or a purchase order, without having to create it from scratch.

Every worksheet is based on a template—until now, you've been using the default Blank Workbook template. It comes with three worksheets, Arial 10 font, and column widths set at 8.43. You can make your own templates containing standard text, formulas, formatting, styles, macros, and custom toolbars.

For example, a company would use a certain form for an expense report for all its sales representatives. You could set up the form with the titles and formulas and formatting and give it to each person to use each week or each month. Another example would be a request for new computer equipment, where the form is filled out and sent around for managers' signatures.

Why: Any time you have to do something over and over, you should set it up to save yourself the trouble. Rather than creating a certain worksheet from scratch every time, save it as a template instead, and simply open it to fill in just the new text and numbers.

CREATE A TEMPLATE

*EXPERT OBJECTIVE: **Create templates***

How: Templates are saved in a specific location with an *.xlt* extension.

1. Set up the workbook the way you want it. Type and format the labels, enter the formulas, and set the print area. You can also start with an existing worksheet, one you use often, and simply erase the places where you want the new information to appear.
2. Add information to help other users know what to enter where.
   - Add comments in cells.
   - Add text boxes explaining how to use the template.
   - Automate any complicated procedures with macros (see Task 2).
3. Choose **File|Save As**. Name the file, and under Save As Type, choose **Template (*.xlt)** as shown in Figure 16.1. Click **OK**.

Figure 16.1 Saving a template

Location for templates

Choose Template.

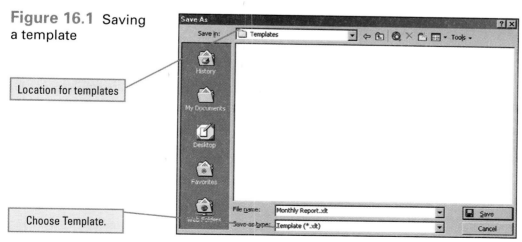

Result: Excel saves the template in the default location for Excel templates: the *Templates* folder in *C:\Windows\Application Data\Microsoft.* The template file has an *.xlt* extension.

Tips from a Pro: If you want to make the template available to other users, you need to save it on a networked drive. Ask your network administrator to save it on the network in a place where everyone in the workgroup can access it.

USE A TEMPLATE TO CREATE A NEW WORKBOOK

Core **O**bjective: *Use templates to create a new workbook*

How: To create a workbook based on a specific template, you must use the menu command, not the button.

1. Choose **File|New**.
2. Choose one of the templates:
   - Click the **General** tab, if necessary, to see your custom template listed.
   - Click the **Spreadsheet Solutions** tab to see a list of Excel's predefined templates (Figure 16.2).
3. Double-click the template you want to use.

Figure 16.2 New
dialog box

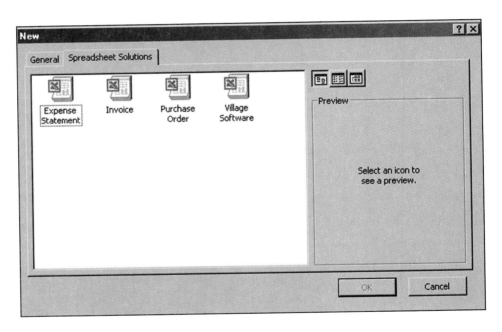

Tips from a Pro: When you use one of Excel's predefined templates, a prompt might appear asking whether you want to enable the macros. This is part of the virus-checking feature, guarding against viruses that are hidden in macros. Because the Excel template's macros come directly from Microsoft, they are safe, so click **Enable Macros**.

Result: A workbook is created from the template you chose. It contains the formatting, formulas, toolbars, and settings it was saved with. Figure 16.3 shows a sample.

Figure 16.3 Sample template

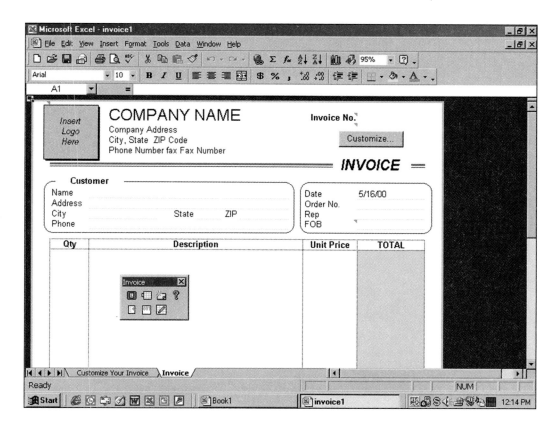

APPLY A TEMPLATE TO A WORKSHEET

EXPERT OBJECTIVE: Apply templates

How: You can apply a custom template that you created to a worksheet in an existing workbook. (This doesn't work with the templates supplied on the Spreadsheet Solutions tab, though.)

1. Select a blank sheet in an existing workbook.
2. Right-click the sheet tab and choose **Insert** from the shortcut menu. This opens the template dialog box shown in Figure 16.2.
3. Click the General tab, if necessary, to see the custom templates. Double-click the template you want to insert.

Result: One or more worksheets are added to your workbook with the formatting, formulas, and cell contents from the template.

EDIT A TEMPLATE

EXPERT OBJECTIVE: Edit templates

How: To make changes to a template, first open it.

1. Click **Open** or choose **File|Open**.
2. In the Open dialog box under Files of Type, choose **All Microsoft Excel Files**, if necessary.
3. Browse to the *C:\Windows\Application Data\Microsoft\Templates* folder or the networked drive where you saved it. Double-click the template name.

Task 1: Use Templates 351

4. Make changes to the formulas, formatting, text, or other settings.

5. Save and close the file.

Result: The template has been modified.

 TIPS FROM A PRO: Excel has an add-in that combines the best of the templates feature with Excel's database functionality. The Template Wizard with Data Tracking sets up a template and a database to collect the information entered on the form. Each time you enter data in the template, Excel automatically saves the information to a database, saving you the trouble of having to retype the information. This way, for example, you can keep track of all employee expenses, month by month, or the purchase orders by vendor.

TASK 2   *Use Macros*

What: Sometimes you need to do the same task over and over, and whether easy or difficult, it is boring. Other times, a task is very difficult for a novice user or so rarely used that an experienced user doesn't want to have to figure it out again. Excel enables you to record the steps to accomplish these tasks and store them as a *macro*. This lets you run them quickly and painlessly by pressing a shortcut key, or by clicking a custom button.

Macros can be stored either in the same workbook as the template or workbook you want to use them with, in a new workbook, or in a Personal Macro Workbook.

Why: Record a macro so you can run it the next time you want to do the same task with a single step.

RECORD A MACRO

 EXPERT OBJECTIVE: Record macros

How: It's a good idea to practice the steps first, and begin to record the macro.

1. Choose **Tools|Macro|Record New Macro**. This opens the Record Macro dialog box shown in Figure 16.4. Enter a one-word name for the macro and specify a shortcut key and where to store it. (You'll learn how to assign the macro to a button in Task 4.)

Figure 16.4 Record Macro dialog box

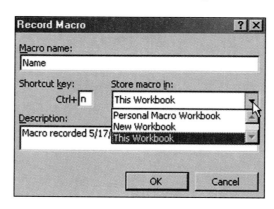

TIPS FROM A PRO: Store the macro in the personal macro workbook if you want to be able to use the macro in any Excel file.

 TIPS FROM A PRO: Shortcut keys allow you to run the macro by pressing two or more keys together, such as Ctrl+M or Ctrl+Shift+M. Pick a shortcut key that you can remember, but be sure not to choose one that's been assigned to another action, such as Ctrl+C for Copy. If you do so, the macro shortcut overrides the default action. For this reason, it's a good idea to try out possible shortcut keystrokes before you begin to record the macro to be sure that they are unassigned.

Figure 16.5 Stop Recording toolbar

2. Perform the keystrokes and mouse actions for the task. As you do this, you see the Stop Recording toolbar on the screen (Figure 16.5).
3. Click the **Stop Recording** button when you are finished.

Result: The many steps you recorded are saved as a macro that you can run with a single action.

 TIPS FROM A PRO: The button to the right of the Stop Recording button enables you to specify whether the actions of the macro are relative (that is, they work on any cells relative to the starting point) or absolute (work only on those specific cells). The button is a toggle: pushed in means relative; not pushed in means absolute.

RUN A MACRO

 EXPERT OBJECTIVE: Run macros

How: When you want to use a macro you've recorded, perform one of the following actions:

○ Press the shortcut key you defined for it when you created it.
○ Choose **Tools|Macro|Macros** or choose **Alt+F8** to access the Macro dialog box (Figure 16.6) and double-click the macro name to run it.

Figure 16.6 Macro dialog box

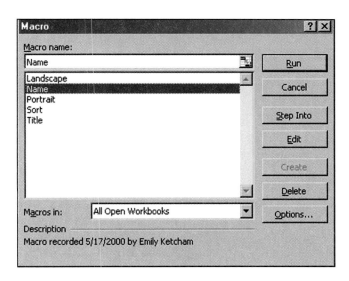

Result: The macro runs, and the commands you recorded are executed. You'll learn how to run a macro using a button in later tasks.

 THOUGHT QUESTION: Can you think of some other examples where macros might be useful? Would you record a macro to repeatedly format a cell to be bold, Arial 30, blue, and centered? Why or why not?

TASK **3** *Modify an Existing Macro*

 EXPERT OBJECTIVE: Edit macros

What: You can change an existing macro by changing its name, making a copy of it, deleting it, or changing the action of the macro. The macro is recorded in a programming language called *Visual Basic for Applications (VBA)*. The VBA code can be changed to modify the action of the macro. The language might be confusing at first, but a closer look shows that the code echoes the actions you took and the selections you made while recording the macro.

Why: Sometimes after you record a macro, you realize the name isn't memorable, or the macro doesn't quite do what you want. You can fix those problems.

DELETE A MACRO

How: Get rid of unwanted macros this way.

1. Choose **Tools|Macro|Macros** or choose **Alt+F8**.
2. Select the macro in the Macro dialog box.
3. Click **Delete**, and click **Close** to close the dialog box.

Result: The macro is removed from the list.

EDIT A MACRO

How: You can easily change the macro's name or the function it performs.

1. Choose **Tools|Macro|Macros** or choose **Alt+F8**.
2. Select the macro in the dialog box.
3. Click **Edit**. When the Visual Basic Editor opens, you see the code that is running behind the scenes, beginning with Sub and the macro name and ending with EndSub. As you see in Figure 16.7, the language looks somewhat familiar, and you can figure out enough to change the cells referred to in the macro.
4. To rename the macro, change **Sub Macro1** () to **Sub NewName** (). (Use a one-word name.)
5. To change the text or function shown in the code, type the replacement between the quotation marks.
6. Close the window.

Figure 16.7 Visual
Basic Editor

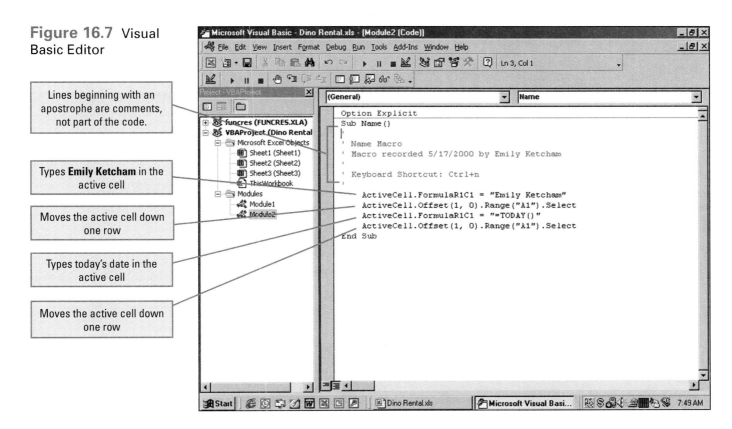

Lines beginning with an apostrophe are comments, not part of the code.

Types **Emily Ketcham** in the active cell

Moves the active cell down one row

Types today's date in the active cell

Moves the active cell down one row

Result: The change is automatically saved. The macro has a different name or performs a different function. The next time you access the Macros dialog box, you'll see the new name listed in place of the old one.

TIPS FROM A PRO: If you need to do more editing than those simple steps mentioned previously, you might find it easier to record the macro again from scratch rather than modify the Visual Basic code. VBA is a programming language well worth learning, but you don't really need to know it to automate tasks in Excel.

TASK **4** *Customize Excel's Toolbars*

EXPERT OBJECTIVE: *Customize a toolbar*

What: Customize Excel by creating a button on a toolbar for a macro or command you use often.

Why: It is much faster and easier to use a toolbar button than to choose a macro from the dialog box or to choose a command from a menu.

CUSTOMIZE THE TOOLBAR WITH READYMADE BUTTONS

How: Add buttons for existing commands using these steps.

1. Click the **More Buttons** button on the toolbar where you want to add a new button. This appears on the right edge of a *docked* toolbar (a tool-

bar that appears along the edge of the window), or on the top-left corner of a *floating* toolbar (a toolbar that appears on top of the document, with its own tiny title bar and Close button), as you see in Figure 16.8.

Figure 16.8 More buttons

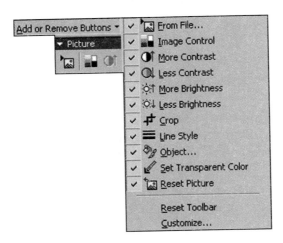

More Buttons button

2. Click **Add or Remove Buttons.** Excel offers buttons from which you can choose that appear on the toolbar, as you see in Figure 16.9.
3. Click the buttons you want to add or remove.

Figure 16.9 Add or Remove Buttons option

Result: A new button appears on the toolbar, or an existing button is removed.

CREATE A CUSTOM TOOLBAR BUTTON

Expert Objective: Assign a macro to a command button

How: Access the Customize dialog box one of these ways:

❍ Click **Add or Remove Buttons** on the toolbar and choose **Customize.**
❍ Choose **View|Toolbars** and click **Customize.**
❍ Choose **Tools|Customize.**
❍ Right-click a toolbar or menu and choose **Customize.**

If the toolbar you want to change isn't on the screen, select the **Toolbars** tab and click to place a check next to its name. Then click the **Commands** tab.

1. Choose the Category containing the command you want, or **Macros** for a macro you created yourself.
2. Choose the command or the **Custom Button** button and drag to the toolbar location. You'll see a bold insertion mark as you drag, as shown in Figure 16.10.

Figure 16.10 Drag to the toolbar

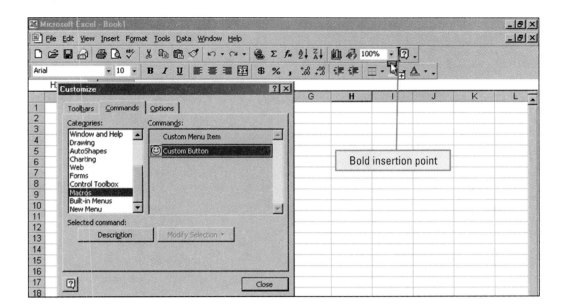

If you used a command, you are finished. Close the dialog box. If you are assigning a macro to the button, continue with the next steps.

3. Click **Modify Selection** to see the Customize dialog box in Figure 16.11.
4. Type a nice short name for the button, if you want to replace macro name that appears by default.
5. Choose **Change Button Image** to pick from several button faces, or choose **Edit Button Image** to create your own button face.
6. Select one of these options:
   - **Text Only (Always)** shows the macro name or command on the button face.
   - **Text Only (In Menus)** shows a square button without words on the toolbar.
   - **Image and Text** displays the button image accompanied by words.

Figure 16.11 Customize dialog box with Modify Selection popped up

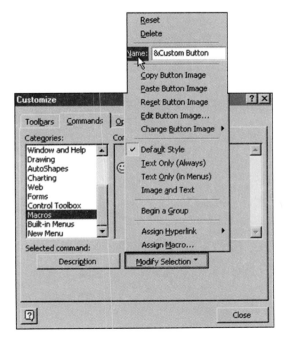

7. Click **Assign Macro** and choose the macro you want to assign to the button. Click **OK**.
8. Close the dialog box.

Result: Your new custom button is available to run the command or macro (Figure 16.12). When you point to it, a ScreenTip shows its name.

Figure 16.12
Custom button on the toolbar

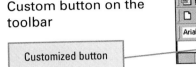

TIPS FROM A PRO: You can easily rearrange a button or remove it from a toolbar with the mouse. To do this, hold down **Alt** while you drag it left, right, or down. You can restore the default toolbar layout by clicking the Reset button on the Toolbars tab of the Customize dialog box.

THOUGHT QUESTION: Is it a good idea to create a custom button face for the standard toolbar buttons? Why or why not?

CREATE A CUSTOM BUTTON ON THE WORKSHEET

How: You can create a button for a macro right on the worksheet.

1. Choose **View|Toolbars** and click to display the **Forms** toolbar (Figure 16.13).
2. Click the **Button** button, and drag a rectangle on the worksheet.
3. In the Assign Macro dialog box, choose the macro name and click **OK** (Figure 16.14).
4. With sizing handles around the button (Figure 16.15), you can type the name of the macro on the button face. Click away from the button to finish.

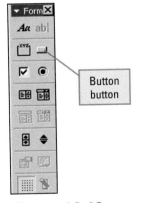

Figure 16.13 Forms toolbar

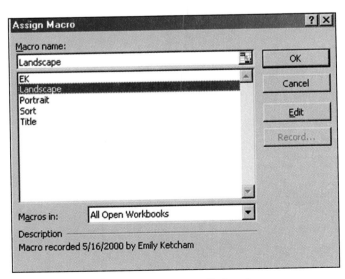

Figure 16.14 Assign Macro dialog box

Figure 16.15 Custom button with sizing handles

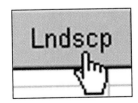

Figure 16.16 Button with mouse pointer

Result: When you place the mouse pointer over the button, it changes into a pointing hand, signifying that it will do some action when you click it (Figure 16.16). To modify the button, right-click the button to get sizing handles around it.

TIPS FROM A PRO: You can also customize a menu using the same technique. Rather than dragging the macro name from the Customize dialog box to the toolbar, drag it to a menu instead.

TASK **5**   *Customize Excel*

What: You can customize other aspects in addition to the toolbars. You can set up Excel so that when it starts it automatically opens a certain worksheet or workspace.

Have you felt frustrated by not having the color you wanted on the color palette, when filling cells or changing charts? You can customize that, too.

In addition, Excel enables you to specify a number of file settings, such as where your files are stored, how many sheets are in each workbook by default, and how many recently used files appear at the bottom of the File menu.

Why: You're an Excel expert now; you deserve to have it the way you like it.

OPEN A FILE AUTOMATICALLY

How: Do you want Excel to automatically open a certain workbook every time it starts? Save the file in the *XLStart* folder. Look for it in either of these locations:

C:\Program Files\Microsoft Office\Office\XLStart
C:\Windows\Application Data\Microsoft\Excel\XLStart

Result: When you start Excel, the workbook opens as well.

CREATE A WORKSPACE FILE

EXPERT OBJECTIVE: Use a workspace

Figure 16.17
Arrange Windows
dialog box

How: Do you often use two or more workbooks open, arranged a certain way on screen? Create a workspace to save the arrangement.

1. Open the files that you will use together.
2. Arrange them on screen the way you like them.
   - Choose **Window|Arrange** and choose an option to place a window of each file side by side (Figure 16.17).
   - Click the **Restore Window** button on the menu bar to reduce the size of each of the windows and drag their borders to size them the way you want them.

3. Choose **File|Save Workspace** and type the name of the workspace. Browse to save it in the desired drive and folder.

Result: Excel saves the arrangement and the names of the files in a workspace file with the extension *xlw*. You still have to save the changes to each file individually; all the workspace does is remember which files are arranged in what way. When you open the workspace file, you open the files it contains, arranged as you saved them, with the same worksheet and cell active as when you saved it.

 TIPS FROM A PRO: Store the workspace file (not the files themselves) in the *Xlstart* folder if you want to open this arrangement of files when Excel starts.

CHANGE A COLOR IN THE COLOR PALETTE

How: Have you got a certain color in mind to use on your worksheet or chart, but it's not one of the standard choices? Customize the color palette.

1. Choose **Tools|Options** and select the **Color** tab (Figure 16.18).
2. Select the color you want to change and click **Modify**.

Figure 16.18
Modifying the color options

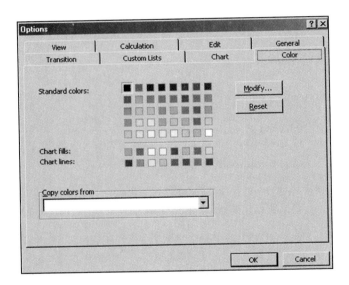

Figure 16.19 Colors dialog box

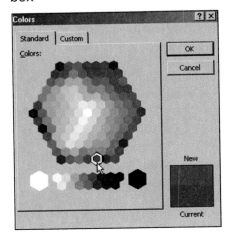

Figure 16.20 Creating a custom color

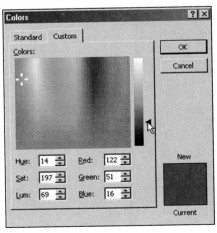

3. In the Colors dialog box (Figure 16.19) choose from over a hundred colors, or click the **Custom** tab (Figure 16.20) to vary the hue and shade. Click **OK** when you have the color you like in the New/Current preview area.

Result: Anything in the worksheet formatted with the original color is changed to the new substitute color. The new color appears in the Color palette for you to choose from when formatting worksheet or chart elements.

MANAGE DEFAULT FILE SETTINGS

How: Choose **Tools|Options** and click the **General** tab to manage these default settings for Excel (Figure 16.21):

○ Change the number of recently used files that are listed at the bottom of the File menu. (You can have up to nine.)
○ Specify the number of sheets in a new workbook, up to 255.
○ Change the default font from Arial 10, if you prefer something else.
○ Select a different location than Excel suggests when you first access the Save As dialog box. If you continually find yourself switching away from *My Documents* to another drive or folder, you can specify it here.

Figure 16.21
General tab of the
Options dialog box

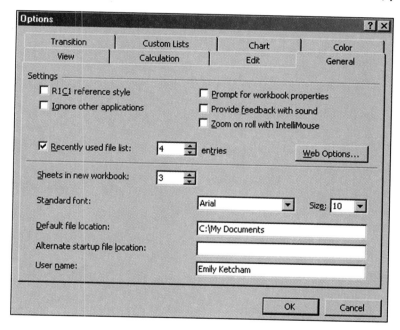

Result: Excel uses the new default setting the next time you start a new worksheet or start Excel.

Use PinPoint

After gaining the skills in this chapter, you can create templates and use them to create standard files, record macros and run them, and customize Excel's toolbars and environment. Now it's time to use the PinPoint software and see what you can do. Remember, whenever you are unsure of what to do, you can reread that portion of the chapter or you can click Show Me for a live demonstration. Check out these skills in PinPoint:

- Apply a template
- Create a new workbook
- Create a template
- Create a workspace
- Customize a toolbar
- Edit a macro
- Edit a template
- Macro command button
- Record a macro
- Run a macro

Key Terms

You can find definitions for these words in this chapter:

Template
Macro
Visual Basic for Applications (VBA)
Docked toolbar
Floating toolbar

Review Questions

You can use the following review questions to test your knowledge and skills. Answers are given in Appendix D.

True/False

Indicate whether each statement is true (T) or false (F).

____ 1. A template is an example file containing standard formulas, formatting, and settings.

____ 2. When you save a template, you have to specify exactly which folder to put it in.

____ 3. To edit or modify a template, choose File|New and choose the template name.

____ 4. To store a group of mouse actions or commands together so you can run them all at once, create a macro.

____ 5. To begin recording a macro, double-click the REC on the status bar.

____ 6. Macros are recorded in the programming language known as COBOL.

____ 7. The name of a macro appears on the bottom line of code, next to End Sub.

____ 8. After you create a macro, you can add it either to a menu or to a toolbar button.

____ 9. You can replace a color on Excel's color palette with any of millions of colors.

____ 10. When you save several files as a workspace, they automatically open when you start Excel.

Multiple Choice

Select the letter that best completes the statement.

___ 1. The file extensions used by Excel are:
   a. *.xls* for a workbook.
   b. *.xlw* for a workspace.
   c. *.xlt* for a template.
   d. *.htm* for a Web page.
   e. All of the above.

___ 2. To use a template that you have created:
   a. Click the New button on the Standard toolbar.
   b. Double-click the New button and choose the template name.
   c. Choose File|New and, on the General tab, double-click the template name.
   d. Choose File|New and on the Spreadsheet Solutions tab click the template name.
   e. None of the above.

___ 3. A toolbar that appears along the edge of the Excel window, such as the Drawing toolbar or Formatting toolbar, is called a(n) _____ toolbar.
   a. Docked.
   b. Edge.
   c. Locked.
   d. Stable.
   e. Stationary.

___ 4. When recording a macro, the Stop Recording toolbar appears with a button that will:
   a. Back up a step in case you make a mistake.
   b. Create a button for the macro on a toolbar.
   c. Create a shortcut key for the macro.
   d. Name the macro.
   e. Stop the recording process.

___ 5. To run a macro you've created:
   a. Choose Tools|Macro|Macros, and double-click the name of the macro.
   b. Click a customized button you've created for the macro.
   c. Press the shortcut key you've created for the macro.
   d. Press Alt+F8 to access the Macros dialog box and choose the macro from the list.
   e. All of the above.

___ 6. When creating a new, custom button for the toolbar, choose:
   a. Show Picture to show a square button without words on the toolbar.
   b. Text Only (Always) to show the name of the macro on the button.
   c. Image and Text to show a square button on the toolbar but text on the menu.
   d. Name (Macro) to show the name of the macro on the button.
   e. Shortcut to show the command on the shortcut menu.

___ 7. To add a different button to a toolbar:
   a. Click the More Buttons button and choose Add or Remove Buttons.
   b. Right-click a toolbar and choose Customize.
   c. Choose Tools|Customize and click Toolbars.
   d. Choose View|Toolbars and click Customize.
   e. All of the above.

8. To rearrange a button on a toolbar so it appears in a different location:
   a. Double-click the button, and then specify Left or Right in the dialog box.
   b. Right-click the toolbar and choose Arrange.
   c. Choose Window|Arrange All.
   d. Hold down Alt while dragging left or right.
   e. All of the above.

9. When you save a file in the XLStart folder:
   a. Excel starts with a different number of sheets in the workbook.
   b. Excel always shows the file name on the bottom of the File menu for easy access.
   c. Excel displays a button for one-click access to the file.

   d. The file opens automatically whenever you start Excel.
   e. All of the above.

10. Using a workspace file is handy because:
    a. When you save the workspace, you don't have to save the files individually.
    b. It enables you to open several files at once in a given arrangement.
    c. It enables you to open files automatically when you start Excel.
    d. It contains standard text, formulas, and formatting you can use over and over.
    e. It enables you to run a series of mouse actions and commands at one time.

Screen Review

Match the letters in Figure 16.22 with the correct items in the list. One answer will be used more than once.

Figure 16.22

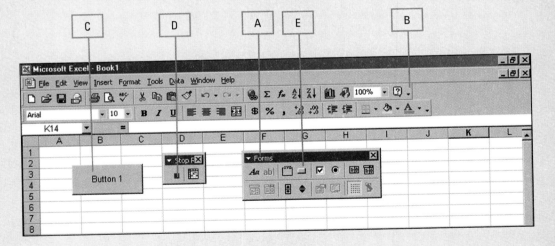

____ 1. Click here to run a macro.

____ 2. Click here to stop recording a macro.

____ 3. Click here to add a button to the toolbar.

____ 4. Look here to see a floating toolbar.

____ 5. Click here to create a button on the worksheet.

____ 6. Look here to see a docked toolbar.

Exercise and Project

Follow these step-by-step instructions to create a template. If you are working in a computer lab, ask your instructor where you should save and print your file.

Exercise

Create a template for a company that rents automated dinosaurs to groups for fund-raising activities. The template will be a form that can be used repeatedly as an invoice for the company. It should resemble Figure 16.23.

Figure 16.23

	A	B	C	D	E
1		Dino Dig			
2	Dates:		Location:		
3	Type	Rental Cost/Day	Days Rented	Total Cost	
4	Tyrannosaurus	$300			
5	Apatosaurus	$250			
6	Deinonychus	$250			
7	Albertosaurus	$200			
8	Camptosaurus	$200			
9	Coelophysis	$200			
10	Allosaurus	$150			
11	Barosaurus	$150			
12	Diplodocus	$150			
13					
14					

Sheet1 / Sheet2 / Sheet3

1. Enter a formula for Total Cost in D4 and copy it down the column.
2. Insert a comment in B2 telling the user to **Enter start and stop dates**. Choose **Tools|Options** and, in the View tab, choose the option to view the Comment & Indicator.
3. Save the worksheet as a template called **Dino Invoice**. If you are using your own computer, save it in *C:\Windows\Application Data\Microsoft\ Templates*. If you are working in a computer lab, ask your instructor where to save it.
4. Close the template.
5. Choose **File|New** and open a new worksheet based on your template. Enter the following values in the Days Rented column: **1,2,3,4,5,6,7,8,9**. Place your name in a header. Print the worksheet and close it without saving it.
6. Now choose **File|Open** (with Files of Type set to All Microsoft Excel Files), navigate to the folder where you saved the template, and open the template. Create a macro that automatically prints the invoice. To do so, choose **Tools|Macros|Record New Macro** and name the macro **Printing**. Assign it to an unassigned shortcut key. Record the steps of choosing **File|Print** and clicking OK. (If you are prompted for the file name and storage location, type the file name and click OK.) Then click the **Stop** button on the Stop Recording toolbar.

7. Add a button on the screen from which to print your macro. To do so, view the Forms toolbar and choose the Button button. Drag a button on the Dino Invoice template. When the dialog box prompts for the macro name, choose **Printing**. Resize the button if necessary and change its text to **PRINT**.

8. Save the template. Run the macro. Close the file.

Project

1. Open the *Dino Invoice* template you created in the exercise for this chapter. (Be sure to open the template rather than a new workbook based on it.) Enable the macros.

2. Create a macro that selects the cells A3:D12 and sorts them alphabetically by Type. Name the macro **Sorting** and assign it a keyboard shortcut.

3. Create a button for the macro. In cell D14, insert a formula to sum the Total Cost column.

4. Customize the Formatting toolbar by adding Increase Font Size and Decrease Font Size buttons.

5. Print a picture of the screen with the new toolbar buttons and the macro button showing. To do this, press the Print Screen key on the keyboard, open Word, and paste. Print. Close Word.

6. In Excel, save the template and close it. Open a new workbook based on the *Dino Invoice* template. Enter some numbers in the Days Rented column. Save the workbook as **Dino Invoice1**. Resize the window to accommodate another Excel sheet.

7. Open a new worksheet. Enter the heading **Dino Totals** at the top of the sheet and save the workbook with that name. Resize it and position it on the screen side by side with the *Dino Invoice1*.

8. Save the workspace as **Dino Info** in the *XLStart* folder so that the files open automatically as soon as you start Excel with the same arrangement of windows. Exit Excel.

9. Start Excel again to see that the *Dino Info* workspace opens automatically. Copy the Subtotal from the *Dino Invoice1* worksheet and use Paste Special to Paste Link them on the *DinoTotals* sheet. On the *Dino Totals* sheet, add a row for Sales Tax by multiplying the Subtotal by .0825 (or whatever your local sales tax rate is). Sum the two Subtotals and Sales Tax.

10. Add your name and class time in a header. Print the two open files. Save them and close them.

11. If you are working in a computer lab, you must restore the computer to its original state. To do this, open Windows Explorer and delete the template and the workspace file. Restore the toolbars by clicking the **Reset** button on the Toolbars tab of the Tools|Customize dialog box.

Collaborate with Workgroups

You've learned how to dash Excel data off to associates without leaving your desk by using email. Still, Excel offers many additional capabilities to simplify the process of sharing information with colleagues and team members. You can share files with others without worrying that any critical data will be inadvertently changed and yet retain the right to see and approve changes.

At the end of this chapter, you will be able to:

C E

- ☐ ☑ Create, edit, and remove a comment
- ☐ ☑ Create a shared workbook
- ☐ ☑ Track changes (highlight, accept, and reject)
- ☐ ☑ Apply and remove worksheet and workbook protection
- ☐ ☑ Apply and remove file passwords
- ☐ ☑ Merge workbooks
- ☐ ☑ Change workbook properties

E   EXPERT OBJECTIVE: *Create, edit, and remove a comment*

What: You can attach a note to a particular cell to remind yourself or a colleague of important information. The comment is not part of the worksheet text and doesn't affect any of Excel's functionality. It is also hidden unless you direct it to become visible.

Why: When you are collaborating or sharing a workbook, it's handy to be able to use comments like electronic sticky-notes. Because the comments are invisible when you print, you don't have to worry about forgetting to remove them when your editing is finished. Additionally, the identity of the person who wrote each comment is automatically recorded along with it.

 TIPS FROM A PRO: The Reviewing toolbar (Figures 17.1 and 17.2) helps to simplify working with comments. To turn it on, choose **View|Toolbars** and click **Reviewing**. The buttons vary depending on the operation that you are performing.

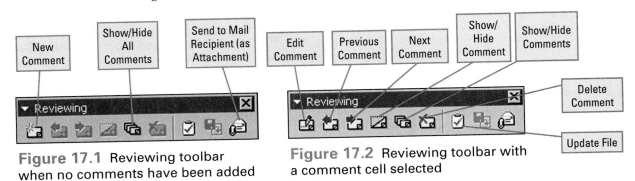

Figure 17.1 Reviewing toolbar when no comments have been added

Figure 17.2 Reviewing toolbar with a comment cell selected

INSERT A COMMENT

How: To insert a comment in a worksheet, use these steps:

1. Select the cell where you want the comment and then access the comment box one of these ways:
   - Choose **Insert|Comment**.
   - Right-click and choose **Insert Comment** from the shortcut menu.
   - Click the **New Comment** button on the Reviewing toolbar.
2. Type in the comment box, as in Figure 17.3, where the insertion point is flashing.
3. When you are finished entering text, click outside of the box to close it and return to the worksheet.

Result: The comment box disappears and a small red triangular *comment indicator* appears in the upper-right corner of the cell.

  TIPS FROM A PRO: Another way to draw attention to a cell is to use the Fill Color button. Comments are handier, though, because they enable you to add an explanation.

Figure 17.3
Inserting a comment

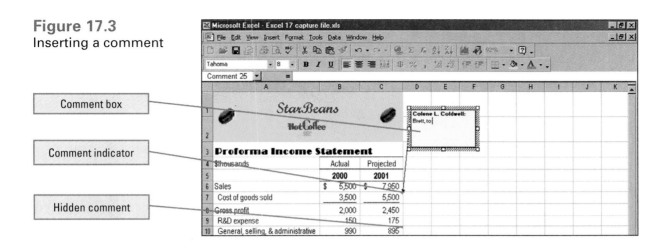

Comment box

Comment indicator

Hidden comment

REVIEW AND REVISE COMMENTS

How: To review or revise comments that have been added to a worksheet, follow these steps:

O To review comments one at a time, place the mouse pointer over the comment indicator and pause. The comment box appears showing the author's name, any text that has been entered, and an arrow leading to the comment cell, as shown in Figure 17.4.

Figure 17.4 Viewing
a comment

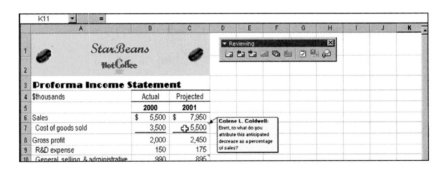

O To review multiple comments consecutively from left to right across the sheet, click in the worksheet. Click the **Next Comment** button on the Reviewing toolbar to move to the closest comment. Click the **Previous Comment** button when you want to move from right to left.

O To see all comments on a worksheet at one time (Figure 17.5), choose **View|Comments** or click the **Show All Comments** button on the Reviewing toolbar. Click the button again to hide all of the comments.

O To edit comment text, right-click the comment cell and choose **Edit Comment,** or click the **Edit Comment** button on the Reviewing toolbar.

O To resize or reposition the comment box, select the box (Figure 17.6), resize and reposition as you learned to do with text boxes in Chapter 9, "Work with Pictures and Objects." (No matter where you drag the box, the arrow still connects the comment box to the cell.)

O To format a comment, select the comment and double-click the border, or choose **Format|Comment.**

Figure 17.5 Viewing all comments

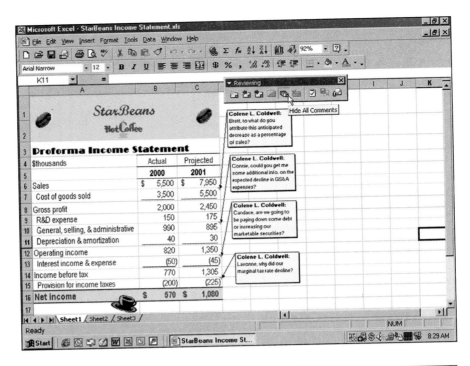

Figure 17.6 A selected comment

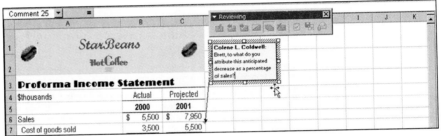

 TIPS FROM A PRO: If you click the Previous Comment or Next Comment button, after clicking Show All Comments, the comment box that you jump to is automatically selected. Now you can resize, format, reposition, or delete the box.

Result: After you have reviewed or revised the comments, click outside of the box and continue working in the worksheet. To delete a comment, select the cell and then use one of these methods.

○ Right-click and choose **Delete Comment.**
○ Click the **Delete Comment** button on the Reviewing toolbar.
○ Select the comment box and press **Delete.** (A selected comment box has a thick border.)

PRINT COMMENTS

How: You can print comments in two different formats—as they lie on the page or listed together on a separate sheet.

1. Choose **View|Comments** or click the **Show All Comments** button on the Reviewing toolbar to display all. (Or right-click individual comments and choose **Show Comment** from the shortcut menu.)
2. Choose **File|Page Setup,** and click the **Sheet** tab.
   • Drop down the arrow beside the Comments box and select **As Displayed on Sheet** to print the sheet with the comments.

- Drop down the arrow beside the Comments box and select **At end of sheet** to print a list of comments on a separate page at the end of the worksheet.

3. Print as usual.

Result: Your comments have been printed as a separate page (Figure 17.7) or as objects on the worksheet pages.

Figure 17.7
Comments printed on a separate page at the end of a sheet

Cell:	C7
Comment:	Colene L. Coldwell:
	Brett, to what do we attribute this anticipated decrease as a percentage of sales?
Cell:	C10
Comment:	Colene L. Coldwell:
	Connie, could you get me some additional info. on the expected decline in SG&A expenses?
Cell:	C13
Comment:	Colene L. Coldwell:
	Candace, are we going to be paying down some debt or increasing our marketable securities?
Cell:	C15
Comment:	Colene L. Coldwell:
	Lavonne, why did our marginal tax rate decline?

TASK 2   *Create a Shared Workbook*

E EXPERT OBJECTIVE: *Create a shared workbook*

What: When you want to team up with others on a project that involves Excel data, you can set up a workbook to allow data sharing. This means that up to 256 people can use the same workbook simultaneously if you save it on a network.

Why: Why hassle with sending around a file and letting people make their changes one at a time? Make one workbook and let various people update their own data at the same time or at their convenience.

THOUGHT QUESTION: When would you use these two techniques for sharing your work with others: creating a shared workbook versus publishing an interactive Excel Web page?

SET UP A WORKBOOK FOR SHARING

How: To set up a workbook for sharing and automatically tracking changes, open the workbook and choose one of the following options:

○ Choose **Tools|Track Changes|Highlight Changes** and select the **Track Changes** check box.

○ Choose **Tools|Protection|Protect and Share Workbook**.

○ Choose **Tools|Share Workbook** to access the Share Workbook dialog box and implement additional conditions.

1. Click the **Editing** tab (Figure 17.8) and select **Allow Changes by More Than One User at the Same Time**.

2. Click the **Advanced** tab (Figure 17.9) to specify the following additional conditions for your shared workbook.

   • **Track changes** enables others to make changes, but Excel keeps a record of everything that is added or deleted so you can review changes for the number of days that you specify (the default is 30 days). If you turn off the change history, you won't be able to merge multiple copies of the workbook or see highlighted updates.

   • **Update changes** enables you to make choices about the frequency with which you want to see the updates made by others.

   • **Conflicting changes between users** enables you to make decisions about how inconsistent changes made to the same cells by different users are handled.

   • **Print Settings** and **Filter Settings** save the options you set.

3. When you finish setting up the workbook, publish it on your organization's network (if you need help with this, contact your system administrator) or distribute copies to the individuals who need them.

Figure 17.8 Setting up a shared workbook: Editing tab

Figure 17.9 Setting up a shared workbook: Advanced tab

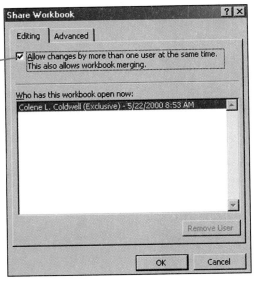

Click to allow multiple simultaneous users.

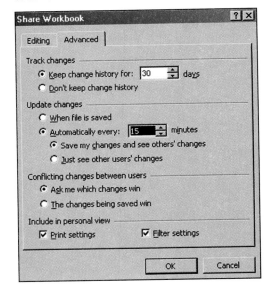

TIPS FROM A PRO: If you don't know how long you will be utilizing the shared workbook, make sure that the number in **Keep change history for __ days** is sufficient. After the days specified have elapsed, you no longer have access to any of the modifications that have been made. Additionally, changes that are older than the specified number of days are simply erased.

Result: The workbook is ready to be updated by many people at one time, and the changes can later be merged together to form one sheet (you learn how to do this in Task 6). The file name on the title bar includes the bracketed word *Shared*.

REMOVE A WORKBOOK FROM SHARING

How: After the project is complete or you want to replace a workbook with something more current, you will want to remove the file from sharing if you have published it on a network. To remove a workbook from sharing:

1. Choose **Tools|Track Changes** and clear the check box or choose **Tools|Share Workbook** to access the dialog box shown in Figure 17.8. Check to make sure that you are the only one listed in **Who has this workbook open now**.
2. Clear the **Allow changes by more than one user at the same time** check box and click **OK**.
3. If you receive a prompt regarding the effect that this change will have on other users, click **Yes**.

Result: The sharing aspect of the workbook has been removed. The file is now a typical workbook.

TASK **3**	*Track Changes*

Expert Objective: Track changes (highlight, accept, and reject)

What: When you set up a workbook for sharing, it automatically turns on a feature that tracks changes others make to it. The reverse is also true—if you turn on Excel's *Track Changes* feature, the worksheet is automatically set up as a shared worksheet. You can also choose to have cells whose contents have been modified encased by a colored border for quick identification.

Why: When people are collaborating to compile workbook information, it's handy to be able to see the kinds of changes that are being made by others. Using the Track Changes feature not only lets you see who made the modifications but it also lets you review the edits before you make the changes permanent.

START TRACKING CHANGES

How: You can start the Track Changes feature when you set up the workbook for sharing, as you learned to do in Task 2. However, when you want to highlight the cells that are being changed you must access the Highlight Changes dialog box as follows:

1. Choose **Tools|Track Changes** and choose **Highlight Changes** to see the dialog box shown in Figure 17.10. Click the top check box to turn on the feature and click **OK**. Now you can do the following:

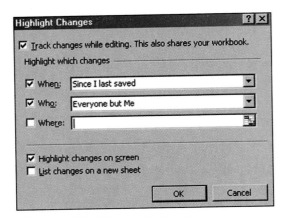

Figure 17.10 Highlight Changes dialog box

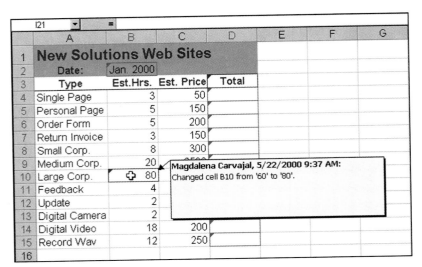

Figure 17.11 Tracking changes

- Choose which changes to highlight during a particular time-frame.
- Choose whose changes to highlight.
- Choose the changes in a particular range of cells to highlight.
- Choose to have the changed cells framed in a colored border with a change mark as shown in Figure 17.11. Each user's changes are shown with a different colored border.
- Have those changes that meet the specified criteria listed on a separate History sheet, as you'll see later in the chapter (Figure 17.21).

2. When you have finished making selections in the dialog box, click **OK**.

Result: The Track Changes feature is on and Excel keeps a record of the changes as they are made to the workbook. If you check the option to highlight changes on screen, modified cells appear with a colored border and a triangular indicator in the upper right corner until you save the sheet. When you run the mouse pointer over the cell, details about the change are displayed as you can see in Figure 17.11.

REVIEW TRACKED CHANGES

How: After others have worked on the file or you've merged several files together, as discussed in Task 6, you need to decide whether to accept or reject the changes. You can choose to move from cell to cell, reviewing each change as you go, or you can accept all or reject all of the changes at one time.

1. Choose **Tools|Track Changes** and choose **Accept or Reject Changes** to see the dialog box shown in Figure 17.12.
2. Use the default settings or revise the review time period, which author's changes to review, and what portions of the worksheet to evaluate and click **OK**.
3. The Accept or Reject Changes dialog box, shown in Figure 17.13, opens with the change options.

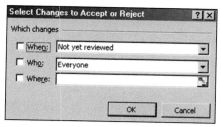

Figure 17.12 Setting up acceptance or rejection criteria for changes

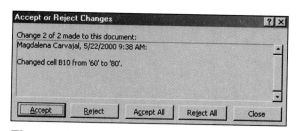

Figure 17.13 Accepting or rejecting changes

- Choose **Reject** to keep the original version and move to the next change.
- Choose **Accept** to keep the change and move to the next one.
- Choose **Accept All** or **Reject All** to do all the changes at one time, and you receive a prompt asking you if you are sure that you want to take this action.

TIPS FROM A PRO: You can also review the changes all in one place by choosing **File|Track Changes**. Make sure that **All, Highlight changes on screen,** and **List changes on a new sheet** are checked. A new worksheet named History appears.

Result: If you accept the change, the highlighting goes away; if you reject the change, the cell data is returned to the previous value. After you finish accepting or rejecting all the changes, the dialog box closes.

TASK 4   *Protect a Workbook*

E   EXPERT OBJECTIVE: *Apply and remove worksheet and workbook protection*

What: When you collaborate with other people to prepare or compile data, they might want to make comments on the workbook, edit your entries, or add fresh entries. However, there might be some cells that you don't want changed. Workbooks and worksheets can be protected to prevent others from changing all or portions of your work without your approval.

Why: Suppose you have created a complicated worksheet that others in your office will use. You don't want them blundering around, making changes to your formulas or erasing things by mistake. You can protect your worksheet from harm like that or accidents. (Have you ever accidentally wiped out some cells as you rushed around trying to mop up the coffee that you spilled on your keyboard?)

Protection is especially useful when you are passing out copies of a workbook to team members and want to limit each member to changing only those portions that concern him or her, such as an expense report or a departmental budget.

ADD PROTECTION AND PASSWORDS

How: Choose **Tools|Protection**, choose what you want to protect, and then one of the dialog boxes shown in Figures 17.14 through 17.16 opens. Choose from three choices.

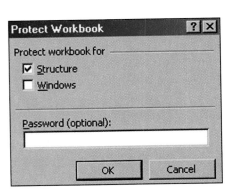

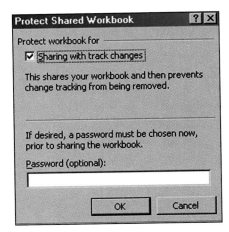

Figure 17.14 Protect Sheet dialog box

Figure 17.15 Protect Workbook dialog box

Figure 17.16 Protect Shared Workbook dialog box

○ **Protect sheet** enables you to protect various aspects of a worksheet. You can also add a password to prevent anyone from removing the protection without authorization.

○ **Protect Workbook** enables you to prevent structural changes, such as deleting sheets or parts of a worksheet, to the entire workbook and/ or to workbook windows. Again, you can add a password to prevent someone from turning off the Protection feature.

○ **Protect and Share Workbook** not only converts the file to a shared workbook but also prevents the sharing and change history tracking from being disabled in a shared workbook. Although this option turns on the shared workbook feature, you can't add a password to prevent the protection from being removed if the workbook is already set up for sharing. Turn off the sharing; then protect and add a password.

When you have finished in the dialog box, click **OK**.

Result: Although nothing seems to change in your workbook, you'll notice the difference as soon as you try to change the contents of a cell that is protected. You receive a prompt telling you that the cell is locked for editing. To remove protection or just protect specific cells, refer to the remainder of this task.

ALLOW INPUT ON A PROTECTED WORKSHEET

How: At times you want others to input numbers on a worksheet but keep the formulas protected. Use the following steps to unlock certain cells so others can type in them:

1. Select the cells that you want to be able to change.
2. Choose **Format|Cells** and click the **Protection** tab.
3. Clear the **Locked** check box and click **OK**.
4. Protect the sheet or workbook as usual.

Result: Now your worksheet has certain cells that can be changed and others that are protected from changes. Figure 17.17 provides an example of worksheet where locking certain cells, while leaving others unprotected, makes sense. Users can enter their data in the shaded cells and see the results, but if they try to change a protected cell, a message appears.

Figure 17.17
Worksheet with locked and unlocked cells.

Unprotected cells

Changing a protected cell produces this message.

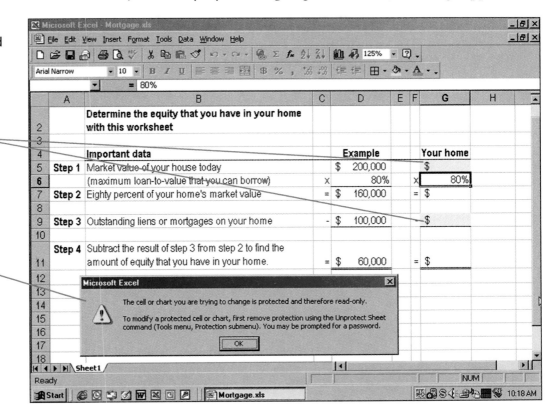

Note: If you want to use this feature in a shared workbook, you must do so before you share the workbook, or you must remove the sharing, protect the cells, and turn the sharing back on.

REMOVE PROTECTION

How: To remove the protection that you've just added, open the workbook and choose **Tools|Unprotect Document**. If you have added a password, it will have to be entered before you can proceed.

Results: The protection has been removed, and any cell can now be changed.

TASK **5**   *Add File Passwords*

E

EXPERT OBJECTIVE: Apply and remove file passwords

What: In Task 4, you learned how to apply passwords to prevent protection from being removed from certain portions of material. You can add another type of password so that no one without authorization can modify or even open a workbook. This feature can be used on normal or shared workbooks.

Why: If you distribute copies of an important but confidential workbook or store it in an unsecured location, you might not want prying eyes examining or modifying your data. Protecting data has become even more relevant with the increasing number of mischievous attacks from computer hackers.

ADD A FILE PASSWORD

How: To add a file password

1. Choose **File|Save as**, click **Tools** (on the menu inside the dialog box), and choose **General Options** to display the dialog box shown in Figure 17.18.
2. Enter the password that you want to use and click **OK**. If the password is for modification only, the file can still be opened but users can read the information, but cannot make changes.
3. When prompted, reenter the password.

 TIPS FROM A PRO: Don't rely on your memory to store your passwords—even the best of memories forgets things from time to time. Store passwords in a location where you can easily find them (of course, this means that you have to remember where they are kept).

 TIPS FROM A PRO: You can also set up workbooks as Read Only. This allows others to open the file and look at it, but prevents them from changing any aspects of the workbook unless they save it with a different name.

Result: The workbook now includes a password. If you required a password to open the file, anyone who tries to open the file sees a message similar to the one shown in Figure 17.19.

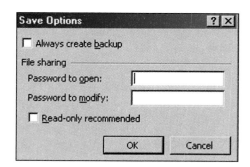

Figure 17.18 Adding a file password

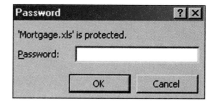

Figure 17.19 Prompt for file password

REMOVE PASSWORDS

How: To remove a file password:

1. Open the workbook (make sure that you don't open it as Read-Only) and choose **File|Save as**, click **Tools**, and click **General Options** to display the dialog box.

2. Remove the password (shown by asterisks) and clear the check boxes. Click **OK** to close the dialog box and **Save** to resave the file.

Result: The file passwords have been removed. The file can be opened and modified as usual.

TASK 6   *Merge Workbooks*

EXPERT OBJECTIVE: Merge Workbooks

What: When you use a shared workbook that isn't published on a network, at some time, you might want to merge all of the workbooks into one to create a compilation of everyone's work. To bring together all changes into a single workbook, use Excel's Merge Workbooks feature.

Why: Comparing multiple versions of a workbook by eye would be tedious and unreliable; it would be easy for you to overlook an important change. Excel performs this task quickly and accurately.

CREATE A WORKBOOK TO ALLOW MERGING

How: Before you can merge a workbook, you must create a file that can be merged, as follows:

1. Create a shared workbook as discussed in Task 2. The Change History must be turned on in the Share Workbook dialog box (refer to Figure 17.9), and it must be within the timeframe selected when you merge the files.
2. Make identical copies for distribution from the file that you just created in step 1 but give each copy a different name (this means different from the original workbook as well).
3. Distribute the copies to the individuals who will enter their data.

Result: You have created and distributed a workbook that can be merged. When the updated copies are returned to you, merge them together using the techniques discussed in the remainder of this task.

MERGE COPIES

How: To merge together copies of the same shared workbook follow these steps:

1. Open the original version of the document you want to merge.
2. Choose **Tools|Merge Documents** (you may be prompted to save the workbook) to access the **Select Files to Merge into Current Workbook** dialog box (Figure 17.20). Click to select a copy of the shared workbook that has changes to be merged, and click **OK**.
3. Repeat Step 2 with each version or select multiple copies to merge by pressing and holding **Ctrl** while you select workbook versions.

Figure 17.20 Select files to merge

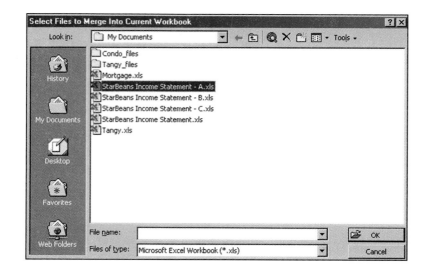

Result: The workbook copies you selected have been merged into one spreadsheet. Each changed cell is framed by a colored border, with a different color for each person who made modifications.

To review the changes that have been made, choose **File|Track Changes**. When you check the check boxes for **All**, **Highlight changes on screen**, and **List changes on a new sheet** are all checked, a new worksheet named History, like the one in Figure 17.21, appears. All the changes that have been made to the sheet are listed. You can create and view the change history and accept or reject changes as you learned in Task 3.

Figure 17.21 Viewing the History sheet

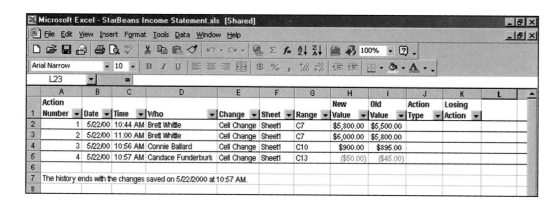

TASK 7   *Change Workbook Properties*

EXPERT OBJECTIVE: Change workbook properties

What: When you've completed a spreadsheet, it's a good idea to record some information about the file, such as who worked on the project, who the client was, and why you were doing the work. Right after you finish with the file, you'll probably think that as soon as you see the title, you'll remember what it was for. However, after some time passes and you have 50 other workbooks in that folder, you may not! To be on the safe side, use Excel's Properties feature to record workbook information.

Why: Not only is this efficient—all the information is stored in one place, with the file—but keywords that you add can be used to find the file later. Excel's *File Properties* feature tracks workbook statistics, including the date and time it was modified and who created it. You can also record comments or other information that relates to the file.

How: You can add keywords and comments to the properties record using the following steps:

1. Choose **File|Properties** and click the **Summary** tab to open the dialog box shown in Figure 17.22
2. Enter information for the fields.
3. Click the other tabs to view or modify properties. Click **OK** when you're finished.

Result: When you change to Properties view in the Open dialog box, as in Figure 17.23, you can see the category, keywords, and comments along with the other workbook statistics.

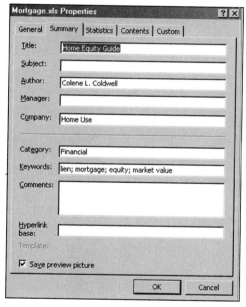

Figure 17.22 Adding workbook properties

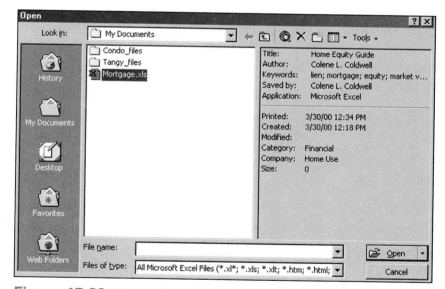

Figure 17.23 Properties view of the Open dialog box

 TIPS FROM A PRO: On the Summary tab, click **Save Preview Picture**, so you can see the contents of the file in Preview view in the Open dialog box.

Use PinPoint

After gaining the skills in this chapter, you can add comments to a worksheet, create a shared workbook, merge together versions of the same file, protect a workbook from change. Now it's time to use the PinPoint software and see what you can do. Remember, whenever you are unsure of what to do, you can reread that portion of the chapter or you can click Show Me for a live demonstration. Check out these skills in PinPoint:

- Add a comment
- Change properties
- Find a comment
- Apply passwords
- Merge workbooks
- Protect cells
- Share lists
- Tracking changes

Key Terms

You can find definitions for these words in this chapter:

Comment indicator
File Properties
Track Changes

Review Questions

You can use the following review questions to test your knowledge and skills. Answers are given in Appendix D.

True/False

Indicate whether each statement is true (T) or false (F).

___ 1. When you turn on the Track Changes feature, modified cells have a colored fill.

___ 2. When you merge workbooks, each file that you plan to merge together must have a different name.

___ 3. After you've added a file password, it can't be removed.

___ 4. If you want to direct attention to the data in a particular cell, add a comment.

___ 5. The Reviewing toolbar is handy when you are looking over tracked changes.

___ 6. File passwords can prevent someone from changing your worksheet.

___ 7. The only workbooks that can be merged using the Merge feature are shared workbooks.

___ 8. A shared workbook can be published on a network and modified by hundreds of people at the same time.

___ 9. Protecting a workbook means keeping it on a secure disk location.

___ 10. When you want to view a single comment, run the pointer over the comment indicator.

Multiple Choice

Select the letter that best completes the statement.

___ 1. To add a file password to a workbook:
    a. Choose Format|Cells|Protection.
    b. Choose Tools|Protection.
    c. Choose File|Save as and Tools|General Options.
    d. Choose Tools|Password.
    e. Both a and b.

___ 2. A workbook that is Read-Only:
    a. Can't be modified as-is.
    b. Can't be opened.
    c. Can be changed if you save it with a different file name.
    d. Can't be protected.
    e. Both a and d.

___ 3. Comments that are inserted into a cell:
    a. Are handy for making notes right on a worksheet.
    b. Can be viewed by running the pointer over the cell.
    c. Are placed inside a text-box-like comment box.
    d. Are identified by the triangular comment indicator.
    e. All of these.

___ 4. The *change history* aspect of a shared workbook:
    a. Refers to the length of time that the workbook can be updated.
    b. Refers to the length of time that information about user changes is kept by Excel.
    c. Is required to be turned on if you want to merge several copies of the same sheet.
    d. Enables you to be notified when anyone is changing the worksheet.
    e. None of these is correct.

___ 5. To set a workbook up for sharing:
    a. Choose Tools|Options and click the Editing tab.
    b. Choose Tools|Share Workbook.
    c. Choose Tools|Track Changes.
    d. Choose Tools|Online Collaboration.
    e. Both b and c.

___ 6. When you are using the Track Changes feature:
    a. The changes that people make are highlighted.
    b. Changes are designated by a colored border *if* you turn on the Highlight Changes feature too.
    c. The workbook also allows sharing.
    d. A history of the changes will always be kept for 30 days.
    e. Anyone with access can accept or reject changes to the workbook.

___ 7. The properties of a workbook include:
    a. Information about the date the file was created.
    b. Information about the author of the workbook.
    c. Information about the various worksheets in the workbook.
    d. Information about the last time the workbook was modified.
    e. All of these.

___ 8. To prevent some cells on a workbook from being changed, select the cells and:

    a. Choose Format| Cells|Protection, clear the Locked check box, and protect the sheet.

    b. Choose Tools|Protection, Unprotect, and click Selected Cells.

    c. Choose Format|Protection|Protect Sheet.

    d. All of these.

    e. Both a and b.

___ 9. Workbook merging:

    a. Refers to the process of bringing together various copies of a different workbook.

    b. Is only possible if the workbook is set up as a shared workbook.

    c. Is only possible if each copy of the workbook has the same file name.

    d. None of these explains this concept.

    e. Both b and c.

___ 10. To remove protection:

    a. Choose Tools|Unprotect.

    b. Choose Format|Cells|Unprotect.

    c. Is impossible; you can't remove it!

    d. Choose Tools|Protection| Unprotect.

    e. Both a and b.

Screen Review

Match the letters in Figure 17.24 with the correct items in the list.

Figure 17.24

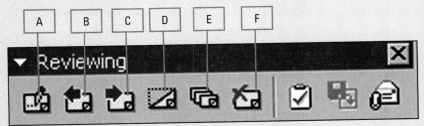

___ 1. Delete a comment.

___ 2. Go to the next comment.

___ 3. Go to the previous comment.

___ 4. Edit a selected comment.

___ 5. Show or hide the selected comment.

___ 6. Show all of the comments on a sheet.

Exercise and Project

Follow these step-by-step instructions to create a workbook. If you are working in a computer lab, ask your instructor where you should save and print your document.

Exercise

1. Open the file called **Cost of Capital.xls** from the *Student\Chapter 17* folder of the PinPoint CD, and turn on the Reviewing toolbar.
2. In cell F5 add this comment: **Equal to the before-tax cost less taxes.**
3. In cell E5 add the following comment: **Equal to the actual cost of the firm's debt, or if unavailable, the cost of similar debt in the market.**
4. Edit the comment in cell C12 to read, **The marginal tax rate is the tax rate paid on the last dollar earned.** Save the file as **Exercise 17A.**
5. Show all comments, and then set up the page so that the comments print on the page.
6. Add your name, the date, and any other relevant information to a header and print this sheet. Hide the comments.
7. Create a shared workbook from the file. Set it up to track changes for 15 days. (Keep the other default settings.) Save the file as **Exercise 17B.**
8. Unlock cells C6-C8, C12, and E6-E8. Protect the worksheet.
9. Turn on the feature to highlight the changes on screen.
10. Change the amount of 2A Corporate bonds to **$8,500** and the amount of common equity financing to **$10,000.**
11. Save the file and show the changes on a separate sheet. Print the change history.
12. Add your name as the manager in the file properties. Add a comment and some keywords, and then save the file.

Project

1. Open **New Solutions.xls** from the *Student\Chapter 17* folder of the PinPoint CD.
2. Insert this comment: **Should we calculate the totals for the customers?**
3. Accept all tracked changes.
4. Calculate the Total by multiplying B4*C4, and print the sheet so the comments appear.
5. Add these file properties: For the Title type **New Solutions**; for the Subject type **Price Table**, and show your name as the **Author.**
6. Protect and share the workbook. Make sure each sheet has the Tools|Share Workbook options on and **Keep change history** checked with the time within proper limits.
7. Either save the file on a networked drive or email it to a classmate. Have him or her open it and change some of the Est. Hrs and add a comment. When the file is returned, merge the workbooks and print the results.

MOUS Skill Guides for Core and Expert Objectives

Each MOUS exam involves a list of required tasks you may be asked to perform. This list of possible tasks is categorized by skill area. The following tables list the skill areas and where their required tasks can be found in this book. Table A contains the Core-level tasks. Table B contains the Expert-level tasks.

C Table A   MOUS Core Skill Guide

Skill Set	Required MOUS Activity	Chapter	Task	Page #
WORKING WITH CELLS				
	Use Undo and Redo	2	9	81
	Clear cell content	2	8	80
	Enter text, dates, and numbers	1	5	49
	Edit cell content	2	6	76
	Go to a specific cell	1	4	48
	Insert and delete selected cells	3	4	97
	Cut, copy, paste, paste special, and move selected cells, use the Office Clipboard	2 3 11	7 2, 3 4	78 92, 95 257
	Use Find and Replace	2	10	82
	Clear cell formats	6	7	156
	Work with series (AutoFill)	2	7	78
	Create hyperlinks	15	2	331
WORKING WITH FILES				
	Use Save	1	7	54
	Use Save As (different name, location, format)	1	8	56
	Locate and open an existing workbook	2	1, 2	68, 69
	Create a folder	1	9	57
	Use templates to create a new workbook	16	1	350
	Save a worksheet/workbook as a Web Page	15	3	334
	Send a workbook via email	15	1	330
	Use the Office Assistant	1	11	58
FORMATTING WORKSHEETS				
	Apply font styles (typeface, size, color, and styles)	2 6	5 3	74 148
	Apply number formats (currency, percent, dates, comma)	2 6	5 1	74 143
	Modify size of rows and columns	2 3	5 5	74 99
	Modify alignment of cell content	2 6	5 4	74 150

C Table A MOUS Core Skill Guide
(continued)

Skill Set	Required MOUS Activity	Chapter	Task	Page #
FORMATTING WORKSHEETS				
	Adjust the decimal place	2	5	74
	Use the Format Painter	6	8	157
	Apply autoformat	6	6	155
	Apply cell borders and shading	6	5	153
	Merging cells	6	4	151
	Rotate text and change indents	6	4	150, 152
	Define, apply, and remove a style	6	8	158, 159
PAGE SETUP AND PRINTING				
	Preview and print worksheets & workbooks	1 5	10 1, 2	58 125, 126
	Use Web Page Preview	15	3	336
	Print a selection	5	1	125
	Change page orientation and scaling	5	4	128
	Set page margins and centering	5	5	129
	Insert and remove a page break	5	8	135
	Set print, and clear a print area	5	3	127
	Set up headers and footers	5	6	131
	Set print titles and options (gridlines, print quality, row & column headings)	5	7	132
WORKING WITH WORKSHEETS AND WORKBOOKS				
	Insert and delete rows and columns	3	4	97
	Hide and unhide rows and columns	3	5	101
	Freeze and unfreeze rows and columns	3	6	101
	Change the zoom setting	3	7	102
	Move between worksheets in a workbook	1	4	49
	Check spelling	2	11	84
	Rename a worksheet	11	2	254
	Insert and Delete worksheets	11	1	253
	Move and copy worksheets	11	3	233
	Link worksheets & consolidate data using 3D References	11	4, 5	257, 258
WORKING WITH FORMULAS & FUNCTIONS				
	Enter a range within a formula by dragging	7	1	168
	Enter formulas in a cell and using the formula bar	2	3	70
	Revise formulas	7	3	170

C Table A   MOUS Core Skill Guide
(continued)

Skill Set	Required MOUS Activity	Chapter	Task	Page #
WORKING WITH FORMULAS & FUNCTIONS				
	Use references (absolute and relative)	4	1	110
	Use AutoSum	1	6	52
	Use Paste Function to insert a function	7	3	170
	Use basic functions (AVERAGE, SUM, COUNT, MIN, MAX)	1 3 7	6 8 1	52 104 168
	Enter functions using the formula palette	7	3	170
	Use date functions (NOW and DATE)	7	2	169
	Use financial functions (FV and PMT)	8	1, 3	186, 192
	Use logical functions (IF)	7	5	176
USING CHARTS AND OBJECTS				
	Preview and print charts	10	10	245
	Use chart wizard to create a chart	10	3	225
	Modify charts	10	7	233
	Insert, move, and delete an object (picture)	9	1	203
	Create and modify lines and objects	9	3, 4	208, 210

E Table B   MOUS Expert Skill Guide

Skill Set	Required MOUS Activity	Chapter	Task	Page #
IMPORTING AND EXPORTING DATA				
	Import data from text files (insert, drag and drop)	12	1	269
	Import from other applications	12	2	273
	Import a table from an HTML file (insert, drag and drop - including HTML round tripping)	15	5	340
	Export to other applications	12	4	276
USING TEMPLATES				
	Apply templates	16	1	351
	Edit templates	16	1	351
	Create templates	16	1	349
USING MULTIPLE WORKBOOKS				
	Using a workspace	16	5	359
	Link workbooks	11	4	258

Table B   MOUS Expert Skill Guide
(continued)

Skill Set	Required MOUS Activity	Chapter	Task	Page #
	Apply number formats (accounting, currency, number)	6	1	143
	Create custom number formats	6	2	146
	Use conditional formatting	7	5	177
PRINTING WORKBOOKS				
	Print and preview multiple worksheets	11	6	262
	Use the Report Manager	14	3	320
WORKING WITH NAMED RANGES				
	Add and delete a named range	4	3	114
	Use a named range in a formula	4	3	113
	Use Lookup Functions (Hlookup or Vlookup)	7	4	173
WORKING WITH TOOLBARS				
	Hide and display toolbars	10	5	228
	Customize a toolbar	1 / 16	3 / 4	47 / 355
	Assign a macro to a command button	16	4	356
USING MACROS				
	Record macros	16	2	352
	Run macros	16	2	353
	Edit macros	16	3	354
AUDITING A WORKSHEET				
	Work with the Auditing Toolbar	4	5	117
	Trace errors (find and fix errors)	4	5	119
	Trace precedents (find cells referred to in a specific formula)	4	5	118
	Trace dependents (find formulas that refer to a specific cell)	4	5	119
DISPLAYING AND FORMATTING DATA				
	Apply conditional formats	7	5	177
	Perform single and multi-level sorts	13	4	290
	Use grouping and outlines	11 / 13	5 / 6	261 / 295
	Use data forms	13	2, 7	286, 296
	Use subtotaling	13	6	294
	Apply data filters	13	8, 9	297, 299

E Table B MOUS Expert Skill Guide
(continued)

Skill Set	Required MOUS Activity	Chapter	Task	Page #
DISPLAYING AND FORMATTING DATA				
	Extract data	13	8, 9	297 299
	Query databases	13	10	301
	Use data validation	13	3	287
USING ANALYSIS TOOLS				
	Use PivotTable autoformat	13	11	306
	Use Goal Seek	6	9	160
	Create PivotChart Reports	13	11	306
	Work with Scenarios	14	2	317
	Use Solver	14	4	321
	Use data analysis and PivotTables	13	11	303
	Create interactive PivotTables for the Web	15	6	341
	Add fields to a PivotTable using the Web browser	15	6	342
COLLABORATING WITH WORKGROUPS				
	Create, edit and remove a comment	17	1	368
	Apply and remove worksheet and workbook protection	17	4	375
	Change workbook properties	17	7	380
	Apply and remove file passwords	17	5	377
	Track changes (highlight, accept, and reject)	17	3	373
	Create a shared workbook	17	2	371
	Merge workbooks	17	6	379

Appendix B

Use MOUS PinPoint 2000 Software

PinPoint 2000 is a software product that provides interactive training and testing in Microsoft Office 2000 programs. It is designed to supplement the projects in this book and will aid you in preparing for the MOUS certification exams. PinPoint 2000 is included on the CD-ROM in the back of this text. PinPoint 2000 Trainers and Evaluations currently run under Windows 95, Windows 98, and Windows NT 4.

The MOUS PinPoint software consists of Trainers and Evaluations. Trainers are used to hone your Office user skills. Evaluations are used to evaluate your performance of those skills.

PinPoint 2000 requires a full custom installation of Office 2000 to your computer. A full custom installation is an option you select at the time you install Microsoft Office 2000, and means that all components of the software are installed.

In this Appendix, you'll learn to:

- Install and start the PinPoint Launcher
- Start and run PinPoint Trainers and Evaluations
- View Trainer and Evaluation results
- Recover from a crash
- Remove PinPoint from your computer

Introduction to PinPoint 2000

The PinPoint 2000 Launcher

Your PinPoint 2000 CD contains a selection of PinPoint 2000 Trainers and Evaluations that cover many of the skills that you may need for using Word 2000, Excel 2000, PowerPoint 2000, and Access 2000.

Concurrency

PinPoint 2000 Trainers and Evaluations are considered "concurrent." This means that a Trainer (or Evaluation) is run simultaneously with the Office 2000 application you are learning or being tested in. For example, when you run a Pinpoint PowerPoint 2000 Trainer, the Microsoft PowerPoint 2000 application is automatically started and runs at the same time. By working directly in the Office 2000 application, you master the real application, rather than just practice on a simulation of the application.

Today's more advanced applications (like those in Office 2000) often allow more than one way to perform a given task. Concurrency with the real application gives you the freedom to choose the method that you like or that you already know. This gives you the optimal training and testing environment.

Trainer/Evaluation Pairs

Trainers and Evaluations come in pairs. For example, there is a Trainer/Evaluation pair for Word 2000 called "Expert Creating a Newsletter." This means that there is both a Trainer and an Evaluation for "Expert Creating a Newsletter."

Pinpoint Word 2000, Excel 2000, PowerPoint 2000, and Access 2000 all have such sets of Trainers and Evaluations.

Tasks

Each Trainer/Evaluation pair, or *module*, is a set of tasks grouped according to level (Core or Expert) and skill set.

Trainers

If you need help to complete the task, you can click the Show Me button and activate the Show Me feature. The Show Me will run a demonstration of how to perform a similar task.

After you attempt the task, the program checks your work and tells you if you performed the task correctly or incorrectly. In either case you have three choices:

- Retry the task.
- Have the Trainer demonstrate with the task's Show Me an efficient method of completing the task.
- Move on to the next task.

After you have completed all of the tasks in the module, you can study your performance by looking at the report that appears when you click the Report tab on the Launcher.

You may take a Trainer as many times as you like. As you do so, the Launcher keeps track of how you perform, even over different days, so that when you run a Trainer another time, the Trainer is set up to run only those tasks that were performed incorrectly on all of your previous run(s).

Evaluations

Since an Evaluation is really a test, it does not give you immediate feedback. You also cannot go back to a previous task or watch a demonstration of how to do the current task. You simply move from task to task until you have attempted all of the tasks in the Evaluation.

When you have finished, you can look at the report in the Reports section to see how you performed.

You can take an Evaluation as many times as you like. While you do so, the Launcher program keeps a record of how you have performed. As a result, if you take a Trainer after the corresponding Evaluation has been taken, the Trainer will set up to run only those tasks that were performed incorrectly on the Evaluation.

System Requirements

Table B.1 shows the system requirements to run PinPoint 2000 software on your computer.

Table B.1 PinPoint 2000 System Requirements

Component	Requirement
CPU	Minimum: Pentium Recommended: 166 MHz Pentium or better
Operating System	Windows 95, Windows 98, or Windows NT 4.0 sp5
Installed Applications	Full Custom Installation of Office 2000* Printer
RAM	Minimum: 16 MB Recommended: 32 MB or higher
Hard Drive Space	Minimum: Installing PinPoint 2000 software requires about 4 MB of hard drive space. Recommended: For efficient operation, however, you should make sure you have at least 100 MB of unused drive space after installing PinPoint 2000.
CD-ROM Drive	4X speed or faster
Video	Minimum: Color VGA video display running at 640x480 resolution with 16 colors. Recommended: Color VGA video display running at 800x600 (or higher) resolution with 16 colors. Note for Gateway computer users: If running a P5 90 (or less) Gateway computer, obtain the latest ATI "Mach 64" video driver from Gateway. This can be downloaded from Gateway's Web site.

*Office 2000 must be installed before installing PinPoint 2000. If a Full Custom Installation of Office 2000 has not been performed, some tasks will not be available because the components required for those tasks will not have been installed. The tasks will not be counted as right or wrong but recorded as N/A.

Run PinPoint 2000

Now that you know what PinPoint 2000 is and what is required to use it, you now see how to install and use the Launcher, and start and run Trainers and Evaluations. You also see how to view Trainer and Evaluation reports. Lastly, you find out how to recover from a crash of PinPoint 2000, if one occurs.

INSTALL THE LAUNCHER ON YOUR COMPUTER

To run the PinPoint 2000 Trainers or Evaluations, you must first install the Launcher program.

1. Start Windows on your computer.
2. Be sure that Office 2000 has already been installed to your computer with a Full Custom Install. If this is not the case, perform this installation before you continue with step 3.
3. Insert the PinPoint 2000 CD into your CD-ROM drive.
4. From the Start menu, select Run.
5. In the Run dialog box, enter the path to the SETUP.EXE file found in the root directory of the CD. For example, if your CD-ROM drive has been assigned the letter E, you would enter E:\setup.exe as shown in Figure B.1.

Note: If your CD-ROM drive has been assigned a letter different from E, use that letter to begin the path in this dialog box. For example, if your CD-ROM drive has been assigned the drive letter D, enter D:\setup.exe in this dialog box.

Figure B.1

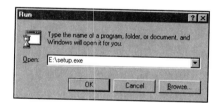

6. Click OK.
7. When the Setup Type screen appears, select Normal Single-User Installation.
8. Click Next to continue.

You are given a choice concerning the location of the PinPoint 2000 folder.

The recommended location of the PinPoint 2000 folder is shown as the default. (*Note:* Two files that initially take up only 109 KB will be placed in this folder.)

If you prefer to use a different path or name for the PinPoint 2000 folder, click the Browse button and navigate to the location you prefer, or rename the folder.

9. Click Next to continue.

After the installation is complete, the PinPoint 2000 program group window appears.

10. Close the PinPoint 2000 program group window.

If the installation has occurred correctly, the following changes have been made to your computer:

○ A PinPoint 2000 shortcut icon has been installed that will enable you to run the Launcher program via the Start menu.

○ A new folder called PinPoint 2000 has been created on the hard drive of your computer (see Figure B.2).

Figure B.2

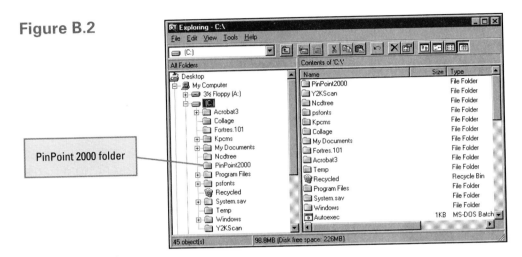

The PinPoint2000 folder contains:

○ An empty database file, CC_Admin.mdb. As you run Trainers and Evaluations, this file records your performance.

○ A small file, Uninst.isu, that is used for removing PinPoint 2000 from your computer.

Note: If your computer is configured so that file extensions are turned off, the CC_Admin.mdb file will appear without the .mdb extension.

Some files necessary for database access have been added to the Windows\System folder.

PREPARE TO RUN THE PINPOINT 2000 LAUNCHER

Before running the PinPoint 2000 Launcher, it is necessary to initialize each of the Microsoft applications (Word 2000, Excel 2000, PowerPoint 2000, and Access 2000) at least one time. If you have already used each of these applications, you can ignore this section.

Initializing these applications enables PinPoint training and testing to run in a more stable environment. You will need to provide user information in the first application that you run.

1. Start Microsoft Word 2000.
2. When the User Name dialog box appears type your Name and Initials.
3. Click OK to confirm.
4. When the Word window is completely set up and ready for use, you can close the application.
5. Start Microsoft Excel 2000.
6. When the Excel window is completely set up and ready for use, you can close the application.
7. Start Microsoft PowerPoint 2000.
8. When the PowerPoint window is completely set up and ready for use, you may close the application.
9. Start Microsoft Access 2000.
10. When the Access window is completely set up and ready for use, you can close the application.

You are ready to run the Launcher program and begin Trainers and Evaluations.

START THE PINPOINT 2000 LAUNCHER

The Launcher program enables you to run Trainers and Evaluations. It also gives you a performance report after you have taken a Trainer or Evaluation.

1. Select Start, Programs, PinPoint 2000, PinPoint 2000 (see Figure B.3).

Figure B.3

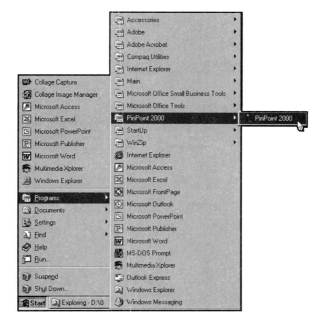

2. Enter a user name and password (see Figure B.4).

Figure B.4

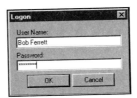

The user name and password can consist of any characters, as long as neither of them exceeds 50 characters. They are NOT case sensitive: It doesn't matter if you use upper- or lowercase letters.

If more than one person will be running PinPoint 2000 from your computer, each person must enter a different user name. However, passwords can be the same.

3. Click OK in the Logon dialog box.

If you are logging on for the first time, you need to enter some information in the User Information dialog box.

4. Enter the requested information and click OK.

The PinPoint 2000 Launcher screen appears (see Figure B.5). Please note that this screen will show the application for the text you are using.

Figure B.5

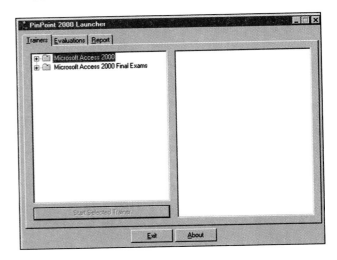

You are now ready to run PinPoint Trainers and Evaluations.

START PINPOINT 2000 TRAINERS AND EVALUATIONS

1. From the PinPoint Launcher, click the Trainers tab if you want to start a Trainer, or the Evaluations tab if you want to start an Evaluation (see Figure B.6).

Figure B.6

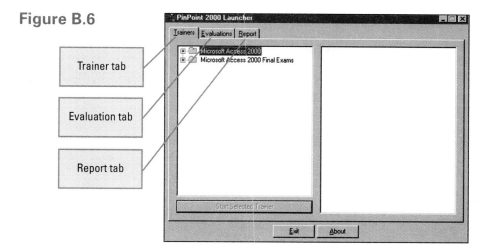

Trainer tab

Evaluation tab

Report tab

Note: Before you run a Trainer or Evaluation for the first time you must initialize each of the applications (Word 2000, Excel 2000, PowerPoint 2000, and Access 2000) at least one time.

---

2. Click the plus sign (+) to open an application's modules and exams. The plus sign becomes a minus sign (-), as shown in Figure B.7.

Figure B.7

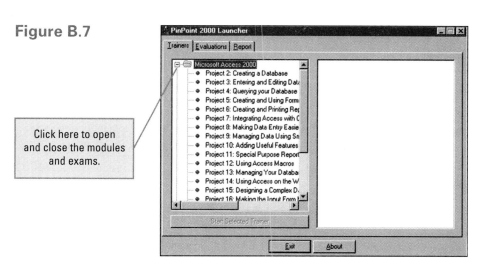

Click here to open and close the modules and exams.

3. Select the module or exam that you want to run.

The individual tasks that are part of the Trainer or Evaluation appear in the pane on the right.

4. If you are running a Trainer without an Evaluation, you can select or deselect individual training tasks by clicking on the box beside the task name (see Figure B.8).

The tasks that are deselected will not run during the Trainer. This enables you to adjust your training to include only those tasks that you do not already know how to do.

When running an Evaluation, however, you cannot deselect individual tasks. All tasks will run.

Figure B.8

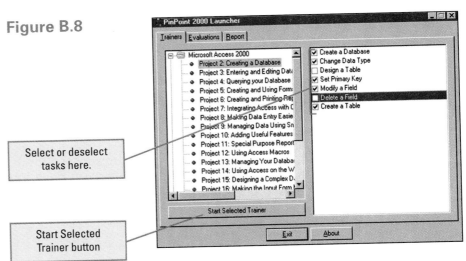

Select or deselect tasks here.

Start Selected Trainer button

5. Click the Start Selected Trainer button if you are starting a Trainer. Click the Start Selected Evaluation button if you are starting an Evaluation.

6. When you start the Trainer, you might encounter a warning message instructing you to change your computer's Taskbar settings (see Figure B.9).

If this message appears, follow its instructions before proceeding. Changing your taskbar settings in this way is necessary for proper functioning of a PinPoint Trainer. You can carry out the instructions given without canceling the box.

Figure B.9

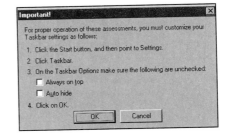

The PinPoint 2000 Launcher dialog box with your name and module selection appears (see Figure B.10).

Figure B.10

7. Click Yes to continue.

The Trainer or Evaluation starts.

Proceed to the next two sections to see how to run Trainers and Evaluations.

RUN A TRAINER

This lesson shows you how to run a Trainer. It also details how to handle some of the situations you might encounter during a Trainer.

1. Once your name and the selected module are displayed, click OK to begin the trainer.

The PinPoint 2000 launcher dialog box appears before a Trainer runs (see Figure B.11).

Figure B.11

2. Click Yes to continue.

The first thing you see is an introduction to how all PinPoint 2000 Trainers work. If you want to see the demonstration of how a PinPoint Trainer works and how to use the PinPoint 2000 controls, press any key or click the mouse to continue.

3. Press Esc to skip the introduction for now and go directly to a task.

 TIPS FROM A PRO: You can exit the introduction at any time by pressing **Esc** and moving straight to the training.

After initializing, the Trainer opens the first selected task.

The task instructions are displayed in a moveable instruction box that hovers over the application (see Figure B.12).

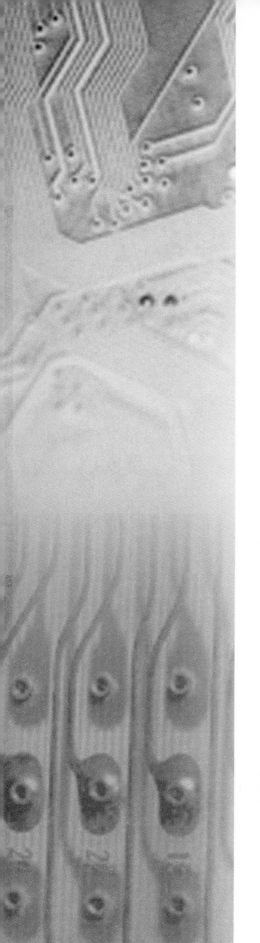

Figure B.12

The instruction box can be moved to different parts of the screen.

TIPS FROM A PRO: If the instruction box is blocking your view of something, you can drag it to another part of the screen. To instantly move the box to the other side of the screen, right-click the instruction box.

Notice the PinPoint control buttons that appear on the perimeter of the instruction box. Use these buttons to interact with the Trainer according to your needs (see Figure B.13).

Figure B.13

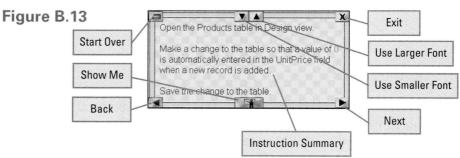

The features of the instruction box in Figure B.13 and their descriptions are listed here:

- The Instruction Summary displays the task to be completed. Instructions remain visible during the task.
- The Start Over button starts the current task again.
- The Back button returns you to the previous task.
- The Show Me button gives you a step-by-step demonstration using a similar example.

- The Use Larger Font and Use Smaller Font buttons enlarge or reduce the size of the box and text.
- The Quit button ends the current training session and returns you to the Launcher.
- The Next button checks a finished task for correct performance and moves you to the next task.

4. Try to do the task exactly as instructed in the PinPoint instruction box.
5. Click the Next button (refer to Figure B.13).

PinPoint 2000 gives you feedback in the Results dialog box.

Whether you performed the task correctly or not, you now have three choices:

- Click the Show Me button to display a step-by-step demonstration using a similar example.
- Click the Try Task Again button to set up the task so you can attempt it again.
- Click the Next Task button to move on and attempt the next task.

If you click the Show Me button, a demonstration of how to perform a similar task is given. This demonstration, called a Show Me, begins with a summary of the steps required to perform the task.

6. Press any key or click the mouse to advance the next Show Me box.

Usually the key concept behind the particular skill is explained during the Show Me.

After the instruction summary (and possibly a key concept), each of the instructions in the summary is explained and demonstrated in detail.

 TIPS FROM A PRO: If you want to exit from the Show Me demonstration at any point, press **Esc** to return to the PinPoint task.

During the Show Me demonstration, the mouse pointer moves and text is entered automatically when appropriate to the demonstration, but whenever the description or action is completed the demonstration halts until the user prompts it to continue with either a mouse click or a key stroke.

After the demonstration is complete, you can perform the task yourself.

7. Continue through the PinPoint Trainer at your own pace, attempting each task and watching Show Me demonstrations when you need help.

When you have finished with the training session, the Trainers screen of the Launcher is visible again. You can see a report of your performance by clicking the Report tab in the Launcher.

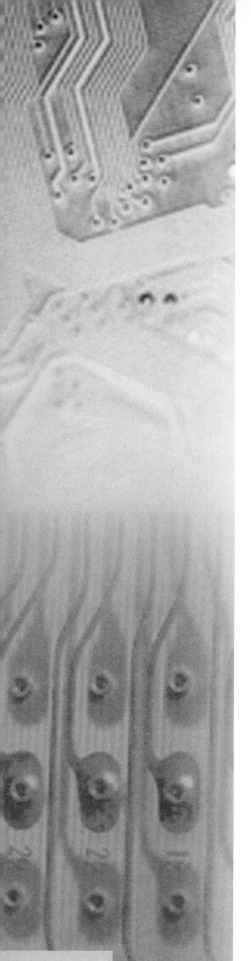

 TIPS FROM A PRO: You are free to exit from the training at any time by clicking the Exit button (refer to Figure B.13). When you attempt to exit a Trainer before it is finished, you are asked to confirm this decision (see Figure B.14).

Figure B.14

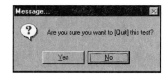

If you want to exit from the trainer at this point, click Yes.

RUN AN EVALUATION

This lesson shows you how to run an Evaluation. It also details how to handle some of the situations you might encounter during an Evaluation.

1. When you start the Evaluation, you might encounter a warning message instructing you to change your computer's Taskbar settings (refer to Figure B.9).

If this message appears, follow its instructions before proceeding. Changing your taskbar settings in this way is necessary for proper functioning of a PinPoint Trainer. You can carry out the instructions given without canceling the box.

2. After you have carried out the steps listed, click OK to continue.

The Pinpoint 2000 Launcher dialog box appears before an Evaluation runs (refer to Figure B.11).

3. Click Yes to continue.

The first thing you see is an introduction to how all PinPoint 2000 Evaluations work. If you want to see the demonstration of how an Evaluation works and how to use the PinPoint 2000 controls, press any key or click the mouse to continue past each screen. If you do not need to see the demonstration, press **Esc** to go straight to the testing.

Like a Trainer, an Evaluation presents you with a task to perform. In an Evaluation, however, the Start Over, Back, and Show Me buttons are all disabled. Therefore, you cannot restart a task, return to a previous task, or run a Show Me demonstration of how to perform the task.

4. After attempting a task, click the Next button to continue to the next task.

Normally, you would attempt all of the tasks in the Evaluation. But if you need to finish early and click the Exit button before you have attempted all of the tasks, the message box in Figure B.14 will display. Click the Yes button if you want to exit the Evaluation and go back to the Launcher program.

5. You can view a report of your performance by clicking the Report tab in the Launcher.

See the next section for details about viewing reports.

 TIPS FROM A PRO: Keep the following in mind for PinPoint 2000 Trainers and Evaluations to run properly:

- Only perform actions that the PinPoint task instructions ask you to perform.
- Do not exit from the Microsoft Office 2000 application in which you are training or testing unless you are told to do so.
- Do not close the example document (the document that PinPoint opens for you when you begin a task) unless you are told to do so.
- Do not run other programs (such as email, Internet browsers, virus shields, system monitors, and so on) at the same time as running PinPoint, unless you are asked to do so.
- Do not change views in one of the Office 2000 applications unless you are asked to do so.
- Do not change the way your Windows operating system or Office 2000 applications are configured by default.
- Do not turn off your computer in the middle of a PinPoint Trainer or Evaluation. Instead, first exit from the Trainer or Evaluation, and then turn off your computer.

VIEW REPORTS IN THE LAUNCHER

After you have taken at least one PinPoint 2000 Trainer or Evaluation, you can view detailed reports at any time concerning your performance on any of the modules that you have taken.

1. If the Launcher is not running, click Start, Programs, PinPoint 2000, PinPoint 2000 to run it. Then log on.
2. Click the Report tab.

The Report screen appears (see Figure B.15).

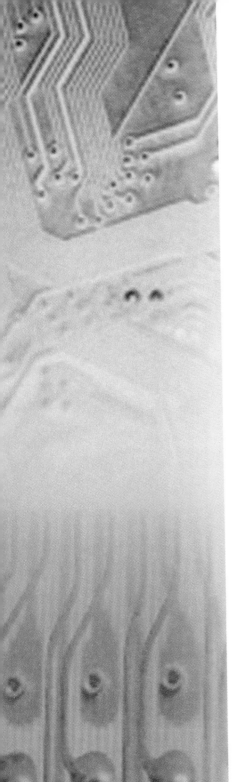

Figure B.15

> Click the Report tab to view a detailed report of your performance.

PinPoint 2000 Launcher

Trainers | Evaluations | Report

Test results for Robert Ferrett:

Microsoft Access 2000 Project 2: Creating a Database - Evaluation (05/04/00 05:15:46 PM)

Summary Information

Total Score: 71%   Working Time: 6 min, 9 sec.   Total Time: 12 min, 21 sec.

No.	Item	Actual Time	Target Time	Correct	Did Show Me
1	Create a Database	105 sec.	25 sec.	No	No
2	Change Data Type	21 sec.	20 sec.	Yes	No
3	Design a Table	56 sec.	45 sec.	Yes	No
4	Set Primary Key	16 sec.	30 sec.	Yes	No
5	Modify a Field	25 sec.	25 sec.	Yes	No
6	Delete a Field	20 sec.	25 sec.	Yes	No
7	Create a Table	126 sec.	60 sec.	No	No

Print...

Exit   About

The very last Trainer or Evaluation that you ran is displayed on screen. The information displayed in the Report screen is as follows:

- *Total Score*—The percentage of the correctly performed tasks out of the total number of tasks set to run.
- *Working Time*—The total time you actually spent working on all of the tasks in the Trainer or Evaluation.
- *Total Time*—The total time you spent running the entire Trainer or Evaluation.
- *Item*—The name of the task.
- *Actual Time*—The time you took to perform the task.
- *Target Time*—A reasonable amount of time required to perform the task by an efficient method.
- *Correct*—Displays Yes if you performed the task correctly; No if you did not.
- *Did Show-Me*—Displays Yes if you ran a Show Me demonstration for that task; No if you did not.

Note: A blank or dotted line running through the task line, or N/A, indicates that the task was not taken.

---

3. If you want to print a report, click the Print button.
4. If you want to see a report for a Trainer or Evaluation that you took previously, select it from the Test results for *<your name>* drop-down list.

The reports are listed in the order in which they were taken.

Note: You will see only your own reports on the Reports screen and not the reports for anyone else using PinPoint on your computer.

Note: An important feature of the PinPoint 2000 Launcher is its capability to keep track of your history of running Trainers and Evaluations. The Launcher uses your history to reconfigure a Trainer each successive time you run it. To "reconfigure" means to change the tasks that will run.

The Launcher does not reconfigure an Evaluation the same way it does a Trainer. No matter which tasks you have performed correctly in the past (on either a Trainer or Evaluation), all tasks are automatically selected to be run when you attempt to take an Evaluation.

RECOVER FROM A CRASH DURING A TRAINER OR EVALUATION

If your computer crashes while you are running a Trainer or Evaluation, all the work you have already done is not wasted. You do not need to start the Trainer or Evaluation over again from the beginning. To recover from a crash during a Trainer or Evaluation, follow these simple instructions.

1. Reboot your computer.
2. Start the Launcher again and log on as usual.
3. When a message like the one in Figure B.16 appears, close the Office application you were working on (if it's still running in the background) by clicking the Close button in the top right corner of the application window.

Figure B.16

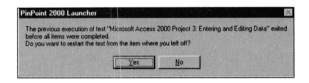

4. Click Yes to close the message box and return to the test.

The Trainer or Evaluation with which you were working will resume at the point where your computer crashed. Continue working on the Trainer or Evaluation as before.

Remove PinPoint 2000

When you have finished training and testing with PinPoint 2000, you may want to remove the Launcher program from your computer. PinPoint 2000 can be removed using the procedure for removing most other applications from your computer.

1. From the Start menu, select Settings, Control Panel.
2. Double-click the Add/Remove Programs icon.

The Add/Remove Programs Properties dialog box is displayed.

3. Select PinPoint 2000.

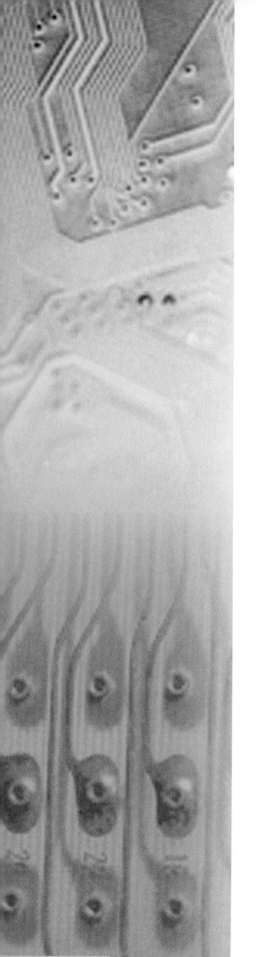

4. Click the Add/Remove button.
5. Confirm the removal of PinPoint 2000 by clicking Yes in the dialog box.
6. If the Remove Shared File? dialog box appears, click the Yes To All button (see Figure 17).

Figure B.17

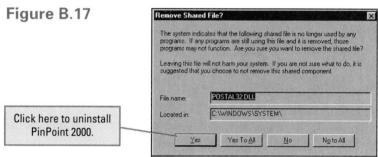

Click here to uninstall PinPoint 2000.

7. When the Remove Programs From Your Computer dialog box reports that the uninstall was successfully completed, click OK.
8. Click OK in the Add/Remove Programs Properties dialog box.
9. Close the Control Panel window.

PinPoint 2000 has now been completely removed from your computer.

Summary

PinPoint 2000 is a very valuable tool for preparing yourself for a MOUS Exam. You've learned how to install and start the PinPoint Launcher. You can now run Trainers and Evaluations, and view a report of their results. You also know what to avoid while running Trainers and Evaluations. You've seen how to recover if PinPoint crashes. And finally, you've learned how to uninstall PinPoint when you no longer need it. You are now equipped to take full advantage of the PinPoint 2000 training and testing software.

Prepare for MOUS Certification

This appendix gives you information that you need regarding the certification exams—how to register, what is covered in the tests, how the tests are administered, and so on. Because this information may change, be sure to visit www.mous.net for the latest updates.

How to Prepare for the Exams

This text is certified for both levels of certification:

- **Core**—You are able to manage a wide range of real world tasks efficiently.
- **Expert**—In addition to the everyday tasks at the Core level, you are able to handle complex assignments and have a thorough understanding of a program's advanced features.

In addition to the Core and Expert levels, Microsoft now offers a Master certification, which indicates that you have a comprehensive understanding of Microsoft Office 2000 and many of its advanced features. A Master certification requires students to successfully pass all five of the required exams: Word, Excel, PowerPoint, Access, and Outlook.

Each exam includes a list of tasks you may be asked to perform. The lessons in this book identify these required tasks with an icon in the margin. You can also review the MOUS Skill Guide in the front of this book to become familiar with these required tasks.

In addition to these icons, this book contains various study aids that not only help you pass the test, but also teach you how the software functions. You can use this book in a classroom or lab setting, or you can work through each chapter on your own using the PinPoint CD-ROM.

The PinPoint CD-ROM includes Chapter Review Tests for each MOUS Exam skill set. The coverage has two parts: a Task and a Show Me. The Task requires you to do something, (for example, format a document) and the Show Me demonstrates how to perform that task. In addition, each PinPoint has a practice test that mirrors the actual MOUS exams.

Use the PinPoint software as an evaluation of your comprehension. If you get stuck, be sure to use the Show Me demonstration.

Registering for and Taking the Exam

All MOUS exams are administered by a MOUS Authorized Testing Center (ATC). Most MOUS ATCs require pre-registration. To pre-register contact a local ATC directly. You can find a center near you by visiting the MOUS Web

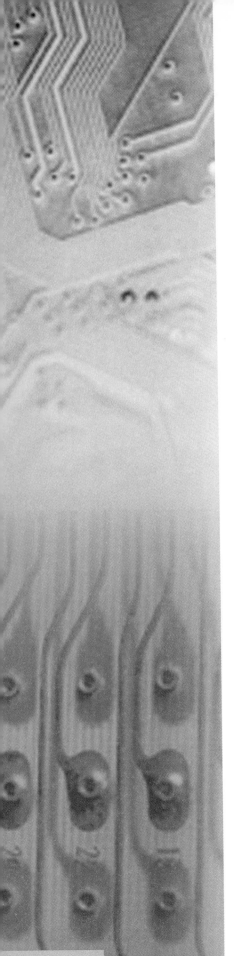

site at *www.mous.net*. Some ATCs accept walk-in examination candidates, allowing on-the-spot registration and examination. Be sure to check with a specific ATC to make certain of their registration policy.

The exam is not written and there are no multiple choice or true-false questions. You perform the required tasks on a computer running the live Microsoft application. A typical exam takes 45 to 60 minutes to complete. You must work through each task in the exam as quickly as you can.

All examination data is encrypted, and the examination process is closely monitored so your test scores are completely confidential. Examination results are provided only to the candidate and to Microsoft.

The Day of the Exam

Bring the following items with you to the testing center on exam day:

- **Picture ID**—driver's license or passport
- **Your MOUS identification number** (if you have take a previous MOUS certification exam)
- **ATC Student ID**, if applicable

At the exam center, you can expect to first complete the candidate information section, which provides the information necessary to complete your MOUS certificate.

After confirming your ID, the administrator will seat you at the test computer, log you onto the test system, and open your test module. You are now ready to begin.

To start the test, click the "Start Test" button and you're ready to begin your certification exam.

The Exam Itself

Instructions are displayed in a separate window on the screen. You can close the instruction window by clicking on it. You can restore it by clicking "Instructions" on the test information bar at the bottom of the screen. Read the test instructions carefully. Once you have started, a box in the bottom right corner of the screen indicates the question on which you are currently working. (For example, "question 3 of 50.")

If anything abnormal happens during the exam, or if the application "crashes," stop immediately and contact the administrator. The administrator will restart the test from where you left off. You will not be penalized any time for this.

When you have completed your exam, the computer will calculate your score. The scoring process takes a short time, and you will be notified onscreen whether you passed or failed. You may then ask the administrator to give you a printed report.

If you complete the exam successfully, your MOUS certificate will be delivered within 2-3 weeks.

General Tips

Unlike earlier MOUS exams, the results of the Office 2000 MOUS exams are expressed as a value on a 1000-point scale, rather than a percentage.

Each activity or question on the Office 2000 MOUS exams is comprised of several individually scored subtasks. A candidate's score is derived from the number of subtasks successfully completed and the "weight" or difficulty assigned to each.

Pay close attention to how each question is worded. Answers must be precise, resolving the question exactly as asked.

You can use any combination of menus, toolbars, and shortcut keys to complete each assigned task. Answers are scored based on the result, not the method you use or the time taken to complete each required task. Extra keystrokes or mouse clicks will not count against your score as long as you achieve the correct result within the time limit given.

Remember that the overall test is timed. While spending a lot of time on an individual answer will not adversely affect the scoring of that particular question, taking too long may not leave you with enough time to complete the entire test.

Answers are either right or wrong. You do not get credit for partial answers.

Important! Check to make sure you have entirely completed each question before clicking the NEXT TASK button. Once you press the NEXT TASK button, you will not be able to return to that question. A question will be scored as wrong if it is not completed properly before moving to the next question.

Save your Results Page that prints at the end of the exam. It is your confirmation that you passed the exam.

 TIPS FROM A PRO: Take note of these cautions:

- DON'T leave dialog boxes, Help menus, toolbars, or menus open.
- DON'T leave tables, boxes, cells "active or highlighted" unless instructed to do so.
- DON'T click the NEXT TASK button until you have "completely" answered the current question.

Lastly, be sure to visit the *mous.net* Web site for specific information on the Office 2000 exams, more testing tips, and to download a free demo of the exams.

Answers to Review Questions

Start with Windows

True/False	Multiple Choice	Screen Review
1. F	1. B	1. D
2. T	2. A	2. H
3. T	3. D	3. C
4. F	4. B	4. A
5. F	5. A	5. G
6. F	6. A	6. F
7. T	7. E	7. E
8. T	8. E	8. B
9. T	9. A	
10. F	10. A	

Chapter 1

True/False	Multiple Choice	Screen Review
1. F	1. A	1. E
2. T	2. E	2. B
3. T	3. C	3. A
4. T	4. A	4. C
5. F	5. D	5. F
6. T	6. C	6. D
7. F	7. C	7. H
8. F	8. A	8. G
9. T	9. D	
10. F	10. D	

Chapter 2

True/False	Multiple Choice	Screen Review 1
1. T	1. E	1. B
2. T	2. B	2. A
3. T	3. C	3. C
4. T	4. B	**Screen Review 2**
5. F	5. A	1. B
6. F	6. B	2. A
7. T	7. E	3. C
8. F	8. E	4. D
9. T	9. C	5. E
10. F	10. E	6. F
		7. I
		8. G
		9. H

Chapter 3

True/False

1. T
2. T
3. F
4. T
5. T
6. T
7. T
8. F
9. T
10. F

Multiple Choice

1. B
2. D
3. E
4. A
5. D
6. A
7. B
8. B
9. C
10. B

Screen Review

1. E
2. A
3. E
4. C
5. D
6. B

Chapter 4

True/False

1. F
2. F
3. T
4. T
5. T
6. T
7. T
8. F
9. F
10. F

Multiple Choice

1. D
2. B
3. D
4. B
5. C
6. E
7. B
8. D
9. C
10. B

Screen Review

1. A
2. C
3. D
4. E
5. F
6. B

Chapter 5

True/False

1. F
2. F
3. F
4. F
5. T
6. T
7. F
8. T
9. T
10. F

Multiple Choice

1. E
2. D
3. C
4. E
5. C
6. C
7. C
8. D
9. E
10. C

Screen Review

1. E
2. D
3. A
4. F
5. H
6. G
7. C
8. I
9. B

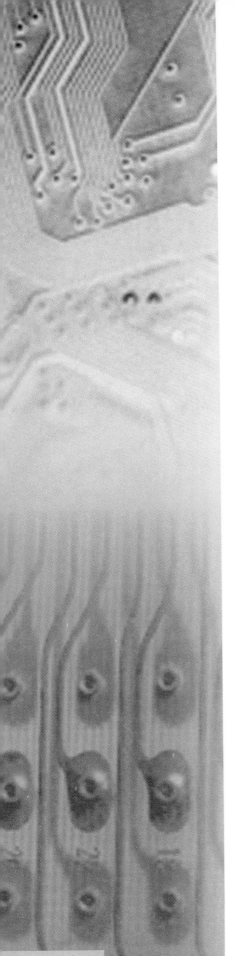

Chapter 6

True/False
1. F
2. T
3. F
4. F
5. T
6. T
7. F
8. T
9. F
10. F

Multiple Choice
1. A
2. C
3. C
4. C
5. B
6. E
7. A
8. D
9. E
10. E

Screen Review
1. H
2. E
3. A
4. B
5. D
6. F
7. G
8. C

Chapter 7

True/False
1. T
2. T
3. F
4. F
5. T
6. T
7. F
8. T
9. F
10. F

Multiple Choice
1. A
2. C
3. B
4. C
5. A
6. A
7. A
8. B
9. E
10. E

Screen Review
1. G
2. A
3. B
4. C
5. F
6. E
7. D

Chapter 8

True/False
1. F
2. T
3. T
4. T
5. T
6. F
7. T
8. F
9. T
10. T

Multiple Choice
1. D
2. A
3. C
4. C
5. D
6. C
7. A
8. D
9. A
10. E

Screen Review
1. G
2. E
3. C
4. B
5. D
6. F
7. A

Chapter 9

True/False
1. F
2. F
3. F
4. F
5. T
6. T
7. T
8. F
9. T
10. F

Multiple Choice
1. D
2. E
3. E
4. A
5. D
6. E
7. A
8. B
9. B
10. A

Screen Review
1. F
2. H
3. A
4. B
5. G
6. I
7. D
8. E
9. C

Chapter 10

True/False
1. T
2. T
3. F
4. T
5. F
6. F
7. T
8. T
9. T
10. F

Multiple Choice
1. D
2. A
3. A
4. B
5. C
6. E
7. C
8. D
9. B
10. D

Screen Review
1. B
2. C
3. D
4. A
5. G
6. F
7. E

Chapter 11

True/False
1. F
2. F
3. F
4. F
5. T
6. T
7. T
8. F
9. T
10. F

Multiple Choice
1. E
2. E
3. A
4. D
5. A
6. A
7. C
8. A
9. D
10. B

Screen Review
1. C
3. D
4. D
5. A
5. E

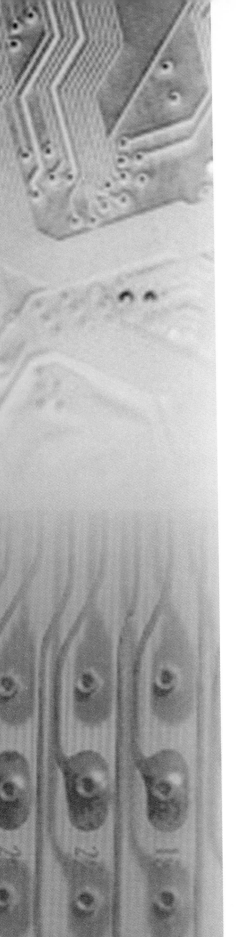

Chapter 12

True/False	Multiple Choice	Screen Review
1. T	1. A	1. A
2. F	2. A	2. C
3. T	3. B	3. B
4. T	4. E	4. A
5. F	5. A	5. C
6. F	6. D	
7. T	7. E	
8. T	8. E	
9. T	9. B	
10. F	10. C	

Chapter 13

True/False	Multiple Choice	Screen Review 1
1. F	1. D	1. D
2. T	2. D	2. B
3. T	3. B	3. A
4. T	4. D	4. C
5. T	5. D	**Screen Review 2**
6. T	6. A	1. A
7. T	7. E	2. D
8. F	8. C	3. B
9. F	9. E	4. C
10. T	10. D	5. F
		6. E

Chapter 14

True/False	Multiple Choice	Screen Review
1. T	1. B	1. A
2. T	2. C	2. E
3. F	3. E	3. B
4. F	4. C	4. C
5. F	5. E	5. D
6. F	6. E	
7. F	7. C	
8. F	8. A	
9. T	9. E	
10. F	10. E	

Chapter 15

True/False
1. T
2. F
3. T
4. F
5. T
6. F
7. F
8. T
9. T
10. F

Multiple Choice
1. E
2. E
3. C
4. A
5. E
6. E
7. A
8. C
9. E
10. D

Screen Review
1. F
2. E
3. D
4. A
5. B
6. C

Chapter 16

True/False
1. T
2. F
3. F
4. T
5. F
6. F
7. F
8. T
9. T
10. F

Multiple Choice
1. E
2. C
3. A
4. E
5. E
6. B
7. E
8. D
9. D
10. B

Screen Review
1. C
2. D
3. B
4. A (and possibly D)
5. E
6. B

Chapter 17

True/False
1. F
2. T
3. F
4. T
5. F
6. T
7. T
8. T
9. F
10. T

Multiple Choice
1. C
2. E
3. E
4. B
5. E
6. C
7. E
8. A
9. B
10. D

Screen Review
1. F
2. C
3. B
4. A
5. D
6. E

Index

C